Carmen *and the Staging of Spain*

ALEJANDRO L. MADRID, SERIES EDITOR
WALTER AARON CLARK, FOUNDING SERIES EDITOR
WALTER AARON CLARK, SERIES EDITOR FOR CURRENT VOLUME

Nor-tec Rifa!
Electronic Dance Music from Tijuana to the World
Alejandro L. Madrid

From Serra to Sancho
Music and Pageantry in the California Missions
Craig H. Russell

Colonial Counterpoint
Music in Early Modern Manila
D. R. M. Irving

Embodying Mexico
Tourism, Nationalism, & Performance
Ruth Hellier-Tinoco

Silent Music
Medieval Song and the Construction of History in Eighteenth-Century Spain
Susan Boynton

Whose Spain?
Negotiating "Spanish Music" in Paris, 1908–1929
Samuel Llano

Federico Moreno Torroba
A Musical Life in Three Acts
Walter Aaron Clark and William Craig Krause

Agustín Lara
A Cultural Biography
Andrew G. Wood

Danzón
Circum-Caribbean Dialogues in Music and Dance
Alejandro L. Madrid and Robin D. Moore

Music and Youth Culture in Latin America
Identity Construction Processes from New York to Buenos Aires
Pablo Vila

Music Criticism and Music Critics in Early Francoist Spain
Eva Moreda Rodríguez

Carmen *and the Staging of Spain*
Recasting Bizet's Opera in the Belle Epoque
Michael Christoforidis and Elizabeth Kertesz

Carmen and the Staging of Spain

Recasting Bizet's Opera in the Belle Epoque

Michael Christoforidis

and

Elizabeth Kertesz

OXFORD
UNIVERSITY PRESS

Oxford University Press is a department of the University of Oxford. It furthers the University's objective of excellence in research, scholarship, and education by publishing worldwide. Oxford is a registered trade mark of Oxford University Press in the UK and certain other countries.

Published in the United States of America by Oxford University Press 198 Madison Avenue, New York, NY 10016, United States of America.

CIP data is on file at the Library of Congress
ISBN 978–0–19–538456–7

1 3 5 7 9 8 6 4 2

Printed by Sheridan Books, Inc., United States of America

This volume is published with the generous support of the Donna Cardamone Jackson Endowment of the American Musicological Society, funded in part by the National Endowment for the Humanities and the Andrew W. Mellon Foundation.

CONTENTS

FIGURES

ACKNOWLEDGMENTS

The origins of this book go back to 1999 when, in the course of a research trip that took us to Madrid, we began to explore how the first Spanish audiences responded to Bizet's *Carmen*. Over a series of conference papers in the following years we realized there was a much larger story to tell about *Carmen*'s interactions with Spain, one that transcended the complex tale of the opera's creation. The viability of this approach was confirmed in discussion with colleagues, and especially in collaboration with Kerry Murphy in the course of proposing a far-reaching research project on the reception of *Carmen*. While that project did not eventuate, we were given the opportunity to tell this story in a book by Walter Aaron Clark, the founding series editor of Currents in Latin American and Iberian Music, and Suzanne Ryan, Executive Editor, Music at Oxford University Press. We thank Walter and Suzanne for their long-standing encouragement, support, and patience in seeing this book to completion. We must also acknowledge our gratitude to Rajesh Kathamuthu and Leslie Safford for shepherding the manuscript (and its authors) through the production process with such thought and consideration.

The research for this volume has led us into many libraries and archives, both physically and virtually. Our heartfelt thanks go to the University of Melbourne libraries, especially the staff of the Louise Hanson-Dyer Music Library, for their support and friendship over many years, including Evelyn Portek, Lena Vigilante, Gordon Dunlop, Christine Webster, Georgina Binns at the Lenton Parr Library, Jen Hill at Rare Music, and the staff of the inter-library loans department of the Baillieu Library. Ben Kreunen at the University of Melbourne's Digitisation Centre was of invaluable assistance in preparing the images.

The research that underpins this book has been shaped by the amazing collections and facilitated by the helpful staff at the National Library of Australia, State Library of Victoria, various departments of the Bibliothèque nationale de France, the British Library, London's Theatre Museum (now the Theatre and Performance department of the Victoria and Albert Museum), and the Metropolitan Opera Archives (New York), especially John Pennino. The riches of Spanish libraries have contributed new narratives to the *Carmen* story, as uncovered in the Biblioteca Nacional de España and its Hemeroteca; the Biblioteca de Catalunya, the Arxiu Nacional de Catalunya, Barcelona's Institut del Teatre and Museu de les Arts Escèniques (MAE) i Centre de Documentació; the Biblioteca de Andalucía, the Centro de Documentación Musical de Andalucía, and the Archivo Manuel de Falla.

The extended life of this project has coincided with the proliferation of internet-based resources, such as the great national digitization initiatives, which have made the historical press accessible even to those in the Antipodes; our debt to these sites is incalculable. We have also appreciated the efforts of private individuals who set up their own websites about entertainment and the press, especially Old Fulton NY Postcards, Papeles Flamencos, and the various incarnations of John Culme's Footlight Notes and Sarah Stovin's Rosario Guerrero Spanish Dancer. In addition to the online resources of the Biblioteca Nacional de España and the Bibliothèque nationale de France's "Gallica" site, we have benefited greatly from the digital offerings of the Library of Congress, the New York Public Library and the National Library of Australia's extraordinary online portral "Trove." The online archives of the Metropolitan Opera (MetOpera Database) and La Monnaie (appropriately named CARMEN) not only helped us pin down key performance dates, but also provided cast information and even reviews, and offer a marvelous resource, especially as they are constantly updated.

Beyond the privilege of arguing with each other over many years, we have been fortunate to exchange ideas about our Carmens within a generous scholarly community. We thank Richard Langham Smith and Lesley Wright for their inspiration and encouragement, and their leadership in the area of Carmen research. Thanks also to Annegret Fauser and Tim Carter, and Roy Howat and Emily Kilpatrick, for their friendship, advice and inspiring research. We are grateful for many fruitful discussions with colleagues and friends at the Melbourne Conservatorium of Music (University of Melbourne), including Kerry Murphy and Melanie Plesch, and especially our former graduate students Geraldine Power and Ken Murray, whose research intersected with ours in so many creative ways. To dance historian Philippa Heale and musicologist John Whiteoak: thank you for sharing your immense knowledge and extraordinary collections of artwork and sheet music with us over the years. Special thanks are due to Suzanne Robinson for her thoughtful and critical reading of the manuscript; needless to say, any faults are entirely our own. Our University of Melbourne colleagues in the School of Culture and Communication and the Spanish studies area of the School of Languages and Linguistics have been supportive. Thank you to Jessica Trevitt and Veronique Murch for their help with French-language sources; to Hispanists José Colmeiro and Stewart King for their interest and encouragement; to

Linda Weste for many conversations about writing, and for following up a lead for us at the National Library in Canberra and to Peter Campbell for guidance and support. Research for this book was undertaken with the assistance of the Australian Research Council, the University of Melbourne, and Spain's Ministry of Culture.

In Spain, we gratefully acknowledge the collegial advice and assistance of present and past staff of the Instituto Complutense de Ciencias Musicales (ICCMU), especially Emilio Casares Rodicio, Javier Suárez-Pajares, Adelaida Muñoz Tuñón, and our dear friend and colleague Yolanda Acker. Other Spanish colleagues who have assisted us, and whose research and lively conversations have broadened our own horizons, include in particular Ruth Piquer Sanclemente, María Palacios, Samuel Llano, Montserrat Bergadá, Teresa Cascudo, Celsa Alonso, Ramón Sobrino, Encino Cortizo, and Luisa Morales. We owe a special debt to Francesc Cortès i Mir of the Universitat Autònoma de Barcelona for his friendship, spirited discussions, and sage advice after reading portions of the manuscript.

This book is dedicated to our parents: Con and Pam Christoforidis, and George and Barbara Kertesz. Their love and encouragement of our research efforts made this journey possible. We are also grateful to Joyce and Neville Sims. To Margaret Kertesz, Peter Tregear, and Marianna DiBartolo—our love and thanks for your companionship and support. Much of the thinking and writing for this project took place in the great cafes of Melbourne, and we would like express our gratitude for the friendly welcome (and superb coffee and refreshments) we have always received from the staff of Dolcetti, Brunetti, and Vanilla Lounge.

INTRODUCTION

Nearly 150 years after its composition, Georges Bizet's *Carmen* remains a potent work, its staging of an imagined Spain enjoyed by audiences around the world. By the end of the Belle Époque, *Carmen* was already a dynamic cultural commodity both within and beyond the world of opera and had become synonymous with Spain. However, the exotic images it conveyed on stage and screen by 1915 were very different from those represented in the opera's initial Parisian incarnation at the Opéra-Comique in 1875. While *Carmen* was French in conception and composition, its creation was shaped by the affairs of Spain and long-standing representations of the country's culture. Over the next forty years, as *Carmen* was produced internationally, the Spanishness of its settings and characters was progressively reimagined, as performers, designers, and directors responded to the fashions for Spanish style that added a unique coloration to the Belle Époque.

In this book we explore the processes of Hispanicization that transformed *Carmen* in the aftermath of its premiere and demonstrate how stagings of the opera intersected with the evolution of staged Spanishness in this cosmopolitan age of spectacle.[1] Although it started its life as an *opéra comique*, *Carmen* quickly transcended both the genre and its national frame. Our narrative traces the agency of a remarkable series of protagonists and a variety of adaptations on the popular stage, as it follows a multiplicity of Carmens between 1875 and 1915, in Paris, different sites in Spain, and traveling between the urban centers of London and New York. It also illustrates the dynamic cycles of influence between opera, popular Spanish entertainments, and other theatrical genres, all of which were undergoing change during this period of burgeoning modernity. The story and characters of *Carmen*, and even aspects of Bizet's music, infiltrated a range of non-operatic genres like popular music theater, spoken drama, ballet, and film from the 1890s into the early 1900s. These spectacles were rarely mounted in Paris, where any treatment of *Carmen* was more tightly controlled by Bizet's widow and the Opéra-Comique.

---

1. "Staged Spanishness" is a term we will use to refer to the theatrical representation of Spanish customs, costumes, characters, and styles of music and dance.

However distant some of the case studies in this volume may seem from the version of Bizet's opera premiered in 1875 at the Opéra-Comique, they all form part of what H. Marshall Leicester terms the "discourse-*Carmen*," a "multiply authored, historically developing tangle of bits and pieces from Bizet, Mérimée, high-art criticism, the folk imagination and the movies; of stock images of Spain, opera, melodrama, femmes fatales and doomed lovers, and heaven knows what else," bits of which "float free of the opera but still carry its name."[2] Yet elements from these other theatrical manifestations of *Carmen* were to shape productions of the opera and impersonations of its principal character.

The role of Carmen is not given an elaborate characterization in Bizet's score, nor in Henri Meilhac and Ludovic Halévy's libretto, nor even in Prosper Mérimée's novella, on which the opera was based. The challenge, and indeed the opportunity, provided by such an open character is that it invites each new interpreter to make her own sense of the protagonist and her motivation. One of the strands of this study traces Carmen's development through the interpretative choices of her impersonators, from Célestine Galli-Marié's strong and sensual reading to the realist yet flirtatious approach of Emma Calvé, which in turn inspired the wild and passionate Carmen of Geraldine Farrar. To this familiar roll call of Carmens, our narrative introduces the Spanish singers Elena Sanz, Elena Fons, and Maria Gay, who were critical in defining Carmen as a Spanish character. We also propose that non-operatic performers like music-hall stars Carolina "la Belle" Otero, Rosario "la Belle" Guerrero, and the English actress Olga Nethersole contributed to the formation of the Belle Époque Carmen. These performers engaged with contemporary dramatic and musical trends, while invoking the constantly changing fashions in Spanishness that threaded through the Belle Époque.

From the 1880s *Carmen* followed two parallel trajectories in Spain, both as an Italian opera, and translated into the national lyric genre of the *zarzuela*. The widely promulgated belief that all Spaniards disliked *Carmen* and its stereotyped representation of their culture, while true of certain fin-de-siècle Spanish intellectuals, is contradicted by the work's popularity with Spanish audiences. This notion is also undermined by the active engagement of Spanish artists in the international "Carmen industry" of production and adaptation during the Belle Époque, and the fact that Bizet's score served as a model for some Spanish composers searching for a national voice.

The evolving representations of *Carmen* in the Belle Époque highlighted in this volume challenge the idea of the opera and Spain as fixed, unchanging exotic constructs, and privilege the largely unrecognized agency of Spanish

2. H. Marshall Leicester, "Discourse and the Film Text: Four Readings of *Carmen*," *Cambridge Opera Journal* 6, no. 3 (1994): 247, 249.

artists in this process of transformation. *Carmen* refashioned more than half a century of stereotypes of Spain and, in turn, over the first forty years of its existence served as a vehicle for evolving projections of staged Spanishness. It thus became a sort of Ruritania, an internationally recognized and constantly updated compilation of clichéd Spanishness, attracting the parodies that provide clear evidence of sustained success. We provide case studies of two parodies—one English (*Carmen Up to Data* of 1890), and one Spanish (*Carmela* of 1891)—that enjoyed remarkable international success, pitching satire of the opera and Spanish customs to two very different audiences. *Carmen* survived this ubiquity more successfully than any other opera of the period, as the stream of parody and adaptation both informed and perpetuated interest in the original work.

This volume is conceived in four parts, beginning with a Prelude that briefly situates the creation of Mérimée and Bizet's *Carmen* within a long tradition of Spanish entertainment in the French capital. We argue that the culture of the Second Empire—when fashions were influenced by the Spanish-born Empress Eugénie and Spanish performers and artists formed part of the cultural landscape—provides a backdrop to the local color of the opera.

Part 1, "*Carmen*'s Early Escapades (1875–90)," follows the new opera from Paris to London, as it overcame its shaky start at the Opéra-Comique and became established in theaters around the world. *Carmen*'s progress from its 1875 premiere to Galli-Marié's triumphant reclamation of the title role in Paris in 1883 is explored in Chapter 1, "Premiere and Revival: Paris, Galli-Marié, and Spanish Affairs." It establishes connections between the opera's changing fortunes in Paris and a range of issues related to Spain and fresh notions of local color, just as Galli-Marié's growth in the role is linked with her "Hispanicization" of Carmen. Chapter 2, "Impersonating Carmen in Victorian London," considers *Carmen*'s important early career on the other side of the channel from its 1878 debut, in light of long-standing local interest in Spanish-themed song and dance. Introducing the subject of parody and adaptation, the chapter focuses on the two-act Gaiety burlesque, *Carmen Up to Data* (1890), a work that stood apart from the minor parodies that proliferated in the years following *Carmen*'s English debut by virtue of its sustained engagement with the opera, and its local and international success.

In Part 2, "Spain Discovers *Carmen* (1887–91)," we interrogate the notion that Spanish audiences and critics rejected *Carmen* as an exoticist abomination. The opera's arrival in Madrid in 1887–88 coincided with significant debates over Spanish cultural identity, and its translation into Spanish for adaptation as a *zarzuela* exposed the fault lines between Bizet's vision of Spain and local concerns about self-representation. "Dueling *Carmens* in Madrid" (Chapter 3) explores the controversies surrounding the opera's Spanish debut, including the dispute over rights between Madrid's two leading lyric theatres. Chapter 4, "Profusion and Parody in Barcelona," indicates just how firmly *Carmen* had become established in Spain's cosmopolitan northern city by the 1890s. In *Carmela* (1891), *Carmen* became the subject of a successful parody that subverted the local color and melodies of Bizet's opera for a Hispanic audience and toured Spain and Latin America for several years.

The opera entered a new phase when its productions began to integrate elements of dramatic approaches that came to the fore in the 1890s. Part 3, "Authenticating *Carmen* in the Age of Verismo (1889–1908)," proposes that these changes occurred in tandem with the emergence of new modes of staging Spain. It takes as its point of departure the seismic shift in depictions of Spanish culture that resulted from the 1889 Exposition Universelle in Paris, most notably with the flamenco performances of Spanish gypsies from Granada. Emma Calvé, the great Carmen of the Belle Époque, takes center stage in Chapter 5, with her compelling reinterpretation of Bizet's protagonist examined in light of her dramatic development in Italy and research into Spain. Alongside Calvé's impersonation, new *Carmen* productions around 1900 began to reflect an image of Spain that drew on Granada's unique history and exotic representations of its gypsy culture.

In the early 1890s Calvé's emergence coincided with the ascent of Spanish dancing stars, Carmencita Dausset and La Belle Otero, on the international music hall circuit. All three achieved renown that took them from Paris across the English Channel and the Atlantic. Their influence can be seen in the two major adaptations that form the subject of "Transatlantic Carmens in Dance and Drama" (Chapter 6). Famed in both London and New York, dramatic actress Olga Nethersole starred in a lurid adaptation of the opera for the legitimate stage in the mid-1890s, while the young Spanish dancer Rosario Guerrero reinterpreted *Carmen* in mime and dance in a ballet version devised for London's Alhambra Theatre in 1903, the dramatic intensity of her performance inflected by newly emerging flamenco styles. Guerrero's fresh Spanish reading of the role finds its counterparts in the interpretations of Sevillian Elena Fons and the Catalan Maria Gay, the first Spanish Carmens to gain international acclaim on the operatic stage. In Chapter 7, "Finding a Spanish Voice for Carmen: Elena Fons and Maria Gay," the focus returns to Spain, where Fons built on her own local heritage to create a new authenticity as Carmen, applauded throughout the Latin world. The influence of verismo in tandem with the acceptance of *Carmen* in Spain was to have an impact on Spanish composers searching for a national operatic voice, often leading to comparison with and ambivalence toward Bizet's opera. The chapter ends with a case study of Maria Gay, the singer who created a reading of Carmen that was both modern and Spanish, defining it as a verismo role while engaging critically with the layers of Hispanic stereotype it had accrued.

The fluidity between the worlds of opera and popular entertainment introduced in Parts 2 and 3 is the main focus of Part 4, "*Carmen* as Popular Entertainment (1900–15)." Chapter 8, "*Carmen's* Music-Hall Embrace," returns to the hybrid Franco-Spanish entertainment scene in Paris, examining the presence of Carmenesque themes in the *chanson* market, in the context of a significant subgenre of Spanish-styled songs. This new Spanish fashion extended onto the stage in the dance-focused *spectacles* of the prewar years. And it is here that we present the case of La Belle Otero, who in the final stage of her stellar career made the rare—although not unprecedented—transition from music-hall Carmen to operatic protagonist. Our journey ends across the Atlantic with "Reproducing *Carmen* in the United States: Geraldine Farrar, the Met, and Beyond" (Chapter 9). Farrar, building on the legacies of Calvé and Gay, enjoyed an unprecedented and unmistakably modern celebrity as Carmen, born of her ability to exploit the confluence of operatic performance, recordings, and the silent film industry. The Met's attempt to stage a genuine Spanish opera in the guise of Enrique Granados's *Goyescas* was undermined by comparison with the vibrant New York traditions of *Carmen* in winter 1915–16, referred to by Carl Van Vechten as "the Spanish blaze."

Winton Dean's 1948 observation that "[o]n the Spanish element [in *Carmen*] much unnecessary ink has been spilt" hints at the extent of the literature on both the opera and its Spanishness over more than a century.[3] While some of this writing is referred to in the text of this volume, we are particularly indebted to the current generation of scholars who have transformed the landscape of *Carmen* and Spanish music studies.

Building on a history of scholarship dating back to the early years of the twentieth century, outstanding biographical work on Bizet has been produced by Hervé Lacombe and Hugh Macdonald.[4] The opera's prehistory has been illuminated in studies by Jean Sentaurens, Peter Robinson, and Robert Clark of Prosper Mérimée's 1845 novella and its adaptation for the lyric stage.[5]

3. Winton Dean, *Bizet* (London: Dent, 1948), 228. Cited in Ralph P. Locke, "Spanish Local Colour in Bizet's *Carmen*: Unexplored Borrowings and Transformations," in *Music, Theater, and Cultural Transfer: Paris, 1830–1914*, ed. Annegret Fauser and Mark Everist (Chicago and London: University of Chicago Press, 2009c), 318.

4. Hervé Lacombe, *Georges Bizet: Naissance d'une identité créatrice* (Paris: Fayard, 2000); Hugh Macdonald, *Bizet*, The Master Musicians (Oxford and New York: Oxford University Press, 2014).

5. Robert L. A. Clark, "South of North: *Carmen* and French Nationalisms," in *East of West: Cross-Cultural Performance and the Staging of Difference*, ed. Claire Sponsler and Xiaomei Chen (New York: Palgrave, 2000); Jean Sentaurens, "*Carmen*: De la novela de 1845 a la zarzuela de 1887; Cómo nació 'la España de Mérimée,'" *Bulletin Hispanique* [104], no. 2 (2002). We would also note the excellent Introduction to the 1997 Spanish edition and Peter Robinson's analysis of the novella in *Georges Bizet*, Carmen, ed. Susan McClary (Cambridge: Cambridge University Press, 1992); Luis López Jiménez and Luis-Eduardo López Esteve, "Introducción," in *Prosper Mérimée*: Carmen, trans. Luis López Jiménez and Luis-Eduardo López Esteve (Madrid: Ediciones Cátedra,

Richard Langham Smith demystified early versions of *Carmen* in his critical edition of Bizet's score, while Ralph Locke has followed the trail of Bizet's Spanish sources in his landmark work on exoticism.[6] Lacombe and Christine Rodriguez have undertaken a detailed exploration of the opera's celebrated "Habanera."[7] The 2013 Overture Opera Guide essays by Langham Smith and Lesley Wright provide a scholarly narrative to the opera's historical contexts, its evolution through the novella and libretto, and its career at the Opéra-Comique.[8] Much modern scholarship has focused on the composition, production, and early reception of *Carmen* in Paris, with scholars such as Lesley Wright—whose *Dossier de presse* is an invaluable resource—and Kerry Murphy offering rich explorations of the opera's Parisian contexts and the enormously complex story of its early performances.[9] James Parakilas and Susan McClary have analyzed the work and the character of *Carmen* in terms of exoticism, gender, and race, and Carmen's gypsy identity has been explored by Lou Charnon-Deutsch and Anna Piotrowska.[10]

Although *Carmen* frequently features in singers' biographies, studies of the performers who really shaped the role are relatively rare, and we have benefited from Wright's research on Célestine Galli-Marié (the first Carmen), and Steven Huebner's work on Emma Calvé, the great fin-de-siècle Carmen.[11] Karen

1997), 9–97; Peter Robinson, "Introduction," in Susan McClary, *Georges Bizet,* Carmen (Cambridge: Cambridge University Press, 1992), 1–14.

6. Georges Bizet, *Carmen: Opéra-Comique in Four Acts*, ed. Richard Langham Smith (London: Peters Edition, 2013); Ralph P. Locke, "Nineteenth-Century Music: Quantity, Quality, Qualities," *Nineteenth-Century Music Review* 1, no. 1 (2004): 2–41; Ralph P. Locke, "Spanish Local Color in Bizet's *Carmen*," 316–60; Ralph P. Locke, "Exotic Operas and Two Spanish 'Gypsies,'" in *Musical Exoticism: Images and Reflections* (New York: Cambridge University Press, 2009b), 150–74.

7. Hervé Lacombe and Christine Rodriguez, *La Habanera de Carmen: Naissance d'un tube* (Paris: Fayard, 2014).

8. Richard Langham Smith, "*Carmen*: From Mérimée to Bizet," and Lesley Wright, "*Carmen* and the Opéra-Comique," in Carmen: *Georges Bizet*, ed. Gary Kahn (Richmond, UK: Overture, 2013), 9–34; 35–55.

9. Lesley Wright, ed. *Georges Bizet,* Carmen: *Dossier de presse parisienne (1875)* (Weinsberg, Germany: Lucie Galland, 2001); Lesley A. Wright, "*Carmen* and the Critics," in *Tan-yin-lun-yue: Conference Proceedings of "Musical Research and Music Practice," 1999* (Taipei: Gao-Tan, 2000); Kerry Murphy, "*Carmen: Couleur locale* or the Real Thing?," in *Music, Theater, and Cultural Transfer: Paris, 1830–1914*, ed. Annegret Fauser and Mark Everist (Chicago and London: University of Chicago Press, 2009).

10. James Parakilas, "The Soldier and the Exotic: Operatic Variations on a Theme of Racial Encounter; Part I," *Opera Quarterly* 10 (1993): 33–56; McClary, *Georges Bizet,* Carmen; Lou Charnon-Deutsch, *The Spanish Gypsy: The History of a European Obsession* (University Park: Pennsylvania State University Press, 2004); Anna G. Piotrowska, *Gypsy Music in European Culture from the Late Eighteenth to the Early Twentieth Centuries*, trans. Guy R. Torr (Boston: Northeastern University Press, 2013).

11. Lesley A. Wright, "Une critique revisitée: Réflexions sur l'accueil de *Carmen* à Paris en 1883," in *Musique, esthétique et société au XIXe siècle: Liber amicorum Joël-Marie Fauquet*, ed. Damien Colas, Florence Gétreau, and Malou Haine (Wavre,

Henson's groundbreaking research on opera singers and performance styles includes an important contribution on Galli-Marié, while Susan Rutherford's essay in Henson's edited volume *Technology and the Diva* discusses Calvé and other Carmens, and Melina Esse considers Geraldine Farrar.[12] Such studies aside, Carmen's trajectory between 1883 and the blockbuster films of 1915 is marked by a slight scholarly hiatus, as research into adaptations of the opera has focused squarely on film, along with the productions and adaptations from the mid-twentieth century to the present day. The cinematic history of Carmen has been the subject of landmark studies appearing as a result of a major project based at the University of Newcastle upon Tyne in the 2000s, led by Ann Davies and Phil Powrie, while Gillian Anderson's reconstruction of the score to the 1915 Lasky/DeMille *Carmen* has facilitated study of this important film.[13]

Developments in Spanish musicology (and contributions from some non-Spanish scholars) over the past generation have opened up new areas of research into nineteenth- and early-twentieth-century Spanish musical culture, many of which are relevant to the present study. Our research is particularly indebted to the groundbreaking work on nineteenth-century song by Celsa Alonso, as well as the revelatory studies on the panorama of nineteenth- and early-twentieth-century Spanish music by Luis G. Iberni, Ramón Sobrino, María Encina Cortizo, Francesc Cortès, and the publications of the Instituto Complutense de Ciencias Musicales (ICCMU) curated by Emilio Casares Rodicio.[14] Our knowledge of the *escuela bolera* and the guitar in this period has

Belgium: Éditions Mardaga, 2007), 187–97; Steven Huebner, "*La Princesse Paysanne du Midi*," in *Music, Theater, and Cultural Transfer: Paris, 1830–1914*, ed. Annegret Fauser and Mark Everist (Chicago and London: University of Chicago Press, 2009), 361–78.

12. Karen Henson, *Opera Acts: Singers and Performance in the Late Nineteenth Century* (Cambridge: Cambridge University Press, 2015); Susan Rutherford, "'Pretending to Be Wicked': Divas, Technology, and the Consumption of Bizet's *Carmen*," in *Technology and the Diva*, ed. Karen Henson (Cambridge: Cambridge University Press, 2016), 74–88; Melina Esse, "The Silent Diva: Farrar's Carmen," in *Technology and the Diva*, 89–103.

13. Most notably, Phil Powrie et al., *Carmen on Film: A Cultural History* (Bloomington and Indianapolis: Indiana University Press, 2007). See also Gillian B. Anderson, "Geraldine Farrar and Cecil B. DeMille: The Effect of Opera on Film and Film on Opera in 1915," in Carmen: *From Silent Film to MTV*, ed. Chris Perriam and Ann Davies (Amsterdam, NY: Rodopi, 2005), 23–35.

14. Celsa Alonso, *La canción lírica española en el siglo XIX* (Madrid: ICCMU, 1998); Celsa Alonso, "En el espejo de 'los otros': Andalucismo, exotismo e hispanismo," in *Creación musical, cultura popular y construcción nacional en la España contemporánea*, ed. Celsa Alonso (Madrid: ICCMU, 2010), 83–103; Luis G. Iberni, *Pablo Sarasate* (Madrid: ICCMU, D.L., 1994); Luis G. Iberni, "Controversias entre ópera y zarzuela en la España de la Restauración," *Cuadernos de música iberoamericana* 2-3 (1996–97): 157–64; Luis G. Iberni, "Cien años de Antonio Peña y Goñi," *Cuadernos de música iberoamericana* 4 (1997): 3–13; Luis G. Iberni, "Verismo y realismo en la ópera española," in *La ópera en España e Hispanoamérica*, ed. Emilio Casares Rodicio and Álvaro Torrente (Madrid: ICCMU, 2002), 2:215–26; Ramón Sobrino, "Alhambrismo musical español de

been enriched by the studies of Javier Suárez-Pajares and Xoán M. Carreira, while the works of Faustino Nuñez, José Blas Vega, and Gerhard Steingress have illuminated the histories of flamenco and the habanera.[15] More specific contributions have been made to the study of *Carmen*'s reception in Spain, and we acknowledge the pioneering work of Jean Sentaurens and Laura Santana Burgos, who makes a major contribution with her work on the Spanish translations of *Carmen*'s libretto.[16]

The impact of Spanish music and musicians in France has been essayed by Christiane Le Bordays and more assiduously unraveled by Montserrat Bergadá, Samuel Llano, and Geraldine Power.[17] Ken Murray has surveyed the reception of Spanish music in London, while Richard Kagan, Walter Clark, Carol Hess, and Kristen Turner have highlighted aspects of the reception of Spanish music in fin-de-siècle New York.[18]

los albores románticos a Manuel de Falla," in *Manuel de Falla y la Alhambra*, ed. Francisco Baena and Yvan Nommick (Granada, Spain: Patronato de la Alhambra y Generalife; Fundación Archivo Manuel de Falla, 2005), 39–69; Francesc Cortés, *Història de la música a Catalunya* (Barcelona: Base, 2011); María Encina Cortizo Rodríguez, "El bolero español del siglo XIX: Estudio formal," *Revista de musicología* 16, no. 4 (1993): 2017–26; María Encina Cortizo and Ramón Sobrino, "Los salones musicales madrileños: Nuevos espacios sociales para el cultivo de la música de concierto en la segunda mitad del XIX," *Ad Parnassum: A Journal of Eighteenth- and Nineteenth-Century Instrumental Music* 13, no. 25 (2015): 209–43.

15. Javier Suárez-Pajares and Eusebio Rioja Vázquez, *El guitarrista almeriense Julián Arcas (1832–1882): Una biografía documental* (Almería: Instituto de Estudios Almerienses, Diputación de Almería, 2003); Javier Suárez-Pajares and Eusebio Rioja Vázquez, eds., *The Origins of the Bolero School*. Studies in Dance History 4, no. 1 (Madison: University of Wisconsin Press for Society of Dance History Scholars, 1993); Maria Teresa Linares and Faustino Nuñez, *La música entre Cuba y España* (Madrid: Fundación Autor, 1998); Faustino Nuñez, "La música española y lo español en *Carmen*," *Carmen* (program of the Teatro Real), (Madrid: Teatro Real, 1999), 140–51; José Blas Vega, *Los cafés cantantes de Sevilla* (Madrid: Cinterco, 1987); José Blas Vega, *Diccionario enciclopédico ilustrado del flamenco* (Madrid: Cinterco, 1988); Gerhard Steingress, . . . *Y Carmen se fue a París* (Cordoba: Almuzara, 2006).

16. Laura Santana Burgos, "Diálogos entre Francia y España: La traducción de los libretos de *Carmen* y *El retablo de Maese Pedro*" (PhD diss., Universidad de Granada, 2013).

17. Christiane Le Bordays, *La Musique espagnole* (Paris: Presse Universitaire de France, 1977); Montserrat Bergadá, "Les Pianistes catalans à Paris entre 1875 et 1925" (Thèse doctorat, Université François Rabelais, 1997); Montserrat Bergadá, "Musiciens espagnols à Paris entre 1820 et 1868: État de la question et perspectives d'études," in *La Musique entre France et Espagne: Interactions stylistiques 1870–1939*, ed. Louis Jambou (Paris: Presses de l'Université de Paris-Sorbonne, 2003), 17–38; Samuel Llano, *Whose Spain? Negotiating Spanish Music in Paris, 1908–1929* (New York: Oxford University Press, 2013); Geraldine Power in "Projections of Spain in Popular Spectacle and Chanson, Paris: 1889–1926" (PhD thesis, University of Melbourne, 2013).

18. Kenneth James Murray, "Spanish Music and Its Representations in London (1878–1930): From the Exotic to the Modern" (PhD thesis, University of Melbourne, 2013); Richard Kagan, "The Spanish Craze: The Discovery of Spanish Art and Culture in the United States," in *When Spain Fascinated America* ([Madrid]: Fundación Zuloaga;

With the rapid approach of the 150th anniversary of the composition of *Carmen*, Bizet's opera continues to inspire new research, notably the project *Carmen Abroad*, which brings together an international network of scholars under the distinguished leadership of Clair Rowden and Richard Langham Smith. It will gather and disseminate archive materials that document the opera's spread across the globe between 1875 and 1945, examining *Carmen* in transnational and transcultural contexts. The collegial exchange of this project has provided us with vital encouragement in the final phases of preparing this book, and promises a bright future for the ever expanding horizons of *Carmen* research.[19]

Gobierno de España, Ministerio de Cultura, 2010), 25–46; Walter Aaron Clark, *Enrique Granados: Poet of the Piano* (New York: Oxford University Press, 2006); Carol A. Hess, "A 'Puzzling Borderline Case?' Manuel de Falla y la cultura de la posguerra en los EE.UU," in El amor brujo, metá*fora de la modernidad*, ed. Elena Torres Clemente, Francisco J. Giménez Rodríguez, and Cristina Aguilar Hernández y Dácil González Mesa (Madrid and Granada: Centro de Documentación de Música y Danza—INAEM/Fundación Archivo Manuel de Falla), 427–54; Kristen M. Turner, "Opera in English: Class and Culture in America, 1878–1910" (PhD thesis, University of North Carolina at Chapel Hill, 2015).

19. For further information about *Carmen Abroad*, see the website, which features an interactive map of *Carmen* productions: http://www.carmenabroad.org/index.html

Carmen *and the Staging of Spain*

Prelude

The Spains of Paris, Mérimée, and Bizet's Carmen

L'ESPAGNE ROMANTIQUE *AND PROSPER MÉRIMÉE*

By the time Prosper Mérimée published his novella *Carmen* in 1845, the French cultural landscape was already crowded with literature, theater, and music that evoked a Romantic image of Spain. *L'Espagne romantique*, with its history and legends; its monuments and art; its customs, music, and dance; and, above all, its women, was a familiar and exotic pleasure to French audiences.[1] Spain had been repeatedly "discovered" by French travelers in the first half of the nineteenth century, when the many soldiers and officials who had traveled to Spain during and after the Peninsular War (and the anti-liberal incursion of 1823) were followed by tourists and writers. A fascination for Spanish art had been awakened by French collectors "rescuing" great works from the wartorn Iberian peninsula, while liberals disenfranchised by the end of the Napoleonic era found in Spain a revolutionary people with freedom in their very nature, and elements of a preindustrial paradise that coexisted with poverty, backwardness, and barbarism.[2]

---

1. In effect, "Spain became à la mode in France between 1800 and 1850." Lou Charnon-Deutsch, *The Spanish Gypsy: The History of a European Obsession* (University Park: Pennsylvania State University Press, 2004), 57.

2. Spanish influence on French literature, theater, and music—both high-status and popular—indicates a continuing cultural exchange. Gustave Larroumet noted the effect of visiting Spain on French painters, and celebrated the various French literary renewals sparked by Spanish-influenced works. Gustave Larroumet, "Carmen et les gitanes de Grenade," in *Nouvelles Études d'histoire et de critique dramatiques* (Paris: Librairie Hachette, 1899), 305. In line with most of the historical sources consulted, we use the term gypsy (and gipsy, *gitana*, *gitane*) instead of Romani or Roma.

At the same time, France was flooded with Spanish exiles and emigrés fleeing the political instability and repression that followed the restoration of the Bourbon monarchy in 1814, the Liberal Triennium (1820–23), and that accompanied the Carlist Wars of the 1830s and 1840s.[3] Spaniards formed a visible and creative group in Parisian culture for much of the nineteenth century, with each successive political upheaval sending a new wave of exiles fleeing northward. Writers and artists also sought out the French capital in order to extend their horizons and seek greater opportunities. The large community of expatriate Spanish artists resident in France recreated the topics of their homeland, "selling" an image of Spanishness that appealed to a public devouring travel writings, poetry, and fiction about Spain by the likes of François-René de Chateaubriand, Victor Hugo, Washington Irving, Théophile Gautier, Alexandre Dumas (*père*), and Prosper Mérimée himself. The first half of the nineteenth century saw the consolidation of stereotyped images of Spanish life and people, like bullfighters, gypsies, smugglers, and bandits, and of course Spanish women glancing coyly from under their lace mantillas or their gypsy counterparts performing exotic dances. It was during this period that the image of the dancing Spanish woman, which defined the character of Carmen, emerged in her modern form.

The theme of *l'Espagne romantique* proliferated on the Parisian stage in the post-Napoleonic era, in dance, plays, and opera.[4] Spanish dances, and more particularly the ballerinas who performed them, achieved astonishing celebrity in the 1830s and 1840s. The Austrian Fanny Elssler sparked the international enthusiasm for these dances when she introduced a *cachucha* (her version of the lively solo Andalusian dance in triple time) as part of a ballet set in Spain, *Le Diable boiteux*, at the Paris Opéra in 1836, and the dance became celebrated for its lascivious southern character (see Figure P.1). A decade later the French dancer Marie Guy-Stephan presented the *jaleo de Jerez*, similar in style to the *cachucha*, and equally popular.[5] The *jaleo* and the *cachucha* represented a style of Spanish dance based on clichés first established

3. See Montserrat Bergadá, "Musiciens espagnols à Paris entre 1820 et 1868: État de la question et perspectives d'études," in *La Musique entre France et Espagne: Interactions stylistiques 1870–1939*, ed. Louis Jambou (Paris: Presses de l'Université de Paris-Sorbonne, 2003), 17–38. For a more general discussion of the pro-French exiles who poured into France after Napoleon's defeat in 1813 and the restoration of Spain's Bourbon monarchy, and the emigration caused by the Carlist Wars, see Henry Kamen, *The Disinherited: The Exiles Who Created Spanish Culture* (London and New York: Allen Lane, 2007), 171–212.

4. For a wide-ranging consideration of the presence of Spanishness in French culture in the first half of the nineteenth century, with a particular emphasis on theater and literature, see Léon-François Hoffmann, *Romantique Espagne: L'Image de l'Espagne en France entre 1800 et 1850* (Paris: Presses Universitaires de France, 1961).

5. Emilio Sala, *The Sounds of Paris in Verdi's* La traviata, trans. Delia Casadei (Cambridge: Cambridge University Press, 2013), 78; Gerhard Steingress, . . . *Y Carmen se fue a París* (Cordoba: Almuzara, 2006), 88–112.

Figure P.1 Fanny Elssler in "La Cachucha" (1836).
Public domain.

by the *escuela bolera* (Bolero School) in the late eighteenth century. Initially characterized by song and dance genres deriving from the theater, which were often based on folk-inspired forms like the *seguidilla* and *bolero*, the *escuela bolera* had evolved by the early nineteenth century to incorporate styles associated with the *género andaluz*. These latter forms include the *tirana* and the *polo*, which can also be traced in the songs of the renowned opera singer and composer Manuel García, whose music was to prove such an important source for Bizet's own Spanish style.[6] They also shaped the Spanish character dances of the Romantic ballet school that evolved in the post-Napoleonic period. International stars like Elssler and Marie Taglioni projected a new balletic incarnation of the Spanish *escuela bolera* dance style beyond the borders of Spain.[7]

Long viewed as a backward country by more "advanced" Western European nations, Spain and its image were reinterpreted during the first half of the nineteenth century. According to José Alvarez Junco, Romantic writers following the lead taken by Gautier and Irving increasingly saw Spain as "a country of strong passions, brave people, banditry, blood and sun." The cast of characters familiar from the "Black Legend"—"the conquistador, the inquisitor, the idle aristocrat"—were "now converted into *guerrilleros*, bandits, Carlist friars, proud beggars, bullfighters," and "represented different things: bravery, pride, dignity, intense religious feelings, closeness to death and scorn for it. All this was epitomized in Mérimée's *Carmen*."[8]

Alvarez Junco argues that this more positive re-evaluation emerged in response to a sense that Spain could meet a growing interest in a commodified exoticism among the new middle classes. Spain's perceived status as a "premodern society" rendered it a conveniently close location for intellectuals seeking to celebrate a primitive paradise, unsullied by "industrialization, urbanization, and capitalism" (see Figure P.2). These notions of Spain incorporated colorful exoticism while simultaneously embracing a culture seen to be true to its roots, and offered relief from the ennui of modern Western society. This ideal Spain was characterized by spontaneity and the joy of living, and indeed by a quite specific understanding of Spanish national character.[9]

6. García was only one among many Spanish musicians who made sustained contributions to French cultural life in the early 1800s; his notable compatriots include the guitarist and composer Fernando Sor, whose ballets were produced at the Paris Opéra in the 1820s.

7. Delfín Colomé, "El ballet en España y Rusia: Influencias mutuas," in *Relaciones musicales entre España y Rusia*, ed. Antonio Álvarez Cañibano et al. (Madrid: Centro de documentación de música y danza, 1999), 130.

8. José Alvarez Junco, "The Nation-Building Process in Nineteenth-Century Spain," in *Nationalism and the Nation in the Iberian Peninsula*, ed. Clare Mar-Molinero and Angel Smith (Oxford and Washington, DC: Berg, 1996), 94.

9. Alvarez Junco, "Nation-Building Process," 94–95.

GIPSIES AT GRANADA

Figure P.2 "Gipsies at Granada" in Henry Blackburn, *Travelling in Spain in the Present Day* (London: Sampson Low, Son, and Marston, 1866), facing 208.

Prosper Mérimée traveled widely in Spain, and during his journey of 1830 he became a close friend of the family of the Count of Teba (later Montijo), forming a special intimacy with Countess Maria Manuela Montijo and her young daughter Eugenia. He tutored Eugenia and her sister in Paris during the 1830s, confirming a lifelong bond that led to preferment once Eugenia had married Napoleon III in 1853, becoming the Empress Eugénie. It seems that in the course of lively conversations, the Countess told Mérimée several stories that combined to form the kernel of his novella *Carmen*: a news story about a man who murdered his lover (a dancer) out of jealousy, and the problem of a relative who had fallen in love with a *cigarrera* (cigar maker).[10] Over subsequent visits to Spain, Mérimée became an *aficionado* of bullfighting. In constructing his *Carmen* narrative, Mérimée was able to incorporate a wealth of cultural referents: banditry and smuggling, gypsy culture (as characterized by exotic stereotypes of fortune tellers, thieves, dancers, and women of easy virtue), bullfighting, and the ubiquitous presence of the military during those years of civil disturbance and guerrilla warfare. His knowledge of these themes was furthered by his association with Spanish authors, in particular the noted purveyor of Andalusian culture, Serafín Estébanez Calderón.[11]

Mérimée overlaid these cultural signifiers on the stories he had heard in Spain, creating an innovative literary form. His *Carmen* was first published in 1845 by the *Revue des deux mondes*, purporting to be a nonfictional account of an actual journey. The first-person narrator, a learned traveler and archaeologist, presents his travel tale, then cedes the central storytelling to José the bandit. This structure of double narrative reduces the eponymous "heroine" to a subsidiary character with no real voice of her own, although she seduces both narrators and becomes their obsession. In 1846 Mérimée added a final chapter focused on gypsy culture and language, underlining the element of linguistic and ethnographic observation that permeated the work. He then published the whole piece in a volume of his own novellas. It was released into a French market saturated with literature on Spanish themes, and gradually came to be seen as Mérimée's masterpiece.[12] Despite its scholarly overlay, this novella fulfilled the vision of *l'Espagne romantique*, as delineated by Léon-François Hoffmann, by narrating the tale of "the ideal Spanish couple: the

10. Luis López Jiménez and Luis-Eduardo López Esteve, "Introducción," in *Prosper Mérimée*: Carmen, trans. Luis López Jiménez and Luis-Eduardo López Esteve (Madrid: Ediciones Cátedra, 1997), 13.

11. Hervé Lacombe and Christine Rodriguez, *La Habanera de Carmen: Naissance d'un tube* (Paris: Fayard, 2014), 23.

12. López Jiménez and López Esteve, "Introducción," 13–18; Peter Robinson, "Mérimée's *Carmen*," in *Georges Bizet*, Carmen, ed. Susan McClary (Cambridge: Cambridge University Press, 1992), 2.

bandit and the gypsy" against a richly drawn background of Spanish regional customs, especially dance and the bullfight. Hoffmann concluded that "all this forms part of the Spanish dream of the collective imagination."[13] These Spanish themes continued to interest French authors of the Second Empire, from the informed criticism of Théophile Gautier to the travel writings of Jean Charles Davillier.

EMPRESS EUGÉNIE'S PARIS AND THE *ESPAGNOLADE*

The fate of Mérimée and his Carmen owed much to the serendipity of Napoleon's 1853 marriage to Eugenia de Montijo, daughter of Countess Maria Manuela, who as Empress Eugénie made Spain the height of Parisian fashion during the Second Empire (1852–70) (see Figure P.3[14]). Parisians still remembered the charming Spanish dances of Fanny Elssler, and the Spanish-themed entertainments of the July Monarchy (1830–48), which are vividly evoked in the chorus and dance of the matadors in Giuseppe Verdi's 1853 opera *La traviata* (act 2, scene 2), in which Gastone and his friends dress up as bullfighters in a scene Emilio Sala considers reminiscent of "a pseudo-Spanish masquerade typical of Paris in the 1840s."[15] Eugénie perpetuated this fashion for Spanishness in dress and popular entertainment, hosting gatherings that included Mérimée, and featured Spanish songs performed by her music master Sebastián Iradier.

Despite Eugénie's departure from her birthplace in early childhood, Granada and its Moorish past continued to be associated with the Empress, and this connection was celebrated by the Romantic poet José Zorrilla in the "Serenata morisca" he dedicated to her on the occasion of her marriage and coronation.[16] By then resident in Paris, Zorrilla was one of a number of Spanish authors who gravitated to the French capital during the Second Empire, taking advantage of the new networks of patronage created by the presence of Eugénie and Spanish noble families that relocated to Paris, and by members of the cultural and commercial elites of the Hispano-American world (in particular from the Spanish colonies of Cuba and Puerto Rico, as well as Mexico and Argentina). The Countess of Montijo was a key figure in this

13. Unless otherwise acknowledged, all translations are by the authors. Hoffmann, *Romantique Espagne*, 134–35.

14. This image appears to be based on Édouard Odier's *Equestrian Portrait of Eugénie* (1849), in which Eugénie is depicted wearing a Spanish riding habit, mounted on an Andalusian horse. Alison McQueen, *Empress Eugénie and the Arts: Politics and Visual Culture in the Nineteenth Century* (Farnham, UK; Burlington, VT: Ashgate, 2011), 78–79.

15. Sala, *Sounds of Paris*, 79.

16. Narciso Alonso Cortés, *Zorrilla: Su vida y sus obras* (Valladolid, Spain: Imprenta Castellana, 1918), 2: 165–66.

Figure P.3 "The Empress Eugénie in Spanish Costume" in Madame Carette (née Bouvet), *My Mistress, the Empress Eugénie, Or, Court Life at the Tuileries* (London: Dean and Son, 1889), 109.

community, at times interceding to promote performances of Spanish works (including the *zarzuelas* of Francisco Asenjo Barbieri).

The influx of Spanish authors and visual and performing artists during the Second Empire, in tandem with the tastes of their patrons and the French public, served to reinscribe the tropes of *l'Espagne romantique*, in particular their depictions of Andalusia, and the performance of styles of music and dance associated with that region. The resulting art and entertainment consolidated the *espagnolade* as a genre in Paris, which became a key site for its international dissemination. While the term *espagnolade* normally denominates foreign evocations of Spain by French (or other foreign) creative and performing artists, its development was in fact nourished by Spanish artists, at times drawing directly on aspects of Spanish culture. The movement known as *costumbrismo*, which flourished during the reign of Isabel II (1833–68), saw Spanish authors and visual artists engaging with local customs and scenes of everyday life in Spain, most notably from the region of Andalusia.[17]

The Parisian *espagnolade* was arguably a unique manifestation of nineteenth-century exoticism because it resulted from continuous cultural exchange, as Spanish artists in Paris both informed the *espagnolade* and were inspired by it. Despite the timelessness associated with Spain in such depictions, manifestations of the *espagnolade* did not remain static and were influenced by changing fashions, both French and Spanish. Unlike the larger Spanish urban centers of Madrid and Barcelona, however, Parisian audiences were more likely to hear newer styles of Spanish song and dance as well as older Spanish forms dating back to the early nineteenth century, such as the *escuela bolera* dances that were institutionalized as part of the Romantic ballet performed at the Opéra.[18]

Dance was the archetypal representation of Spanishness, and the early 1850s saw an influx of new Spanish dancers in Paris. This trend is attested to by the increasing number of specifically Andalusian names and genres in programs, like "La Granadina" dancing *fandangos* in 1853 or Pepa Vargas performing a *soleá granadina* in 1854. By this time, according to Lou Charnon-Deutsch, gypsies had come to be seen as a "key element" in every kind of Spanish dance, and some of the Andalusian dancers appearing in Paris in the 1850s, such as Pepita de Oliva (famed for her *jaleo*), were given a "gypsy" epithet (see Figure P.4).[19] As more Andalusians and "gypsies" appeared in entertainment venues, Spanish dance embarked on a process of

17. There were earlier and later manifestations of *costumbrismo*, and in terms of music it is most often associated with genres of the lyric stage, including the *zarzuela* and the shorter, often comic, *género chico*.

18. Celsa Alonso, *La canción lírica española en el siglo XIX* (Madrid: ICCMU, 1998), 233–76; Steingress, *Carmen*, 163–86.

19. Charnon-Deutsch, *Spanish Gypsy*, 48.

Figure P.4 Pepita de Oliva dancing "El ole" (*c.* 1850).
Credit: From the New York Public Library, Jerome Robbins Dance Division, https://digitalcollections.nypl.org/items/55f93d80-d711-0132-5789-58d385a7bbd0.

Orientalization that removed it decisively from the sphere of the Romantic ballet, which had been championed by cosmopolitan stars like Elssler. This process of Orientalization and hybridization of Spanish dance in Paris (and companies performing between Spain and Paris), formed a substrate for the evolution and staging of flamenco dance in the second half of the nineteenth century.[20]

In terms of Spanish song, the *género andaluz*, which had gained prominence in the first half of the nineteenth century, still held sway in Paris. The continuing influence of the genre was in part due to the efforts of performers such as Pauline Viardot and other members of the García clan (including Maria Malibran and Manuel García junior), and French theatrical works that perpetuated forms like the *seguidillas, tiranas,* and *polos*. Of even greater importance to the development of Spanish song in the Second Empire was the composer Sebastián Iradier, who had been associated with the Madrid court and went on to become Eugénie's singing teacher. He developed the existing body of Andalusian songs, at times performed in the dress of a matador, and introduced new elements to the genre. But perhaps his greatest contribution to the *espagnolade* was in the dissemination of the habanera, that sensuous song-dance form that superimposes (and juxtaposes) triple and duple rhythmic figures.[21]

The habanera originated in Cuba through the Creolization of the European contredanse, and elements of this style were first presented to Parisian audiences in the late 1840s through the works of the New Orleans pianist Louis Moreau Gottschalk.[22] From the mid-nineteenth century the habanera also became a popular Spanish urban song and dance form, commonly referred to as an *americana*, but was not principally construed as an exotic genre, because Cuban culture was still strongly identified with Spain.[23] It belonged to the category of *canciones de ida y vuelta* ("round-trip" songs), reflecting the repeated journey between the Iberian peninsula and the New World, along with several other popular or flamenco song and dance styles performed in the nineteenth century. By the 1860s, the habanera had been subjected to Hispanicization, integrating features of Andalusian song.[24] In Europe it became a social dance and song style, and a favorite in aristocratic salons of France's late Second Empire, where it clearly denoted Spanishness.[25] The fact that the habanera was in part popularized in the court of Napoleon III and his Spanish wife, and

20. Steingress, *Carmen*, 13–23.

21. Alonso explores the *género andaluz* and its evolution in Paris in her groundbreaking volume on Romantic Spanish song: Alonso, *La canción lírica*, 233–76.

22. Lacombe and Rodriguez, *La Habanera de Carmen*, 91–103. Lacombe and Rodriguez also point out the slightly earlier piano works of Julian Fontana published in Paris in the mid-1840s.

23. Even after the loss of Cuba as a colony in 1898, Manuel de Falla included a "Cubana" as one of his *Cuatro piezas españolas* (1906–8). See also Linares and Nuñez, *La música entre Cuba y España*, 191–92.

24. Lacombe and Rodriguez, *La Habanera de Carmen*, 103; Alonso, *La canción lírica*, 264–67.

25. Dozens of editions of Iradier's songs appeared in Paris, with major collections released *c.* 1857 and in 1864. The covers of the sheet music name singers who performed Iradier's music (including Maria Malibran, Pauline Viardot, and Adelina

in the leading salons of Paris, casts doubt on modern claims that this "Creole" or "African-Cuban" form was principally associated with the ill repute of the Parisian cabaret.[26] However, it can be viewed as an "Orientalized" form of Spanishness, as were the *chansons maures* that appeared in French salons from the 1860s, a Spanish development in the wake of the Moroccan campaigns of the 1850s, which aligned with a wave of Arab Andalusian nostalgia. These had their French counterparts in the *chansons mauresques* of the 1860s by the French composer (of Spanish parentage) Francisco Salvador Daniel, some of which were identified as *chansons andalouses*, or Arab Andalusian songs from Spain's Moorish diaspora.

The *chansons maures* were also performed by Spanish guitarists and vocalists associated with Parisian salons during the Second Empire, such as Jaime Bosch (see Figure P.5) and Lorenzo Pagans, who were painted by Édouard Manet and Edgar Degas respectively. Another of the famed Spanish classical guitarists present in the Hispanic circles of Paris was Trinidad Huerta, who, like Julián Arcas, had received the patronage of Queen Isabel II. Arcas included habaneras and protoflamenco forms in his repertoire, conforming with the tastes of Isabel II.[27] By the mid-nineteenth century the guitar was viewed increasingly as a Spanish instrument in Paris, and was intimately associated with the soundscape and imagery of Spain.

From around 1850 several generations of Spanish painters resident in Paris contributed to the success of the *espagnolade*, which in the visual arts coalesces around the Exposition Universelle of 1855.[28] Parisians' fascination with Spanish music and dance was complemented by revivals of interest in historic Spanish painting and engagement with Spanish themes by French painters such as Manet, who often depicted Spanish performers and was closely associated with Eugénie's court. Encouraged by the markets created through *l'art pompier* (academic paintings, especially on historical themes), and the Second Empire vogue for the *espagnolade*, a second wave of Spanish artists began to arrive in Paris in the 1860s. By the early 1870s some of the leading Spanish artists known to the French public included Mariano Fortuny with his Orientalist visions of Spain, the realist painter Eduardo Zamacois y Zabala, and the Spanish-born Daniel Vierge, who published many illustrations

Patti) while making claims that the songs were performed at the leading salons of Paris and London. Alonso, *La canción lírica*, 317–18.

26. Susan McClary, *Georges Bizet,* Carmen (Cambridge: Cambridge University Press, 1992), 51–52.

27. Isabel II also had a penchant for the emerging flamenco song forms accompanied by guitar, and in 1866 one of the leading exponents of the artform, Silverio Franconetti, performed for her.

28. Alonso, *La canción lírica*, 305; Carlos González López and Montserrat Martí Ayxelá, *Pintores españoles en París: 1850–1900* (Barcelona: Tusquets, 1989), 13–54.

Figure P.5 J. Bosch, *Plainte Moresque*, op. 85 (1862); cover image by Édouard Manet
Credit: From the New York Public Library, https://digitalcollections.nypl.org/items/510d47da-41be-a3d9-c040-e00a18004a99

in *Le Monde illustré*.[29] The fashion for folk-inspired or antiquated Spanish dress (perpetuated by costume balls) and the reintroduction of bullfights to Paris in the late 1850s further reinforced the picturesque elements of Spanishness, as did the *costumbrista* paintings created by Spanish artists.

29. Orientalist visions of Spanish Morocco by Spanish artists like Fortuny both drew upon and influenced French painters like Henri Regnault.

The popularity and oversaturation of the espagnolade is attested to by the number of parodic stage works on Spanish themes produced during the Second Empire, including the *folies-concertantes* and operettas by Hervé (Florimond Ronger). However, by the mid-1860s Spanish-themed entertainments began to lose favor, coinciding with the declining fortunes of Napoleon and Eugénie's regime, although there were more pointed references to the regime in works by Jacques Offenbach, at times with a Spanish theme aimed at Eugénie (as was the case with *La Périchole* of 1868).[30] This was only a temporary setback, because the exile of Queen Isabel II to Paris from 1868 (made permanent by her abdication in 1870) provided renewed patronage for Spanish artists. A prominent sponsor of the arts (especially works drawing on popular culture) during her long reign in Spain, Isabel continued these activities in the company of the noble families who relocated with her to Paris. In the wake of the 1867 Exposition Universelle, these developments provided further encouragement for the large number of Spanish musicians gravitating to Paris.

Albums of Spanish songs were in demand in Paris, especially from the late 1860s, building on the growing market for both popular and classical music in Spain itself during the years of the *Sexenio Democrático* (dating from the revolution of 1868 to the Bourbon restoration in 1874). During this period numerous collections of folk and popular songs—often known as *cancioneros*—were published in Spain, some of which were also popular in Paris. This era also marks the beginnings of travel writers describing some of the flamenco genres that had begun to be disseminated in the *cafés cantantes* (taverns with musical entertainment and usually dancers) of the 1870s. These venues, especially after 1870 when Silverio Franconetti opened the first of his establishments in Seville, created the contexts for the coalescing of flamenco forms, their modes of performance, and staging, while contributing to the professionalization of flamenco song (*cante*), dance (*baile*), and guitar playing (*toque*).

PROJECTIONS OF SPAIN IN GEORGES BIZET'S *CARMEN*

Bizet's choice of Mérimée's *Carmen* as the subject for his new *opéra comique* appears almost quixotic, as it posed his librettists Henri Meilhac and Ludovic Halévy a significant challenge.[31] Not only were they faced with the delicate task of reimagining Mérimée's well-known and rather brutal story for the

---

30. Steingress, *Carmen*, 13–23.
31. Lesley Wright, "*Carmen* and the Opéra-Comique," in Carmen: *Georges Bizet*, ed. Gary Kahn (Richmond, UK: Overture, 2013), 43.

bourgeois audience of the Opéra-Comique, but they also had to construct an effective drama with just enough Spanish local color to entertain a public perhaps slightly weary of a topic still associated with the overthrown Second Empire. Meilhac and Halévy were, however, celebrated writers of the French theater (authors of many Offenbach operettas), capable of incorporating spectacle, topical elements, and humor while still allowing the human drama of the story to play out.

By commissioning a new opera from Bizet, Meilhac, and Halévy in 1872, Camille Du Locle, director of the Opéra-Comique, was attempting to renovate the theater's repertoire and breathe new life into the traditionalist opéra comique style.[32] His company, which performed in the Salle Favart on the Place Boïeldieu, was dedicated to lighter operatic subjects, with spoken dialogue, differentiating their offerings from the staple of grand opera featured at the nearby Opéra. The subject of Carmen broke with the trend for opéras comiques on historical themes, in which the heroes were almost always noble or royal. This approach did not change until around 1879, when works celebrating the lower classes began to appear, and may have materially affected the reception of Carmen when it reappeared on the Parisian stage in 1883.[33] It is possible that the librettists consciously injected a satirical element in their portrait of the two main characters, as the downfall of ineffectual northerner José because of his obsession with the showy southern gypsy Carmen reflected the widespread belief that Napoleon III lost his throne as a result of allowing his Spanish wife, Eugénie, to exercise too much power.[34] In their collaboration with Offenbach, Meilhac and Halévy had already alluded to the excesses of the Second Empire and the power of the Empress, especially in La Grande Duchesse de Gerolstein (1867) and La Périchole (1868, revised 1874, based on a play by Mérimée). The protagonist of La Périchole is a poor Hispanic street singer who uses her wits to avoid the lecherous advances of the Viceroy of Peru and the plot allowed Offenbach to include a seguidilla and bolero among the numbers.[35]

32. Steven Huebner, French Opera at the Fin de Siècle: Wagnerism, Nationalism, and Style (Oxford and New York: Oxford University Press, 1999), 197. See Wright's essay for further discussion of the Opéra Comique from the late 1860s to 1875: Wright, "Carmen and the Opéra-Comique," 36–42.

33. Spies observes conservative tendencies in his study of libretti of both the Opéra and the Opéra-Comique, but identifies liberalizing changes after 1879 at the Opéra-Comique only. André Michael Spies, Opera, State and Society in the Third Republic, 1875–1914 (New York: Peter Lang, 1998), 8.

34. This idea is suggested by Nelly Furman in "The Languages of Love in Carmen," in Reading Opera, ed. Arthur Groos and Roger Parker (Princeton, NJ: Princeton University Press, 1988), 169.

35. La Périchole sings the line "Il grandira, car il est Espagnol" (which was thought to refer to Eugénie's advancement of Spaniards, or possibly be a compliment to her son,

Carmen's less than heroic leading man aside, Meilhac and Halévy created a cast of characters both to entertain and touch the heart: Escamillo provides a welcome swagger as the colorful bullfighter, while the addition of Micaëla— extraneous both to the central love triangle and the opera's projection of Spain—contributes an unthreatening and wholesome foil to Carmen, and stands in for José's absent and loving mother. Carmen herself is a new kind of protagonist. Her identity transcends that of the femme fatale, for she is an entertainer who performs Spanishness in nearly all her numbers, whether through her sensuality, the abandon of the dance, or gypsy superstition. Despite her narrative of independence and famous solo arias, closer examination of the words reveal that Carmen has little subjective or first-person lyric utterance, and although she may ruin José, she is equally clearly the victim of inescapable destiny.

Meilhac and Halévy's simplification of the dramatic structure, contrasting with the complexity and detail of Mérimée's novella, led to criticism of their efforts. According to Halévy, playwright Jean Henri Dupin complained,

> Here is a man who meets a woman … he finds her pretty, that's the first act. He loves her, she loves him, that's the second. She doesn't love him any more, that's the third. He kills her, and that's the fourth.
>
> And you call that a play! In a real play you have to have surprises, misunderstandings, adventures, things that make one ask "what is going to happen in the next act?"[36]

Yet this was to become the most familiar of operatic stories, renowned for its strong dramatic narrative. Dupin seemed to miss the opera's underlying theme of inexorable and tragic fate, which stemmed from the implication of both the ancient Greek epigraph about woman's bitterness that opens the novella, and Mérimée's closing sentence, in which he blames Carmen's tragic destiny on her gypsy race. French Hispanist Jean Sentaurens defends the libretto, declaring it a "faithful and intelligent reading" of Mérimée's work, in which Meilhac and Halévy simply reduced José's long narrative to its fundamental

the young Prince Napoleon). Arturo Delgado Cabrera and Emilio Menéndez Ayuso, "*Saynete, opérette, fête*: En torno a Mérimée y Offenbach," *Anales de filología francesa* 17 (2009): 155.

36. Jean Henri Dupin, who had been a noted collaborator of Eugène Scribe, was affronted by the work's inattention to basic tenets of construction: he criticized the continuity of the score, which left too few places for applause, and he was enraged by the shortcomings of the plot. Visiting the librettists the day after the premiere, he expressed his exasperation, as recalled by Halévy in this quotation. Ludovic Halévy, "La Millième Représentation de *Carmen*," *Le Théâtre* 145 (January [I] 1905): 10.

schema, concentrating the action in four spectacular episodes that represent the stages in the tragic confrontation between the two protagonists.[37]

Meilhac and Halévy took Mérimée's realist descriptions of a lawless and at times savage Spain, and transformed them into *l'Espagne romantique*, neatly packaged for the bourgeois theater, abandoning the various locations of the original in favor of a clear focus on Seville, the archetypal site of Spanish exoticism. To the existing Spanish stereotypes of bandits smuggling in the mountains and sensual gypsy women, they added sufficient local color—a few additional gypsy characters and a bullfight, that compulsory emblem of Spain—to sell the story on the Opéra-Comique stage. This predigested exoticism synthesized all the main elements of local color, within the librettists' attempt to ameliorate the plot's essential violence by avoiding scenes that would discomfit a polite audience, a process that led some critics to comment on their active exclusion of the "harsher reality" of Mérimée's original.[38] In the opinion of the renowned Italian critic and godfather of operatic verismo, Amintore Galli, Meilhac and Halévy had faithfully adapted Mérimée's novella (with the exception of their invention of Micaëla). Galli argued that "[o]ne needs to recognize that their reduction was made with great knowledge of the theater."[39] Indeed, taken in the context of contemporary operatic exoticism featuring spectacular settings in Egypt or the Far East, their employment of local color could be viewed as restrained. The familiarity of the Spanish stereotypes meant that they could be fully integrated into the production, allowing Bizet to create a coherent and recognizable world, a setting sufficiently familiar that it did not detract attention from the drama itself.

Bizet also wished to renew the *opéra comique* genre, doing away with vocal display and effect for its own sake and as a means to draw applause from the audience. According to Halévy, he sought instead to imbue the work with the maximum "truth and passion, movement and life."[40] *Carmen*'s first act is

37. For an overview of the adaptation, see Edgar Istel and Janet Wylie Istel (trans.), "Carmen: Novel and Libretto: A Dramaturgic Analysis," *Musical Quarterly* 7, no. 4 (1921): 493–510. See also Chapter 2, "The Genesis of Bizet's *Carmen*," in McClary, *Georges Bizet, Carmen*, 15–28; Jean Sentaurens, "*Carmen*: De la novela de 1845 a la zarzuela de 1887; Cómo nació 'la España de Mérimée,'" *Bulletin hispanique* [104], no. 2 (2002): 857. For a lively synopsis coupled with a detailed examination of the work's adaptation from novella to libretto, see Richard Langham Smith, "*Carmen*: From Mérimée to Bizet," in Carmen: *Georges Bizet*, ed. Gary Kahn, 11–34.

38. Mina Curtiss, *Bizet and His World* (New York: Vienna House, 1958), 383; Kerry Murphy, "*Carmen*: Couleur locale or the Real Thing?" in *Music, Theater, and Cultural Transfer: Paris, 1830–1914*, ed. Annegret Fauser and Mark Everist (Chicago and London: University of Chicago Press, 2009), 309.

39. Amintore Galli, "*Carmen*: Dramma lirico in quattro atti . . . ," *Il teatro illustrato*, 16 December 1880, 3–4, 7; reproduced in Sergio Viglino, *La fortuna italiana della "Carmen" di Bizet (1879–1900)* (Torino: EDT, 2003), 88.

40. Halévy, "La Millième Représentation de *Carmen*," 8.

recognizable as an *opéra comique*, with its conventional plot and clearly defined numbers, especially the duet between Micaëla and Don José. The later
acts, however, depart more and more radically from the traditional forms,
with only some numbers like the "Toreador Song" in act 2 and Micaëla's aria
in act 3 operating within the familiar style. The almost continuous musical
fabric of the final act heightened its shocking drama and further distanced the
work from *opéra comique* conventions.

The radical conception of the opera's final act indicates the librettists' sensitivity to changing representations of Spain in music and literature. Mérimée led
his unhappy couple to a deserted hillside for an unobserved final confrontation,
whereas Meilhac and Halévy provided an almost Oriental setting for the death of
Carmen by moving it to a spectacular and public location, set against the tumult
and excitement of an invisible but audible bullfight. The Opéra-Comique's set
designers contributed a magnificent design with three great quasi-Arab arches
to frame the murder of Carmen, bringing to mind images from Henri Regnault,
Georges Clairin, and Fortuny's celebrated Orientalist paintings of the early 1870s
that portrayed the massacre of the Abencerrajes, the despotic final Moorish dy-
nasty of fifteenth-century Granada. In an ironic cultural twist, the representation of Arab despotism in these paintings, especially in the case of Regnault, may
have been inspired by the bloody suppression of the Paris Commune, and is dis-
tantly echoed in the 1875 poster for *Carmen*, which depicts her corpse framed by
a great Arab archway (see Figure P.6).

Bizet may have emulated Mérimée in employing sources that were already
part of the musical panoply of *l'Espagne romantique* and the *espagnolade*. He
constructed the local color of his score from recognizable and remembered
Spanish music, and if he adapted classic, familiar, even conventional song
forms, these choices may explain why the French critics at the opera's premiere did not find the Spanish forms in themselves remarkable.

Bizet's musical depiction of Spain seems to be based on direct musical
borrowings from published sources in only two instances, but as Locke has
demonstrated, the identification of Bizet's sources is perhaps less interesting
than the way he adapted and transformed them. The first of these borrowings,
in terms of the opera's compositional chronology, occurs in the entr'acte to
act 4; the entr'acte is based on elements of Manuel García's early nineteenth-
century *polos* "Cuerpo bueno, alma divina" and "El contrabandista." The second
is Carmen's immortal "Habanera" (act 1), which marks the beginning of her
relationship with José and the inclusion of which was indebted to the intervention of the first Carmen, Célestine Galli-Marié.[41] This late addition to the
opera was adapted from "El arreglito" by Iradier, whose works enjoyed great

41. For discussion of Galli-Marié's involvement in the composition of *Carmen*, see
Karen Henson, *Opera Acts: Singers and Performance in the Late Nineteenth Century*
(Cambridge: Cambridge University Press, 2015), 52–53; Hervé Lacombe, "La Version

Figure P.6 Prudent Louis Leray, poster for premiere of *Carmen* (1875).
Credit: Bibliothèque Nationale de France.

primitive de l'air d'entrée de Carmen: Réflexion sur la dramaturgie et 'l'autorialité' d'un opéra," in *Aspects de l'opéra français de Meyerbeer à Honegger*, edited by Jean-Christophe Branger and Vincent Giroud (Lyon, France: Symétrie, 2009), 29–45. In addition to discussing Galli-Marié, Ralph P. Locke provides a detailed examination of Bizet's borrowings in "Spanish Local Color in Bizet's *Carmen*: Unexplored Borrowings and Transformations," in *Music, Theater, and Cultural Transfer*, ed. Fauser and Everist (Chicago and London: University of Chicago Press, 2009c), 316–60.

vogue in Paris and who was best known for another of his habaneras, the ever popular "La paloma." The marked Spanish character of Carmen's "Séguedille" from the end of act I, sung to inveigle José into letting her escape custody, shows its roots in the *seguidilla*, a Spanish song and dance form that was popular in France in the first half of the nineteenth century.[42]

It has become commonplace to perceive aspects of flamenco in the music of *Carmen*, and this association has been reinforced by productions of the opera over the twentieth century. The protagonist expresses herself through song and dance, and she is typically depicted as a flamenco performer, but flamenco as we recognize it today was largely unknown to Bizet. None of the song and dance forms employed by Bizet can be classified as flamenco, an art form that was just coalescing in Spain when *Carmen* was composed. The Parisian public caught glimpses of this new style in some of the dance spectacles of the Second Empire—particularly in the evolving Orientalization and gypsification of dance styles from the *escuela bolera*—and through the travel writings and images of Spain being disseminated in the 1860s and 1870s. What we have in *Carmen* is reference to a number of song forms—especially the *polo*—that form part of the preflamenco era of the *género andaluz*, which in turn nourished and informed some of the flamenco forms (or *palos*). But in a process that paralleled the evolution of flamenco forms and dance styles, Bizet dramatized and Orientalized elements that he had drawn from the *género andaluz* and other sources in his depiction of Spain.[43] Bizet's new orchestral stylization of Spanish music in turn facilitated the use of his music as a backdrop for flamenco dance performances by 1900, either within the opera or in danced adaptations, thereby consolidating the nexus between *Carmen* and flamenco.

One of the markers of the *género andaluz* was the Andalusian cadence, a stepwise descending chordal progression over a four-note figure, or tetrachord (i–VII–VI–V in relation to a minor key, and often expressed as the chords of A minor, G major, F major, and E major when played on the guitar). The Andalusian cadence, more often used as an ostinato or repeated chord progression, forms the harmonic basis of a number of flamenco *palos*. Bizet clearly and dramatically enunciated this progression in the midst of the entr'acte to act 4, played *fortissimo* in the orchestra with the descending line emphatically proclaimed by the trumpets and trombones. In addition to such presentations

---

42. Locke speculates that the lyrics of Carmen's "Séguedille" are related to Iradier's "El arreglito." Locke, "Spanish Local Color," 353–58.

43. Locke argues that Bizet may have referred to a transcription of another preflamenco form in the guise of the "Malagueña" transcribed by P. Lacome in *Echos d'Espagne: Chansons & danses populaire*, collected and transcribed by P. Lacome and J. Puig y Alsubide (Paris: Durand et Fils, n.d.). See Locke, "Spanish Local Color," 320.

of the Andalusian cadence in its original form, Bizet also adapted it and placed it into a variety of musical contexts throughout the score.

The "fate" motive, which is first heard in the overture and is employed dramatically throughout the opera, has been repeatedly referred to as one of the Orientalized or Arab elements of Bizet's score. The early-twentieth-century French composer and Hispanist Raoul Laparra described it as "a swarthy type with its interval of the augmented second.... It seems to exhale a strong and magical breath of Africa. It has something of the desert and the devastated soul of Don José.... It is also Carmen."[44] Closer to Bizet's time it had also been identified as a distinctly Arab element of the score by the Spanish composer and critic Felipe Pedrell and the Italian critic Galli, who claimed that it was based on a descending tetrachord of the Arab Asbein mode.[45] However, it is more likely that Bizet—an experienced purveyor of musical exoticism in operas such as *Djamileh* and *Les Pêcheurs de perles*—actually chromaticized his Spanish sources, in this case inserting an augmented second (that ubiquitous musical marker of the Orient) into the falling tetrachord of the Andalusian cadence to fashion the fate motive. Bizet applied this process of chromatic inflection to his other Spanish borrowings, including the vocal line of Carmen's "Habanera," possibly with the intention of further Orientalizing or dramatizing the original sources.

The Andalusian cadence is alluded to as a harmonic ostinato in passages of the "Chanson bohème" (act 2), although it is augmented temporally with each chord repeated over several bars. The employment of an ostinato bass in this number echoes long-standing associations of repetitive harmonic patterns such as the *folia* or the *romanesca* with Spain (as noted by some of the early critics of the opera), and contemporary evocations of a gypsy dance, or *romalis*, although this last form is more specifically referenced by Carmen's number in act 2, "Je vais danser en votre honneur." Building from the simple flute strains of its quiet entry, and adding new instrumental color as the energy intensifies with each new stanza, the "Chanson bohème" literally speeds toward its ecstatic climax. This acceleration to the finish accords with the practice of some flamenco *bailes* (as well as representations of gypsy dance music from the latter part of the nineteenth century), a device that further accommodated its later staging as a flamenco spectacle.

Another key component of the *género andaluz* was the employment of the guitar or its evocation. Elements of this style were to be developed and refined by guitarists performing in Paris in the 1860s and 1870s, and Bizet was

44. Raoul Laparra, *Bizet et l'Espagne* (Paris: Librairie Delegrave, 1935), 12–13.
45. F. P. [Felipe Pedrell], "La quincena musical," *Ilustración musical hispano-americana* 1, no. 2 (1888): 10; Amintore Galli, "Del melodrama attraverso la storia e dell'opera verista del Bizet," *Il teatro illustrato* 4, no. 9 (March 1884): 34–36, reproduced in Viglino, *La fortuna italiana della Carmen*, 111.

familiar with these effects through hearing performances or studying piano imitations of such music. Passages of Bizet's score reflect guitar tuning and the harmonic practices associated with the instrument in the *género andaluz*. The idiosyncratic tuning of the open strings is hinted at in sections of the "Chanson bohème," while the entr'acte to act 4 references some of the harmonic peculiarities that arise from strumming a chord that includes some open strings, and then shifting the fingered chord shape up and down the fret board against the unchanging pitch of the open strings.[46] The "Chanson bohème" and the entr'acte to act 4 also provide examples of Bizet evoking the sonority of the guitar, principally via pizzicato strings and harp, which are at times accompanied by the *tambour de basque*, adding a further touch of Spanish color. Castanets, another quintessential marker of Spain, also feature in Bizet's score, most notably played by Carmen to accompany her *romalis* in act 2.

Even beyond his imitation of the guitar, Bizet invested the local color of *Carmen* with a new orchestral garb and dynamism that brought his instrumental writing to the fore as a key marker of Spanishness, relaunching the orchestral showpiece on Spanish themes that traced its origins to Mikhail Glinka's *Capriccio brilliante on the Jota aragonesa* (1845). Reviewing the premiere of *Carmen*, Victor Fournel claimed that orchestration, which had usually been nothing more than an "accompagnement subaltern" at the Opéra-Comique, was taken to a new level by Bizet, perhaps going so far as to convert the opera from a dramatic to a symphonic work.[47] The orchestral color and filigree of *Carmen* was even lauded by Spanish critics, and became a model for Spanish composers. The symphonic evocation of Spanish forms by French composers had gained momentum in the 1870s, in particular in works such as Édouard Lalo's *Symphonie Espagnole* (1874). A key figure in this enterprise was the virtuoso violinist Pablo Sarasate, one of a new wave of Spanish performers arriving in Paris during the Second Empire, who was well received by French audiences and accepted as a peer by the musicians associated with the Société Nationale de Musique (see Figure P.7). He had performed with Bizet in this forum in 1873 and is thought to have suggested a folk source that was adapted by Bizet into Carmen's "tra la la la" riposte to Zuñiga and José in the penultimate number of act 1.[48] Sarasate prefigures the complicity and agency of Spanish artists, most notably Isaac Albéniz and Enrique Granados,

46. Locke, "Spanish Local Color," 345. Locke has argued convincingly that Bizet could have observed this practice in his copy of P. Lacome and J. Puig y Alsubide's *Echos d'Espagne*.

47. Victor Fournel, "Les Oeuvres et les hommes," *Le Correspondant* (Paris), 10 March 1875, in Lesley Wright, ed., *Georges Bizet,* Carmen: *Dossier de presse parisienne (1875)* (Weinsberg, Germany: Lucie Galland, 2001), 100.

48. María Nagore Ferrer, *Sarasate: El violín de Europa* (Madrid: ICCMU, 2013), 186.

Figure P.7 Pablo de Sarasate (after a photograph by Fr. Hanfstängl), in *Die Gartenlaube* 7 (1886): 113.

in the consolidation and evolution of Spanish musical tropes in Western concert music.

Bizet's score is also filled with brilliant evocations of local color without necessarily having direct recourse to Spanish musical styles: for instance, in the chorus numbers and crowd scenes that open acts 1 and 4. Likewise, his masterful use of fanfares and marches not only indicates the military presence in Seville (act 1), but also sets the stage for the disembodied bugle call that reminds José of his duty when he is tempted to stay with Carmen in act 2. Bizet probably composed original fanfares imitating military practice, although he may have also had in mind the long-standing musical traditions of depicting Spanish military fanfares (especially the retreat).

The bullfight, while not actually depicted on stage, is used by Bizet as a musical frame for the opera, from the evocative fanfares and marches of the overture to the boisterous music of the final act. In Escamillo's "Toreador Song" (act 2), Bizet describes all the pageantry and drama of the bullfight before breaking into the jaunty, swaggering march that quickly became one of the opera's most popular numbers. Although not a *pasodoble*, which is the type of march traditionally performed at and during a bullfight, it gained such popularity (even in Spain) that it has on occasion been played at real bullfights during the twentieth century. Likewise, the march that begins the overture to *Carmen* could be construed as evoking a *pasodoble*.[49] In the stunning denouement to the opera, fragments of this march and the "Toreador Song" are reprised, a reminder of the bullfight playing out offstage that breaks in waves of sound across the final, fatal confrontation between Carmen and José. It is the perfect union of local color, drama, and the staging of Spain.

49. Some of Bizet's fanfares may also suggest the fanfares that punctuate the commencement and different *tercios* (thirds or sections) of a bullfight.

PART I

Carmen's Early Escapades (1875–90)

CHAPTER 1

cⱴɔ

Premiere and Revival

Paris, Galli-Marié, and Spanish Affairs

Carmen was finally premiered at the Opéra-Comique on 3 March 1875, after a difficult six-month rehearsal period, but failed to establish itself at the Opéra-Comique. By the eve of the opera's debut, the theater's Director, Camille Du Locle, had become increasingly nervous about the whole production and was clearly aware of the work's potential to create a scandal.[1] As a whole, the opera posed its Opéra-Comique audience challenges aplenty, from genre disruption and musical innovation to its controversial subject matter and, above all, Célestine Galli-Marié's realist performance style in the title role. But there were multiple factors behind the celebrated "failure" of *Carmen*'s premiere, including cultural politics connected with the theater and the broader political resonances of the opera's plot and setting. While the opera employed Spanish local color in familiar settings like the square, tavern, and bullring, and was populated by smugglers, gypsies, and bullfighters—themes that had been worked and reworked in literature and on the Parisian stage throughout the nineteenth century—Bizet and his librettists found new ways to dramatize the representation of Spain and Spanishness. It was to take the passing of seven

---

1. Du Locle's nerves were exacerbated by the extra preparation required by the expanded chorus, which struggled to cope with the difficulties presented by Bizet's music, and with the dramatic movement required of them. Even the librettists were anxious, and sought to soften both the harsh realism of the opera's brutal ending, and the frank sensuality of the title character. For further details, see Mina Curtiss, *Bizet and His World* (New York: Vienna House, 1958), 389–92; Hugh Macdonald, *Bizet*, The Master Musicians (Oxford and New York: Oxford University Press, 2014), 210–12; Lesley Wright, "*Carmen* and the Opéra-Comique," in Carmen: *Georges Bizet*, ed. Gary Kahn (Richmond, UK: Overture, 2013a), 47.

years and a new wave of Spanish fashion to reconcile the Opéra-Comique to what eventually became its most enduring and popular work.

CARMEN'S EARLY CONTRETEMPS

It must have been a very long night at the Opéra-Comique for the audience on 3 March 1875, with four substantial acts interspersed by half-hour intermissions and the addition of encored numbers. The tale of the public's evolving response to the opera has often been told: act 1 was greeted with enthusiasm, and after responding positively to the Habanera, the children's march, and José and Micaëla's duet, the opening-night audience also welcomed the entertaining aspects of act 2, like the opening dance and song sequence of the "Chanson bohème," Escamillo's couplets (the famous "Toreador Song") and the smugglers' quintet. But the musically fluid encounter between José and Carmen may have been a little challenging, breaking as it did with the Opéra-Comique's conventions of a simpler number structure. In act 3 the familiar, arguably "Gounodesque" quality of Micaëla's prayer aria, "Je dis que rien ne m'épouvante," was applauded, but after the longeurs of this act, even the colorful Spanish gaiety of the start of act 4 could not prevent a sense of cold indifference, tinged with outrage, from hanging over the entire final act. After the opening crowd scene, the success of act 4 rests squarely on the dramatic and musical ability of José and Carmen, and its impact was undoubtedly weakened on this occasion by Paul Lhérié's unconvincing performance as José, in addition to the continuous music and unconventional tragic ending.[2]

The staging of Spain in the Opéra-Comique, or indeed any popular Parisian theater of this era, was both popular and familiar. The 1875 production of *Carmen*, however, was considered exceptional for its beautifully executed decor, in which critics noted the work of artists rather than hack theater designers.[3] Galli-Marié's costumes were designed by Georges-Jules-Victor

2. Karen Henson, *Opera Acts: Singers and Performance in the Late Nineteenth Century* (Cambridge: Cambridge University Press, 2015), 164; Lesley A. Wright, "*Carmen* and the Critics," in *Tan-yin-lun-yue: Conference Proceedings of "Musical Research and Music Practice," 1999* (Taipei: Gao-Tan, 2000), 50; Paul de Saint-Victor, "Revue dramatique et littéraire," *Le Moniteur universel* (Paris), 8 March 1875, quoted in Lesley Wright, ed., *Georges Bizet, Carmen: Dossier de presse parisienne (1875)* (Weinsberg, Germany: Lucie Galland, 2001), 48. Wright's article "*Carmen* and the Critics" provides a compelling and nuanced analysis of the premiere, employing the useful concept of how the opera and its performers positioned and repositioned the audience. The classic narrative of the premiere can be found in Curtiss, *Bizet and His World*, 389–92.

3. Evan Baker, "The Scene Designs for the First Performances of Bizet's 'Carmen,'" *19th-Century Music* 13, no. 3 (1990): 230–42.

Clairin, who had accompanied the artist Henri Regnault on his celebrated 1868 trip to Spain, while the dragoons' costumes were assigned to a noted military artist, Jean-Baptiste Édouard Detaille.[4] Although lithographs of the stage designs by Auguste Lamy survive in the archive of Bizet's publisher, Choudens, it is unclear whether he was in fact the artist responsible, and the artist's name was not promoted in the press as a drawcard for the opera. Unlike later productions, for which designers were sent to Spain to purchase costumes and make sketches on location, in 1875 the Opéra-Comique was satisfied with a less direct "authenticity" (see Figure 1.1). No ragged or scantily clad chorus members affronted the bourgeois sensibility of this respectable audience. Instead, well-dressed actors played against backdrops that displayed fine stone architecture and recreated an image of *l'Espagne romantique* that had become a stereotype during the Second Empire. This theatrical Spain was apparently untouched by the harsher realities described by travelers and depicted by artists like Gustave Doré or in contemporary French photographs of poverty-stricken gypsies and Sevillian tobacco workers. The barren mountain pass that formed the backdrop to act 3 was the only exception to *Carmen*'s benign picture of Spain, but even this scene lacked originality, because of its striking similarity to the set of Offenbach's *Les Brigands* (1869), recently revived at the Variétés, which was instantly noted.[5] Some critics praised the fresh realism of the production, pointing to its similarities with images by Spanish artists then in vogue in Paris. Albert de Lasalle casually observed that the picturesque quality of the decors and costumes was reminiscent of leafing through a picture album by Mariano Fortuny or Daniel Vierge, while Paul de Saint-Victor declared that the gay local color of the tavern scene (act 2) and the procession of bullfighters that opened act 4 "could have been signed by Fortuny or [Eduardo] Zamacois."[6]

The link between *Carmen*'s visual style and well worn tropes of Spanish-styled entertainment is made explicit in critical praise for the gypsy revelry of act 2. Set in a rather fine patio, complete with decorative stone balcony and palm tree, the Opéra-Comique managed to squeeze only two dancers onto the tiny stage amid the chorus. Surprisingly, several critics singled this scene out as being so realistic that "you will think you are in Spain."[7] Spanish dance was in a period of transition, and it is difficult to determine exactly what

4. Curtiss, *Bizet and His World*, 204, 379.

5. Ibid., 391.

6. Albert de Lasalle, "Chronique musicale," *Le Monde illustré* (Paris), 20 March 1875; de Saint-Victor, "Revue dramatique et littéraire," cited in Wright, ed., *Dossier*, 48, 138. See also Blaze de Bury, "Revue musicale," *Revue des deux mondes* (1829): 477.

7. Blaze de Bury, writing in the *Revue des deux mondes*, as translated in Kerry Murphy, "*Carmen: Couleur locale* or the Real Thing?" in *Music, Theater, and Cultural Transfer: Paris, 1830–1914*, ed. Annegret Fauser and Mark Everist (Chicago and London: University of Chicago Press, 2009), 311.

N° 2 ACTE I____ CARMEN « L'amour est un oiseau rebelle »

Figure 1.1 Act 1—Carmen, "L'amour est un oiseau rebelle," from Georges Bizet, *Carmen: Opéra en 4 actes; Partition piano et chant* (Paris: Choudens fils, 1875), [Plate] no. 2.
Credit: National Library of Australia, MUS HELM I/186.

dances were performed as part of the 1875 production. Illustrations suggest a salon-style Spanish dance, along the lines of the performances of the famous Spanish dancer Lola de Valence, popular in Paris during the 1850s and 1860s. Such choreography, while more folkloric than that of Fanny Elssler, still appears largely balletic, with some arm gesture and no use of heels, unlike

Figure 1.2 Act 2—Carmen, Don José, "Je vais danser en votre honneur!" from Georges Bizet, *Carmen: Opéra en 4 actes; Partition piano et chant* (Paris: Choudens fils, 1875), [Plate] no. 7.
Credit: National Library of Australia, MUS HELM I/186.

the newer flamenco dance styles performed in Spanish *cafés cantantes* in the 1870s (see Figure 1.2). Likewise, the women's costumes would already have been clichéd in the 1850s—the long skirts with little bolero jackets in act 1 have little connection to Spanish fashions of the 1870s, nor even to the depictions of gypsy Spain so current in France. It remains unclear whether the production team was trying to depict contemporary Spain or employ a stylized historicism to match the era in which the opera is set.

Galli-Marié was photographed in her ornate costume for act 2 and seated on a table with legs swinging and hand on her hip (see Figure 1.3). Clearly differentiated from her act 1 garb, this outfit also deviates from contemporary images of staged Spanishness or even representations of Spanish gypsies in the visual arts, despite the presence of castanets at her side and *madroños* (bobbles) edging the bodice. The large pendant earrings, necklace of coins, and armband adorning her bare arms suggest a more Orientalized vision of the gypsy, sharing features with contemporary images of gypsies from Eastern Europe and the Ottoman Empire.[8] But it is Galli-Marié's pose that strengthens the message of sensuality created by the exotic costuming in this image. Her jutting elbow emphasizes her rounded hips and breasts while suggesting an unfeminine sense of power. The stance, which is found in many depictions of Spanish dancers and becomes typical of Carmen portraits, signals to the viewer that this character is not afraid to transgress the limits of accepted feminine behavior.[9]

Galli-Marié's portrayal of Carmen was the most controversial aspect of the production—if not also the key to the opera's lasting success—because it was she who lifted the veil created by Mérimée's literary artifice and narrative frames.[10] Her mature and expressive sensuality, epitomized by the swaying of her hips, was a sign of the character's feisty independence and presented the gypsy in full sunlight, both "embodied" and "envoiced." Considered too provocative for the Opéra-Comique stage, Galli-Marié reminded many critics of Paris's seedy street life, of the visible and working-class immorality of women on street corners in the suburbs; she portrayed a "common" woman.[11] Even the scene outside the bullring was connected by one critic with a particular Parisian street and described in terms of a local crime report.[12]

Galli-Marié certainly tried to communicate the subversive, disruptive potential of her character in her interpretation of the role, but if she had played

---

8. Galli-Marié's act 2 costume also bears some resemblance to Adelina Patti's costume for the title role of Fabio Campana's *Esmeralda* (c. 1870).

9. Susan Rutherford, "'Pretending to Be Wicked': Divas, Technology, and the Consumption of Bizet's *Carmen*," in *Technology and the Diva*, ed. Karen Henson (Cambridge: Cambridge University Press, 2016), 80.

10. See also Henson, *Opera Acts*, 49.

11. Wright, "*Carmen* and the Critics," 55, 60–63; Daniel Bernard, "Théâtres," *L'Union*, 8 March 1875, translated from Wright, ed., *Dossier* in Henson, *Opera Acts*, 48.

12. Wright, "*Carmen* and the Critics," 60–61. André Michael Spies, *Opera, State and Society in the Third Republic, 1875–1914*, Studies in Modern European History (New York: Peter Lang, 1998), 147ff.

Figure 1.3 Céléstine Galli-Marié in costume for act 2 of *Carmen*, photograph by A[lphonse] Liébert (1875).
Credit: Private collection.

Carmen simply as exuberant exotic stereotype, perhaps she might not have caused such offence. Karen Henson describes her interpretation as "actorly," relying more on carefully judged nuance than grand gesture, drawing on a family heritage of thoroughly researched stagecraft, and summoning an ability to make up with convincing physicality for any vocal limitations.[13] As described by Blaze de Bury, Galli-Marié's performance was "skilled, truthful, always simple; no screams, no melodrama," until she finally appeared to be exhausted and overcome.[14] This refusal of artifice confronted the protected bourgeois wives and daughters who attended the Opéra-Comique with a new sense of realism on a stage that had always promised them escapist entertainment.[15] Its effect was perhaps exacerbated by the disjunction at the heart of the work, foreshadowed by the abrupt shift from gaiety to tension in the overture, and culminating in the swing from exuberant spectacle to shocking violence in the final act.

An alternative explanation for the coolness of Carmen's initial reception lies in the possibility that the opera was seen as an allegory of recent events in French political life. By 1875 France was still slowly recovering from its humiliating defeat in the Franco-Prussian War, followed by the bloody Paris Commune in the first half of 1871 and its long aftermath.[16] There is a strong case to be made for the impact of the Commune on the character of Carmen and aspects of the opera, and Delphine Mordey claims that allusions to the Commune are carried over into some of the misogynist lexicon employed by critics when describing the opera's protagonist.[17] But it could also be argued that there were parallels with contemporary Spanish figures in the characterization of Carmen. French critics were used to reading operas set in distant times and places as allegories of the problems of contemporary France, while Meilhac and Halévy were known for lampooning the government in their *opéras bouffes*. As foreshadowed in the Prelude, it is possible that Carmen's appearance so soon after the fall of the Second Empire may have been seen as a comment on the reign of Eugénie and Napoleon III. Many blamed the Emperor's failure to save France from this fate on his essential weakness, too easily led by his beautiful but (in the public's opinion)

13. Henson, *Opera Acts*, 54, 56, 67.

14. Henri Blaze de Bury, "Revue musicale," *Revue des deux mondes* 45 (15 March 1875): 475–80, translated from Wright, ed., *Dossier* in Henson, *Opera Acts*, 50.

15. Wright, "*Carmen* and the Critics," 60–62; Spies, *Opera, State and Society*, 147ff.

16. In a decade of international economic downturn, France's Conservative leadership continued to pursue the Communards through the courts, and Republican parties did not gain government until 1879. Charles Rearick, *Pleasures of the Belle Epoque* (New Haven, CT: Yale University Press, 1985), 7; David Thomson, *Europe since Napoleon*, rev. ed. (Harmondsworth, UK: Penguin, 1966), 396.

17. Delphine Mordey, "Carmen, Communarde Bizet, 'Habanera' (Carmen), Carmen, Act I," *Cambridge Opera Journal* 28, no. 2 (2016): 215–19.

untrustworthy Spanish wife. She was described as "the Spanish whore" by her detractors, and blamed for the decisions that led to France's 1870 defeat under her regency. Harsh caricatures proliferated, attacking Eugénie as a woman who meddled in politics, focusing specifically on her Spanish identity (see Figure 1.4).[18]

The beautiful Empress Eugénie was seen by many of her French subjects as a Spanish woman who was both powerful and capricious, thus embodying some of the characteristics of Bizet's Carmen. Also like Carmen, the exiled former Spanish monarch Isabel II, resident in Paris from 1868, was notorious for her string of lovers, populist musical tastes, and political maneuverings on behalf of both French and Spanish royalist interests. Isabel's behavior, alongside Eugénie's reputation, perpetuated complaints about Spain meddling in French affairs of state. This political subtext may have further undermined any chance that *Carmen* could serve that time-honored function of an *opéra comique*: allowing the audience to forget the practical and political problems of life in a France still recovering from the horrors of war and the Commune.

Carmen's debut may have been scheduled to coincide with the re-establishment of diplomatic relations between France and Spain, after the disruption caused by the restoration of the Spanish monarchy and accession of Alfonso XII to the throne in December 1874. This state occasion, which took place on the morning of the premiere, presented the opportunity to promote Bizet's new opera as a sign of engagement between the two nations and pay a subtle compliment to the new regime of Alfonso XII. Du Locle, however—nervous about the opera's "immorality" and anxious to avoid any diplomatic tension— withheld invitations from visiting Spanish dignitaries and their counterparts in the French government.[19]

Political undercurrents aside, many have ascribed the opera's initial difficulties to the way its title character's loose behavior, exacerbated by explicit representations of violence and murder, violated the sensibilities of a family-oriented theater, consecrated to the entertainment of the bourgeoisie. These factors possibly caused greater moral outrage than any exotic or Spanish element of the work's sensuality and violence. Despite the belief expressed in some quarters after Bizet's death that the work had been destroyed by overwhelmingly negative reviews, Lesley Wright concludes that although "a few critics were thoroughly vitriolic and dismissive," in general the opera was "damned with faint praise," and positive commentary appeared alongside responses ranging from "tepid" to downright "disapproving."[20] As for Bizet's

18. Alison McQueen, *Empress Eugénie and the Arts: Politics and Visual Culture in the Nineteenth Century* (Farnham, UK; Burlington, VT: Ashgate, 2011), 271–87.

19. Henri Malherbe, *Carmen* (Paris: Albin Michel, 1951), 190.

20. Wright, *Dossier*, vi.

LA V.... ESPAGNOLE

Figure 1.4 Zut [Alfred Le Petit], "La V … Espagnole" (1870–71). The Empress Eugénie depicted as a warmongering Spanish cow in partnership with (her rider) Prime Minister Émile Ollivier, wreaking havoc on her husband (Napoleon III) and son (Louis Napoléon, Prince Imperial).

Credit: Universitätsbibliothek Heidelberg, Truebner 1::1, *Collection de caricatures et de charges pour servir à l'histoire de la guerre et de la révolution de 1870–1871*, vol. 1, 50, CC-BY-SA 3.0.

music, most of the critics devoted little space to the score, largely confining their "musical" commentary to praise of the principal singers and disparagement of Bizet's choral writing, which was far too difficult to be successfully executed by the Opéra-Comique's chorus.[21]

21. Macdonald, *Bizet*, 226.

The management's lack of support for Bizet's new work was clearly a factor in the difficulties of the first-night reception, but accounts of later performances suggest a much more appreciative audience, despite the controversy surrounding the premiere.[22] *Carmen* managed a creditable thirty-five performances between March and June 1875, but with the addition of only a further thirteen by the end of the 1875–76 season. Having failed to attract and maintain large audiences, it was dropped from the Opéra-Comique's repertory after a final outing on 15 February 1876.[23] Bizet's disappointment, indeed heartbreak, at *Carmen*'s initial reception, and his tragic death only three months later, quickly became part of the mythology surrounding the opera, typically related by international critics introducing a new production, and it played a crucial role in the work's promotion when it was finally relaunched in Paris.

The French capital may have abandoned *Carmen* in 1876, but the opera swiftly achieved international success.[24] In foreign theaters, audiences valued elements in *Carmen* that had failed to inspire Parisians, and in truth, very few saw the same work that had premiered at the Opéra-Comique in spring 1875. Bizet's publisher, Éditions Choudens, was aware that foreign performances might require recitatives to replace the spoken dialogues typical of an *opéra comique*, so these were commissioned from the composer Ernest Guiraud. The critic Achille de Lauzières undertook the translation into Italian, still the predominant language of many international opera theaters.[25] To be staged as a grand opera, *Carmen* also required ballets, for possible use in acts 2 and 4, so Guiraud interpolated three dances, reorchestrating two numbers from Bizet's incidental music to *L'Arlésienne* and adapting the "Danse bohémienne" from Bizet's opera *La Jolie Fille de Perth* (1867).

The first production of *Carmen* outside Paris took place on 23 October 1875 at the Wiener Hofoper, conducted by Hans Richter, and the work immediately became an annual fixture in the program of the Viennese court theater. It was performed in German, and as Guiraud's recitatives did not arrive in

22. The initial reception of *Carmen* is discussed at length elsewhere. See, for example, Wright, *Dossier*; Wright, "*Carmen* and the Critics;" Susan McClary, *Georges Bizet, Carmen* (Cambridge: Cambridge University Press, 1992).

23. Wright cites thirty-five performances between March and June 1875, and another thirteen between November 1875 and February 1876. Wright, "*Carmen* and the Critics," 51; Curtiss, *Bizet and His World*, 427.

24. For a list of *Carmen*'s national premieres, see Alfred Loewenberg, *Annals of Opera, 1597–1940*, 3rd ed. (London: J. Calder, 1978), col. 1043–44.

25. This Italian version was first performed in Saint Petersburg in February 1878. Edgar Istel reflected on the differences between the original and the version with recitatives in his 1921 article: Edgar Istel and Janet Wylie Istel, trans., "*Carmen*: Novel and Libretto; A Dramaturgic Analysis," *Musical Quarterly* 7, no. 4 (1921): 493–510.

time to be translated and rehearsed, the premiere featured spoken dialogue and additional dances by Carl Telle. Halévy described it as having become "un opéra-ballet à grand spectacle" to suit Viennese tastes. Indeed, act 4 included not only a danced divertissement set to music from *La Jolie Fille de Perth* but also a magnificent procession of bullfighters, including picadors mounted on live horses.[26]

Carmen's second international staging was in Brussels on 3 February 1876, initially with Maria Derivis as Carmen, but soon starring Galli-Marié. This French-language production followed the Opéra-Comique in style of presentation, featuring neither ballets nor horses. It delighted local audiences and enjoyed no fewer than twenty-five performances before the season finished in May. Antwerp's first *Carmen* closely followed, and in October 1876 Budapest staged it in Hungarian. Stockholm, London, Dublin, and New York welcomed *Carmen* in 1878, and 1879 saw its debut in the Antipodes, to enthusiastic Melbourne audiences. It finally reached Germany in the early months of 1880, first Hamburg, then Berlin, to enjoy what John Klein described as the "unparalleled popularity of Bizet's masterpiece in Germany."[27]

Galli-Marié herself went on to perform Carmen throughout Europe and the French provinces, and created the role at its Italian premiere on 15 November 1879 at the Bellini Theater in Naples. *Carmen* did not meet with immediate success in Italy, because of uneven performances, inappropriately large theaters, and sometimes inadequate staging, but its Italian publisher, Edoardo Sonzogno, persevered and the opera was performed widely throughout the country. During the 1880s—once audiences had grown to appreciate its musical originality—Italian critics acknowledged *Carmen* as both new and modern. The chief catalyst for this positive reception was Galli-Marié's performance in the November 1881 production at Genoa, famously attended by Friedrich Nietzsche. Galli-Marié had introduced *Carmen* to Spain the preceding summer, and perhaps her newly minted "Spanish" touches added to the work's appeal and underscored Nietzsche's appreciation of the Mediterraneity of Bizet's score. Galli-Marié's Carmen proved influential, her tireless international touring assuring the opera's impact. However, her performances in Italy were precursors to the new and distinctive performance styles that were to develop around operatic verismo.[28]

26. Ludovic Halévy, "La Millième Représentation de *Carmen*," *Le Théâtre* 145 (January [I] 1905): 12.

27. Loewenberg, *Annals of Opera, 1597–1940*; John W. Klein, "Bizet's Admirers and Detractors," *Music & Letters* 19, no. 4 (October 1938): 410.

28. Karen Henson also links the increased interest in realism to the brief moment of French Naturalism on the 1890s operatic stage. Henson, *Opera Acts*, 50–51. For a useful discussion of the difficulty of defining verismo and naturalism in relation to

Italian audiences recognized *Carmen* as a successor to Verdi in its treatment of "common" people living their everyday life (the workers in the tobacco factory), its expression of raw emotion, and its working out of subjects
like love, duty, and betrayal. Bizet is in turn credited with a generative role in
the development of operatic verismo, as *Carmen*'s success in Italy coincided
with the rise of Italian literary verismo, and the work was championed
by Sonzogno's artistic director, Amintore Galli. An eminent musicologist
and critic, Galli in turn fostered Pietro Mascagni's early operatic efforts.[29]
Furthermore, it was *Carmen*'s establishment in the Italian repertory that
facilitated its international dissemination. Once translated and adapted to
the norms of Italian opera (mainly by replacing spoken dialogue with recitative), works like *Carmen* could be taken up by any of the vast network of
Italian theaters and companies (whether touring or locally based) across the
world.[30] As *Carmen* began its slow but triumphant international conquest,
Paris was about to embrace a new wave of Spanish entertainment, which was
to prepare the audiences of the Opéra-Comique for a new start with Bizet's
wayward gypsy.

CHANGING LANDSCAPES OF SPANISH ENTERTAINMENT: THE EXPOSITION UNIVERSELLE OF 1878 AND BEYOND

As the 1870s progressed, French attitudes to Spain began to change, no
longer associating it with the end of the Second Empire and ensuing political instability. Gradually the Third Republic settled in, and the restoration
of the Spanish monarchy in 1874, after the uncertain period of the *Sexenio
Democrático*, reduced the constant and destabilizing intrigues of exiled
Spaniards in Paris. The scene was set for a fresh injection of Spanish entertainment, and Parisians were more than ready for some fun. The 1878 Exposition
Universelle, which ran from May to November, was the occasion of great
festivities after years of somber rebuilding.

Before the Exposition even opened, the festival atmosphere was
ignited by a new sensation in Spanish entertainment: a large ensemble
of serenading Spanish musicians calling themselves the Estudiantina

---

opera of this period, see Steven Huebner, "*La Princesse Paysanne du Midi*," in *Music,
Theater, and Cultural Transfer*, ed. Fauser and Everist, 364.

29. Hervé Lacombe, "La Réception de l'oeuvre dramatique de Bizet en Italie," *Mélanges
de l'école française de Rome* 108, no. 1 (1996): 192–93; Sergio Viglino, *La fortuna italiana
della Carmen di Bizet (1879–1900)* (Torino: EDT, 2003), 65–82. Lacombe quotes from
Rodolfo Celletti's article on "Verismo" in *Enciclopedia dello spettacolo* (Rome, 1962).

30. Lacombe, "La Réception," 171–72, 182–83.

española.[31] This group traveled up from Madrid in early March 1878 to play on Parisian streets during Carnival. A typical *estudiantina* formation, with plucked string instruments at its core, it predominantly employed *bandurrias, laúdes,* and guitars, with the occasional addition of violins, flutes, castanets, and *tambours de basque,* and some of the ensemble members singing and dancing as well. Spanish *estudiantina* ensembles were often associated with outdoor music, and while their historical precedents lay in Spanish student groups dating back to medieval times, in the latter part of the nineteenth century these traditions were recast in the changing urban contexts of the Iberian peninsula. They gained an international stage in the wake of the Parisian triumph of the Estudiantina española, and their immense popularity in the last two decades of the nineteenth century made them integral to the international projection of Spanish popular musical styles and associated dances.

Consisting of sixty-four students from Madrid's Conservatorium and from various faculties of the University of Madrid, the Estudiantina española planned its visit to Paris to coincide with Carnival festivities and preparations for the 1878 Exposition Universelle, which was to commence in May.[32] They took their cue from the activities undertaken by *estudiantinas* in previous Madrid Carnivals. Despite the well-to-do bourgeois background of the group's membership, it seems that the Spanish monarchy and government had reservations about the trip, given the propensity for pranks among university students.[33] Under the leadership of Ildefonso de Zabaleta and Joaquín de Castañeda, and aware that their activities in Paris would reflect upon Spain, the students drafted a strict code of conduct, and named themselves the Estudiantina española.

Rather than put together their own ad hoc student dress from bygone eras, they commissioned Lorenzo Paris, the principal costumier of the Teatro Real (Madrid's royal opera house), to design and fabricate a costume that reflected elements of Renaissance student dress, such as the ruffled collar. When combined with a number of anachronistic elements, like the eighteenth-century bicorne hat, this luxurious uniform became a nineteenth-century theatrical representation of a university student

31. See Michael Christoforidis, "Serenading Spanish Students on the Streets of Paris: The International Projection of Estudiantinas in the 1870s," *Nineteenth-Century Music Review* 15, no. 1 (2017): 23–36.

32. "Nuestros Grabados: La Estudiantina española en París; La quincena parisien," *Ilustración española y americana* 22, no. 10 (1878): 171, 74; "Paris: La Estudiantina española dando serenata en la plaza de la Ópera," *Ilustración española y americana* 22, no. 11 (1878): 187; "D. Ildefonso de Zabaleta y D. Joaquin de Castaneda, presidente y vicepresidente de la estudiantina española en Paris," *Ilustración española y americana* 22, no. 12 (1878): 213, 215.

33. Ignacio M. de Narvarte, "Le Estudiantina española," *Euskal Erria* 72 (1915): 170–73.

Figure 1.5 "Les étudiants espagnols à Paris" (The Spanish students in Paris), *L'Illustration: Journal Universel* (16 March 1878), cover.

from the Spanish Golden Age and formed the basic template for future *estudiantina* groups (see Figure 1.5).[34]

On arriving in Paris on 2 March 1878, members of the Estudiantina española (or "Estudiantina espagnole" as it was dubbed in French) directed themselves to the Spanish Embassy, performing along the boulevards and suspending traffic on the Quai d'Orsay. This form of street music and dance dominated their activities over the next few days. They serenaded outside the

34. The anachronisms of the uniforms were noted by some of the Spanish and foreign press in 1878. Some *estudiantinas* or *tunas* wear variants of this dress to the present day.

residences of leading Spanish and French dignitaries, such as the palaces of the French President Patrice Maurice de MacMahon and the exiled Isabel II, and the homes of the famous opera singer (and mistress of Alfonso XII) Elena Sanz and the renowned author Victor Hugo. They also spent their time being fêted by—and serenading—leading French citizens and nobility, including the visiting Prince of Wales (the future King Edward VII). A fancy dress ball was held in the ensemble's honor, attended by leading figures from the Hispanic colony and the "artistic *demi monde*" and sponsored by Josep Oller, the famous entertainment impresario of Spanish origin.[35] Concerts were given in their honor at the Théâtre-Italien, during which Sanz joined the *estudiantina* "singing *jotas* and habaneras from her homeland."[36] But what drew the largest crowds of Parisians were the impromptu performances at some of the principal sites of the French capital, which included parts of Montmartre, the Place de l'Opéra, and the Jardin des Tuileries, where the *estudiantina* attracted an estimated crowd of 50,000 people on 6 March.[37]

Like their counterparts in Spain, the repertoire of the Estudiantina española consisted primarily of arrangements of Spanish airs, including instrumental versions of *boleros, jotas,* and *seguidillas,* as well as *zortzicos* and *malagueñas,* at times accompanied by song. They also incorporated urban popular styles such as waltzes and habaneras, marches, and *pasodobles.* Some of these Spanish airs were taken from *zarzuela* arrangements, composed popular scores, or the new wave of *cancioneros.* The Estudiantina española and its subsequent imitators had the effect of reinvigorating well-known Spanish folk and popular song and dance styles, as well as introducing fresh styles to a new generation of Parisian and international audiences. A number of European composers also wrote piano and orchestral works inspired by the sonority of the *estudiantinas,* the most popular of which was Emile Waldteufel's *Estudiantina Waltz* op. 191 (1883). Another work of the same year inspired by the plucked-string sonority of the *jotas* of the *estudiantinas* was Emmanuel Chabrier's orchestral showpiece *España,* and this sonority was also to infuse some of the dances

35. *La correspondencia de España,* 12 March 1878, cited in Félix O. Martín Sárraga, "Crónica del viaje de la Estudiantina Española al Carnaval de París de 1878 según la prensa de la época," accessed 24 April 2015, http://tunaemundi.com/index.php/component/content/article/7-tunaemundi-cat/166-cronica-del-viaje-de-la-estudiantina-espanola-al-carnaval-de-paris-de-1878-segun-la-prensa-de-la-epoca.   Oller   went on to found famous Parisian entertainment venues in the late 1880s, including the Moulin Rouge and the Olympia. For further information on *estudiantinas* see also Félix O. Martín Sárraga, *Mitos y evidencia histórica sobre las tunas y estudiantinas* (Lima: Cauces, 2016).

36. This performance occurred between renditions of the second act of Flotow's *Marta* and the second and third acts of Verdi's *Ernani.* Édouard Noël and Edmond Stoullig, "Théâtre-Italien," *Les Annales du théâtre et de la musique [1878]* 4 (1879): 201–2.

37. *Revue et gazette musicale de Paris* 45 (1878): 78.

from Jules Massenet's *Le Cid* (1885). The success of the Estudiantina española spawned a multitude of imitators who remained on the international popular music stage until World War I. Most of these subsequent *estudiantina* ensembles were made up of professional entertainers and ranged in size between ten and twenty players, although they were at times as small as a trio.[38]

Several Paris newspapers noted that the Spanish students had done much to revive the spirit of Carnival in the French capital, and that exuberant crowds of this size had not been seen on the streets of Paris since the fall of the Second Empire.[39] After the ravages of the Franco-Prussian War the Spanish students represented a less threatening invasion, one that was welcomed by the extensive Hispanic colony in Paris and was seen by the press as strengthening the bonds of *Latinité* and Franco-Spanish fraternity.[40]

The 1878 Exposition celebrated France's recovery on a grand scale, and Spaniards made a significant contribution to its entertainment programs. Serious music by Spanish composers was represented by the official music delegate, noted writer and critic Antonio Peña y Goñi, while the government also sent the Quartet Society and the Concert Society of Madrid, the latter being a hundred-piece orchestra.[41] In addition, the Catalan composer Manuel Giró (resident in Paris from 1875) conducted the Orchestre de l'Exposition on 13 July 1878 in a program of Spanish music. More popular Spanish entertainment was provided by the numerous troupes drawn to Paris by the Exposition, and the injection of their novel representation of Spanish entertainment began to shift French attitudes toward Spanish music. A dance troupe directed by Manuel Guerrero appeared at the Gymnase, while the Palais du Trocadéro hosted several Spanish companies, including a quintet that performed popular Spanish music in national costume.[42] The performers at the Gymnase presented a number of Spanish *danzas regionales*, most notably from Galicia, Seville, and Valencia. Critic Édouard Fournier observed that these local dances reached their perfection only once they had been polished and transformed by the dance schools of Seville, agreeing with the celebrated Spanish traveler

---

38. Professional *estudiantinas* were also present in Spain, although the Estudiantina española helped consolidate the tradition of the university *estudiantina* and the festive visits of such groups to cities within the Iberian peninsula. It also gave the impetus for the formation of amateur groups by Spaniards in the Americas.

39. "Affairs in France (From Our Own Correspondent) Paris, March 4,"; text from *Le Figaro*, translated in *La correspondencia de España*, 10 March 1878, cited in Martín Sárraga, "Crónica del viaje."

40. *La correspondencia de España*, 10 March 1878; "Les Étudiants espagnols: Troisième Journée," *Le Gaulois* (Paris), 7 March 1878.

41. Montserrat Bergadá, "Les Pianistes catalans à Paris entre 1875 et 1925" (Thèse doctorat, Université François Rabelais, 1997), 55.

42. Ibid., 57.

Baron Davillier that only in Seville could one find the true dancer, with "honey in her hips."[43]

The Spanish mezzo-soprano Elena Sanz, beloved star of Paris's Théâtre-Italien, was a leading figure in the Spanish entertainments that occurred around the Exposition in 1878.[44] An established and respected opera singer, during the 1870s she had sung at Milan's La Scala and Madrid's Teatro Real (in Julián Gayarre's company), and had toured internationally. She was a regular member of the Théâtre-Italien and was renowned for her roles in Donizetti's *La favorita* and in Verdi's operas (see Figure 1.6). Having made Paris her home, Sanz was often heard in concert and private performances, and she was the driving force behind many Spanish-themed events held in Paris from the late 1870s into the 1890s.

Sanz's stage career was interrupted in the 1870s by her long liaison with Alfonso XII of Spain, with whom she had two children in the early 1880s. Alfonso insisted that Sanz retire from the stage in late 1878 and she did not reappear in operatic roles until after his untimely death in 1885, although she occasionally appeared in concerts from 1883. Sanz was widely recognized as the best Carmen never to sing the role on the stage of the Opéra-Comique. However, as early as 1878 she had performed the "Habanera" from *Carmen*, along with several "romances espagnoles" and operatic selections, at her benefit concert on 18 June, which was attended by luminaries such as Isabel II.[45] Would it have been acceptable for a woman widely acknowledged as the established mistress of Alfonso XII to appear in an opera like *Carmen*, in Paris, with Isabel II and her considerable Spanish aristocratic entourage in attendance? Sanz's social status was well known, and her casting might have upset the notoriously bourgeois audiences of the Salle Favart.[46] Despite not impersonating Carmen on the Paris stage, Sanz did perform the role in the provincial centers of Spa and Rouen, and continued to sing numbers from the opera in concert. A celebrated exponent of Spanish popular song styles, Sanz was able, according to contemporary accounts, to modulate her vocal and performance styles to accommodate the lyricism of opera, salon song styles, and the inflections and modes of delivery of Spanish song forms. A performance given by Sanz in Madrid in April 1883 highlights her versatility: she sang Italian songs by Saverio Mercadante and Salvatore Scuderi and a Neapolitan serenade

43. Édouard Fournier, "Revue dramatique," [unknown], 12 August 1878, Ro. 12314, Bibliothèque nationale de France. Fournier referred to the famous travelogue by Jean Charles Davillier, illustrated by Gustave Doré, *L'Espagne* (Paris: Hachette, 1874).

44. Noël and Stoullig, "Théâtre-Italien," 96–211. The Théâtre Italien operated in Paris from 1801 until the company folded in 1878 for want of sufficient audience after the closure of the Exposition.

45. Ibid., 209–10.

46. The company of the Opéra-Comique performed in a theatre known as the Salle Favart throughout the nineteenth century, although it was rebuilt twice during this period.

Figure 1.6 Elena Sanz as Amneris in *Aida* at the Théâtre-Italien, in *Paris-Théâtre* 1, no. 99 (8–14 March 1877): cover.

by Émile Paladilhe, and then she responded to "enthusiastic applause from the public, who asked that she sing a Spanish song and another in a *flamenco* style, which she performed at the piano accompanying herself." On that occasion she performed the song *La moza del temple* by José Inzenga (one of the great Spanish song composers and folksong arrangers of the mid-nineteenth century) and some *malagueñas*. The critic of *La época* declared, "What a great pity that Elena Sanz has retired from the theater, where she has gained so many triumphs."[47] Whether in the company of *estudiantinas* or accompanying

47. "En la sala de audiciones del señor Zozaya," *La época*, 17 April 1883, 2, cited in María Encina Cortizo and Ramón Sobrino, "Los salones musicales madrileños: Nuevos

herself at the piano, Sanz was a key figure in the dissemination of a range of Spanish song styles in the salons and concert venues of Paris in the 1870s and again from the mid-1880s. Her social status and aristocratic connections reinforced her projections of Spanishness, and as we will see in later chapters, aspects of her approach to Spanish song (and the numbers from *Carmen*) were to shape the conception of future Carmens, both French and Spanish, from the 1890s onward.

Coinciding with Sanz's years in Paris, another Spaniard had a dominant presence at the Opéra and was to be painted on several occasions by Degas. This was the ballerina Rosita Mauri, a virtuoso in a variety of styles, who reigned as *première danseuse* at the Paris Opéra between 1878 and 1898.[48] Her training in Barcelona allowed her to develop a mastery of Spanish regional dance—including the more classicized Bolero school—as well as Franco-Italian ballet traditions. She came to Paris as a recognized international performer, having danced in the leading opera ballet companies of Barcelona, Vienna, Berlin, and Milan during the 1870s, and she was renowned for being extremely supple, energetic, and dramatic. Charles Gounod saw her dance at La Scala in 1877 and persuaded the Opéra to hire her for the premiere of his opera *Polyeucte*, in which she made her Paris debut the following year. Her dancing in Charles-Marie Widor's ballet *La Korrigane* (1880) raised her to the forefront of Paris ballet. At times Mauri's Spanish background and much-admired dark hair provided the excuse for casting her in exotic roles, as when she performed a pantomimic dance as a Moorish slave to a habanera in Ambroise Thomas's *Françoise de Rimini* in 1882. A number of ballets or *divertissements* within operas were written expressly for Mauri, most notably the suite of regional Spanish dances composed by Jules Massenet for act 2 of *Le Cid* (1885).[49] Here Mauri performed in the style of Spanishness that had been adapted to the Romantic Ballet earlier in the century, while adding her own choreographic touches (see Figure 1.7). Musically, Massenet adopts the rhythms and ornamental melodic writing associated with a number of regional styles, and he employs a habanera rhythm in the "Andalouse." The suite is cloaked in a vibrant orchestration that at times alludes to the Spanish sonorities then in vogue, including the sounds of the *estudiantina* in the "Castillane." Critics noted Massenet's sense

espacios sociales para el cultivo de la música de concierto en la segunda mitad del XIX," *Ad Parnassum: A Journal of Eighteenth- and Nineteenth-Century Instrumental Music* 13, no. 25 (2015): 235.

48. For a detailed account of Mauri's career, see Ferran Canyameres and Josep Iglésies, *La Dansarina Roseta Mauri (1850–1923)* (Reus, Spain: Edicions Rosa de Reus, 1971).

49. See Michael Christoforidis, "Reimagining the *Reconquista*: Massenet's *Le Cid* and the 1900 Exposition Universelle," in *The Eighteenth-Century Italian Opera Seria: Metamorphoses of the Opera in the Imperial Age*, ed. Petr Macek and Jana Perutková (Prague: KLP, Koniasch Latin Press, 2013), 264–71.

Figure 1.7 Rosita Mauri in costume for Jules Massenet's *Le Cid* (1885), based on a photograph by Mr. Benque.
Credit: Private collection.

of bold anachronism in the ballet: "He has not feared to mix with Spain of the eleventh century all of modern Spain, with its *toreros*, its *cachuchas*, its *fandangos*, its *estudiantinas*, and the rest."[50]

In the late 1870s, Pablo Sarasate also began to project his Spanishness on the concert stage in the wake of his collaboration with Lalo and the death of Bizet, and especially after the reinvigoration of Spanish song that resulted

50. See Adolphe Jullien, "Académie nationale de musique: *Patrie* et *Le Cid*," *Le Théâtre* 41 (September 1900 I): 4–8.

from the phenomenal success of the *estudiantinas*. This was achieved through Sarasate's composition and performance of a series of folk-inspired concert pieces. In 1881 he combined this recent interest with an established genre—the operatic paraphrase—to create one of his most popular works, the *Carmen Fantasy* op. 25. In this typically virtuosic operatic potpourri, Sarasate opened with the theme from the entr'acte to act 4, but thereafter selected only motives sung by Carmen. From act 1, he took the "Habanera," Carmen's exchange with Zuñiga (possibly based on a folk theme that Sarasate had brought to Bizet's attention), and the "Séguedille," as well as the "Chanson bohème" from act 2. It is almost as if Sarasate had wanted the violin to impersonate the gypsy protagonist.[51]

Sarasate's *Carmen Fantasy* was enormously popular in Paris and throughout Europe, encouraging the further dissemination of the music of *Carmen* on the concert stage. Here is a clear example of one of the great virtuosi of his age reclaiming his Spanishness through the music of *Carmen* and in the process highlighting the Spanishness of his colleague's score. In 1881, and again in early 1887, Madrid critics responded coolly to the *Carmen Fantasy*—in sharp contrast to its rapturous audience reception—and demanded that Sarasate play more of his own Spanish works as encores.[52] "[T]he habanera of *maestro* Iradier" was judged to be a "completely Spanish" work that had "nothing to do with Bizet."[53] But this comment predated the arrival of *Carmen* in Madrid, and it could be argued that Sarasate's *Carmen Fantasy* would in some small measure prepare the ground for both the Madrid premiere and the Paris revival of the opera.

GALLI-MARIÉ AND CARMEN'S TRIUMPHANT RETURN TO THE OPÉRA-COMIQUE

For seven long years after its 1875 premiere, *Carmen* was banished from the Parisian stage, but audiences in the French capital were again engaging with Spanish entertainment and Bizet's music was not forgotten. Although none of Bizet's works were revived in Paris after their initial performances until the 1880s, Parisian music lovers were able to familiarize themselves with

51. Luis G. Iberni, *Pablo Sarasate* (Madrid: Instituto Complutense de Ciencias Musicales, D.L., 1994), 153.

52. Among mixed reviews, few critics thought it had any merit—indeed one declared it "pale and a bit odd." *El liberal*, 9 October 1887; *El imparcial*, 4 April 1887; "Sociedad de conciertos," *El diario éspañol* (Madrid), 3 April 1887; "Sociedad de conciertos," *El imparcial* (Madrid), 4 April 1887.

53. G. O., "Setimo concierto del Príncipe Alfonso," *La correspondencia musical* 1, no. 16 (1881): 3–4. Iberni identifies G.O. as R. Gil. Osorio. Iberni, *Pablo Sarasate*: 78n6.

Carmen's key numbers while waiting for its 1883 revival. Sheet-music versions of many numbers were released, and were played or sung in private homes, in the salons and even in *cafés-concerts*. As Charles de Sivry observed in 1883, "[n]o society lady, nor even a bourgeois one, with the slightest shred of a voice fails to sing—more or less—the famous Habañera."[54]

While pursuing her tireless advocacy of Bizet's masterpiece outside France, Galli-Marié appeared as Carmen some 350 times between 1875 and 1883.[55] On 2 August 1881 she introduced *Carmen* to Spain, appearing in the title role at Barcelona's Teatro Lírico.[56] A quiet debut, this national premiere was soon all but forgotten, even though *Carmen* was to dominate Barcelona's theatrical life a decade later. On this occasion Galli-Marié appeared with a visiting French company, and her starring roles in five operas (including *Faust* and *Mignon*) were acclaimed by the Barcelona public.[57] Not unaware of the significance of premiering Bizet's "Spanish" opera south of the Pyrenees, she took the opportunity to study local dance and song, taking daily dance lessons from the *maestro de ballet* at Barcelona's Gran Teatre del Liceu, despite the punishing summer heat. But what style of "authentic" Spanish dance would she have learned from such a master? Not the newly emerging flamenco, we can be sure. In Barcelona's leading opera theater, the Liceu's dancing master would have espoused a balletic and stylized form of national dance, as exemplified by the theater's one-time star, Rosita Mauri.

Whether or not this training shaped Galli-Marié's performances in the Catalan capital, she was complimented by the local press on her characteristic and dramatic execution of a role thought difficult for an artist who had not been born in Spain.[58] In the context of an imperfect production—marred by lack of rehearsal, inadequate orchestra (not enough violins), and inappropriate costumes—her reading of the role was considered unexaggerated, and she escaped any accusation of perpetrating an *espagnolade*. She played Carmen for four nights to enthusiastic applause, and was called to repeat the "Habanera" at each performance.[59]

54. Charles de Sivry, "Reprise de *Carmen*," *Ville de Paris*, 23 April 1883, 2, quoted in Lesley Wright, "Rewriting a Reception: Thoughts on Carmen in Paris, 1883," *Journal of Musicological Research* 28, no. 4 (2009): 292.

55. Wright, "Rewriting a Reception," 293.

56. The Gran Teatre del Liceu is referred to by its Catalan name (rather than the Spanish Liceo) although the Teatro Lírico (Sala Beethoven) is given its more commonly used Spanish title.

57. Critics speculated that, occurring at the very end of the season, the four performances of *Carmen* were given almost as an afterthought, perhaps at Galli-Marié's insistence. *El correo catalan* (Barcelona), 1 August 1881, 2.

58. *Diario de Barcelona* (edición de la tarde), 5 August 1881, 1.

59. *El correo catalan*, 5 August 1881, 1; J. Rodoreda, "La *Carmen*, de Bizet," *La ilustració catalana* 2, no. 40 (1881): 326.

Galli-Marié further proved her "Spanish" credentials with her encore on the last night of her Barcelona engagement, a benefit performance of *Mignon*. Accompanying herself at the piano, she sang a well-known habanera, "La Habana se va á perder," with clear and correct pronunciation, and was called for an encore.[60] The singer herself was pleased with her Catalan reception, writing to Bizet's widow—with whom she had remained in touch as she continued to lobby for the work's reinstatement—that "we have had another great success, this time in Carmen's own country."[61]

Back in Paris, Bizet's great supporter Léon Carvalho had been made director of the Opéra-Comique in 1876, but despite having commissioned *Les Pêcheurs de perles* and the incidental music to *L'Arlésienne* some years before, he had no great fondness for *Carmen*, and thought it unsuitable for his family-oriented theater. Carvalho had found Galli-Marié's portrayal too realistic and believed that the tavern in act 2 represented a brothel, an immoral place he would never countenance on the stage of his theater.[62] Halévy tried repeatedly to change his mind, but Carvalho always declared that the foreign productions must have changed the libretto dramatically and that no one would ever dare stage it in France. In 1878, however, provincial theaters took courage, led by Marseilles and Lyons, and this argument lost its weight. By the early 1880s, both the Parisian press and the subscribers of the Opéra-Comique, galled by watching the opera achieve success after success not just abroad, but in the French provinces as well, had realized it was high time they reclaimed *Carmen*. So Carvalho relented, on condition that a singer other than Galli-Marié could be found to play Carmen, and he reluctantly staged an expurgated version of the work on 21 April 1883.

Some critics suggested that Carvalho had set *Carmen* up for another failure, opening after insufficient rehearsal, toward the end of the season, when it was overshadowed by the debut of Léo Delibes's *Lakmé* only the week before. The whole production was toned down, with worn sets and costumes, respectable ballerinas for the dance in Lillas Pastia's tavern, a pedestrian musical performance, and a demure blond soprano—Adèle Isaac—as Carmen.[63] The deficiencies of the production notwithstanding, critics and audience embraced the opera warmly, ensuring its seventeen performances were a resounding success, but anger was directed at Carvalho for treating the work so shabbily. Some critics were forced to reverse their negative judgments of 1875, declaring that *Carmen* should henceforth form a permanent part of the Opéra-Comique's repertory, reserving residual criticism for Galli-Marié's role

60. *La renaixensa (Diari de Catalunya)* (Barcelona), 11 August 1881, 2–3; *Diario de Barcelona*, 11 August 1881.

61. Curtiss, *Bizet and His World*, 430.

62. Ibid., 429; Halévy, "La Millième Représentation de *Carmen*."

63. Curtiss, *Bizet and His World*, 432–34; Wright, "Rewriting a Reception," 285.

in the original production. Spanishness was not at issue this time, and the critical response focused on reclaiming for France a work that was now internationally acknowledged as a masterpiece, by a composer who since his death was beginning to receive the recognition that had eluded him while alive.

Galli-Marié herself by now claimed to have developed a gentler manner in the role, even offering to respond to any criticisms that might be harbored by Meilhac, Halévy, and Carvalho, by shaping her interpretation to their direction in a production near Paris.[64] The pressure evidently became so intense, and the likelihood of the opera making serious money so certain, that Carvalho reengaged Galli-Marié and mounted a "new" production at the Opéra-Comique. *Carmen* received its true revival, uncut, with new costumes and sets, on 27 October 1883.[65] Galli-Marié's return to the role featured what some critics saw as a more considered and accomplished characterization, in which—according to Alphonse Duvernoy—she "rendered the passionate, bizarre, dynamic, cruel portrait of this girl of the streets with a power and an ease that compel admiration."[66] Initially booked for only twenty performances, she stayed on until the end of the year, and on 22 December *Carmen*'s hundredth performance was celebrated.[67]

Galli-Marié's performance now included refinements based on her study and observation of Spanish life and culture. She adorned her Carmen with a carnation, replacing the rose of earlier productions, because she said this was the flower preferred by *manolas* (typical Madrid women, especially around 1800). She insisted on using a real knife, despite suffering repeated injuries. Indeed, she later claimed to have injured three of her Don Josés over the years as well.[68] Furthermore, she adopted the kiss-curl, and associated herself even more closely with the character she impersonated by claiming a superstitious belief in its talismanic quality: she told the press that the state of her hair dictated her mood and performance, and insisting that this coquettish curl plastered to her cheek must stay in place (see Figure 1.8).[69] She was accorded further authenticity in the role when a critic likened her hip-swaying image to a "filly from the studs of Cordoba," echoing the phrase in Chapter 3 of

64. Ibid., 431–32.

65. Wright, "Rewriting a Reception," 293n40.

66. Édouard Noël and Edmond Stoullig, "Théâtre Nationale de l'Opéra-Comique," *Les Annales du théâtre et de la musique [1883]* 9 (1884): 83; Alphonse Duvernoy, "Musique," *La République française*, 31 October 1883, 3, quoted in Wright, "Rewriting a Reception," 293.

67. Curtiss, *Bizet and His World*, 434; Noël and Stoullig, "Théâtre Nationale de l'Opéra-Comique."

68. Édouard Beaudu, "La Carmencita," *La Presse* (Paris), 26 September 1905, 1.

69. Un monsieur de l'orchestre [Arnold Mortier], "La Soirée théâtrale: Galli-Marié dans Carmen," *Le Figaro* (Paris), 28 October 1883, 3. We are indebted to Lesley Wright for sharing this review with us.

Figure 1.8 "Mme Galli-Marie," photograph by Adolphe Jullien Nadar (c. 1883), reproduced in *Le Théâtre*, 164 (October [II] 1905): 4.
Credit: State Library of Victoria.

Mérimée's novella.[70] All these stories circulating in the press surely served to enhance her cachet in the role.

This second revival, with Galli-Marié's triumphant return to the title role, transformed the reputation of Bizet's opera. After making Galli-Marié the scapegoat for the work's initial failure, some critics had to execute a volte-face in order to praise her. After the work's thousandth performance in late 1904, Félix Duquesnel rewrote history by declaring that the 1875 failure had occurred "*despite* the remarkable interpretation of Madame Galli Marié, who realized the ideal type of the heroine, the fickle cigarette girl."[71] No longer a shocking and immoral tale about the seduction of an innocent and unworldly

70. "[E]lle s'avançait en se balançant sur se hanches comme une pouliche du haras de Cordoue." This much-quoted phrase is found in Chapter 3 of Mérimée's *Carmen* but was quoted in this instance in Noël and Stoullig, "Théâtre Nationale de l'Opéra-Comique," 74.
71. Félix Duquesnel, "La Quinzaine Théâtrale," *Le Théâtre* 145 (January [I] 1905: 4. Our emphasis.

man by an exotic and dangerous femme fatale, Bizet's masterpiece was increasingly an opera *about* Carmen, and the title role became the focal point of each new production. Galli-Marié had imbued her with fire and passion, but also with humanity, allowing the character to express fear and anger. Each new singer who engaged with the role was to project a personal identification of some kind, and for many Carmen's Spanishness became their point of departure.

The success of Galli-Marié's interpretation became part of the mythology of the opera's rejection and reincarnation. As *Carmen* found its place at the heart of the Opéra-Comique's repertory, the opera was recognized as an institution not only of that theater, but of France's national lyric heritage as well. The furor that surrounded the 1890 inauguration of a statue of Bizet illustrates this shift. While the Parisian daily *Le Gaulois* coordinated subscriptions, the management of the Opéra offered to mount an extraordinary performance of *Carmen* as a benefit for the fund. It should be noted here that as an *opéra comique*, *Carmen* had never been staged anywhere in Paris but the Opéra-Comique theater itself, and it is an indication of the prestige now attached to Bizet's final opera that the Opéra should have sought it out.[72] The management of the Opéra-Comique was much disturbed at the prospect of losing the monopoly of a work that was one of their most consistent earners, and quickly moved to announce a gala performance of *Carmen* with a stellar cast on 11 December 1890. Galli-Marié herself came out of retirement to sing the title role,[73] Nellie Melba appeared as Micaëla, Jean de Reszke impersonated Don José, while Jean Lassalle reprised his celebrated turn as Escamillo. A *grand divertissement*, added to the fourth act, allowed the appearance of ballerinas from the Opéra, led by Rosita Mauri, along with the Opéra-Comique's own corps de ballet. The band of the Republican Guard played in the foyer, where refreshments, fans, and sweets were provided free of charge. A gala night indeed, it raised 42,000 francs for the cause, and enhanced both the theater's prestige and its exclusive claim to Bizet's masterpiece in the French capital.[74]

72. The Opéra finally staged part of *Carmen* in 1900, when act 2 was performed at a gala on 11 November. The entire work was presented at the Opéra at a gala on 29 December 1907, and then played with Guiraud's recitatives on 10 November 1959. Spire Pitou, *The Paris Opéra: An Encyclopedia of Operas, Ballets, Composers and Performer; Growth and Grandeur, 1815–1914; A–L*, vol. 3 (Westport, CT: Greenwood Press, 1990), 201.

73. This was not Galli-Marié's finest hour, as she apparently found it hard to recover from some kind of vocal mishap and appeared too old and tired for the demands of the role after several years in retirement. Adolphe Jullien, "Mme Galli-Marié," *Le Théâtre* 164 (October [II] 1905): 4.

74. Noël and Stoullig, "Théâtre Nationale de l'Opéra-Comique," *Les Annales du théâtre et de la musique [1891]* 16 (1891): 119–20. This performance seems to have used the Guiraud recitatives. Nicole Wild and David Charlton, *Théâtre de l'Opéra-Comique Paris: Répertoire 1762–1927* (Sprimont: Mardaga, 2005), 178.

CHAPTER 2

༄

Impersonating Carmen
in Victorian London

*C*armen arrived in the capital of the British Empire in 1878, and the opera's subsequent proliferation on London's stages made a unique contribution to its international dissemination. The vibrant local theatrical scene also launched Bizet's gypsy on a journey through adaptation into non-operatic genres, some of which will be traced throughout this book. This chapter introduces early treatments of the work in light of British engagement with Spanish entertainment, culminating in an examination of the spectacularly successful Gaiety burlesque of 1890, *Carmen Up to Data*.

SPANISH FASHIONS AND *CARMEN'S* LONDON PREMIERE

Nineteenth-century British audiences were well acquainted with the sights, sounds, and history of Spain. From their involvement in the Peninsular War (1808–14)—in which many British soldiers fought against the French occupation of Spain—to the ongoing British presence in Gibraltar, Great Britain welcomed a significant influx of Spanish refugees and exiles. A growing interest in all things Spanish, fed by Romantic writers like Lord Byron and consolidated into the mid-century with the enduring popularity of volumes like Washington Irving's *Tales of the Alhambra* (1832) and George Borrow's *The Zincali: An Account of the Gypsies of Spain* (1841) and *The Bible in Spain* (1843). Richard Ford's *A Handbook for Travellers in Spain, and Readers at Home* (1845) sought to encourage tourism to the Iberian lands. The armchair traveler could also enjoy Spanish topics brought to life on the stage, although the authors of these theatrical and choreographic scenarios were less concerned with accurate depiction than travel writers were. Audiences of Spanish-themed entertainment learned that Spain was a land of contrasts, populated by picturesque characters like bullfighters, bandits, and dark-eyed women who worked in the tobacco industry. The fascination of the exotic cigarette girl was exceeded only by interest in the Spanish gypsy, who was as likely to indulge in murderous knife fights as to break forth into song and dance.

The Romantic ballet's love affair with characteristic national dances found its Spanish dance style in the *escuela bolera*, and the international ballet stars of the 1820s, 1830s, and 1840s were renowned for their Spanish dances, particularly the *bolero* itself, which was often incorporated into full-length ballets.[1] Chief among the exponents of this style was Fanny Elssler, who introduced her celebrated Cachucha to London in 1836. London audiences went on to applaud the *boleros* and *cachuchas* performed by her colleagues Marie Taglioni and Marie Guy-Stephan in the late 1830s and early 1840s.[2] By 1843, a critic for the *Times* looked back and described their Spanish dances as "ornamented and modified by the artists of France and Italy." Overcome by the charms of the "Spanish" dancer Lola Montez (in reality the Irish performer Eliza Gilbert), who was billed as coming direct from Madrid's Teatro Real in the summer of 1843, the same critic enthused at the prospect of "a Spanish dance by a Spaniard, executed after the Spanish fashion."[3] Montez offered a new take on Spanish dance, her affectation of a solemn hauteur compensating for her lack of balletic technique, and she enjoyed a sensational, if checkered, career as a "Spanish" dancer, one of many who adopted a Hispanic identity in order to capitalize on the enduring popularity of this mode of entertainment.[4]

Although Spanish dance was less at the forefront of English taste in the 1860s and 1870s, it remained a regular specialty of local dancers, a popular subject for burlesquing by comic performers, and a picturesque topic for dance companies, as when the Alhambra Theatre offered a "Divertissement Espagnol" (featuring a knife fight) in 1865.[5] A wide variety of Spanish

1. Michael Christoforidis and Elizabeth Kertesz, "*Cendrillon*, Cinderella and Spectacle: Insights into Sor's Most Successful Work," in *Estudios sobre Fernando Sor*, ed. Luis Gásser (Madrid: Instituto Complutense de Ciencias Musicales, 2003), 134.

2. A review of this decade of "Spanish" dance in London is provided in "Her Majesty's Theatre," *Times* (London), 5 July 1843, 6, quoted in Kenneth James Murray, "Spanish Music and Its Representations in London (1878–1930): From the Exotic to the Modern" (PhD thesis, University of Melbourne, 2013), 37.

3. "Her Majesty's Theatre," *Times*, 5 June 1843, 6.

4. Bruce Seymour, *Lola Montez: A Life* (New Haven, CT: Yale University Press, 1996).

5. Ivor Guest, *Ballet in Leicester Square: The Alhambra and the Empire 1860–1915* (London: Dance Books, 1992), 16.

artists continued to tour, including the grotesque act of the one-legged dancer Signor Donato, who won over audiences in Covent Garden's 1864 Christmas Pantomime, accompanying his Spanish cloak dance with castanets. In 1876 a Madrid troupe called the Casanobas danced with the inevitable castanets and tambourines in the Alhambra's burlesque extravaganza *Don Juan*.[6] The 1879 tour of the Spanish Royal Ballet set a more dignified tone, beginning with a divertissement between acts of *Don Giovanni* at Covent Garden, but critics hoping for Spanish fire were not satisfied with their generous use of castanets, when presented in the context of graceful and balletic choreography.[7] The Spanish Royal Ballet then moved to the Alhambra, where it offered "The Torrera or Spanish Bull Fight," a ballet that played throughout the month of December.[8]

So established were Spanish topics in entertainment that the young composer Arthur Sullivan chose them for his first full-length opera in 1867. Written in collaboration with burlesque writer F. C. Burnand, *The Contrabandista, or The Law of the Ladrones* picked up on the rich comic potential of the story of a hapless English tourist who finds himself lost in the world of Spanish bandits, where musicians and dancers perform *boleros* and *cachuchas*—with castanets (of course). Despite the exotic color, and topical reference to the steadily increasing tourism industry stimulated by travel writers, the work was not a great success, achieving a respectable seventy-two performances and only a few revivals to 1880.[9]

Given this otherwise receptive environment for theatrical works on Spanish themes, the appearance of *Carmen* on the international scene, enjoying success in cities like Vienna and Brussels, stirred interest among the managers of London's various opera companies in the late 1870s. Paris's Opéra-Comique may have failed to recognize *Carmen*'s appeal, but English impresarios were quick to sense a potential goldmine. Keen to stage the local premiere, long-time manager of the Royal Italian Opera, Frederick Gye, made the first move, announcing a Covent Garden production of *Carmen* starring Adelina Patti in his March 1878 prospectus.[10] Not to be outdone, in May 1878 Colonel James Henry Mapleson of the Italian opera company at Her Majesty's Theatre in the Haymarket declared that his company would stage Bizet's celebrated opera "for the first time in England."[11] He did not even name the singer who would

---

6. Murray, "Spanish Music," 39–41; "Alhambra," *Standard* (London), 6 March 1876, 6.

7. "Her Majesty's Theatre," *Times*, 14 November 1879, 8.

8. *Standard*, 27 November 1879, 4.

9. Murray, "Spanish Music," 70–71.

10. "The Italian Opera Season," *Monthly Musical Record*, 1 August 1878, 118; "Music and Musicians," *Queen, The Lady's Newspaper* (London), 29 June 1878, 476.

11. "The Opera Season," *Monthly Musical Record*, 1 May 1878, 71.

create the first Carmen in the British Isles, the twenty-six year old American singer, Minnie Hauk.

If we are to believe Hauk's memoirs, it was her personal determination to create Carmen in London that led to the British premiere at Her Majesty's, but Mapleson had seen her sing the role in Brussels, and was keen to capture both singer and opera.[12] Hauk relates that she left a successful four-year engagement in Berlin when the management refused to program *Carmen*. Taking up a contract at the Théâtre de la Monnaie in Brussels, she established herself in other works while studying *Carmen* in French in preparation for her debut as Bizet's gypsy in midwinter of the 1877–78 season. She had no qualms about the castanet work, nor her ability to embody the movement of a Spaniard, because of her Viennese experience as Angèle in Daniel Auber's *opéra comique Le domino noir*, a role that features a *bolero*, a *jaleo*, and a "Ronde aragonaise" often performed with castanets.[13]

Hauk claimed to have modeled her costumes on gypsy clothing from the time of Mérimée, but in a widely disseminated image from about 1880 she appears in a costume—and composition—apparently based on the Orientalized look of Galli-Marié's act 2 portrait (see Figures 2.1 and 1.3).[14] Hauk's combination of intelligent acting and beautiful singing delivered her instant recognition, and she quotes *L'Étoile belge* describing her as a "real gypsy girl, with her vivid passions, her quickly changing emotions, and the sudden fancies of the amorous courtesan."[15] With her appearances as Carmen sold out for the rest of the Brussels season, Mapleson concluded their lengthy negotiations, acceding to Hauk's demands that she reserve the right to choose her stage manager and costars.

In contrast to Hauk's enthusiasm for Bizet's opera, Mapleson found it difficult to fill the roles of Escamillo and Don José for the London production. Although both must be first-rate singers, neither role features the star turns typical of an operatic lead. Mapleson recalled,

> On sending [Italo] Campanini the *role* of Don José (in which he afterwards became so celebrated), he returned it to me stating he would do anything to oblige,

12. Hermann Klein, *Thirty Years of Musical Life in London 1870–1900* (London: William Heinemann, 1903), 86.

13. Emilio Sala, *The Sounds of Paris in Verdi's* La traviata, trans. Delia Casadei (Cambridge: Cambridge University Press, 2013), 79.

14. Turner suggests that early US productions (and possibly even Mapleson's London premiere) may have been based on the original Paris designs. Kristen M. Turner, "Opera in English: Class and Culture in America, 1878–1910" (PhD thesis, University of North Carolina at Chapel Hill, 2015), 313–15.

15. Unless otherwise acknowledged, the information on Minnie Hauk is taken from her memoirs. Minnie Hauk, *Memories of a Singer* (New York: Arno Press, [1925] 1977), 144–49, 157–65. The quotation is from *L'Étoile belge*, as quoted by Hauk on page 149.

MINNIE HAUK AS "CARMEN."

Figure 2.1 Minnie Hauk in costume for act 2 of *Carmen*, clipping from unidentified English or US periodical.
Credit: Private collection.

but could not think of undertaking a part in an opera of that description where he had no romance and no love duet except with the *seconda donna*. Shortly afterwards [Giuseppe] Del Puente, the baritone, entered, informing me that the part of Escamillo, which I had sent him, must have been intended for one of the chorus, and that he begged to decline it.[16]

Eventually both Campanini and Del Puente were persuaded, and their performances in *Carmen* were to bring them both international success. But first they had to endure a rehearsal process in which Hauk sought both musical and dramatic control, working with her Belgian stage manager to create "a performance in which acting and scenic effects would go hand in hand with singing" (see Figure 2.2). She recalled the challenge of cajoling some of the cast to attempt some naturalistic acting in place of their accustomed Italian-style "traditional windmill acting." She later praised Del Puente, a Spaniard, for embodying Escamillo so effectively that "in appearance and acting he was a pure type of the Spanish bullfighter," who would have been "at home on the *Plaza de Toros* of Seville."[17]

Hauk assessed her London season as a huge success, and felt that she had introduced London audiences to something quite new in terms of stage action in her "realistic" interpretation of the "Spanish cigar-girl."[18] According to her memoirs, the opening-night audience at Her Majesty's on 22 June 1878 was reduced to total silence by the "innovations in regard to the action," even forgetting to applaud. But, in a reversal of the audience's reaction to the Paris premiere, enthusiasm grew as the work progressed and there was a standing ovation and many calls once the curtain had fallen on act 4.[19] The reviews suggest that Hauk's performance was a highlight of the production, although the dramatic power of her realist style brought out the "demonic" aspects of the character and confirmed some critics in their disgust at the opera's subject matter. The critic of the *Times* recalled no such distaste, but praised Hauk for modeling her interpretation on Galli-Marié, declaring her "the wild, uncontrollable 'Bohemienne' to the life."[20] In phrases that suggest a milder version of the outrage visited on the opera by some Parisian critics in 1875, the *Queen, The Lady's Newspaper,* described *Carmen* as a "risqué" and "spectacular melodrama," featuring "from beginning to end a wild scene of voluptuousness and

16. James Henry Mapleson, *The Mapleson Memoirs: The Career of an Operatic Impresario, 1858–1888,* ed. Harold Rosenthal (London: Putnam, [1888] 1966), 116–17.

17. Hauk, *Memories of a Singer,* 164.

18. "The Creatress of Carmen. An Interview with a Prima Donna," *Pall Mall Gazette,* 22 June 1888, 2, quoted in Susan Rutherford, "'Pretending to Be Wicked': Divas, Technology, and the Consumption of Bizet's Carmen," in *Technology and the Diva,* ed. Karen Henson (Cambridge: Cambridge University Press, 2016), 78.

19. Hauk, *Memories of a Singer,* 164.

20. "Her Majesty's Theatre," *Times,* 24 June 1878, 8.

Figure 2.2 Minnie Hauk in costume for act 3 of *Carmen*, *The Graphic*, 13 July 1878, 36.
Credit: Private collection.

debauchery" and a murderous finale that could have been used by "the propri-
etor of the *Police News* for next week's illustration."[21] The opera's tragic ending
provided "a splendid moral for young ladies in general," warning them against
indulging in vanity and an excessive desire for admiration.[22] Hauk reveled in
the character's wickedness and vulgarity, which she based on a "loyal" reading
of Mérimée's novel, regardless of the risk she might estrange her audience.[23]

21. "Music and Musicians," *Queen*, 29 June 1878, 476; Carados, "Dramatic and
Musical Gossip," *Referee* (London), 23 June 1878, 3.
22. Caliban, "Music and the Drama," *Pictorial World* (1878): 286.
23. "The Creatress of Carmen," 2.

The Spanish elements of the production met with approval from a public fond of local color:

> The music is delightful, full of a character presumed to be Spanish, well scored, and highly dramatic. The opera is well placed upon the stage, scenery and costumes being alike elegant and picturesque; but even had it been only indifferently mounted, the acting and singing of Mlle. Minnie Hauk would have made it remarkable, and would have secured for it the proud position of being the rage of the town.[24]

Despite Hauk's convincing performance, the *Times* critic identified the reliance on local color as a flaw in the opera's characterization of its protagonist. He deplored the "undue prevalence of the national or local over the purely human element. A heroine whose deepest emotion finds expression in a popular Spanish song cannot be said to fulfil the demands of high dramatic art."[25] Other critics recognized the skillful orchestration that incorporated distinctively Spanish instrumental effects in Bizet's interweaving of "the tones of guitars, castagnettes, and the tambours de basque ... with our modern instruments." A comment on "snatch[es] of Moorish coloring" suggests an awareness of the Orientalizing element in Bizet's Spanish dances, which differentiated Bizet's musical evocation of Spain from more familiar scores.[26]

Even the baritone and singing teacher Manuel García, named after his father whose *polo* had formed part of Bizet's score, was drawn to Mapleson's *Carmen*. He attended the opera in the company of critic Hermann Klein, who recorded his impressions. García was "astonished" by the "degree of real Spanish color in the music," especially when compared with other operas set in Seville such as *Don Giovanni* or *Il barbiere di Siviglia*. He praised Hauk for capturing "the peculiarities of the Spanish type, the coquettish manners and the defiant devilry of the wayward gipsy."[27]

Klein claims that the "real popularity [of *Carmen*] in Europe" dated from its London premiere, and this initial production did lead to several key developments in the work's dissemination. In August 1878 Mapleson took Hauk and the company on tour, and on 23 October they introduced *Carmen* to New York audiences in a season at the Academy of Music. They soon found themselves in competition with the Strakosch Italian Opera Company, which launched its own *Carmen*, starring Clara Kellogg, in Philadelphia that same week, leading to a very public battle over performance rights.[28] These

24. "The Italian Opera Season," *Monthly Musical Record* (1 July 1878): 102.
25. "Her Majesty's Theatre," *Times*, 24 June 1878, 8.
26. "Music and Musicians," *Queen*, 29 June 1878, 476.
27. The younger Manuel García had been resident in London from 1848. Klein, *Thirty Years*, 86, 89.
28. Turner, "Opera in English," 351–53.

performances established *Carmen* as one of the most popular modern operas on New York's stages during the 1880s, and Hauk became such a favorite that she sang the role for her farewell performance at the Metropolitan Opera in April 1891, just a couple of years before the young Emma Calvé transfixed American audiences with her fresh take on Carmen.[29] Despite some criticisms that her voice was too small, Hauk's strikingly dramatic interpretation of the role made her one of the most influential Carmens after Galli-Marié, and she sang the role some 500 times throughout her long career.[30] Thanks to Mapleson and Hauk, *Carmen* established itself not only in New York but reached a substantial new audience across the United States as well.

A PROFUSION OF *CARMENS*

After the success of the 1878 premiere, *Carmen* proliferated in London, and was translated into the vernacular. Unlike many European capitals where the opera was usually licensed to only one theater, exclusive rights to perform *Carmen* in London remained unclaimed until they were purchased by Augustus Harris in 1888.[31] Although Covent Garden delayed staging the work until 1882, Londoners were not deprived of Carmen by Hauk's departure, as she was succeeded at Her Majesty's by the French contralto Zélia Trebelli, who had introduced London audiences to the habanera from act 1 before the opera itself was known. Trebelli's less confronting interpretation of the eponymous gypsy was rendered even more charming by its vocal beauty, and audiences flocked to hear her in weekly performances of *Carmen* during the 1878–79 winter season. Summer 1879 saw Hauk return to Her Majesty's, consolidating Carmen's place—and her own—in the affections of London audiences.[32]

A new production to compare with Mapleson's appeared in February 1879, when the Carl Rosa Opera Company mounted *Carmen* translated into English (again at Her Majesty's). It starred Selina Dolaro, an experienced and popular performer, who was making her debut in "opera properly so-called."[33] Born Selina Simmons, she was able to capitalize on her supposed

---

29. John Dizikes, *Opera in America: A Cultural History* (New Haven: Yale University Press, 1993), 214–15.

30. H. Wiley Hitchcock and Katherine K. Preston, "Hauk, Minnie," *Grove Music Online: Oxford Music Online*; Robert Baxter, "The Pathé Opera Series: Bizet *Carmen*," accessed 4 October 2009, http://www.marstonrecords.com/carmen/carmen_liner.htm.

31. Hermann Klein, *The Golden Age of Opera* (London: George Routledge & Sons, 1933), 63–65.

32. Klein, *Thirty Years*, 85; "Operas in Italian: Winter Season," *Monthly Musical Record*, 1 December 1878, 181.

33. "Carmen the Third," *Pall Mall Gazette*, 13 February 1879, 11.

Spanish heritage with the stage name Dolaro when she came to play Carmen. It was her dramatic skill, however, that brought her praise in the role.[34] She had honed her craft at theaters like the Islington and the Gaiety, which from the late 1860s into the 1880s specialized in both burlesque and translations of French *opéra bouffe* by successful composers like Jacques Offenbach and Charles Lecocq, which provided opportunities for "attractive actresses who could combine sophisticated comedy and vocal talents of an operatic level."[35] In the stratified theatrical world of the Victorian era, these genres were considered "lower" than either opera or the legitimate (spoken) stage, but should not be confused with the later American burlesque and its risqué associations. In nineteenth-century Britain, burlesque represented an es-tablished parodic tradition, which subjected operas, classical themes, and well-known tales, plays, and novels to comic treatment, and included sub-stantial musical numbers.[36]

Despite the widespread expectation that Dolaro would "burlesque" the role of Carmen, or at least "treat it in the buffo style," she took the role seri-ously. Praised for her "spirited realism" and "sprightly grace," Dolaro offered an acting ability that more than compensated for her voice being lighter than the two fully operatic Carmens London had heard thus far.[37] The *Times* critic differentiated them as follows: "Mdlle. Hauk *is* Carmen, while Madame Trebelli *sings* Carmen" and "Madame Dolaro *acts* Carmen."[38] Singing in Italian with recitatives, Hauk and Trebelli presented truly operatic Carmens, but Meilhac and Halévy wrote libretti for Offenbach as well as Bizet, and Dolaro may have revealed new possibilities for the interpretation of the role by speaking the di-alogue in the audience's own language. As with the Spanish *zarzuela* versions

34. Dolaro married Isaac Dolaro Belasco, an Italian Jew of Spanish descent, at the age of sixteen. Michele Siegel, "Selina Dolaro," Jewish Women's Archive, accessed 17 January 2014, http://jwa.org/encyclopedia/article/dolaro-selina.

35. Dolaro was not the only *opéra bouffe* specialist to embrace the role: Emily Soldene, who specialized in genres like *opéra bouffe, opéra comique,* and early Gilbert and Sullivan, took on the title role of *Carmen* during the 1879 tour of her "English and Comic Opera Company," which introduced the English version of the opera to the British provinces. Kurt Gänzl, "Soldene, Emily (1838?–1912)," in *Oxford Dictionary of National Biography* (Oxford University Press, 2004).

36. Although the burlesque has been somewhat neglected by musicologists and lit-erary scholars, the following references constitute substantial contributions to the subject: Roberta Montemorra Marvin, "Verdian Opera Burlesqued: A Glimpse into Mid-Victorian Theatrical Culture," *Cambridge Opera Journal* 15, no. 1 (March 2003): 33–66; *Victorian Theatrical Burlesques*, ed. Richard W. Schoch (Aldershot: Ashgate, 2003), i–xlvi; Michael R. Booth, *Theatre in the Victorian Age* (Cambridge: Cambridge University Press, 1991), 196ff; V. C. Clinton-Baddeley, *The Burlesque Tradition in the English Theatre after 1660* (London: Methuen, 1952).

37. "Carmen the Third," *Pall Mall Gazette*, 13 February 1879, 11; "Her Majesty's Theatre," *Times*, 13 February 1879, 8; "'Carmen' in English," *Era*, 9 February 1879, 12.

38. "'Carmen' in English," *Times* (London), 6 February 1879, 10.

of *Carmen* (which will be discussed in Chapters 3 and 4), the adaptation of the work into the vernacular resulted in it entering the realm of operetta performance, taken up by singing actors who could exploit the full dramatic potential of the characters even if their vocal abilities could not compare with their operatic colleagues. Perhaps this versatility contributed to *Carmen*'s sustained appeal as a subject for adaptation and parody, well beyond the usual ephemeral interest provoked by a sensational premiere. Secure of its place in the operatic repertoire, *Carmen* and its themes, both musical and narrative, quickly became sufficiently well known to anchor many forms of referential comedy. Whereas most burlesques used the characters and settings of their subject simply as an excuse for popular songs and generic comic stage business, *Carmen* provided a model in which the underlying plot was intelligible and dramatically fruitful.

Like many successful operas before it, *Carmen* had inspired parodies from the start: its dramatic outline was free from confusing twists and turns and could be easily compressed, while its colorful principal characters lent themselves readily to contrasting caricatures. Even audience members who had not seen the opera would have been familiar with its plot and most famous musical numbers via more popular modes of transmission, such as renditions by street performers and affordable sheet-music arrangements.[39] The renowned translator and adaptor Henry Llewellyn Williams built on the work's currency when he published a "novelized" version in 1880, entitled *Carmen: The Death of the Gypsy*.[40]

One of the first London parodies was Robert Reece's *Carmen, or Sold for a Song*, which ran concurrently with the Carl Rosa season starring Dolaro in early 1879 (see Figure 2.3).[41] With the opera condensed into four scenes, the parody's comic appeal lay in the "grotesque mimicry of the modern operatic tenor" and the sight of a bull chasing the cowardly Escamillo out of the bullring. Despite the restrictions on using Bizet's score, some items were both

39. Reductions of the opera for piano and for piano and voice were only the beginning of its broader dissemination within the first few years after *Carmen*'s debut, as individual numbers (particularly the "Habanera" and the "Toreador Song") were released in arrangements for voice or violin and piano, and various marches appeared set for wind bands. Numerous fantasies and potpourris also appeared.

40. Henry Llewellyn Williams, *Carmen. The Death of the Gipsy. Founded on the … Romance by Mérimée and the … Opera*. (London: E. Ashman, [1880]).

41. Robert Reece's burlesque ran at London's Folly Theatre from 25 January 1879 until the end of the season on 15 March. Its success was sustained by a mid-run "reconstruction" from 23 February, which introduced "new music," "novel effects," and "comic situations." "Theatrical Chit Chat," *Reynolds's Newspaper* (London), 19 January 1879; "Classified Advertisement for Folly Theatre," *Reynolds's Newspaper* (London), 2 March 1879. In mid-March it was picked up by the Royal Park Theatre in Camden Town (*Era*, 16 March 1879) and staged at Dublin's Gaiety Theatre in October of that year (*Era*, 30 October 1879).

Figure 2.3 "Scene from the Burlesque of 'Carmen' at the Folly Theatre," *Illustrated Sporting and Dramatic* News, 8 February 1879, 504.

irresistible and easily quoted, so Escamillo also delivered "many snatches of the popular 'Torreador' song."[42]

Greater longevity was enjoyed by *Cruel Carmen, or the Demented Dragoon and the Terrible Toreador*, which toured the United Kingdom for a year from

42. The music for *Carmen, or Sold for a Song* was arranged by M. Connelly, presumably following the standard burlesque practice of drawing from a wide variety of sources. "Folly Theatre," *Era*, 2 March 1879.

March 1880, with several revivals up until 1885.[43] This production also boasted a Carmen whose singing could have qualified her for the operatic stage, but its comedy peaked in act 4, when the bull, played by a comic actor, sat and laughed at the bullfighters he had thrown around the stage.[44] The bullfight seems to have been one of the main attractions to these early parodists, for as late as February 1884 a three-act burlesque entitled *Little Carmen* appeared briefly at the Globe Theatre, in which an elephant replaced the bull.[45]

The proliferation of *Carmen* coincided with the appearance of a new sensation in Spanish entertainment. After conquering Paris the previous year, the "Spanish students" crossed the English Channel in 1879 and the Estudiantina Figaro undertook a residency at the Alhambra Theatre, while also playing in various other venues, including the Rose Show at the Crystal Palace.[46] In black costumes of doublet, breeches, and cloak, the performers confirmed stereotypes associated with the serenading Spaniard (like Figaro or Don Juan). They performed a wide range of accessible and attractive items, including internationally popular repertoire (like waltzes, mazurkas, polkas, and operatic overtures or arias) alongside distinctly Spanish pieces (from *jotas* and *pasodobles* to flamenco-based genres like the *malagueña*, and excerpts from the Spanish operetta tradition).[47]

By the mid-1880s British audiences were embracing multiple incarnations of Spanishness. Hauk and Dolaro had injected fresh realism into their interpretations of Carmen, reinforcing the image of Spain as both dramatic and sensual. The *estudiantinas* embodied the energy of modern Spanish art while visually referencing old Spain and playing contemporary popular works with great precision. These newer ways of performing Spain coexisted on British stages with the older style of dance and song that had held sway from mid-century through to the late 1870s. The *escuela bolera* style could still be seen in the Spanish numbers of Romantic ballets, while the charming, often nostalgic Spanish songs of the earlier era, as exemplified

43. J. Wilton Jones's burlesque *Cruel Carmen, or the Demented Dragoon and the Terrible Toreador* toured the provinces of England, Scotland, and Ireland almost continuously from March 1880 until May 1881 and again in the second half of 1882, and was briefly revived in late summer 1885.

44. "Cruel Carmen," *Era*, 4 March 1880.

45. Alfred Murray's *Little Carmen*, Globe Theatre, 7 February 1884, with music by Edward Belville. "Miss Bella Howard's Matinee," *Era*, 9 February 1884; Marvin, "Verdian Opera Burlesqued," 65; William Davenport Adams, *A Book of Burlesque, Sketches of English Stage Travestie and Parody* (London: Henry, 1891), 188.

46. The Estudiantina Figaro played twelve nights at the Alhambra, performing a "selection of waltzes, habaneras, national airs etc." "Classifieds," *Times* (London), 16 July 1879, 8.

47. Murray, "Spanish Music," 118–21.

by Iradier's habaneras, remained popular. The great Spanish-born soprano Adelina Patti, for example, favored Iradier's lively "La Calasera" in her encores, alongside her celebrated rendition of "Home, Sweet Home," and she was known for her delightful performance of Hispanic songs, honed during her youthful tours with the pianist Louis Moreau Gottschalk (see Figure 2.4).

Despite Gye's announcements in 1878, Patti did not fulfill her dream of singing Carmen until 1885. By then, when she was well past her prime and singing in her twenty-fifth London season, she found herself a casualty of these changing tastes in Spanishness. Patti's status at Covent Garden

Figure 2.4 Adelina Patti, photograph by N[apoleon]. Sarony (*c.* 1881).
Credit: Library of Congress, https://www.loc.gov/item/2004670844.

was unrivaled, acknowledged as the established queen of operatic repertoire from Donizetti, Bellini, and Rossini to Meyerbeer and Verdi, and beloved for her flexible vocal technique, her beautiful tone, and the charm of
her stage presence. She did not realize, however, that London audiences
would expect something different from her as Carmen, and declared herself
eager to prove her "Spanish" credentials in dance and castanet playing. To
Klein Patti admitted she had longed to sing *Carmen* "for years," and loved
all aspects of the work, from its story and music to its "Spanish scenes
and types."[48] In the Covent Garden production, however, despite the grace
of her dancing, her flirtatious manner was over-determined, lacking any
tenderness, and she struggled to project the more dramatic aspects of the
role. She was roundly criticized for her inability to convey the character's
essential Spanishness: her "bursts of anger lacked the dignity of intense
passion. There was nothing of the volcanic fierceness of Southern nature."
Lacking a strong lower register, she transposed numbers up to suit her effortless soprano range, and applied her usual added ornamentation. This
anachronistic approach to Bizet's score met with little favor from London
audiences.[49]

Just as the 1889 Paris Exposition was hosting an explosion of Spanish entertainment, long-standing trade relationships between Spain and Britain received a boost when a consortium of businessmen staged a "Spanish Exhibition"
on the fairgrounds at Earls Court. Running from June to November, it enjoyed
only limited financial success—perhaps due to the meager offerings of the
trade and industry stalls—but the entertainments it offered were warmly received.[50] While the exhibit of Spanish art was perhaps its most notable highbrow feature,[51] there were also recreations of parts of the Alhambra and a
colorful Spanish marketplace. These displays were enlivened by performances
of Spanish music by *estudiantinas* and the inevitable dance troupes featuring
"Andalusian girls" and staged both daily and nightly in the attractive, well-lit
gardens.[52]

48. Hermann Klein, *The Reign of Patti* (New York: Century, 1920), 225–27.
49. "Royal Italian Opera," *Times*, 16 July 1885, 8.
50. Kirsty Hooper, "'Moorish Splendour' in the British Provinces, 1886–1906: The
Spanish Bazaar, from Dundee to Southampton," in *Contact and Connection Symposium*
(Coventry, UK: University of Warwick Institute of Advanced Study, 2013), 1–10.
51. The art display featured paintings and sculpture by Spanish artists both old and
new, including major names like Diego Velázquez, Bartolomé Esteban Murillo, and
Francisco de Zurbarán; the works were accompanied by paintings on Spanish themes
by British artists. "La exposición española de Londres," *La dinastía* (Barcelona), 12
June 1889, 2.
52. "La exposición española de Londres," *La dinastía*, 12 June 1889, 2; "The Spanish
Exhibition," *Times*, 3 June 1889, 6.

English musicians used comedy as a vehicle for their own versions of the *espagnolade*, and when Arthur Sullivan ventured back into this territory in 1889, at the height of his collaboration with W. S. Gilbert, it resulted in perhaps their most successful work: *The Gondoliers*. Set both in Venice and on an imaginary Spanish island, the operetta offered characters with names like "The Duke of Plaza-Toro" and "Don Alhambra del Bolero," while the most explicit play on Spanish themes can be found in "Dance a cachucha, fandango, bolero," a chorus and dance in act 2. Sullivan went on to revive *The Contrabandista* in 1894, renamed *The Chieftain*, reworking the score to include allusions to some of the new genres of Spanish entertainment.[53]

As the Spanish topic continued to exercise its attraction on English audiences for both high and low art, *Carmen* remained a favorite work that spanned this divide for performers and audiences alike. When in 1890 it became the subject of a Gaiety Theatre burlesque, entitled *Carmen Up to Data*, it achieved a runaway success. Florence St. John, who had already made her name in light opera and by 1892 was dubbed the "Patti of the comic opera stage," starred as Carmen.[54]

CARMEN UP TO DATA: A GAIETY BURLESQUE

The Gaiety Theatre had been renowned for its regular contributions to the burlesque genre since John Hollingshead took up management of the theater in 1868. Although burlesques constituted just one element of the Gaiety's mixed theatrical programs, he boasted their importance in his memoirs, claiming that he had "always endeavoured to keep the sacred lamp of burlesque burning."[55] From 1880 Hollingshead began to extend the Gaiety's burlesque offerings to two and three acts, creating lavish productions with elaborate dance numbers and a greater focus on continuous storytelling.[56] These substantial burlesques became the main attraction of the nightly entertainment, often preceded by an operetta. As institutionalized at theaters like the Gaiety, the genre employed a preexisting storyline and characters to provide a loose thread upon which to hang comic business, elaborate wordplay, dance numbers, and musical items from sources as varied as opera and music

53. Murray, "Spanish Music," 16.

54. Richard Traubner, *Operetta: A Theatrical History* (New York: Routledge, 2004), 58, 66; Erskine Reid and Herbert Compton, *The Dramatic Peerage 1892: Personal Notes and Professional Sketches of the Actors and Actresses of the London Stage* (London: Raithby, Lawrence, 1892), 196.

55. John Hollingshead, *Gaiety Chronicles* (London: Constable, 1898), 400.

56. Traubner, *Operetta*, 187. The first three-act burlesque was *The Forty Thieves* (1880) by Robert Reece.

hall. Burlesques exploited the basic parodic practice of ridiculing operatic convention, laughing at the serious, and rendering the frivolous with absolute solemnity.[57]

This tradition of "pasticcio burlesque," as continued at the Gaiety, was flexible and topical, but its appeal to the largely male audience rested on two essential elements: the dancing chorus girls in revealing costumes, who were to become internationally renowned in the 1890s as the more elegant—and respectably dressed—Gaiety Girls,[58] and the "travesty" tradition featuring the "principal boy" (or burlesque boy), actually a female performer specializing in comic trouser roles. The travesty tradition allowed both principals and dancing chorus to wear fitted costumes that revealed both curvaceous figure and leg without provoking moral outrage, adding to the burlesque's attractions.[59]

After George Edwardes took over the Gaiety's management in 1886, his search for a "new style of entertainment" produced a generation of burlesques in which the entire score—including the songs—was composed by the Gaiety's house composer, Meyer Lutz.[60] Although the most successful numbers were often other composers' preexisting works interpolated into the shows, Lutz provided what Kurt Gänzl describes as a "body of efficient, tulle-weight tunes and songs which served prettily to illustrate the comic high-jinks and girlie antics of the 'new burlesque' genre."[61] Literature and fairy tale were frequent sources, but *Carmen* was not the first operatic target, notably preceded by *Faust Up to Date* in 1888.[62]

Carmen Up to Data followed a tested formula and was the second Gaiety burlesque from George R. Sims and Henry Pettitt, who had written *Faust Up to Date*, and could almost be dubbed the English Meilhac and Halévy for their

---

57. William Adams declared "the *raison d'être* of theatrical burlesque [to be] that it shall satirise the exaggerated and the extreme." Adams, *Book of Burlesque*, 219.

58. Traubner, *Operetta*, 190.

59. Mark Perugini describes the dance traditions at the Gaiety as "step-dancing of the characteristic and admirable English school, quite distinct from the classic ballet style, with its pointe work," and observes that the Gaiety's much-loved *pas de quatre*—a barn dance for four dancers—which appeared in innumerable Gaiety productions, was a very "bright and inspiriting dance." Mark E. Perugini, *A Pageant of the Dance and Ballet* (London: Jarrolds, 1946), 214.

60. Serving as the Gaiety's house composer and music director from 1869 to 1894, Wilhelm Meyer Lutz (1829–1903) selected, arranged, and conducted music for the burlesques, but composed complete original scores for the "new" burlesques, which included *Monte Cristo, Jr* (1886); *Miss Esmeralda, or The Maid and the Monkey* (1887); *Frankenstein, or The Vampire's Victim* (1887); *Faust Up to Date* (1888); *Ruy Blas and the Blasé Roué* (1889); *Carmen Up to Data* (1890); *Cinder Ellen Up Too Late* (1891); and *Don Juan* (1892). His retirement from the Gaiety coincided with the rise of the musical comedy and demise of the burlesque.

61. Kurt Gänzl, "Lutz, (Wilhelm) Meyer (1829–1903)," in *Oxford Dictionary of National Biography* (Oxford University Press, 2004).

62. Lutz's score for *Faust Up to Date* included the enduring "Pas de quatre."

success as theatrical writers across a variety of genres.[63] The phrase "up to date" gained currency only from the late 1880s; indeed, *Faust Up to Date* is cited as its first usage with the meaning "in a condition abreast of the times in respect of qualities, style, knowledge, presentation of facts, etc."[64] The use of "data" rather than "date" seems to have been an attempt to make the *Carmen* burlesque sound Spanish, a joke heavily exploited in the wordplay of the libretto.[65] Employing such contemporary slang in the title underlined the burlesque enterprise of taking classic or celebrated works and rendering them both contemporary and local.

Edwardes's choice of *Carmen* as the subject for his 1890 burlesque offering played into the growing fashion for all things Spanish on stage and in society. With *Carmen* now ensconced in the repertory at Covent Garden (albeit in Italian), and the undeniable success of *The Gondoliers*, the stage was set for the proliferation of Spanish-inflected acts in the 1890s music hall. All this would have suggested to Edwardes that he had backed a winner with a Gaiety burlesque of Bizet's opera. Despite the enduring popularity of Spanish dance acts, London audiences had as yet hardly been exposed to the new and challenging flamenco styles introduced in Paris by the Granadine gypsies in 1889, which may have influenced Edwardes's decision to stick to the familiar and charming vision of Spain perpetrated in productions of the opera. Humorous digs at Spanishness aside, the subject offered opportunities for colorful and entertaining visual spectacle that would surely prove irresistible to the Gaiety's audience. In fact, much of the work's success can be ascribed to its unprecedentedly close adherence to the opera's strong storyline, prompting one critic to describe it as a "parallel" rather than a burlesque.[66]

63. The following discussion of *Carmen Up to Data* is based on a version of the vocal score published in 1890 and a typescript of the libretto held in the New York Public Library. A Gaiety burlesque was not a fixed entity; it changed during its season, and was altered for every new town where it was performed, so these sources are not taken as indicating any "authoritative" version. When used in conjunction with contemporary press responses to the show, they enable some assessment of the nature of the work. Meyer Lutz, *Carmen Up to Data, Burlesque Opera* [vocal score], ed. P. F. Campiglio (London: E. Ascherberg, 1890; New York: Novello, Ewer, 1890), George R. Sims, Henry Pettitt, and Meyer Lutz, "Carmen Up to Date [typescript]," New York Public Library Performing Arts Research Collections—Theatre ([1890]), NCOF+ p.v.493.

64. The growing popularity of stage works set in the present day is illustrated by the fashion for what Ivor Guest terms the "up-to-date" ballet, which featured "topical themes" and "English settings" and had its heyday between 1891 and 1897. Guest cites Hollingshead's *Up the River* (1892) at the Alhambra as an example. Guest, *Ballet in Leicester Square*, 8, 47, 104–14; "Up to date," in *Oxford English Dictionary Online* (Oxford University Press, 2000).

65. As the troop of soldiers enters in act 1, scene 1, José gives them orders in fake Spanish: "Haltidad, eyes rightidad—Intimidad—Imperiales, / Attentionales, Colorado, Maduro, Claro— / Oh, hang the Spanish—you can stand at ease!" Sims, Pettitt, and Lutz, "Carmen Up to Data [typescript]," NCOF+ p.v.493, act 1, scene 1, 7.

66. *Illustrated Sporting and Dramatic News*, 1 November 1890, 6.

Carmen Up to Data incorporated the main events of Carmen's love affair with José, her later dalliance with Escamillo, the cigarette girls and smugglers, and the bullfighting finale. In contrast to the opera, however, Carmen survives, despite being threatened by José with a great array of knives. Their last exchange before the sung Finale is the closing installment in a running gag about José's attachment to his mother, in clear parody of the operatic character:

CARMEN: You cannot be my husband—be my brother!
JOSÉ: Never! (Turns to go)
CARMEN: Where are you going?
JOSÉ: Home to Mother![67]

The action was compressed into two acts, each of the four scenes providing scope for spectacular design and almost exactly matching the acts for the opera, with the one shift of the rocky mountains to a coastal locale:

Act 1   Scene 1: Square in Seville

Scene 2: Courtyard of gipsy club

Act 2   Scene 1: A rocky retreat on the sea-coast

Scene 2: Exterior of the bull ring

Described variously as "exceptionally picturesque," "a triumph of scene painting," and even "captivating," the set designs, one critic suggested, had reached a level of "artistic excellence" that elevated them far above the level of the "singing, dancing and banter" that had long characterized such burlesques.[68] In the context of pervasive verbal humor, which relied heavily on wordplay based on topical references to current people and events, Sims and Pettitt engaged humorously on the Spanish topic and Mérimée's characters.[69]

When Carmen tries to "mash" (or flirt with) José to secure her release from arrest, she—like Mérimée's Carmen—feigns northern Spanish origins. The list of Spanish place names in their duet, "Are You Made of Rock" seems tame when compared with the painful punning of the preceding dialogue:

67. Sims, Pettitt, and Lutz, "Carmen Up to Data [typescript]," NCOF+ p.v.493, act 2, scene 2, 7.
68. *Daily News* (London), 6 October 1890, 6; "Through the Opera Glass: Carmen Up to Data," *Pick-Me-Up*, 22 November 1890, 118; C. M. B. M., "Masterful Stage Art," *Sun* (New York), 19 April 1891, 15.
69. The script made humorous reference to recent plays, wars, prominent people in sports, law, politics, and colonial affairs, and even such modern items as portable cameras (Detectives and Kodaks).

CARMEN: Do you come from Navarre?

JOSÉ: I navarre heard of the place!

CARMEN: You are a native of Catalonia?

JOSÉ: I never saw a cat alone here—there's generally a dog after them!

CARMEN: You are from the country?

JOSÉ: No, although a soldier I am a servillian![70]

In a timely joke about the burgeoning travel industry that led ever increasing numbers of upper-middle-class tourists to "brave" the Iberian penin- sula in search of the picturesque and the exotic, Micaëla's message from José's mother requests more "bad money" for her to pass off to the English tourists.[71]

There was a daring and contemporary quality about some of the costumes and spectacle in *Carmen Up to Data*, and the lively opening scene did not delay the audience's gratification. As the curtain rose on the square of Seville, the opening chorus, "Seville Is Gay Today," accompanied the fol- lowing luscious spectacle: "Young ladies run on and instantly merge them- selves in a perplexing wilderness of underclothing, and then other young ladies with trousers on enter and try to make believe they're young men."[72] The color and flair of the costumes, coupled with choreographed stage groupings, created striking visual effects, and the book of costume plates indicates a huge variety of costumes, referencing every visual stereotype of Spanishness.[73] These ranged from flowers, combs, and mantillas for the girls' headdresses, to short bolero-style jackets, laced bodices, and scarves around the hips, frequently adorned by *madroños* (bobbles). The "men" of the chorus line were poured into tight-fitting pantaloons with short jackets and cummerbunds or heavily embroidered sparkly bullfighting costumes (see Figure 2.5).

Like the many English parodies that preceded it, *Carmen Up to Data* took great delight in lampooning the bullfight, a spectacle that was considered bar- baric by many outside Spain, even in a society whose upper class defended its hereditary right to fox hunting. The travesty tradition of burlesque and dance enabled much fun at the expense of the most *macho* character of the opera, the bullfighter Escamillo, as impersonated by an attractive young

70. Sims, Pettitt, and Lutz, "Carmen Up to Data [typescript]," NCOF+ p.v.493, act 1, scene 1, 16.

71. Ibid., 11–12.

72. "Through the Opera Glass," *Pick-Me-Up*, 22 November 1890, 118.

73. Seventy-eight costume plates (drawings in watercolor, pen, and ink) from the pro- duction that toured Australia in 1892 are preserved in a volume held by the National Library of Australia. "Album of Costume Designs for a Production of *Carmen Up to Data*," J. C. Williamson Collection (*c.* 1892), R9469–R9546, R9469–R546, National Library of Australia, Canberra.

Figure 2.5 "Alphonze," *Carmen Up to Data: A Souvenir of the Gaiety Theatre*, souvenir post-card set with sketches by Percy Anderson (1890).
Credit: Private collection.

woman. Cross-dressing this character seems to have been irresistible to the English, just as it would be when staged as a ballet at London's Alhambra in 1903. Likewise, José's costumes were conceived to heighten the sense of the ridiculous, from his appearance as a stylized "masher" (a Victorian dandy

Figure 2.6 (a) "Captain Zuniga (Mr. Arthur Williams) and José [Mr. E. Lonnen]"; (b) "José in Act III," in "Sketches of 'Carmen Up to Data,' at the Gaiety Theatre," *Illustrated London News*, 25 October 1890, 524.

or stage-door Johnny) when catching Carmen's turn at the gypsy club to his outlandish brigand's outfit (see Figure 2.6).

Notwithstanding the visual delights, relentless wordplay, and an excess of "brisk and bustling burlesque business," the work's chief attraction was its music.[74] "*Carmen Up to Data* might perhaps be more properly called Meyer Lutz up to everything" wrote one critic,[75] while another praised his music as "by turns vivacious and sentimental ... always effective and melodious."[76] Prevented by copyright law from using any of Bizet's music, Lutz still managed to create an entertaining score, which hinted at some themes from the opera by using incipits and rhythmic reminiscence, while evoking an exotic mood when necessary. The press observed the unfairness of this situation when street musicians had free rein with the opera's music: "Mr. Meyer Lutz, who presides in the orchestra at the performances of *Carmen Up to Data*,

74. *Daily Chronicle* (London), 6 October 1890.
75. *Illustrated Sporting and Dramatic News*, 1 November 1890, 6.
76. *Daily Chronicle*, 6 October 1890.

dares not appropriate a bar of M. Bizet's score," yet "an Italian musical 'Bogie Man' outside the Gaiety doors may be grinding away at 'Vivat le Torero' to his heart's content."[77]

In fact, Lutz did make limited use of Bizet's model, most notably in the case of the celebrated "Toreador Song." Entitled "Here He Comes, the Gallant Hero," this chorus heralds Escamillo's entrance. The first bar is melodically identical to Bizet's original tune, and the remaining phrases echo its distinctive rhythmic pattern, while deviating slightly from the famous melody. Lutz also used rhythmic reminiscence as a subtle reminder of the Bizet in the opening number, "Seville Is Gay Today," the text of which recalls the opening soldier's chorus ("Sur la place, chacun passe," act 1, scene 1). Several numbers replicate the dramatic function of items in Bizet's score, like the chorus of boys who enter with the soldiers ("Avec la garde montante," act 1, scene 2), but these generally bear no musical similarity to their models.

Carmen's first number, however, serves as a clear proxy for Bizet's celebrated habanera. In "Ask Me to Marry, I Laugh Ha! Ha!" Lutz presents a dramatic minor-mode introduction, opening with a dotted habanera rhythm in the bass line. When the voice enters, it matches the rhythm and phrase structure of Bizet's habanera almost exactly, but the charming, insinuating melodic line only echoes its famous model in the fourth phrase, which opens with three steps of semitonal descent, before following an original melodic profile to reach its cadence.[78] The mildly exotic flavor of this section then gives way to a far more conventional major-mode waltz, in which the lilting and flirtatious vocal line is ornamented with triplet figures and semitonal inflections to convey a Spanish tinge.

Lutz's "Spanish style" seems to owe something to passages of Bizet's unique score. The celebrated "Pas de quatre," indicated with the subtitle "Spanish" in the score, is reminiscent of the march style of the entr'acte to act 4 of the opera.[79] The nominally "Spanish" numbers, whether sung or danced, intimate their exotic status by musical markers of the most generic kind: frequently in minor keys, they feature triplet turns and figures, dance rhythms, and melodic lines colored by the gypsy or Andalusian scale.[80] The "Cigarette Girls' Chorus," marked "Tempo di polacca," demonstrates the close relationship between this familiar dance and Spanish genres like the *bolero*, which share the same characteristic

77. "Theatres," *Graphic*, 8 November 1890, 529.

78. Where Bizet's line continues the semitone descent, dropping a fourth, Lutz was less audacious, reverting to the last three notes of the minor scale, tracing the fall of a fifth in his phrase. Lutz, *Carmen Up to Data, Burlesque Opera*: no. 5, 23–29.

79. Lutz, *Carmen Up to Data, Burlesque Opera*: no. 10, 54–59.

80. This scale might include the exotic sounds of the flattened supertonic or the augmented second.

rhythmic pattern.[81] The accompaniments to these generic dance styles invoke the strumming of a guitar, so that appropriately costumed cigarette girls could still represent Spanishness even while dancing "alla polacca." The "Calasera," a number declared "thoroughly Spanish in character,"[82] allows Carmen to deploy song, dance, and castanets to persuade José to ignore the call of the bugles and stay with her at the gypsy tavern.[83] For this crucial exotic set piece, Lutz employs the triple time and rhythmic patterns reminiscent of so many Spanish dance types, including the *jota*. The exotic feel comes from the ornamentation, especially of cadential figures, with triplet turns and Phrygian inflections.[84]

The generic requirements of the Gaiety burlesque called for musical numbers like patter songs, Irish songs, sentimental songs, novelty numbers (like Mercedes's "The Farmyard"), and a wide variety of dance styles, including the smugglers' hornpipe and those Gaiety favorites, the "Pas de quatre" and the "Pas de huit" (dubbed the "cachucha de ocho" during the run. See Figure 2.7). In typical burlesque fashion, popular songs from other sources were interpolated throughout the action. The Spanish theme did not prevent the undoubted hit of the show being an Irish-style song entitled "Hush! The Bogie!" that provided a star vehicle for the comic E. J. Lonnen, who played José.[85] The heroine's obligatory sentimental songs distanced her from the character in the opera,[86] but Florence St. John, who performed the role relatively straight, earned great praise for her singing: she "looks, acts, and sings as a genuine Carmen.... I doubt whether any better operatic impersonator of the real character could be found. She is not the least bit burlesque."[87]

Carmen Up to Data became one of the Gaiety's most successful burlesques. After a short out-of-town run in Liverpool it opened in London on 4 October 1890, was refreshed with a "second edition" on 2 February 1891, and played until 4 July 1891, when the theater closed for renovations.[88] The Gaiety's

81. Lutz, *Carmen Up to Data, Burlesque Opera*: no. 4, 18–22.

82. *Daily Chronicle*, 6 October 1890.

83. Adelina Patti was renowned for her performances of Iradier's "La calasera" as an encore throughout her career, including during the Second Empire, and recorded it in 1905.

84. Lutz, *Carmen Up to Data, Burlesque Opera*: no. 15, 77–80.

85. Some critics were aware that, despite being published under Lutz's name, "Hush! The Bogie!" had been heard in London a decade earlier, and was in fact by the American writing/composing partnership of Harrigan and Braham. It was written in 1880 as "Whist! The Bogie Man" for a play called *The Mulligan Guards' Surprise*. The Gaiety had in fact obtained permission to use the song. For the original song, see David Braham and Edward Harrigan, *Collected Songs, 1873–1882* (Madison, WI: published for the American Musicological Society by A-R Editions, 1997), 1: 137–39, 310. "The Bogie Man in the Courts," *Sun* (New York), 6 November 1890, 3.

86. *Observer*, 5 October 1890, 6.

87. "A Pair of Spectacles," *Punch, or the London Charivari*, 6 December 1890, 268.

88. *Carmen Up to Data* opened at the Shakespeare Theatre in Liverpool on 22 September 1890.

Figure 2.7 "Mercedes," *Carmen Up to Data: A Souvenir of the Gaiety Theatre*, souvenir post-card set with sketches by Percy Anderson (1890).
Credit: Private collection.

various touring troupes then took the work around the United Kingdom and abroad, playing in Australia as late as July 1893.[89]

Hollingshead credited George Edwardes with pioneering the existing notion of "new editions," whereby new songs and dances refreshed the program during a burlesque's long run. This practice ensured the success of extended runs, so that *Monte Cristo, Jr.* ran for over a hundred nights, *Faust up to Date* for nearly two hundred, and *Carmen Up to Data* for almost two hundred fifty. Hollingshead, *Gaiety Chronicles*, 400; *Victorian Theatrical Burlesques*, xlivn41.

89. The Gaiety company played *Carmen Up to Data*, alongside several other works in their repertory, around Australia for nearly a year, starting in Adelaide in July 1892

For a work that played so strongly on local references and humor, *Carmen Up to Data* was remarkably successful on tour, perhaps because of the common culture of the English-speaking empire.[90] It is clear from the libretto of *Faust Up to Date* (published in Melbourne during the Gaiety's tour of 1892) that local references were inserted into the text where possible.[91] But touring companies from the Gaiety, announced as the "Royal English Burlesque Company," took the work beyond the English-speaking world. It was announced for a season in Brussels, and the sheet music (vocal score and piano arrangement) was advertised in the Brussels journal *Le Guide musicale* as the "great success of the Alhambra-Eden."[92] Farther east, it played as *Carmen von Heute* (*Carmen of Today*) at the Imperial and Royal Carl Theater in Vienna in September 1892. The work would have appealed to the Viennese taste for light opera and Spanish-inflected entertainment, as evidenced by the warm response to the first *estudiantinas* in 1878 (see Chapter 1). The Gaiety company performed in English, but the theater published a booklet in which both the song lyrics and prose summaries of the plot were translated into German.[93] The critic of the *Wiener Zeitung* noted that it was English not only in speech and song, but also very much after English taste in the arrangement of action, mime, and dance. Despite these comments, the Viennese public laughed and applauded heartily, appreciating the work's "careful and artistic" execution and the charming versatility of the singing and dancing female cast (including the travesty Escamillo):[94]

> It evoked immense enthusiasm. All the leading ladies in the company were presented with flowers and received recalls. "Ta-ra-ra Boom-de-ay" was

and performing in Melbourne, Sydney, and Brisbane. "Opera House: 'Carmen Up to Data,'" *Brisbane Courier*, 5 September 1892, 5.

90. When the Gaiety company toured Australia in 1892–93, it left behind extensive collections of sheet music and costume designs, now held in the J. C. Williamson collection of performance materials at the National Library of Australia. The *Carmen Up to Data* items include orchestral parts, interpolated numbers, marked-up conductors' scores, and multiple vocal scores, as well as the previously mentioned album of seventy-eight watercolor costume designs from the show [R9469–R9546].

91. Unfortunately, no libretto of *Carmen Up to Data* has been located for this tour. George R. Sims, Henry Pettitt, and Meyer Lutz, *Faust Up to Date: A Burlesque in Two Acts* (Melbourne: J. J. Miller, 1892).

92. Also advertising *Faust Up to Date*, the last line reads "Le gran success de l'Alhambra-Eden!," referring to one of the largest theaters in Brussels. "[Advertisement] Nouveautés musicales en vente chez Breitkopf & Haertel," *Le Guide musical*, 27 November 1892.

93. George R. Sims, Henry Pettitt, and Meyer Lutz, *Carmen von Heute: Burlesque in vier Akten* (Vienna: Verlag des k.k. priv. Carl-Theaters, 1892). The booklet was also published by Bernstein in Berlin.

94. "Theater und Kunst," *Wiener Abendpost [Beilage zur Wiener Zeitung]* (Vienna), 2 September 1892, 3.

rendered, and it carried the audience away. It received three encores which is an astonishing occurrence for Vienna.[95]

This international success suggests that the work was seen as comparable to parodic and light-opera traditions on the Continent.

A further indicator of the show's popularity was the volume of sheet music it generated. The London publisher Ascherberg released several vocal scores, reflecting the changing numbers that emerged from the work's evolution during its initial run at the Gaiety. Numerous arrangements of individual songs were published as sheet music for solo piano, voice and piano, and a variety of combinations that included violin, piano, banjo, guitar, and mandolin. The large number of plucked-string arrangements (for solo and various mixed ensembles) catered to the burgeoning popularity of the *estudiantina* and BMG (banjo, mandolin and guitar) movements. Some of the vocal scores of *Carmen Up to Data* included line drawings of characters and scenes from the burlesque, while the Ascherberg catalogue offered piano arrangements for dancing, in which a number consistently titled "Hush! the Bogie, and Carmen Up to Data" appeared under headings as varied as the schottische, waltz, lancers, polka, and quadrille.[96]

In *Carmen Up to Data*, George Edwardes managed to repackage the Gaiety Theatre's familiar product. The opera's strong and dramatic storyline provided an ideal framework for all the elements that had long secured the Gaiety burlesque's popularity, among them the Irish tenor, the chorus line, the low comic, and the principal boy. The Gaiety's commercial success with *Carmen Up to Data* was the result of an inspired merger of what were in effect two established theatrical brands, namely *Carmen* itself and the "up-to-date" burlesque, and resulted in perhaps the ultimate "anglicization" of Bizet's opera, with its localized humor, its distinctively English dance styles, and even its localized version of exotic inflections.

This substantial manifestation of the late Gaiety burlesque in fact pointed the way toward a new kind of musical theater. As the burlesque waned, Edwardes developed the "up-to-date" idea in a work generally recognized as the first "musical comedy": *In Town* (1892), which starred Florence St. John. Edwardes followed this success with *A Gaiety Girl* (1893) and *The Shop Girl* (1894), and the new genre was established. Based on contemporary settings with topical plots, and offering an appealing combination of comedy, romance, and song and dance numbers featuring the newly named "Gaiety Girls," these

95. "Music and Drama Abroad," *New York Times*, 4 September 1892.

96. The production was accompanied by lavish programs and merchandise, like the deluxe souvenir postcard set, which featured beautifully colored lithograph plates of the characters in costume, as seen in Figures 2.5 and 2.7.

works incorporated the best of the variety stage, the most popular elements of operetta, and the new dramatic ground of the 1890s drawing-room drama.[97] By 1896 *The Geisha* indicated the inclusion of exotic subjects alongside the local tales of everyday people, and the enduring appeal of the Carmenesque storyline is seen in the 1901 hit *The Toreador*, with songs by the composers Ivan Caryll and Lionel Monckton. Set in Spain, among bullfighters and foreign tourists, it ran in London until mid-1903, becoming the last show ever staged at the old Gaiety Theatre, and enjoyed international success. Edwardes's dedication to his winning formula meant that it still included a travesty role and the inevitable cast of beautiful girls, but even in the new genre of the musical, the Spanish theme established on the Anglo-American entertainment scene by *Carmen* and its spin-offs retained its appeal and versatility.

The development of musical comedy occurred in a later stage of *Carmen's* translatlantic journey, but by 1890—when *Carmen Up to Data* premiered in London—the opera's literary and musical texts had become so well known that they could be parodied and travestied around the world. The Iberian peninsula was by then in the first flush of its belated love affair with Bizet's opera, which had commenced with a battle over copyright that recalled the experience of Mapleson and Strakosch in the United States. *Carmen's* success in Spain was to inspire a different kind of parody, one that had currency in the Hispanic world, in the form of Salvador María Granès's *Carmela*.

97. Andrew Lamb and John Snelson, "Musical," in *Grove Music Online: Oxford Music Online*; Traubner, *Operetta*, 189.

PART II

Spain Discovers *Carmen* (1887–91)

CHAPTER 3

⌀

Dueling *Carmens* in Madrid

B izet's *Carmen* was slow to arrive in Spain, its putative home, and when
it did the opera became a battleground for debates about national identity and its cultural expression.[1] Even as Spanish critics questioned the way
in which Bizet and *Carmen* staged Spain, Spanish entrepreneurs and writers
were beginning to adapt the opera into local genres, like the *zarzuela*, writing
the debates quite literally into the texts of the work itself. As we have seen,
Carmen's largely unnoticed Spanish premiere took place in Barcelona on 2
August 1881 and it finally found its way on to Madrid's stages in late 1887,
to be greeted with both controversy and enthusiasm. From the outset, it was
much more than just another foreign opera or an *espagnolade* to be reviled
for its caricature of Spanish customs. Capturing the imagination of press and
public, the opera was quickly woven into a rich web of contemporary and
local associations, many of them from the world outside the theater, from
industrial relations in the tobacco industry to furious debates over the cultural representation of Spanish identity. The immediate recognition that in
Carmen Bizet had portrayed stereotypes of Spain within a unique and innovative musico-dramatic framework ensured lively engagement with the work.

A MATTER OF STATE: THE CONTESTED PREMIERE
OF *CARMEN* IN MADRID

Even before its Madrid debut, *Carmen* created a scandal, with the city transfixed
by the spectacle of two well-known impresarios brawling over the exclusive

1. Some of the material presented in this chapter was first published in Elizabeth
Kertesz and Michael Christoforidis, "Confronting *Carmen* beyond the Pyrenees: Bizet's
Opera in Madrid, 1887–1888," *Cambridge Opera Journal* 20, no. 1 (2008): 79–110.

right to stage the Madrid premiere of Bizet's last opera. The Conde (Count) Ramón de Michelena of the Teatro Real and Felipe Ducazcal of the Teatro de la Zarzuela engaged in legal machinations and public relations campaigns, attracting (and exploiting) huge interest from the local and national press, including the comic papers. Although both gentlemen represented state-owned institutions in central Madrid, they were in charge of very different theaters.

Michelena was impresario of the "royal" theater on the Plaza de Oriente from 1885 to 1896. Situated across the square from the Royal Palace, it attracted the cream of Madrid society to hear foreign opera performed in a palatial auditorium that seated nearly three thousand people. The high standards of performance at the Teatro Real under Michelena's management were due in no small part to the musical direction of one of the theater's greatest conductors, Luigi Mancinelli, who held the post from 1886 to 1893.[2] The Teatro Real was dominated by Italian opera and performers during this period, although French grand opera was also performed, mainly in Italian translation. The 1887–88 season ran from 1 October until 22 March, opening with Meyerbeer's *Les Huguenots* and closing with *Carmen*.[3] Ponchielli's *La gioconda* was popular, and the program included works by Verdi and Donizetti, and even Wagner's *Lohengrin*.[4] The Teatro Real was considered by many to be artistically moribund in this period, so staging *Carmen* was something of a coup. Antonio Peña y Goñi, the foremost musical critic of the day, saw the company's performance of this "jewel" of an *opéra comique* as a welcome break in the routine of the season. "In short," he wrote, "last night *Carmen* was like a dose of smelling salts for the Real's public, which seemed to groan under a powerful anesthetic."[5]

Locally composed works were rarely heard at the Teatro Real, but the Spanish national genre—or *zarzuela*—had its own home at the Teatro de la Zarzuela on the Calle de Jovellanos, adjacent to the Congreso de los Diputados (Spanish parliament) on the other side of town from the royal palace. The *zarzuela* is a Spanish theatrical genre that includes both sung numbers and

2. Vicente Bermejo López and Rosa María Valiente Moreno-Cid, "El Teatro Real de Madrid, 1850–1998," accessed 14 January 2007, www.ucm.es/info/hcontemp/madrid/teatro%20real.htm; Ramón Sobrino, "Mancinelli, Luis," in *Diccionario de la música española e hispanoamericana*, ed. Emilio Casares Rodicio (Madrid: Sociedad General de Autores y Editores, 1999–2002).

3. The Teatro Real staged the fully sung Italian version of *Carmen*, the principal vehicle of the opera's global dissemination.

4. The two most frequently performed operas in the Real season were *La gioconda* with twelve performances and *Les Huguenots* with ten. *Carmen*, premiered in the last month, received only five. Joaquín Turina Gómez, *Historia del Teatro Real* (Madrid: Alianza, 1997), 397–400.

5. Antonio Peña y Goñi, "Teatro Real: Carmen," *La época*, 15 March 1888.

spoken text. During the mid- and late nineteenth century, *zarzuelas* often featured specifically Spanish subjects, regularly drawing on Spanish popular culture. The 2,500-seat Teatro de la Zarzuela was established in 1856 to foster the genre and in the 1880s attracted a less exclusive clientele than the Teatro Real. Felipe Ducazcal took over its lease for the 1887–88 season with grand plans to revive the *zarzuela* tradition. A noted theatrical impresario, Ducazcal enjoyed a high profile in Madrid not only because of his success as an animator of popular entertainment, but also because he was notorious as a political operator.[6] He proposed to commission and stage new two- or three-act *zarzuelas* by "authors and artists of true merit" to fulfill his vision of "opera cómica española."[7]

Knowing it would take time to develop new works, Ducazcal intended to launch his first season with a mixture of classic *zarzuelas* and masterpieces of the European operatic tradition "in their primitive form of *óperas cómicas*," translated into Spanish by the most renowned playwrights.[8] Performers were to be drawn both from Spain and abroad, so Ducazcal craved indulgence of foreign accents in the spoken Spanish dialogue. A large orchestra of sixty players was to be gathered under the distinguished baton of Gerónimo Giménez, noted musician and *zarzuela* composer, recently returned from Paris.[9] The highlights of the season were the new Spanish-language version of *Carmen* and the sensational debut of Ruperto Chapí's new *zarzuela* *La bruja* (The Witch).[10] Despite these successes, Ducazcal's increasing political responsibilities forced him to sublet the theater after only one season and his valiant attempt to revive the genre was forgotten as the Teatro de

6. Ducazcal was a key supporter of the democratic government during the Sexenio (1868–74), but ingratiated himself with Alfonso XII after the restoration of the monarchy, and in April 1886 he was elected as a deputy for Madrid in the Congreso de los Diputados. He was involved in a family publishing business and achieved outstanding success with summer theaters and the *género chico* in the early 1880s. Among Ducazcal's many enterprises, he had turned around the fortunes of the Teatro Apolo (1880–84) and built his own hugely successful summer theater, the Felipe (which opened in 1885). Emilio Casares Rodicio, "Ducazcal Lashieras, Felipe," in *Diccionario de la zarzuela: España e Hispanoamérica*, ed. Emilio Casares Rodicio (Madrid: ICCMU, 2002–03), 678–79; Carmen del Moral Ruiz, *El género chico: Ocio y teatro en Madrid (1880–1910)* (Madrid: Alianza, 2004), 64–66.

7. The prospectus for the season can be found in the Museo del teatro de Almagro, and is cited by Luis G. Iberni, *Ruperto Chapí* (Madrid: ICCMU, 1995), 148–49.

8. In this somewhat unusual category Ducazcal included Beethoven's *Fidelio*, Weber's *Der Freischütz*, Mozart's *The Marriage of Figaro* and *The Magic Flute*, Thomas's *Mignon*, Gounod's *Faust* and, most importantly, Bizet's *Carmen*.

9. Iberni, *Ruperto Chapí*, 149.

10. *La bruja* premiered on 10 December 1887 and played until February of the following year.

la Zarzuela succumbed to the new craze for the *género chico* (literally: little genre). This one-act subgenre of the *zarzuela* featured distinctively local humor and became the most popular form of theatrical entertainment in 1880s Madrid. It attracted large, popular audiences, and was run on a system called *teatro por horas* (theater by the hour), in which each short work had a low admission charge. Full-length *zarzuelas* struggled to find market share at the height of the *género chico*'s success.

In 1887, however, Ducazcal was a determined and substantial competitor with the management of the Teatro Real for the opportunity to introduce *Carmen* in the capital.[11] Michelena landed the first blow when on 10 September 1887 the copyright holder for Bizet's *Carmen*, Choudens of Paris, agreed to lease him performance rights for the 1887–88 Madrid season, in a contract reputedly worth 5,000 francs.[12] *Carmen* was to be sung in Italian at a premiere planned for early November, and the Teatro Real management announced on 11 October that the company was busy preparing for the new production.[13] These plans notwithstanding, the Teatro de la Zarzuela announced its own *Carmen* premiere for 27 October 1887.[14] It was rumored that Ducazcal had approached Michelena with a proposal to split the rights so that he could put on a Spanish version, but as no agreement was reached Ducazcal then claimed the right to present *Carmen* in the "provinces."[15] Michelena was incensed and took his complaint to the Duque de Frías, Civil Governor of Madrid, who upheld his claim to the rights.[16] Ducazcal in turn contested this ruling, and both gentlemen submitted supporting documentation to Frías. Michelena had by now enlisted the help of local publisher Benito Zozaya, the Madrid representative of Choudens. The ensuing escalation of the contest drew in an ever-widening circle of international diplomats (Choudens asked the French ambassador to Madrid to speak for Michelena to the Spanish

11. For more detailed accounts of the ensuing "battle" to stage *Carmen*'s Madrid premiere, see Kertesz and Christoforidis, "Confronting *Carmen*," 85–88; Laura Santana Burgos, "Diálogos entre Francia y España: La traducción de los libretos de *Carmen* y *El retablo de Maese Pedro*" (PhD thesis, Universidad de Granada, 2013), 155–87.

12. "Carmen," *La Iberia*, 28 October 1887, 1.

13. *El anunciador universal*, 11 October 1887.

14. As advertised in "Espectáculos," *El liberal*, 27 October 1887.

15. The basis of this claim was that Ducazcal had purchased the rights to perform *Carmen* in Mallorca and the Balearic Islands from a certain D. José Álvarez, in a contract that reportedly authorized performances in "Mallorca and in the provinces of Spain," and Ducazcal argued that as Madrid was a province of Spain, he was empowered to announce a premiere at the Teatro de la Zarzuela. Álvarez had purchased these rights from Choudens, but in the end did not stage a production. "Carmen," *La Iberia*, 28 October 1887, 1; José Subirá, *Historia y anecdotario del Teatro Real* (Madrid: Fundación Caja Madrid, [1949] 1997), 393; Fernanflor, "Madrid: Cartas a mi prima," *La ilustración ibérica* 5, no. 253 (1887): 706; "Más sobre 'Cármen,'" *El país*, 30 October 1887.

16. Subirá, *Historia y anecdotario del Teatro Real*, 393. The following paragraphs are based on the report in "Carmen," *La Iberia*, 28 October 1887, 1–2.

Minister of State) and government departments, as copyright law and registration were invoked.[17] As Michelena's rights were vindicated and Ducazcal's contract proved invalid outside the Balearic Islands, Ducazcal preempted the government's suspension of his advertised premiere—and Choudens's threat to confiscate all the parts—by postponing it himself, blaming a sudden attack of laryngitis that prevented his Carmen, Eulalia González, from performing. He continued to declare that the premiere would go ahead as soon as she recovered.[18] Clearly convinced that he was in the right, Michelena wrote an open letter to the press, stating that Choudens should pay him damages if the premiere at the Zarzuela went ahead in breach of his exclusive contract.[19] Ducazcal, however, seemed undeterred by threats of prohibition, or even confiscation of receipts.[20]

As October turned to November, the tide seemed to be turning in favor of the Teatro Real when it was confirmed that *Carmen* had been properly registered by Choudens, meaning that the rights to the music were protected in Spain.[21] Ducazcal's response to these events was decisive. He released to the press a certificate from the Ministry of Works, dated 27 June 1887, upon which he based his claim that *Carmen* had not been properly registered after all, and that the registration listed only Italian and German, a clause that meant that the rights for performances in Spanish were in the public domain until someone deposited a Spanish translation.[22] Such was the public interest

17. Michelena's contract provided him with exclusive rights to mount not only *Carmen* in Madrid during the 1887–88 season, but also *Les Pêcheurs de perles* and *Roméo et Juliette* (this provision presumably refers to rights for Gounod's opera of this name, although *La Iberia* says all three operas are by Bizet). The whole package cost Michelena 8,000 francs, but Choudens undertook not to enter into any other contracts with respect to *Carmen* and *The Pearlfishers* with any other theater in Madrid. "Carmen," *La Iberia*, 28 October 1887, 2. The press list no fewer than three ministries dragged into the case: State, Works, and Government.

18. "Carmen," *La Iberia*, 28 October 1887, 2; "Carmen," *La Iberia*, 31 October 1887, 2; "Conflicto entre dos empresas," *El liberal*, 1 November 1887, 2–3.

19. Michelena continued to declare that his theater was already engaged in the preparation of costumes, sets, and props for *Carmen*. "Un estreno malogrado," *El país*, 28 October 1887; "Más sobre 'Cármen,'" *El país*, 30 October 1887.

20. According to *La Iberia*, Article 25 of the Spanish intellectual property laws provided for confiscation of income from ticket sales and payment of same to the copyright holder if an unauthorized public performance took place. "Carmen," *La Iberia*, 29 October 1887, 1.

21. The full text of the registration is reproduced in *La Iberia*, listed as No 402. It was also revealed that Álvarez's contract was valid only for the Balearic Islands, and provided for a penalty of 10,000 francs if the material was used anywhere else. Choudens ordered its Madrid agents Vidal and Llimona to confiscate all materials relating to *Carmen* from the Teatro de la Zarzuela, and launched proceedings against Álvarez. "Carmen," *La Iberia*, 31 October 1887, 2.

22. As *La Iberia* points out, this rather confusing set of claims implied that even if Ducazcal might legally present a Spanish translation of the libretto, his singers would

in the story that a pack of journalists waiting outside the Ministry of State reported even the nebulous statement that a proposed solution to the "conflict of the two *Carmens*" was at that time being sent to the French ambassador for consideration.[23] Despite rumors of the governor's resignation, the dispute was mysteriously resolved in Ducazcal's favor, although the authorities were reported to have seized 5% of his receipts in case of future claims in the courts.[24] After all this drama, the Teatro de la Zarzuela staged its new Spanish translation of Bizet's *Carmen* on 2 November 1887. *El imparcial* commented,

> At last . . . Carmen was presented in her homeland . . . followed by her retinue of *toreadores, cigarieres, bohemiens . . . contrebandiers* and her troupe of hispanicized French characters and Latin quarter flamenco types.[25]

What a night it must have been on the Calle de Jovellanos for *Carmen*'s Madrid premiere. A more highly charged atmosphere could hardly be imagined. People attended in full expectation that the performance would be suspended again, yet the blaze of publicity had provided the most effective promotion Ducazcal could have wished for: *Carmen* played until 22 November, always to full houses.[26] On that first night, the excited audience was more heterogeneous than the typical *zarzuela* public, mingling high society with journalists and musicians, literati and the general public.[27] The critic for *La Iberia* observed that despite a packed auditorium the stalls were largely a male domain, perhaps because the "ladies" feared a commotion.[28] The hecklers, mainly in the gallery, "made their presence in the theater felt from the first scenes, whistling or booing at inopportune moments; but the public protested against such inconvenience with great applause that resonated from stalls to boxes and silenced those ill-advised ones."[29] Another account suggests that a claque actually supported the performance, loudly applauding all González's numbers

not have been permitted to perform the music itself. "Carmen," *La Iberia*, 31 October 1887, 2.

23. "Conflicto entre dos empresas," *El liberal*, 1 November 1887, 2–3.

24. *El mundo* states the figure as 10%. "En la Zarzuela," *El mundo*, 3 November 1887, 1; "Notas," *Unión católica*, 3 November 1887, 2; "Carmen en la Zarzuela," *La Iberia*, 3 November 1887, 2.

25. "Teatro de la Zarzuela: *Carmen*," *El imparcial*, 3 November 1887.

26. Toward the end of its successful run, on 17 November, the *infanta* (princess) Isabel graced the theater with her presence, and the management tried to replicate the premiere by making sure González sang the title role. "Entre bastidores," *La opinión*, 18 November 1887.

27. "Teatro de la Zarzuela: *Carmen*," *El imparcial*, 3 November 1887; "Cármen," *El día*, 3 November 1887; "En la Zarzuela," *El mundo*, 3 November 1887, 1.

28. "Carmen en la Zarzuela," *La Iberia*, 3 November 1887, 2.

29. "Zarzuela," *La publicidad*, 4 November 1887.

as Carmen despite the poor quality of her singing. This critic also attributed the work's "near success" to the efforts of the secret police in repressing any unseemly behavior such as foot stamping or booing, while another noted the presence of more policemen than usual.[30]

In a curious echo of *Carmen's* 1875 Paris debut, after greeting the first act with considerable warmth, the enthusiasm of the Madrid audience waned through the long evening (the curtain didn't rise on act 4 until twenty minutes after midnight).[31] Unlike Paris, however, the goodwill of the Spanish spectators may have been sapped by the increasingly colorful (and Frenchified) depictions of Spanish life, or exacerbated by the clumsiness of the translated libretto. Tomás Bretón, one of the leading Spanish musicians and a composer of *zarzuela* and opera, left an account of the premiere in his diary:

> I spent last night at the Zarzuela where they were performing *Carmen*, at last! The first act was very lively and pleasing; the first half of the second act as well, but from there on it began to fall away and become boring without ever recovering. The reason is obvious. The music is mostly characterless, the pompous speeches are ridiculous as are the costumes and the characters who wear them. The libretto is false and clumsy, and the performance labored, bad. The whole audience agreed and many asked what this international conflict was all about![32]

Despite Bretón's misgivings, the major musical numbers were well appreciated, especially the "Habanera" the children's march, and the duet between José and Micäela, which were repeated.[33] In fact, encores and curtain calls greeted every act.[34] Some critics described the audience as reserved at the end, not lavishing applause on the performers, but others simply observed that they were exhausted by such a lot of nonsense. Opening-night nerves may have contributed to shortcomings in the performance, and there was a general sense that the cast had not fully met the demands of the score,

30. "Zarzuela," *El mediodía*, 3 November 1887; "En la Zarzuela," *El mundo*, 3 November 1887, 1.

31. "Zarzuela," *El mediodía*, 3 November 1887.

32. Tomás Bretón, *Diario (1881–1888)* (Madrid: Acento, 1995), 660, quoted in Santana Burgos, "Diálogos entre Francia y España," 189.

33. "En la Zarzuela," *El mundo*, 3 November 1887, 1; "Teatro de la Zarzuela," *El liberal*, 3 November 1887.

34. In act 2 both sung numbers and Fuensanta Moreno's dance were encored, the principals received two curtain calls at the end of both acts 1 and 3, and the sets of the first and final acts inspired ovations. According to *El mundo*, encores included the Quintette (act 2), the Trio (act 3), and the final duet (act 4). "Carmen en la Zarzuela," *La Iberia*, 3 November 1887, 2; "Zarzuela," *El mediodía*, 3 November 1887; "En la Zarzuela," *El mundo*, 3 November 1887, 1; "Zarzuela," *La publicidad*, 4 November 1887.

although a more charitable critic suggested they might do better in later performances.[35]

> The most harmonious disorder reigned among the critics, with respect to the music. Some say that this opera will never acclimatize in Spain, because of the lack of verisimilitude in the characters and the lack of local color in the music; others affirmed that that our public will enjoy, in other performances, the beauties of the score[.][36]

Reflecting that better singers—at the Teatro Real, for example—might establish the work more securely with Spanish audiences, this prescient critic gently summed up the fiery debates that were to surround *Carmen* in its first Madrid season. Many others were to echo his observation that Bizet's opera lacked verisimilitude and accurate local color, in the form of harsh accusations that *Carmen* was based on absurd French constructions of a nonexistent Spain.

CARMEN AND LA "ESPAGNE" ROMÁNTICA

> The author has taken for the argument of the drama a Spanish subject that is not at all true. The characters are false, the scenes are also false, and the whole is disjointed and deformed, because whatever is presented on the stage has never taken place in this ... land.[37]

This trenchant criticism resonates with contemporary debates not only about Spanish identity but also about the way Spain was perceived by the outside world. Many Spaniards enjoyed bullfights and flamenco, and were entertained by their portrayal under the aegis of *costumbrismo*. But the Spanish intelligentsia was increasingly sensitive to foreign depictions of such customs in a context of local color that reinforced images of Spain as somehow backward and primitive, rather than as a modern and enlightened nation. The perceived difference between a French exoticist portrayal of such archetypally Spanish themes and the way Spanish *costumbrista* writers and composers would have depicted such themes clearly affected the reception of *Carmen*.

In the 1880s the rapidly expanding Spanish capital engaged in a process of industrialization and modernization and these changes added urgency to

35. *La Iberia* thought González had sung the title role in half voice throughout, perhaps due to nerves. *La opinión* also noted that she sang with reduced volume. "Carmen en la Zarzuela," *La Iberia*, 3 November 1887, 2; "Carmen," *La opinión*, 3 November 1887, 3.

36. Fernanflor, "Madrid: Cartas a mi prima," *La ilustración ibérica* 5, no. 254 (1887): 722.

37. "Carmen," *La opinión*, 3 November 1887, 3.

long-standing debates about national identity. One source of friction was that during the nineteenth century powerful interests had begun to locate their understanding of what constituted Spanishness in the idea of Andalusia. This southern Spanish region provided an ideal focus for such nation making because it projected a recognized Orientalist and exotic image with great potential as a cultural symbol—admittedly partially based on foreign perceptions—but did not harbor a strong separatist movement.[38] Signifiers of *Andalucismo* included gypsies, flamenco, bullfighting, and fiestas,[39] so richly evoked in *Carmen* but also commonly featured in the *zarzuela*. The attempt to promulgate this image as a unifying symbol of Spanish national identity was largely supported by the landowning class, but it was increasingly opposed by intellectuals who supported liberal republicanism and Europeanization.[40]

One example of the predilection for Andalusian themes was the representation of bullfighting in the *zarzuela*. Barbieri himself had written a famous and respected *zarzuela grande*, *Pan y toros* (1864, *Bread and Bulls*), which featured three celebrated bullfighters as central characters, including Pepe-Hillo, one of the most renowned bullfighters of the late eighteenth century, who was also the eponymous hero of several subsequent *zarzuelas*.[41] Some of the most celebrated *zarzuela* composers of the age turned their hand to this subject, notably Federico Chueca and Joaquín Valverde, who wrote a series of bullfighting *zarzuelas* in the 1870s and 1880s, and successfully characterized many Spanish types in their *género chico* hit, *La Gran Vía* (1886).[42] Many popular *zarzuelas* involving bullfighting were produced in the 1880s, extending into the realm of parody and comedy.[43]

38. Manuel González de Molina and Miguel Gómez Oliver, *Historia contemporánea de Andalucía (Nuevos contenidos para su estudio)*, 2nd ed. (Granada, Spain: Proyecto Sur de Ediciones, 2000), 313. For further discussion of the identification of *Andalucismo* with the idea of *castizo* culture, in relation to the arts and specifically to music, see Celsa Alonso, *La canción lírica española en el siglo XIX* (Madrid: ICCMU, 1998), 233ff.

39. González de Molina and Gómez Oliver, *Historia contemporánea de Andalucía*, 312.

40. This debate was already alive in 1887, as evidenced by the Congreso Literario Internacional (8–15 October; see the discussion later in this chapter), but it did not reach full strength for another decade, when the "Generation of '98" began to espouse it much more powerfully in response to Spain's defeat in the Spanish-American war, and the loss of its last colonial possessions.

41. *Pan y toros* was marked by pronounced anti-French sentiment, set in the 1790s at a time of high tension between France and Spain, just before the Peninsular War. A later *zarzuela* composed by Guillermo Cereceda was entitled *Pepe Hillo* (1870).

42. *La Gran Vía* (literally: The Great Way) was a *revista* (review) in the form of a *género chico zarzuela*, with a plot predicated on longstanding plans to build a grand new thoroughfare in Madrid, featuring some of the affected streets as characters. After innumerable delays, construction finally began in 1910 and stretched over several decades, but the Gran Vía is a major feature of the contemporary Spanish capital.

43. Antonio Barrios lists no fewer than eighteen *zarzuelas* on bullfighting from the 1880s alone (and his avowedly incomplete list does not provide dates for every work it includes). Many of the bullfighting *zarzuelas* were described in their subtitles

Spain's strongest bullfighting traditions were to be found as much in Madrid as in southern Spain, so *zarzuela* audiences in the capital would not countenance earnest but nonsensical depictions of their beloved *fiesta nacional*.[44] The librettists' use of "toreador"—a word that does not even exist in Spanish, in which *torero* is the generic term for bullfighter—provoked extreme ridicule, repeated as it was throughout the celebrated march. In Mérimée's novella, Lucas is only a *picador* (a mounted member of the *cuadrilla*, or bullfighting troupe, who lances the bull in the opening *tercio*, or third, of the bullfight), but Meilhac and Halévy promoted their replacement character Escamillo to the status of *torero* (the bullfighter himself). Satirist Espoleta described the Toreador Song as a "de profundis flamenco"—an ironic description of the very cheerful and lively march in an unmistakably *opéra comique* style.[45]

Bizet and his librettists trespassed on well-marked theatrical territory when their clumsy, foreign version of bullfighting was presented to a Madrid audience. *Carmen* suffered from inevitable comparisons with familiar and affectionate representations of tauromachy in the contemporary *zarzuela*. Also identified among Bizet's inauthentic cast of characters were French imitations of *majas* (a woman of Madrid dressed in turn-of-the-nineteenth-century costume) and *chulas* (a characteristic "type" of the Madrid lower-class and stock character of the *zarzuela*, typified by dress, style, and a confident, witty manner).

> We who have Barbieri who achieved success with Pepe-Hillo, and who without depriving them of character or originality, has described with great elegance *majas*, *toreros* and *chulas*. Could we see these very characters falsified?
>
> Those who admire, with good reason, the musical naturalism of Chueca, would they admit Bizet's notes to types that have been so well characterized by the author of *La Gran Vía*?[46]

A very different attitude to *costumbrista* representations of Spanish identity was expressed in debates connected with the Congreso Literario Internacional,

as "cómico-lírico," "cómico-lírico-taurino," or even longer chains of such descriptors. Tauromachy also attracted the conductor of the 1887 *Carmen* production, Gerónimo Giménez, who composed *Caballeros en plaza* (1887), and Tomás Reig, who was to compile the music for Granés's *Carmen* parody *Carmela* (1891) and who had composed his own *Las toreras* (1888). Antonio Barrios, "Los toros en la *zarzuela*," *Gaceta Taurina* 2, no. 9 (1997): 11–13.

44. *Fiesta nacional* is a term applied to bullfights, and taurine spectacles more generally. See Carrie B. Douglass, *Bulls, Bullfighting, and Spanish Identities* (Tucson: University of Arizona Press, 1999), 21; 34–35.

45. Espoleta, "Pitos y Palmas: CARMEN ópera cómica en cuatro actos y varias latas," *La avispa*, 9 November 1887.

46. Allegro, "En el teatro de la Zarzuela: Cármen," *El país*, 3 November 1887, 3.

an international conference held in Madrid from 8 to 15 October 1887. This prestigious event gave Spanish intellectuals the opportunity to promote a fresh image of Spain to representatives of the outside world. The high-minded morning program discussing matters of intellectual property was supplemented by lighter activities such as banquets, excursions to Toledo and El Escorial, a ceremony at the statue of Cervantes, and performances at the Teatros Real and Español. Former Spanish president and republican politician Emilio Castelar hinted at their goals in his speech at the closing banquet. In a clear reference to Romantic constructions of Spain and the negative images perpetrated by the Black Legend, he expressed his hope that the delegates would "contribute to the disappearance of so many errors and injustices that circulate abroad about Spain.... You can say that you have encountered a nation that is free, cultured, generous, that wants to reclaim its past glories, living the life of freedom and democracy."[47]

In apparent contradiction of these lofty aspirations, delegates were also invited to a bullfight held in honor of the conference and to a flamenco performance after the final banquet. The debate this invitation provoked was crucial to the genesis of the *antiflamenquismo* movement (which regarded flamenco and bullfighting as being among the key sources of Spain's problems), and it came to a head when the President of the Association of Writers and Artists, Gaspar Núñez de Arce, wrote to *El imparcial* on 30 October 1887 to deplore the delegates' exposure to flamenco and *bailes gitanos* (gypsy dances).[48] The *antiflamenquistas* were reacting to the proliferation of flamenco *cafés cantantes* in Madrid in the 1880s, a trend that had converted the Spanish capital into one of the key sites of flamenco's development. These cafes, which had been established in Seville in the 1870s and spread to many of the major urban centers of Spain by the following decade, were crucial in the dissemination of flamenco to a broader Spanish public and to the professionalization of the genre (see Figure 3.1). The decor and costumes associated with the *cafés cantantes* also perpetuated and reinscribed the imagery associated with Andalusia for a national audience.

Just three days after the *antiflamenquista* letter was published in *El imparcial*, *Carmen* made its debut at the Teatro de la Zarzuela. Given this context, it is no wonder that the opera became the focus for fierce criticism of the *espagnolade*. French exoticist literature was lambasted by critics who considered *Carmen* to be the nadir of the tradition:

> The libretto of Carmen is the biggest absurdity which could have come from
> the French imagination. Even putting together all the absurd articles written

47. "El banquete del Ayuntamiento de Madrid," *El liberal*, 16 October 1887.
48. Gaspar Núñez de Arce, "[Letter to the Editor]," *El imparcial*, 30 October 1887, 1.

Figure 3.1 *Café cantante* [El Burrero, Seville], photograph by Emilio Beauchy (*c.* 1888).
Credit: Private collection of Carlos Teixidor Cadenas, CC BY-SA 4.0.

on Spain by Frenchmen who have visited us, we could not have come up with a more unfortunate work.[49]

The worst excesses of the genre represented by *Carmen* were blamed on French writers in general, and Alexandre Dumas (*père*) in particular:

> That torero with the knife in his belt, the smugglers and gypsies are purely French conceptions, types that existed only in the mind of Dumas, and that, portrayed by him, have been accepted by our neighbors as real and actual.[50]

The original novella was, however, distinguished from the libretto. Mérimée's output was familiar to Spanish critics, who acknowledged his understanding of Spanish customs, gained through time spent in their country and his long

49. "Carmen en la Zarzuela," *La Iberia*, 3 November 1887, 2.
50. "Carmen," *La opinión*, 3 November 1887, 3. The critic Allegro attempts to excuse Dumas by placing his writings in historical context: "Spain made a bad impression on Dumas because he encountered such vicissitudes during his voyage in Spain, at a time when there were no trains, and he was at the mercy of stagecoaches." Allegro, "En el teatro de la Zarzuela," *El país*, 3 November 1887, 3.

Figure 3.2. Cover of first Spanish translation of Mérimée's *Carmen*. *Cármen: Novela de Prosper Mérimée*. Translated by D. Cristóbal Litrán. 2nd ed. Barcelona: López, 1891.

association with the Empress Eugénie. The novella was not published as a volume in Spanish until 1890, when Cristóbal Litrán published his translation in Barcelona (see Figure 3.2).[51] Despite this delay in translation into Spanish, *Carmen* was well known in the original French, and Mérimée was

51. Luis López Jiménez and Luis-Eduardo López Esteve, "Introducción," in *Prosper Mérimée: Carmen*, trans. Luis López Jiménez and Luis-Eduardo López Esteve (Madrid: Ediciones Cátedra, 1997), 63, 90; Santana Burgos, "Diálogos entre Francia y España," 118–36.

acknowledged for having been "in a position neither to fantasize too much nor to over-exaggerate the local color that so many foreigners abuse to inspire themselves over matters of our land."[52] The critic for *El país*, who wrote under the pseudonym Allegro, found himself unable to exonerate Mérimée quite so completely, stating that even though "he was inspired by the land," he still "vacillated between painting us naturally and pleasing his countrymen by gratifying their ideas about us, and opted for the second."[53]

Despite these reflections on the original novella, most critics blamed Bizet's librettists for the infelicities of the scenario and libretto. Meilhac and Halévy, like Mérimée before them, felt they had to paint a colorful picture, but while the librettists employed the broad brushstrokes needed to achieve maximum dramatic effect in an opera, they lacked the local experience and nuanced description that had rendered the original novella more acceptable to contemporary Spanish critics. Even though this first Madrid production was based on a new adaptation, the critics were clearly familiar with the French libretto and used their pre-performance notices to criticize many elements of the story, before they had even heard the Spanish translator's judicious attempt to adapt the work for a local audience.[54]

The critic for *El mundo* felt that despite a promising beginning with act 1, in which "the story, although simple, is completely satisfying," the work suffered because its French authors were inextricably caught up in their exoticist attitudes. He declared their libretto "full of absurdities and inexactitudes which cannot get past a Spanish public," and even when it "paint[s] Spanish customs," they are painted "in a French manner."[55]

Allegro agreed in principle, but he viewed the whole problem from a modern perspective, mocking the stereotypes:

> Upon reading all that has been written about Spain by the French, one would believe that it is almost impossible to reach this country, that we are separated from the neighboring Republic by an immense distance, that there is no railway between the two countries, and that all that has been written about us has to be believed completely.[56]

Complaining that "the great majority of French writers describe us like this," Allegro declared it "unforgivable that they don't know us better." Through a comparison of modern Spain with Dumas's imagined Spain, Allegro

52. J. O. Picón, "Teatro de la Zarzuela: Estreno de 'Cármen.'" *El correo*, 3 November 1887.

53. Allegro (Pascual Millán), "En el teatro de la Zarzuela," *El país*, 3 November 1887, 3.

54. Allegro quoted the French text in order to ridicule it. Ibid., 3.

55. "En la Zarzuela," *El mundo*, 3 November 1887, 1.

56. Allegro, "En el teatro de la Zarzuela," *El país*, 3 November 1887, 3.

attacked the myth of its timelessness, rejecting the idea that the picturesque backwardness described by early nineteenth-century travelers persisted unchanged.

Some elements of the opera—the women smoking and cigarette workers in particular—had strong parallels with aspects of contemporary Spanish life and art. As a familiar Spanish "type," the *cigarrera* was popular as a fancy-dress character, particularly in Seville's famous fiestas (see Figure 3.3). Although the tobacco factory in Seville is better known, its counterpart in the Embajadores area of central Madrid employed up to 8,000 workers, almost all of them women, and images of their workers were widely disseminated in the visual

Figure 3.3 *La cigarrera (type d'après nature)*, photograph by J. Laurent, Province of Seville (*c.* 1863).
Credit: Library of Congress, https://www.loc.gov/item/94512224.

arts and early photography.[57] The Compañía Tabacalera (the Spanish state tobacco monopoly) was a national firm, and after various changes of status during
the nineteenth century the government leased it to private enterprise in April
1887, with the intention that they achieve greater efficiencies, possibly through
mechanization.[58] On 5 October 1887 the Madrid tobacco workers walked out
of the factory at 2 p.m. to gather in their thousands, shouting and jostling,
in protest at deteriorating pay and working conditions, and the ever-present
fear that their jobs would be replaced by machinery. Their threat to march on
the royal palace to seek the protection of the queen regent was prevented by
the call-out of cavalry and infantry divisions to keep order in the streets,
but the next day windows were broken in the empty factory. After several days
of unrest and negotiation, the matter was settled through the intervention of
the Governor of Madrid. These disturbances were not uncommon, for the cigarette workers had no other means to arrest the gradual deterioration in their
working conditions consequent on privatization and mechanization.

The way Bizet's chorus burst out of the factory in act 1, scene 8, after the
knife fight that caused Carmen's arrest, could not have failed to recall the recent
spectacle of demonstrating tobacco workers on the streets of Madrid. Both the
strike and the operatic scene were described as a *motín* (riot) in the press,[59] but
the action of the real-life *cigarreras* (female cigarette maker) was declared "utterly
Spanish" in the extensive coverage of the dispute.[60] The modernity of industrial
workers threatening civic order while bargaining collectively through chosen
spokespeople contrasts richly with popular depictions of the *cigarrera* as a time-
less Madrid character. Caricatures of the *cigarrera*'s appearance and speech demonstrate that journalists sometimes preferred to impose some illusion of control
by exoticizing this disruptive class of women, rather than addressing the modern
industrial confrontation they brought into focus. However, the *cigarreras* were
also described in the contemporary press as "legitimate descendants of the
antiguas manolas," perhaps in reference to Goya's portraits from the beginning of
the century, and provided inspiration for Spanish authors of *costumbrista* literature and *género chico zarzuelas* (see Figure 3.4).[61]

57. This estimate of employees in Madrid's tobacco factories is based on the contemporary press, where *El imparcial* lists 7,500 workers, and *El día* says their
numbers approach 8,000. "El motín de las cigarreras," *El imparcial*, 6 October 1887, 2;
"Las cigarreras," *El día*, 6 October 1887, 1.

58. Marta Macías, "Privatization and Management Accounting Systems Change: The
Case of the 19th-Century Spanish Tobacco Monopoly," *Accounting Historians Journal*
29, no. 2 (2002): 38.

59. The parody of *Carmen* in the comic journal *La avispa* also refers to cigarette girls
emerging "mutinously" from the factory in act 1. Espoleta, "Pitos y Palmas: CARMEN
ópera cómica en cuatro actos y varias latas," *La avispa*, 9 November 1887.

60. Fernanflor, "Madrid: Cartas a mi prima," *La ilustración ibérica* 5, no. 250
(1887): 658.

61. "Las cigarreras," *El día*, 6 October 1887, 1; Jean Sentaurens, "Des effets pervers
d'un mythe littéraire romantique: À Séville, toutes les cigarières s'appellent Carmen,"
Bulletin Hispanique 96, no. 2 (1994): 454n2.

Figure 3.4 [Carlos Ángel] Díaz Huertas, *Tipos populares de Madrid: Las cigarreras* (Popular characters of Madrid: The cigarmakers), (1890).
Credit: Private collection.

Carmen was premiered at the Teatro de la Zarzuela just a few weeks after these dramatic events. The wild scenes at the tobacco factory had been freshly reported, and the operatic characterization of Carmen and her coworkers must have touched a raw nerve. Allegro insisted that the opera's "absurd" scenes should not be believed, "especially when there is a knife handled by women."[62] This comment is undermined by an incident reported during the strike in which two workers armed with a knife confronted a subaltern within the factory.[63] Yet Bizet's dreamy chorus of *cigarières* ("Dans l'air nous suivons des yeux / La fumée") was as far removed from such brutal realities as the Chilean women celebrating a fiesta in Manuel Fernández Caballero's popular 1877 *zarzuela, Los sobrinos del Capitán Grant (Captain Grant's Nieces)*, in which a chorus of women sing cheerfully about the vice of smoking.[64] Oddly enough, the way Bizet introduced Carmen—singing a habanera that followed the cigarette workers' chorus—would have resonated with contemporary Spanish audiences because of the strong Cuban associations with Spanish tobacco trade. However, the habanera had a complex relationship with Spanish identity in the late nineteenth century.

While the libretto's resonance with contemporary events heightened Spanish sensitivities to the exoticizing elements of the plot, the translation only exacerbated this situation. As the generally sympathetic critic of *La Iberia* concluded,

> [o]ne must ... confess that if *Carmen* had been presented in Italian at the Teatro Real it would have had a different fate. The atrocities of the libretto, veiled by the Italian language, would not have caused such pain to the soul of our public, and the musical interpretation would have been better.[65]

CARMEN AS ZARZUELA: LIERN'S ADAPTATION OF THE LIBRETTO

Never did a writer face a more ungrateful task than Rafael María Liern when— at the request of his friend Ducazcal—he undertook the Spanish translation for *Carmen*'s premiere at the Teatro de la Zarzuela (see Figure 3.5).[66] An

---

62. Allegro, "En el teatro de la Zarzuela," *El país*, 3 November 1887, 3.
63. Fortunately no injury resulted. "El motín de las cigarreras," *El liberal*, 7 October 1887.
64. Coro de fumadoras (Chorus of smokers), "Si es en el hombre un vicio," *Los sobrinos del Capitán Grant*, act 2, scene 3. Music by Manuel Fernández Caballero, libretto by Miguel Ramos Carrión, based on a novel by Jules Verne.
65. "Carmen en la Zarzuela," *La Iberia*, 3 November 1887, 2.
66. An unattributed manuscript libretto entitled "Carmen: Zarzuela en cuatro actos, arreglada a la escena española ..." exists in the archives of the Sociedad General de Autores y Editores (SGAE), Archivo Lírico, Materiales MMO/2234. It bears the stamp of "Compañia de Zarzuela: Empresa Juan Orejon," and seems to have been used for later touring productions. Reference to reviews of the 1887 Teatro de la Zarzuela production reveals that this is in fact the Spanish translation prepared by Liern, as it contains altered character names and passages of dialogue unique to this version. Sentaurens also refers to this manuscript source. Jean Sentaurens, "*Carmen*: De la

Figure 3.5 Ramón Cilla, caricature of Rafael María Liern, *Madrid Cómico. Periódico festivo ilustrado*, 277 (9 June 1888): 1.
Credit: Biblioteca Nacional de España, Madrid.

established writer and theater producer, he already had many *zarzuela* libretti to his credit, including *género chico* and parody works. He was also known for his comic articles and bullfighting journalism in the contemporary periodical

novela de 1845 a la zarzuela de 1887; Cómo nació 'la España de Mérimée,'" *Bulletin Hispanique* [104], no. 2 (2002): 860n12. For a thorough analysis of this text and the way that Liern's text was adapted in production at the Zarzuela, see Santana Burgos, "Diálogos entre Francia y España."

press.[67] Even though he was widely recognized as a skilled and experienced dramatist,[68] the press gave his version of *Carmen* no quarter:

> The lyrics are of the most absurd that exist, despite the translation and adaptation of Sr Liern; suffice it to say that it is based on Spanish topics and given the poor estimation of us by foreign writers, that says it all; soldiers, gypsies, toreros, tobacco workers, and other flamenco types are drawn into the story, which is like an indecipherable charade.[69]

In adapting *Carmen* as a *zarzuela*, Liern endeavored to combine a faithful translation with some amelioration and even explanation of the book's more fanciful representations of Spanishness, tackling anything from characterization to problems with the scenario while infusing the text with Spanish *gracia* (wit, charm).[70] Liern's careful adaptation can be viewed as the first Spanish step in the gradual process of Hispanicizing *Carmen*, and his major changes indicate the points where Spanish identity collided with French *espagnolade*. By reworking the lyrics of the main arias, Liern attempted to remove the most offensive references to gypsies and bullfighting without damaging the opera's dramatic and lyric fabric.

Liern's most basic change was to rename three of the characters, to avoid the kind of satirical response that was to greet the Teatro Real's 1888 *Carmen*:

> Invention beyond the Pyrenees has coined the characters El Dancaire and Lilas Pastia.... We should hold a philological, ethnographic, etymological and genealogical competition in Madrid to try and find the origin of this Dancaire and that Lilas Pastia perpetrated by Mérimée, Meilhac and Halévy and immortalized by the adorable music of Bizet.[71]

---

67. Liern's connection with Ducazcal is further attested to because he dedicated to the impresario his parody of *La Gran Vía*, entitled *Efectos de la Gran Vía* (1887). José A. Aguilón Martínez, "Rafael María Liern y Cirac," accessed 26 March 2007, http://es.geocities.com/mizarzuela/Liern.htm; Maria Luz González Peña, "Liern y Cerach, Rafael María," in *Diccionario de la zarzuela: España e Hispanoamérica*, ed. Emilio Casares Rodicio (Madrid: ICCMU, 2002–03); Sook-Hwa Noh, "Doña Juana Tenorio: Imitación burlesca de escenas de Don Juan Tenorio, en un acto y en verso, original de Don Rafael María Liern," *Revista de Folklore* 18a, no. 208 (1998): 1. See also the biographical sketch in Santana Burgos, "Diálogos entre Francia y España," 216–19.

68. "Carmen," *La opinión*, 3 November 1887, 3.

69. M. Corral, "Espectáculos," *La provincia* 1, no. 5 (1887): 20.

70. Sentaurens suggests that Liern's aim was to replace the *espagnolade* of the French local color with a *costumbrismo* more recognizable to *zarzuela* audiences. Sentaurens, "*Carmen*," 859.

71. Peña y Goñi, "Teatro Real: Carmen," *La época*, 15 March 1888. Spanish writers often use "Lilas" instead of the more common "Lillas," but according to Santana Burgos both spellings can be found in French libretti. Santana Burgos, "Diálogos entre Francia y España," 235n68.

In Liern's adaptation, Lillas Pastia was renamed Sebastián, Frasquita became Currilla, and Escamillo was replaced by Joselillo, a name that subtly recalled the bullfighter Pepe-Hillo but also suggested a gentle humor at work.

Liern also paid close attention to the character of José, who is referred to both in the Mérimée and the French libretto as "Don José" from the northern region of Navarre. His presumption of Basque nobility and clear bloodline would not have impressed a Castilian audience, for Castile abounded in men whose noble blood gave them the right to use such an honorific.[72] Accordingly, Liern erases any trace of José being a "Don," and the sergeant simply claims that his family was "modest but honorable." The apparent ease with which the Opéra-Comique's José enlists after fleeing a possible murder charge in Navarre suggests a tolerance for criminality in the Spanish army, but Liern's José actually obtained a pardon through high connections before starting his military career. This episode dramatizes the fault lines between north and south that run through the various stagings of *Carmen*, and Liern's text intimates that differently situated audiences might identify with different sides. In the French versions, José is aligned with the more "advanced" civilizations of France or even Europe, in contrast to Carmen's unmistakable identification with the southern regions of a lawless and backward Spain, where Carmen's Andalusian exoticism is only magnified by her gypsy blood.[73] It should be noted, however, that Spain's modern centrist capital embraced a large Andalusian population, which formed a crucial element in the identity of Madrid's popular classes and inspired a homely exoticism often represented in the *zarzuela*. A Madrid audience of the late 1880s may have viewed Navarre as more remote than Andalusia, and related to the opera's characters accordingly. In line with this identification, Liern subtly alters Carmen's local color by reconfiguring her generic gypsiness into a more specifically Andalusian characterization.[74]

Carmen's lyric utterances define her character and Liern translated her infamous "Habanera" almost literally, with one crucial change: he omitted the central stanza that refers to love as a lawless gypsy child ("L'amour est enfant de Bohême, / il n'a jamais, jamais connu de loi"). According to Liern, love might be

72. José calls himself an old Christian (*vieux chrétien*), implying that there is neither Jewish nor Moorish "contamination" in his ancestry. This pretension was to provide ample material for comedy in the *zarzuela* parody *Carmela* (1891), which will be discussed in Chapter 4. Salvador María Granés and Tomás Reig (music), *Carmela: Parodia-lírica de la ópera "Carmen" en un acto y tres cuadros* (Madrid: Velasco, 1891).

73. James Parakilas, "The Soldier and the Exotic: Operatic Variations on a Theme of Racial Encounter; Part I," *Opera Quarterly* 10 (1993): 40.

74. For Sentaurens, Carmen loses her subversive power when her gypsy identity is downplayed, and he accuses Liern of "censoring" the diabolic element in her character. Sentaurens, "*Carmen*," 860–61.

a wild bird, known to be contrary, but nothing more. The "Chanson bohème," on the other hand, is completely rewritten. Meilhac and Halévy composed a lyric in the third person, a vivid description of generic "bohemian" gypsies singing and dancing with complete abandon. The text reflects the gypsy tavern scene on stage, and provides non-Spanish audiences with a colorful tableau in sight and sound. Liern created a contrasting and uniquely Spanish effect by writing for Carmen in the first person and removing overt reference to gypsies from her text, retaining only the stage direction that gypsies dance during the chorus. By means of southern Spanish argot and reference to sung forms typical of the *cante andaluz* (flamenco song), he typecast her as "quién de verdá es andaluz" ("someone who is truly Andalusian").[75] In the lyric Carmen reflects on how she feels when singing and dancing, activities to which she was born and that wipe away all her tiredness and pain. For Spanish audiences of the time, these lyrics may not have conveyed an exotic scene; rather, they could have performed a Hispanicizing function, authenticating Carmen as both Andalusian and *aflamencada* (partaking of the revelry and social contexts associated with flamenco performance).

Liern, who had written extensively on bullfighting, must have anticipated that local critics would ridicule the libretto's clumsy treatment of tauromachy.[76] To this end, he zealously reworked the relevant scenes in acts 2 and 4, adding humorous touches where he could. Meilhac and Halévy's Escamillo may have just triumphed at the Granada bullfights, but Liern's Joselillo was playing for a local crowd in Spain's capital. He is declared "the best matador in the world," to which Carmen dryly responds, "So he's come from Madrid then."[77] This is a nicely judged pleasantry for Madrid audiences, who believed they were the best arbiters of bullfighting.

While the original French text for the relentlessly popular "Toreador Song" had employed the third person to describe a bullfight to an audience unfamiliar with its action, Joselillo's lyric seems truncated in comparison. Liern's use of the first person lends power to the dramatic text, and just a few pithy expressions suffice to describe the same bullfight to a knowing Spanish audience.[78] Joselillo's text contains Andalusian inflections that color the characterization, such as dropped final consonants and alteration of consonants within a word.

75. Liern refers to flamenco forms like *alegría, soledad,* and *caña,* and puns on the last one, which also means a drinking glass.

76. Allegro singled out the treatment of the bullfighters in the libretto, laughing at the crowd scene and procession in act 4. Allegro, "En el teatro de la Zarzuela," *El país,* 3 November 1887, 3. Millán was also a bullfighting critic.

77. Rafael María Liern, "Carmen: Zarzuela en cuatro actos," in Autograph libretto (SGAE, Madrid, [1887]), Carmen/SGAE/MMO/2234, act 2, scene 1.

78. The lyric refers in passing to details that might seem technical to a foreigner: for example, the bull emerging once the President lets fall his white kerchief.

All this effort to touch up the work for a Spanish audience is overshadowed by Liern's heroic attempt to rationalize the nonsensical aspects of act 4's scenario. In brief, no Spanish audience would have recognized a parade of bullfighters outside the bullring, for the members of the *cuadrilla* (the bull-fighting troupe) usually processed directly into the arena to take their places for the bullfight. Allegro noted that this scene caused great hilarity among Spaniards who saw it in theaters outside Spain.[79] In order to rationalize the onstage procession that must occur outside the bullring (because its interior is never depicted), Liern concocted a story—conveyed in lengthy spoken dialogue—about an aristocrat complaining of traffic problems outside the bullring, so that carriages were stopped at some distance from the gate.[80] He also tackled the absurdity of Joselillo emerging from the bullring to find Carmen dying after he had killed only one bull, given that a matador normally faced at least two bulls.[81] Liern's elaborate if still slightly implausible tale committed Joselillo to a second bullfight that day, in Ronda, a town with a renowned bullring.

Allegro observed Liern's struggles with the absurdities of the French original, commenting that "when the author tries to break these shackles that constantly bind him, he has to digress at length."[82] Nonetheless, he simultaneously criticized him for reproducing "the greater part of the improprieties of the libretto" and following the French original "step by step." These comments demonstrate the difficulty of Liern's task, for the circumlocutions required to explain the plot work against his general intent of paring the work back. He had tried to correct even the smallest detail: although unable to change the inappropriate portrayal of women smoking in public as they left work, which was such a popular French image of the Spanish working class, he did rewrite the tavern menu, replacing sweetmeats with the typically Spanish fried fish, in fidelity to Mérimée.[83]

79. Allegro, "En el teatro de la Zarzuela," *El país*, 3 November 1887, 3.

80. The number of dignitaries involved in this parade was ridiculed in the cartoon parody of *La avispa* and in the daily press. "Carmen en la Zarzuela," *La Iberia*, 3 November 1887, 2; Espoleta, "Pitos y Palmas: CARMEN ópera cómica en cuatro actos y varias latas," *La avispa*, 9 November 1887.

81. Several critics noted the oddity of the *torero* killing only one bull that afternoon, among them, "Carmen en la Zarzuela," *La Iberia*, 3 November 1887, 2.

82. Allegro uses a picturesque and peculiarly Spanish turn of phrase here: "y cuando el autor pretende romper el círculo de hierro que constantemente le cerca, se va, como vulgarmente se dice, por los cerros de Ubeda." Allegro, "En el teatro de la Zarzuela," *El país*, 3 November 1887, 3.

83. In act 2, scene 1, the soldiers order sherry and fish, while in scene 6 Carmen orders all the sherry in the house, along with various fish and shellfish for herself and José. The satirical journal *La avispa* asks coyly how the lovers were ever to come together without lobsters and *manzanilla*. Espoleta, "Pitos y Palmas: CARMEN ópera cómica en cuatro actos y varias latas," *La avispa*, 9 November 1887.

Despite his herculean effort to render the text palatable to a Spanish audience, Liern's painstaking transformation of the libretto was largely ignored by Madrid critics and he did not appear when called to take a bow at the end of the performance.[84] Although the press remained poised to criticize the distorted depiction of Spain and the shortcomings of the musical performance, the production's overall success could not be denied. The critic of *El mundo* concluded,

> There is no need to stress that the music of Bizet had to be good to make the public listen in silence to so many tasteless depictions. In the end, however, the public applauded. It was a success, not because of the work, but despite the work. With another libretto *Carmen* would become an eternal fixture.[85]

CONTESTING THE SCORE: BEYOND "SPANISH" LOCAL COLOR IN *CARMEN*'S MUSIC

The upsurge in interest created by the legal proceedings surrounding *Carmen*'s premiere at the Teatro de la Zarzuela—which were extensively reported across Spain—inspired the work's revival in Barcelona, where it had not been performed since its (almost forgotten) Spanish premiere in 1881. The Gran Teatre del Liceu, Barcelona's leading opera theater, introduced two of Bizet's works in that winter season, staging *Les Pêcheurs de perles* early in November 1887, and then launching a new production of *Carmen* on 26 January 1888, sung in Italian, with a mixed French, Italian, and Spanish cast.[86] Although the singing was considered weak, the orchestra was good, allowing the quality of Bizet's music to be recognized. The Liceu had long been the home of European opera, dominated by Italian traditions, with some French works, and a slow upsurge in Wagner production from the 1880s into the new century. The mixed critical response nonetheless suggests that in Barcelona, *Carmen* was viewed within the broader (international) operatic context in contrast to the more parochial (or national) debates that dominated the opera's reception in the Madrid press. Welcomed as a relief from the decadence of Italian opera and the rise of Wagnerism, it was also criticized for a monotony resulting from too great a reliance on the model of Gounod.[87]

---

84. "No obstante el Sr. Liern ha llevado a término uno de los trabajos de Hércules." "Carmen," *La opinión*, 3 November 1887, 3; Allegro, "En el teatro de la Zarzuela," *El país*, 3 November 1887, 3.

85. "En la Zarzuela," *El mundo*, 3 November 1887, 1.

86. It was conducted by Juan Goula, while Mme Frandin sang the title role. "Crónica," *La vanguardia* (Barcelona), 1 November 1887, 6848;

87. J. P., "Gran teatro del Liceo: Carmen del Maestro Bizet," *La vanguardia* (Barcelona), 27 January 1888; "Los estrenos: Gran teatro del Liceo; Cármen," *La dinastía* (Barcelona), 28 January 1888.

Barely six weeks later, on 14 March 1888, *Carmen* finally appeared at the Teatro Real and played to packed houses at the very end of the season.[88] After the long buildup, some concluded that the night's success was a foregone conclusion, "a victory without a struggle," but Michelena proved himself as canny an impresario as Ducazcal by making *Carmen's* first night a charity benefit for the "Asilos del Pardo."[89] This gesture enabled him to disclaim any hope of monetary gain, turning it into a social event that attracted a "numerous and most distinguished" audience.[90]

Peña y Goñi described the premiere as a "truly triumphant entrance" before a "unanimous and enthusiastic public," while another critic predicted that "*Carmen* will become a repertory work in our Teatro Real."[91] In comparison with the earlier production at the Zarzuela, this was a magnificent staging "sung by singers of indisputable merit."[92] Now that it was performed in Italian with accompanied recitatives, and with an orchestra superbly conducted by the renowned Mancinelli, audience and critics could be carried away by the work's dramatic and musical power. Peña y Goñi declared that "to cite the beauties of the opera would entail listing all its pieces."[93]

Some of the variations in response to these early Spanish productions may have been related to differences between their audiences, and the forms of patronage that supported the theaters in question. Unlike the two Madrid theaters we have considered, the Liceu was privately owned by its shareholders. Their shares took the form of seats or boxes, and they appointed a board, which selected the Liceu's impresario. The contrast between Madrid's Teatro Real and Teatro de la Zarzuela might also be related to the political allegiances and class profile of their respective patrons. The Teatro Real audience, with its royal connections, aristocratic subscribers, and a more unified class identity, may have been less discomfited by the opera's exoticization of Spain than the more liberally inclined public of the Teatro de la Zarzuela.

Allegro had judged that *Carmen* would inevitably fail as a *zarzuela*, but he embraced the Teatro Real's production. He concluded that essentially the

88. The production was admired, especially the set for act 4. "Carmen," *La Iberia*, 15 March 1888, 2.

89. "Desde el paraiso," *La opinión*, 15 March 1888; "Carmen," *La Iberia*, 15 March 1888, 2. The Asilo del Pardo seems to have been an institution for the poor and the sick, and a regular beneficiary of theatrical performances. We are indebted to Ruth Piquer for this information.

90. "Teatro Real," *El imparcial*, 15 March 1888.

91. Peña y Goñi, "Teatro Real: Carmen," *La época*, 15 March 1888; "Desde el paraiso," *La opinión*, 15 March 1888.

92. The critic of *El imparcial* declared the two productions as different as night from day. "Teatros: Real," *La regencia*, 12 March 1888; "Teatro Real," *El imparcial*, 15 March 1888.

93. Peña y Goñi, "Teatro Real: Carmen," *La época*, 15 March 1888.

same work pleased so much more as an opera than as a *zarzuela* because "in opera, the music is everything; the rest has no importance. If the score is good, it all goes smoothly."[94] Coupled with the distancing effect of being sung in Italian, the cultural distortions that resulted from a Frenchman's attempt to create Spanish local color—which had so troubled audiences in a vernacular theater—were simply accepted in an opera house:

> In a theater where they speak and sing in Spanish, one cannot present falsified toreros and Sevillian cigarette girls invented in Paris. But in the opera one can; it will be one more convention, a score on a Spanish subject that is sanctioned by all the audiences of the world and we ourselves must not reject it.[95]

Arguing that opera audiences were more accustomed to convention than to an imitation of reality, Allegro explained that the construction of operatic scenarios required the reimagination of historical (and literary) figures in order to accommodate the dramatic demands of the libretto. The acceptance of this practice obliged opera audiences to listen impassively to ridiculous texts, applaud when they were sung well, and ignore any offence.[96]

If we assume some overlap in public between the two Madrid theaters, then the simple factor of increased familiarity may also have played a role in *Carmen*'s more positive reception at the Teatro Real. As the critic J. O. Picón observed in response to the 1887 *zarzuela* version, "it is impossible [for the public] to savor in one day important musical works. We are, then, entirely sure that *Carmen* will put down roots in Madrid, and that it will be better liked the more it is heard."[97]

Despite the lapse of more than a decade since its 1875 Paris debut, Bizet's *Carmen* remained a confronting novelty for Madrid's audiences in its drama and compositional techniques. But in the context of a rich local tradition of Spanish-themed lyric works, perhaps the most imaginative—and contested— element of *Carmen* was Bizet's musical characterization of Spain, specifically his representation of gypsy song and dance, and his attempt to compose music associated with the bullring. Madrid audiences had first heard music from *Carmen* as early as 1881, when the virtuoso violinist Pablo Sarasate performed his recently completed Fantasy on *Carmen* while touring Spain. Although

94. Allegro, "En el teatro de la Opera: 'Carmen,'" *El país*, 15 March 1888, 3.
95. Ibid.
96. Ibid. Allegro's main example was Vasco de Gama, that "intrepid navigator" who created no particular sensation as a historical figure, but who, when represented in Meyerbeer's *L'Africaine*, became a "type of Portuguese tenor who as easily fell in love with a white woman as with a negro," and was sure to create an effect with the audience.
97. Picón, "Teatro de la Zarzuela: Estreno de 'Cármen,'" *El correo*, 3 November 1887. "Neither *Gioconda*, heard today to great applause, nor *Les huguenots*, now so justly and widely praised, conquered suddenly the spirit of the public."

Sarasate set the most characteristically Spanish numbers of the opera, they failed to make any impression on Madrid's expert listeners, abstracted from their as yet unknown dramatic context.

Critical carping notwithstanding, in 1887 it was the opera's most overtly Spanish numbers that were most often encored: "It is impossible to ask for anything more in four acts with a sentimental, romantic score packed with Spanish airs and orchestrated by a masterly hand.... Many of the numbers display the perfect study that the author has made of national airs," wrote the critic in *El imparcial*.[98] Critic and composer Felipe Pedrell—a key ideologue of Spanish musical nationalism—also found much to admire in the "Spanishness" of Bizet's score. As an important advocate of Spain's folk music, Pedrell believed that Spain's musical heritage could be traced only through forms that predated the influence of Italian opera in the nineteenth century, especially music that incorporated folk elements. Pedrell later defined this music, along with transcriptions and settings of Spanish folk music, as Spain's *cancionero musical popular* (popular/folk musical songbook), and believed it should inform Spanish composers. According to Pedrell, Bizet "knew how to write genuinely popular Spanish music" and demonstrated "admirable facility" for it in the crowd scenes. The composer "divined the musical color, character, melodic turns, modulations and rhythm of our *cancionero musical popular*, to the extent to which its specific orientalism is valued and so well heard" by Bizet.[99]

Praise for Bizet's extensive use of Spanish material is supported by comments on specific scenes: Carmen's seduction of José had "marked Spanish character," and the entr'acte to act 4 was based on "a very characterful Spanish theme; treated with much understanding of our music."[100] The provenance of the entr'acte theme in Manuel García's *polo* was not discussed by Madrid critics,[101] but they were well aware that Carmen's "Habanera" was based on Sebastián Iradier's "El arreglito" (1864). Critics noted the enormous success of the "Habanera" after the November 1887 premiere, in which it was repeatedly encored, but certain malicious parties queried whether Iradier's estate was receiving rights for its use.[102] In the *Diario de Barcelona* Carmen's first aria was considered an apt sketch of her character and clearly Spanish,

---

98. "Teatro de la Zarzuela: *Carmen*," *El imparcial*, 3 November 1887.

99. F. P. [Felipe Pedrell], "La quincena musical," *Ilustración musical hispano-americana* 1, no. 2 (1888): 10.

100. "Carmen," *La opinión*, 3 November 1887, 3. *El imparcial* concurred in 1888: "Of the Spanish themes the work has only one which is really notable and beautiful, the entr'acte to Act Four, which was admirably performed and repeated to applause." "Teatro Real," *El imparcial*, 15 March 1888.

101. García's *tonadillas* would have been long forgotten in late 1880s Madrid.

102. Subirá, *Historia y anecdotario del Teatro Real*, 394.

with "the air of a habanera."[103] Indeed, by 1887, Iradier's habaneras, also called *americanas*, had been superseded in Spain by new works in the genre. The habanera itself was still very popular, and in its more contemporary form was frequently used as a characteristic number in late-nineteenth-century *zarzuelas*, especially in the *género chico*. One of the most famous Spanish habaneras of the *género chico* was the "Tango de la Menegilda (Pobre chica)" from Chueca and Valverde's *La Gran Vía* (1886).[104] This was the backdrop against which Bizet's "Habanera," playing to audiences so familiar with the form, was inevitably judged:

> Bizet has developed Spanish motives working wonders with melody and instrumentation, but he did not know, and this is not strange, how to give them that animation, that air, that local flavor to which we are accustomed. The tango of the first act had undoubted merit, but it cannot stand comparison with that other more modest, but much more *gracioso* [witty, charming], by the inspired Chueca.[105]

Pedrell, on the other hand, disliked Bizet's "Habanera" for its "French" coquetry, declaring it both "wretched" and "insipid." He deemed the genre unsuitable for Bizet's purpose, because the habanera had become an urban popular style, degraded by overuse and removed from its folk roots.[106]

Dance was a crucial element in the miscellany of Spanish topics from which *Carmen* was formed, and some critics protested that a Frenchman should presume to describe such a uniquely Spanish phenomenon as a *juerga* (a riotous gathering characterized by drinking, singing, and Andalusian or gypsy entertainment).[107] Fuensanta Moreno, a seasoned exponent of Spanish dances (including Andalusian and flamenco styles) on the popular stages of Madrid, danced Maestro Guerrero's choreography of the "Chanson bohème" to great applause at the Teatro de la Zarzuela. Nevertheless, *El mediodía* labeled it a dance with a "flamenco veneer,"[108] and Espoleta made fun of its instrumental backing, describing it as a noisy combination of drum, cymbals, tabor,

103. "Teatro del Liceo: Cármen, ópera cómica de Bizet," *Diario de Barcelona*, 28 January 1888, 1308.

104. Menegilda is cast as a *chula* domestic servant in *La Gran Vía*. Achieving comparable popularity a few years later was Tomás Bretón's charming habanera "Dónde vas con mantón de Manila" from *La Verbena de la paloma* (1894).

105. *El resumen*, 3 November 1887, quoted in Sentaurens, "Carmen," 869.

106. Pedrell's criticism encompassed the comment that it had been "soldered into the work, so they say, because it pleased the artist who created the principal role of the opera." F. P. [Felipe Pedrell], "La quincena musical," 10.

107. The critic in question exclaimed, '¡Una *juerga* descrita por un francés!' "Carmen en la Zarzuela," *La Iberia*, 3 November 1887, 2.

108. "Crónica de teatros: Real," *El mediodía*, 20 March 1888.

tambourine, and handclapping.[109] This description closely parallels Bizet's orchestration, in which he progressively adds tambourine, triangle, timpani, and finally cymbals as the "Chanson bohème" reaches its climax. Such colorful orchestration was more akin to the French and Russian traditions of representing Spanishness (along with gypsy or even oriental revelry) than contemporary Spanish practice. Even within *zarzuela* scores, gypsy music was more commonly evoked by imitating—or at times incorporating—the sound of the guitar or *estudiantina*, creating a quite different sonic stylization.

A ubiquitous trope of popular theater and literature in Spain, the homegrown auto-exoticism represented by *Andalucismo* focused on images of Andalusian identity and local color, and often typified them musically with gaiety and exuberance in the light entertainment of the *zarzuela chica*. Whereas the habanera was a widely recognized marker of southern identity in the *zarzuela* of the time, the polonaise, the mazurka, and the *chotis* (a local adaptation of the schottische) were commonly used to indicate Madrid identity in *género chico zarzuelas*. In this context, some judged Bizet's employment of a more dramatic musical style to convey the same subject matter too somber. "The flamenco fiesta at the start of the second act is beautiful, above all the crescendo with which it ends, even though there are moments that seem more like sad Arab melodies than joyful Andalusian tunes."[110] The category of Arab style distinguishes between gay Andalusian folk music and the greater melancholy of *arabismo*, a trend that reached its height in popular Spanish song during the 1870s and 1880s and has some parallels with Bizet's Orientalization of Spanish sources.[111] Pedrell suggested that greater recourse to this "Arab" style would have lent a passionate ferocity to José's jealousy, lamenting that Bizet's principal characters were not infused with the "popular" Spanish music he found so pleasingly characteristic in the crowd scenes.[112]

These comments point to the stylistic distinctions applied by some Spanish critics to representations of Andalusian scenes, including the smugglers and bullfight procession:

> In the third act the music is too serious for the scene which represents the gypsies, bandits and toreros in the interior of the mountains. [The fourth act] was received coldly, given that the setting and the characters called for merry tunes and Spanish airs, which were generally lacking in the score.[113]

109. Espoleta, "Pitos y Palmas: CARMEN ópera cómica en cuatro actos y varias latas," *La avispa*, 9 November 1887.

110. "Zarzuela: Carmen," *La regencia*, 3 November 1887. Optimism and joie de vivre were counted as essential Andalusian traits by Blas Infante in *El ideal andaluz* (Seville, 1915), as cited in Alonso, *La canción lírica*, 233.

111. Alonso, *La canción lírica*, 397.

112. F. P. [Felipe Pedrell], "La quincena musical," 10.

113. "Zarzuela," *La publicidad*, 4 November 1887.

Allegro also found the opening of act 4 inauthentic, despite its undeniable energy, and his criticism encapsulated the problematic comparison between Bizet's opera and the *costumbrista zarzuela* tradition:

> To what end has the author of *L'Arlésienne* written inspired dances and marches for the bullfight procession, if they were to be performed here, where we have real *cante jondo, sevillanas* and *pasos dobles* with more color than a painting by Velazquez!
>
> It is French music, very apt for those French toreros and *demoiselles* tobacco workers painted by Meilhac. But would this music suit real toreros and tobacco workers, sung in Spanish and dressed as God decrees? . . .
>
> In one word, does the score of *Carmen* have sufficient merit to make us applaud a torero converted into a *monsieur* and a *cigarrera* into *mademoiselle*?[114]

Allegro was not alone in suggesting that Bizet's Frenchness handicapped him in representing popular Spanish types. Some of the harshest critics declared that it was impossible for a Frenchman to compose music for such essentially Spanish scenes.

Despite the "vigor and arrogance" of the music accompanying the entry of Joselillo/Escamillo, Bizet was accused of lacking a deep musical understanding of the Spanish nationality, a failure that somehow falsified the characters of Carmen and her bullfighter.[115] Another even claimed that only a Spanish composer could truly set the music of the bullfighter:

> In the second act [at] the entrance of the matador Joselillo . . . the music is bright and does not lack a certain gallantry, but for Bizet to have interpreted it well, it would not have been enough to have lived for a few months in Seville, it would have been necessary to have been born under the limpid sky of Andalusia and for his blood to have been mixed with the golden *Jerez* [sherry] and the tasty essence of the pallid *Manzanilla* [a variety of sherry]: it would have been indispensable, at the very least, to have been Spanish, because in this land we all have something of the Andalusian in us . . . and we all hope desperately to be considered *flamenco*.[116]

This declaration indicates the extent to which characteristics of Andalusia and its music, at times with recourse to the nascent flamenco style, had permeated the *zarzuela* and formed part of the psyche of the Spanish capital.

---

114. Allegro, "En el teatro de la Zarzuela," *El país*, 3 November 1887.
115. *El mundo*, 27 October 1887; P., "Gran teatro del Liceo: Carmen del Maestro Bizet," *La vanguardia*, 27 January 1888, 2.
116. "Carmen," *La opinión*, 3 November 1887, 3.

While *Andalucismo* was at the heart of critical debates surrounding *Carmen* at the Teatro de la Zarzuela, it became less prominent after the grander operatic productions at Barcelona's Liceu and Madrid's Teatro Real, when the discussion of local color assumed a different tone.

An unsubstantiated rumor that the Teatro Real planned to set its production in Naples—a suitably exotic locale for a Spanish audience, albeit still infused with Hispanic associations—suggests that the management was anxious to avoid a repetition of this critical distraction.[117] But some detractors still took Bizet to task for failing to seek enough inspiration for his local color in actual Spanish sources:

> [The work] has an exuberance of melody and harmony and almost complete absence of inspiration in everything that is based on Spanish airs. Only outside of these is Bizet's genius to be found.... Given the heights achieved by Bizet, it should have been relatively easy for him to find in the immense treasury of Spanish [folk] songs something more salient and characteristic than that which was incorporated into the score of *Carmen*.[118]

In his review of the Teatro Real production, Peña y Goñi addressed these critical misgivings about the opera's use of local color, insightfully questioning not only what constituted a Spanish opera, but also casting doubt on the Spanish musical pedigree of the very *zarzuelas* that had been compared so favorably with *Carmen*.

> Some Madrid musicians (those of low aspirations and accidental amateurs) attack *Carmen* for not being very Spanish. For these gentlemen, the work with a Spanish plot should consist of an inexhaustible collection of *polos*, *manchegas*, *vitos*, *boleros* and *peteneras*; a species of gypsy *Cosmorama* of "ayyys," "Oles" [and the like].

Peña y Goñi identified the inconsistency in this argument, when viewed in the context of operas set in Spain:

> Yet they will also proclaim as masterpiece of masterpieces Rossini's *Barber of Seville*, in which the great maestro was simply content to write an immortal work, which is about as Spanish as we are Chinese. The same gentlemen will demonstrate indignation at the seguidilla in *Carmen*, without taking into account

---

117. Manuel Giró, "La ópera española y los compositores españoles," *Diario de Barcelona* (1888): 1155–57.

118. "Teatro Real," *El imparcial*, 15 March 1888. See also "[t]he music is notable at some moments, but insubstantial when it is based on Spanish motives." Ignoto, "Espectáculos," *La provincia* 2, no. 11 (1888): 41.

Figure 3.6 Giuseppina Pasqua (*c.* 1888).
Credit: Centre de Documentació i Museu de les Arts Escèniques de l'Institut del Teatre (MAE).

the much-applauded polonaises of so many Spanish maestros. Let's forget about
these musical craftsmen, given that the true aficionado will savor the beauties of
Carmen without making an exhaustive study of her baptismal record.[119]

The greater forbearance of local color in foreign works on Hispanic themes
at the Teatro Real allowed imported performers to achieve success in the roles,
especially if they were able to render their characters *more* Spanish. The Italian
singer Giuseppina Pasqua became an audience favorite, and gained a form of
honorary naturalization for her exceptionally characteristic performance of
Carmen (see Figure 3.6). Called repeatedly at the end of every act on opening

119. Peña y Goñi, "Teatro Real: Carmen," *La época*, 15 March 1888.

night, she rendered the difficult part with all the charm, wit, and "picaresque character that could be asked of a foreign singer performing a genuinely Spanish type."[120] Peña y Goñi set the seal of approval:

> When Pasqua sings Carmen outside of Spain one will be able to say that Bizet's character will have Spanish blood in her veins, inoculated in Madrid with her successes here over the past decade. Then, surely, there will be no one who will be able to compete with her in that role.[121]

The last performance of *Carmen*, which coincided with the last night of the opera season, was a benefit for Pasqua. In her encore she proved her Spanish credentials by singing, in Spanish, a Spanish song entitled "Lo que Dios da ...," which she had to repeat amid a great ovation.[122] Pasqua thus paved the way for future Hispanicized, and even Spanish, Carmens.

120. Peña y Goñi, *La época*, 15 March 1888; "Carmen," *La Iberia*, 15 March 1888, 2.
121. Peña y Goñi, "Teatro Real: Carmen," *La época*, 15 March 1888.
122. "Entre bastidores," *La opinión*, 23 March 1888, 3.

CHAPTER 4

✧

Profusion and Parody in Barcelona

Barcelona proved to be a key location for *Carmen*'s acceptance in Spain, less because it had hosted the opera's Spanish debut in 1881 than for the way it seized the momentum created by Madrid's competing productions of 1887–88. As Spain's most cosmopolitan city in the late nineteenth century, Barcelona could also claim to be its undisputed opera capital. Barcelona's many theaters were highly attuned to international cultural developments and quickly adopted the latest trends from Paris, London, Vienna, Italy, and the New World. While its operatic culture focused on the Gran Teatre del Liceu (Liceo Theater) and the Principal Theater, numerous other theaters flourished around them, staging everything from opera and classic drama to music-hall acts and up-to-the-minute theatrical parodies.[1]

As the 1890s dawned, Barcelona's theaters provided the impetus for *Carmen*'s Spanish enculturation, and its integration into key native genres of the time: first the *zarzuela grande* (following the example set by the Teatro de la Zarzuela in Madrid), and then the popular *género chico* that was sweeping Spain's urban centers. At times the unique perspective provided by Catalan cultural identity colored local reception of Bizet's opera, contrasting with the responses the work had inspired in Madrid. This chapter traces how *Carmen* was domesticated through translation, adaptation, and parody in Barcelona's theaters, as Spanish artists began to "recompose" Bizet's opera to reflect their own images of theatrical Spain.

---

1. Apart from the Gran Teatre del Liceu, some of the Barcelona theaters referred to in this chapter are given Spanish nomenclature (in line with the practice in most of the historic sources consulted).

CARMEN TAKES HOLD IN COSMOPOLITAN BARCELONA

Carmen was staged in Barcelona against the background of a flourishing Catalan resurgence. With roots early in the nineteenth century, the Catalan *Renaixença* revived interest in and identification with the distinct language, culture, and literary traditions of the region, idealizing the medieval past when the Kingdom of Aragon commanded a Mediterranean empire and its culture flowered in the courtly arts of the troubadours. An important trading city, Barcelona was the focus of Catalonia's growing economic and industrial productivity in the nineteenth century, driven by a burgeoning middle class, whose educated members were sympathetic to viewing themselves as separate from Spain and Hispanic stereotypes. Rejecting Spain's image as isolated and backward, Catalan artists and intellectuals were keen to identify with modern Europe.

From the late 1880s, high culture in Barcelona also began to be shaped by the new artistic trends of *Modernisme*, a particularly Catalan take on Art Nouveau and Jugendstil, also influenced by the Pre-Raphaelites and Symbolism, the exponents of which included Santiago Rusiñol and the young Antoni Gaudí. Artists and intellectuals of this generation looked to Europe, and particularly to Paris, for inspiration.[2] A Barcelona audience might thus have been able to view and rationalize Bizet's opera as exotic, rather than as a slight on their own culture.

Right from the 1881 production of *Carmen* at the Teatro Lírico, the Catalan-language press reviewed the opera from a Catalanist perspective, clearly distinguishing local audiences from the nation so cruelly caricatured by Bizet, Meilhac, and Halévy. The respected local critic José Rodoreda explained that "there exists a region within Spain, which is discredited by these ignorant Frenchmen, for it is rich, industrious, honorable, hard-working and peaceful. As Catalans, we can thus tolerate this libretto, if not accept it [because it doesn't apply to us]."[3]

Although criticism of the libretto in 1881 did not reach the heights of outrage later attained by Madrid's press, some did feel the need to defend Spanish honor against the perception that Spain was populated by whores, thieves, and thugs, and to decry the complete ignorance of Spanish life and customs manifested by French writers. Rodoreda was concerned that the silly names of the characters would make the audience laugh, and that the lack of propriety in the libretto would alienate them, but his fears were unfounded. The beauty of the music and the excellence of the singers' interpretation carried the work, and he repeated his belief that "the opera is the music,"[4] a conviction

2. Robert Hughes, *Barcelona* (New York: Alfred A. Knopf, 1992), 391.
3. J. Rodoreda, "La *Carmen*, de Bizet," *La ilustració catalana* 2, no. 40 (1881): 326.
4. Ibid.

upon which his deep appreciation of the emotion and drama of the score was founded. Recognizing some element of Spanishness in the opera, Rodoreda praised the effective local color in the "Chanson bohème" of act 2 and the entr'acte to act 4, and noted the great success of Galli-Marié's renditions of the "Habanera," which were encored at each performance.[5] The critic for *La ilustración* qualified his praise for Galli-Marié's performance with a broadside at the Teatro Lírico's management for presenting inappropriately dressed *cigarreras, gitanas, majos,* and *toreros* to a Spanish audience that did not appreciate seeing its national costumes and customs ridiculed.[6]

The year after *Carmen* made its quiet Spanish debut at the Teatro Lírico, however, a new operatic force was presented to Barcelona's audiences in the shape of their first fully staged Wagner operas: *Lohengrin* played in 1882 and 1883, and was followed by productions of *Tannhäuser* and *Der fliegende Holländer*. Wagner's music was already familiar to the Catalan public from concert selections, and the activities of various Wagner societies. His glorification of the medieval past, coupled with a modernity of artistic expression, offered a model to the kindred enterprise of the *Renaixença*. Art historian Robert Hughes concludes that "Barcelonans saw in Wagner their own desire to create a myth of national identity."[7] Progressive Catalans also identified with German industriousness and industrialization, as it underscored their developing narrative of difference from the rest of Spain.

Attracting support from a broad cross section of Catalan nationalists in the late nineteenth century, the main ideologues of Spanish opera engaged critically with Wagner's music and its potential to serve as a template for their nationalist aspirations in the lyric art. Ardent Wagnerism shaped responses to *Carmen* by key thinkers and composers of the period, such as Madrid-based writer and music critic Peña y Goní or the Catalan musicologist and composer Felipe Pedrell, who produced his 1891 opera manifesto, *Por nuestra música (For Our Music)*, to coincide with the launch of his operatic trilogy *Los Pirineos (The Pyrenees)*, and espoused a style that was to combine elements of Wagnerian leitmotiv with national folklore.[8] J. P. in *La vanguardia* explained that Catalan audiences were more discerning as a result of their knowledge of Wagner: they demanded from their operas both intelligence and underlying philosophy, rather than just a string of pretty melodies, and became impatient with the never-ending series of Italian operas served up to them.[9]

5. Ibid.

6. "Variedades," *La ilustración* 40, no. 1 (1881): 331.

7. Hughes, *Barcelona*, 454.

8. Francesc Cortès, "La ópera en Cataluña desde 1900 a 1936," in *La ópera en España e Hispanoamérica*, ed. Emilio Casares Rodicio and Álvaro Torrente, (Madrid: ICCMU, 2002), 2:325–62.

9. J. P., "Gran teatro del Liceo: Carmen del Maestro Bizet," *La vanguardia*, 27 January 1888, 2.

Figure 4.1 Maurici Vilomara, set design for *Carmen* act 1, Teatre Liceu, Barcelona (1888).
Credit: Centre de Documentació i Museu de les Arts Escèniques de l'Institut del Teatre (MAE), (escF 8).

Wagner's introduction to Barcelona's operatic stages in the 1880s caused Bizet's *espagnolade* to be seen and heard in quite a different context from that which shaped Madrid's response. When the Liceu mounted a new production in January 1888, probably in response to the upsurge in interest sparked by Madrid's well-publicized *Carmen* wars, it met with a lukewarm reception in some quarters.[10] Pedrell was concerned that the comparison with Wagner would impede *Carmen*'s appreciation by local audiences. Against the background of steadily increasing interest in Wagner, he speculated that the formal Germanic grandiloquence and background symbolism of operas like *Lohengrin* had a dulling effect on Catalan audiences' ability to really appreciate the "shining filigree" of Bizet's score. In fact, the set design for act 1 of the Liceu *Carmen* production seems to betray some of the characteristics associated with Wagner operas in contrast with the local color of the Parisian premiere (see Figure 4.1). Despite the opera's revival at this less than opportune moment, Pedrell remained convinced that *Carmen*'s score displayed enough characteristic local color in depicting its Spanish subject matter to truly engage the interest of the public.[11] Audiences and critics alike enjoyed the Liceu's staging and showed their appreciation of the Spanishness of *Carmen* and

10. "Los estrenos: Gran teatro del Liceo; Cármen," *La dinastía*, 28 January 1888, 2.
11. F. P. [Felipe Pedrell], "La quincena musical," *Ilustración musical hispano-americana* 1, no. 2 (1888): 10.

Bizet's music in particular. The critic of the *Diario de Barcelona* wrote, "It's not strange that [the author] chose for the protagonist of the drama a *cigarrera andaluza*, a woman voluble and capricious who promotes quarrels," and described Escamillo's song as "an air of *jaleo* (revelry)," which Señor Carbonell gave "with élan."[12]

The January 1888 Liceu production led to a spate of *Carmens* in Barcelona's theaters over the next few years, and in some ways Bizet's opera came to share a cultural space with the similarly burgeoning Spanish-themed entertainment in the city's flourishing cafe and theater scene. This vibrant industry found itself ideally situated in a bustling port town, and Barcelona was a destination for performers from across Spain—like the young Carolina Otero (of whom more later), or flamenco artists emerging from the *cafés cantantes* of Andalusia—in the hope of discovery by scouts for the international circuit.

Catalan critics and audiences viewed Andalusian and gypsy entertainment as exotic, perhaps a little crude and primitive, and certainly foreign. Like their equivalent attractions in Paris, Andalusian performers working in Barcelona, whether gypsy or not, shared with their Parisian counterparts the base of an established and dynamic local community. Barcelona was home to a significant Andalusian population, which retained its outsider status at this time, unlike its Madrid equivalent, where Andalusian-inflected *chulos* established a hybrid identity that became part of the capital's cultural character.[13]

Local commentator Federico Rahola observed the "invasion" of Barcelona by flamenco (and all its accoutrements), sparking a trend that reached its height in the mid-1880s as Catalans embraced not only flamenco song and dance, but Andalusian costume, *manzanilla*, bullfighting, and *juergas* along with it. As fashion changed, however, the French style began to dominate in the *cafés cantantes* and *cocottes* displaced *gitanas* with their can-can and pirouettes instead of Andalusian tangos and *vueltas de pecho* (chest turns). Yet Rahola described a curious dynamic on Barcelona's popular stage in early 1888:

> One must remember that this is a neutral country, as distant from the *chulo* [masculine of *chula*] as from the *maqreau* [French equivalent of *chulo*, specifically a pimp]; the French style and the flamenco style battle it out here like belligerents, yet both are exotic in this land. It may be that today's losers will be tomorrow's victors.
>
> The good thing is that living in close quarters there is a transfer of peculiarities of character, such that flamenco performers return to their country

12. "Teatro del Liceo: Cármen, ópera cómica de Bizet," *Diario de Barcelona*, 28 January 1888, 1308.

13. Barcelona's Andalusian population was to expand in the early twentieth century and during the Franco years. See Luis Cabrera Sanchez, *Catalunya serà impura o no serà* (Barcelona: Portic, 2010).

displaying cancan-esque airs, and the French reenter their nation flaunting their flamenco-ness.[14]

This hybridization is seen in the late 1880s programming of variety theaters like the Teatro del Circo and the Eden-Concert, which offered international variety programs with some Spanish inflection. Alongside flamenco singing and dancing, Barcelona audiences could enjoy acts direct from Paris nightclubs, troupes from far-flung countries like Japan, acrobats, and short lyric works from *zarzuela* companies.

By 1887 the flamenco acts were well established and familiar, referred to as "the indispensable *canto y baile flamenco*," but clear distinctions were still made between the varieties of Spanish song and dance on offer. *Baile español*, probably referring to Spanish regional dance, is listed separately from the *cuadros flamencos*, and the Café Restaurant del Concierto Barcelonés advertized its *cuadro* (or flamenco troupe) as including the "principal *cantaores* (flamenco singers) from Seville, Malaga and Granada," thus claiming authenticity based on drawing performers from the main centers of this emerging style.[15]

In 1892 the English writer and music-hall aficionado Arthur Symons visited a humble Barcelona music hall, the Alcazar Español. He described it as "the most characteristic place [he] could find," and his vivid recollections of the evening he spent in this small *café cantante* reveal a heterogeneous program that replicates the tendencies outlined by Rahola a few years earlier and possibly not unlike the venue depicted by Ricardo Canals in 1890 (see Figure 4.2).[16] A distinctively Spanish overture introduced a *zarzuela* sketch, followed by French-style turns that ranged from comic songs to a "Lilliputian [puppet] theater."[17] One of the local dance troupes seemed to integrate can-cans with high kicks and pirouettes into their Spanish dances. There were brackets for Spanish solo guitar (not in flamenco style), as well as Andalusian songs like the *malagueña*, with flamenco inflections in the vocal line, which were accompanied by the theater's small orchestra, rather than by guitars. This representative and hybrid program corroborates the fluidity Rahola identified, in which elements of French or more generally international turns were absorbed into Spanish acts, while flamenco inflected the vocal performance of Spanish songs, drawing on developments in the performance of flamenco in such venues as the *cafés cantantes*. Symons may not

---

14. Federico Rahola, "La rota de lo flamenco," *La vanguardia*, 1 February 1888, 1.

15. "Crónica," *La vanguardia*, 7 October 1887, 6288–89; "Crónica," *La vanguardia*, 15 September 1887, 5787; "Espectáculos," *La vanguardia*, 16 September 1887, 5810.

16. Arthur Symons, "A Spanish Music-Hall" [1892], in *Cities and Sea-Coasts and Islands* (New York: Brentano's, 1919), 146.

17. A "turn" was the allotted appearance on a variety program of a particular performer or troupe, and might consist of various short items.

Figure 4.2 Ricardo Canals, *La Danse de la Poule* (*c*. 1890).
Credit: Private collection.

have been fully aware of the process of hybridization he was observing, but his descriptions remain a valuable documentation of this phenomenon.

Symons visited a Barcelona that had been galvanized a few years earlier by its hosting of the 1888 Exposició Universal, which ran from May to December and showcased Catalan industry and architecture to the world. The local entertainment industry received a parallel boost from the influx of visitors for the exposition. Internationally renowned Spanish acts like the dancer Carmencita Dausset and the Estudiantina Figaro performed a short but brilliant season at the Tivoli, while the young Carolina Otero was spotted and given her international break, moving to dance in Marseilles, an engagement that in turn enabled her graduation to the bright lights of Paris. After the Liceu's decorous *Carmen* production just weeks before the opening of the Exposició, it is possible that the explosion in cultural activity and popular entertainment that took place during that landmark year prepared the ground for the subsequent proliferation of productions. And so *Carmen* was to be embraced by a city that boasted audiences with a nuanced understanding of the ways in which Spanish culture could overlap with cosmopolitan entertainment.

THE *CARMEN* PHENOMENON IN BARCELONA

The summer of 1889 saw the beginning of a run of competing and successful *Carmen* productions in Barcelona, starting with a new production at the Tivoli Theater, which was known for a consistent offering of popular *zarzuelas* and French and Italian operas, along with some mixed programming. The Tivoli presented an Italian *Carmen* (with Italia Georgio in the title role), but sought to create a new kind of "authenticity" in the visual aspects of the production, which included a historical vision of Spanishness. Critics praised the realistic scenery, especially the sets of the tobacco factory and the bullring,[10] but the Tivoli had also announced new costumes with designs based on Mérimée's novella.[19] Designer Lluís Labarta i Grané created a fresh look for the characters by adjusting the dress to reflect early-nineteenth-century fashions, deliberately matching the period in which Mérimée had placed the action.[20] Sketches of Labarta's costumes survive in Barcelona's Institut del Teatre, revealing a thoughtful attention to realistic detail (in particular in the designs for the street vendors in act 1), which resists incongruous ideas of luxury (so often a feature of Carmen's outfit at the bullring in act 4).[21] These were costumes that a knowledgeable Spanish audience could recognize and condone (see Figure 4.3).

The Tivoli's artistic team also highlighted their inclusion of the dance numbers "written by Bizet" just before the bullfight in the final act.[22] The critics

18. "Barcelona," *Diario de Barcelona*, 22 July 1889, 9132–33.
19. "Barcelona," *Diario de Barcelona*, 19 July 1889, 9018.
20. "Barcelona," *Diario de Barcelona*, 22 July 1889, 9132–33.
21. While Labarta is clearly named as the designer of the costumes for the 1889 Tivoli production, the date of the sketches reproduced in Figure 4.3 is 1888, and they are catalogued by the Centre de Documentació de l'Institut del Teatre as pertaining to the 1888 Liceu production. It is possible that both theaters used Labarta's designs.
22. "Barcelona," *Diario de Barcelona*, 19 July 1889, 9018.

Figure 4.3 Lluís Labarta i Grané, *Figurins*. Costume designs for *Carmen* production at Gran Teatre del Liceu, Barcelona, 26 January 1888: (a) Escamillo—Torero; (b) act 4 vendors, selling lemonade, oranges, fans, and hazelnuts; (c) Don José as smuggler in act 3; (d) Carmen in act 2 and act 3 [and act 4].

Credit: Centre de Documentació i Museu de les Arts Escèniques de l'Institut del Teatre (MAE), (escF 8).

(c)

(d)

Figure 4.3 Continued.

judged this "baile de gitanas" (gypsy dance) slightly monotonous because the dancers' movements were too naturalistic.[23] Their apparent lack of stylization must have seemed dull or even clumsy to Spanish audiences accustomed to classicized Spanish dance as exemplified by dancers like Rosita Mauri. The critics' descriptions are cursory, but it is possible that the choreography was more rustic than was usual on the operatic stage (in line with the style of the costumes), probably incorporating elements of flamenco *baile*.

The Tivoli production presented competing authenticities: historically informed costuming combined with elements of a modern dance style (given that flamenco was anachronistic in an 1830s setting). It thus attempted to engage with *Carmen* as a work that represented elements of Spanish history and culture, in the context of contemporary entertainment. There was no questioning its success: described in August as "the fashionable opera of the moment," it played on until early October.[24]

The Liceu presented *Carmen* again in November 1889, but by spring 1890 a concentration of interest suggests that Barcelona was in the grip of a *Carmen* craze. The Tivoli built on the success of the previous summer by remounting its *Carmen* production in March 1890, while the Gayarre Theater presented the opera with an Italian troupe in the same month. The competing companies fought it out with ever-increasing hype in the advertising columns—the Gayarre announced exuberant decor and costumes—as both claimed extraordinary success. As March turned to April, the *zarzuela* company of the Teatro del Circo took the *Carmen* competition to the next level by announcing rehearsals of a new, Spanish version, arranged for the Spanish stage by the respected Barcelona writer and journalist D. P[atricio] Eduardo de Bray. Although initially billed as a *zarzuela*, it is then consistently referred to as an "opera cómica," linking it more closely to the original Bizet. Many of its performers had appeared in the various earlier productions, and the Teatro del Circo sought to assure its success by presenting the Tivoli's Italia Georgio in the title role, singing it in Spanish for the first time. Their advertising didn't miss anything: this new production was to feature, along with lavish new costumes, "a chorus of men and women, corps de ballet, military band, numerous extras, horses and all the properties befitting the importance of the work.[25]

Bray's translation corrected some of the more ridiculous aspects of Mérimée's *espagnolade* and is perhaps best viewed in comparison with

23. C. C. de S., "Los teatros: Teatro del Tivoli; Carmen," *La dinastía*, 23 July 1889, 2; "Barcelona," *Diario de Barcelona*, 22 July 1889, 9132–33.

24. *Diario de Barcelona*, 12 August 1889, 9977.

25. "Ecos teatrales: Espectáculos," *La dinastía*, 2 April 1890, 3; "Espectáculos," *La dinastía*, 6 April 1890, 3.

Liern's earlier attempt at a Spanish version.[26] Although both took the Opéra-Comique's original version, with its spoken dialogue, as a starting point, Bray's text is far more polished and "literary" than Liern's. Whether in spoken dialogue or sung lyric, he applies an elaborate and varied end-rhyming scheme throughout, an approach that reduces the sense of naturalism.

The crucial issue of Hispanicization can be summed up with a few observations. Bray kept most of the character names as written, although the tavernkeeper Lillas Pastia becomes the much more Andalusian Curro Flores. Carmen's Spanish and gypsy identity is variously delineated and suppressed: Bray avoids any reference to mysticism and religion, but he allows her to order a Spanish feast for her tryst with José, abandoning her Parisian taste for sweetmeats in order to enjoy olives, fried anchovies, sausages, and good wine (act 2, scene 5).[27] Despite adding informal language and colloquialisms to the text, and even a few words of Romaní (the gypsy language) to the dialogue, Bray suppresses even more of the opera's references to gypsies than Liern had eliminated. The habanera loses all mention of gypsies, although elsewhere in the opera Carmen still declares herself a gypsy and *gitanillas* dance to the guitars in the translation of the "Chanson bohème," a lyric in which Bray stays closer to the spirit of the original French text than Liern had. The bullfight remains an exoticized spectacle for Bray; lacking Liern's expertise, he keeps the text vague and suggests that it is mainly an opportunity for drinking. Clearly designated as a Spanish translation of an *ópera cómica*, Bray's *Carmen* met with success in Barcelona, playing ten performances over the three weeks following its 6 April opening and granting *Carmen* the by now familiar accolade of the "success of the season."[28]

Meanwhile, the Tivoli had no intention of losing its place as the premier theater for seeing *Carmen* in Barcelona. Always competitive in price—general entry cost 50 céntimos as opposed to the 75 charged by many of the Tivoli's competitors—the management did not intend to rely on the continuing success of its 1889 production. Accordingly, on 10 April it announced rehearsals of *Carmen* the "zarzuela española," with a Spanish libretto based on Mérimée's novella by Rafael María Liern. It was staged by a company led by the respected and experienced composer and impresario Guillermo Cereceda, which claimed

---

26. For a close study and minutely detailed comparison of the Liern and Bray translations, examining both text and musical setting, see Laura Santana Burgos, "Diálogos entre Francia y España: La traducción de los libretos de *Carmen* y *El retablo de Maese Pedro*" (PhD thesis, Universidad de Granada, 2013), 234–345. The Bray text formed the basis for the 2014 revival of *Carmen* at the Teatro de la Zarzuela in Madrid.

27. D. P. Eduardo de Bray, *Carmen: Zarzuela en 4 actos y en verso, basada en la ópera del mismo nombre; Letra de D. P. Eduardo de Bray; Música del maestro Georges Bizet* (Barcelona: José Cunill, 1890), 45.

28. "Espectáculos," *La dinastía*, 6 April 1890, 3.

to have performed the work no fewer than sixty-eight times in various parts of Spain.[29] The competing Spanish translations led to the inevitable legal dispute between the two theaters,[30] and may have contributed to the production's short season in Barcelona.

Liern's *Carmen* was not given a warm reception in the Catalan capital. Unlike Madrid, where audiences had been introduced to *Carmen* via this translation, Barcelona had a public that already knew the work well. Its crimes against Spanishness had been sufficiently abstracted by repeated performances in a foreign language, and even by Bray's flowery style and rhyming verse, but Liern's dialogue was too vernacular for local tastes. He was taken to task for accentuating the "*nota flamenco* (flamenco note) that is found in the opera's libretto" and for his own additions to the plot, which were found implausible and farfetched. Although the main musical numbers were applauded, and the arrangement judged "not lacking in merit," the production was not found attractive.[31] It must be speculated that the performance as a *zarzuela*, with the attendant difference in musical and vocal standards, could not compete with the operatic quality of most of the other Barcelona productions. Santana Burgos concludes that Liern and Bray each in his own way offered "interpretations of Bizet's work that appropriate the original *Carmen* and translate it as much into [Spanish] culture as into the [Spanish] language."[32]

SALVADOR GRANÉS'S PARODY: *CARMELA*

The summer hiatus of 1890 did not break *Carmen*'s momentum in Barcelona. The indefatigable Italia Georgio appeared yet again as the Spanish gypsy in an August production at the Teatro Gayarre, featuring the Tivoli's sets. Barcelona's apparently inexhaustible appetite for the work, coupled with its high profile in Madrid, made the appearance of a burlesque or theatrical parody inevitable, given that the opera had already been lampooned in comic literary publications such as Madrid's *La avispa* as early as 1887. And so in the following winter, *Carmela* appeared. Written by the renowned parodist Salvador María

29. "Ecos teatrales," *La dinastía*, 10 April 1890, 2, 3; "Espectáculos: Tivoli," *Diario de Barcelona*, 12 April 1890, 4586.

30. "Teatros: Tivoli," *La vanguardia*, 13 April 1890, 5; "Espectáculos," *La dinastía*, 6 April 1890, 3.

31. "Ecos teatrales: Teatro del Tivoli," *La dinastía*, 14 April 1890, 3.

32. Santana Burgos, "Diálogos entre Francia y España," 285. "Desde una perspectiva más amplia, podríamos entender ambos libretos, en principio, como interpretaciones de la obra de Bizet que se apropiaron de la *Carmen* original y la desplazaron tanto hacia nuestra cultura como hacia nuestra lengua meta."

Granés, in collaboration with the composer Tomás Reig, *Carmela* was a one-act *parodia lírica* consisting of three tableaux.[33] It premiered in Barcelona on 24 January 1891 at the Principal Theater, followed by productions throughout the Iberian peninsula and in parts of Latin America within the following year, proving so popular that a second edition was published as late as 1901.[34] This work was composed at the height of the *género chico*'s reign in Spain's popular theaters, where the genre had dominated throughout the 1880s. Written and performed throughout the Spanish-speaking world, these *zarzuelas chicas* were irresistibly popular because of their one-act format, cheap ticket prices, and consistent reliance on topical humor. They were also the ideal vehicle for theatrical parody. Reig and Granés exploited the musical appeal of a *Carmen* parody, presenting clear references to Bizet's score alongside popular numbers from operas and *zarzuelas*.

The action of *Carmela* takes place in Madrid, the spiritual home of the *género chico* genre. Granés's lyric parody tells us much about Spanish responses to *Carmen*, as it normalizes many of the themes and characters that had appeared exotic in the French opera, and simultaneously integrates contemporary issues and nationalist debates into the fabric of the work. The basic plot and principal characters are retained, with some slight changes to their names: Carmela (a more colloquial form of Carmen) and Don José, Zuñiga, Micaëla, Frasquita, Escamón for Escamillo, and Lilas Patrás (which sounds like "you're going backwards") for Lillas Pastia. Apart from Carmela, the name changes involve wordplay, as exemplified by Escamón, a name that suggests a suspicious character or fraudster, undermining his claims to be a great and courageous bullfighter. The character of Micaëla is retained for her comic potential, but her lyrical sung numbers—those artifacts of the *opéra comique*—were dispensed with. While the work's eponymous heroine is depicted as a witty and appealing local type, José is made over into a peasant from Galicia in the distant rural north, the butt of every joke.

The generic structure provided for a comic play with sung numbers, which allowed Reig to articulate his fairly conventional *género chico* score with versions of all the key "Spanish" items from Bizet's opera. He avoided breaching copyright by relying on limited quotation of the most famous themes, presenting instantly recognizable incipits that rework parts of Bizet's score, and following them up with newly composed music in which thematic or rhythmic reminiscence reinscribed the relationship with the operatic original. Reig's quotations from the Bizet score are far more extensive than Meyer Lutz's references in *Carmen Up to Data*. The plot adheres to the opera in broad outline, inasmuch as

---

33. Salvador María Granés and Tomás (music) Reig, *Carmela: Parodia-lírica de la ópera "Carmen" en un acto y tres cuadros* (Madrid: Velasco, 1891). Manuscript vocal and full scores are held by the Sociedad General de Autores y Editores of Spain.

34. *Carmela* was produced in Barcelona by the Julián Romea company.

José releases Carmela from custody and is punished, then joins the smugglers, and finally loses her affection to the bullfighter.

As an operatic parody, *Carmela* picks up on certain details from the Bizet but is largely concerned with the content of the plot, resisting the temptation to make fun of the genre itself. A gentle dig at operatic convention may be inferred from the jealous exchange between José and Escamón that precedes their knife fight (tableau 2, scene 7), in which Escamón declares, "You have lost her love: I've already told you in speech, now I'll tell you in song, and you will understand it better."[35] Other theatrical allusions include multiple references to the *género chico* hit *La Gran Vía* and to the mid-nineteenth-century classic reworking of the Don Juan theme, *Don Juan Tenorio* by José Zorrilla.[36]

The action takes place in contemporary Madrid, as Granés implicitly rejects any reference either to gypsies or Seville and transforms both characters and subject matter to create a quintessentially local comedy. The soldiers become policemen (*guardias municipales*), characters who might typically appear in a *zarzuela*, while Carmela and her friends appear as *chulas madrileñas* who work in the tobacco factory. Granés sharpens this characterization by adding speech inflections of working-class Madrid to their dialogue. Carmela's sassy, sharp-witted character embodies the hybrid Andalusian–Madrid identity that emerged in the late nineteenth century as a result of internal migration and became a stereotype of theatrical representations of Spanish national character.

Whereas Bizet's (or perhaps Meilhac and Halévy's) Carmen was conceived as an exotic cipher and femme fatale, Carmela, like Liern's Carmen before her, is liberated from this marginal status. Neither Carmela nor any of her friends are represented as gypsies; they are instead working women, from an industry whose low pay forces involvement with smugglers. Carmela thus becomes a representative type of Spanish womanhood, gifted with *gracia*, her identity further marked by the use of the emerging urban Madrid argot that characterized the *chula*. This culturally specific identity enhances her dry, almost swaggering humor and differentiates Carmela and her friends from mere coquettes. Granés presents a comic theatrical version of the conditions of working-class life in the suburbs of the capital, a characterization that was part of the *género chico*'s undoubted appeal to Hispanic audiences, along with the cheap ticket prices.

Granés discusses contemporary working conditions with both a comic and a serious edge, as the policemen complain in the opening number about standing around in all weather for low pay,[37] and Carmela and the chorus of

35. Granés and Reig, *Carmela*, 30, "Perdiste su amor: / antes te lo he dicho hablado, / ahora lo diré cantado, / y lo entenderás mejor."

36. Alonso Zamora Vicente, "Asedio a 'Luces de Bohemia' primer esperpento de Ramón del Valle Inclán" (Biblioteca Virtual Miguel de Cervantes, 2002; Madrid: 1967), 23; accessed 14 August 2016, http://www.cervantesvirtual.com/nd/ark:/59851/bmcrb717.

37. Granés and Reig, *Carmela*, tableau 1, scene 1, "¡Rabia da! ¡voto va!"

chulas sing about wanting money and the difficulties of being a cigarette maker when the company supplies poor-quality tobacco to work with.[38] The women freely acknowledge their involvement in petty crime, including smuggling, and their desire to attach themselves to men with money, but simultaneously declare themselves to be "honorable girls."[39]

PRIMERAS	Cada cual de nosotras
	Tiene su apaño.
	No es extraño.
SEGUNDAS	Yo tengo novios marqueses.
PRIMERAS	Yo timo como el que más.
TERCERAS	Yo he estado presa seis meses.
TODAS	Me paece que semos muchachas honrás.
	Y así, de cuando en cuando,
	también metemos
	contrabando[40]

(Firsts: Every last one of us / has our trick. / It's nothing strange.
Seconds: I have marquis boyfriends.
Firsts: I swindle like anyone.
Thirds: I've been in jail for six months.
All: It seems to me we are honorable girls. / And as such, from time to time, / we also get mixed up in / smuggling.)

Carmela's big numbers provide opportunities for topical humor rather than exotic color, although they retain at least the opening phrases of Bizet's distinctive melodies. The Habanera uses one statement of the famous semitonal descent before departing from the Bizet, but also presents four bars of the major-mode second theme that accompanies "L'amour est enfant de Bohême" in the opera.[41] Granés's new text revolves around Carmela's preference for men with money over men with title, its inspired and rhythmic wordplay including the chorus:

CARMELA	Mas para mí
	es la cuestión
	que tengan dín,
	aunque no tengan don.[42]

---

38. Ibid., tableau 2, scene 1, "Carmela la bonita soy,"
39. Ibid., tableau 1, scene 3, no. 4, "Me paece que semos muchachas honrás." Note use of *chulo* argot.
40. Ibid., 12.
41. Ibid., tableau [cuadro] 1, scene 3, no. 4. "Cuando yo, columpiando el talle," marked "Tempo de Tango."
42. Ibid., 12.

(More to me / is the question / whether they have money [dín], / although they have no title/talent [don])

The second tableau opens in Lilas Patrás's *merendero* (outdoor bar), with guests seated at tables and drinking, and evidence of a long night of partying. The "Chanson bohème" of the tavern scene retains the obligatory dancers, with Carmela singing of her love for the *juerga*, but the chorus conclude that first they need money. Despite this light mood, Granés transforms the second stanza into a political statement, as Carmela complains about the industrial problems in the tobacco industry, closing with the trenchant comment that the government provides them with worthless tobacco to work with.[43]

The parody of the "Chanson bohème" is given a special musical impact not only by starting with an almost literal quotation of sixteen bars from the original Bizet (including the instrumental introduction), but also because the chorus enters to the tune of musical references to Verdi's famous aria "La donna è mobile" (woman is fickle) from *Rigoletto*,[44] bound together by Reig's original material. This rich musical pastiche adds emphasis to the text, which successfully combines fun, wit, and a serious comment on contemporary conditions.

Even as Carmela is adopted or enfranchised as a true Spaniard, Granés renders José an outsider. In a complete reversal of cultural authority, José (and indeed his whole troop) become country bumpkins from the northern Spanish region of Galicia, figures of fun to the Madrid populace. Their status is represented musically by the inclusion of a *gallegada* in the score when they march onstage—a folk tune over a drone bass, imitating the sound of a Celtic bagpipe from Galicia—an effect that is also interpolated into the children's chorus.[45] In this parody, the *gallego* José represents the uncivilized periphery, having lost any vestige of superiority, while *madrileña* Carmela and her companions are located firmly in the centre.

José is caricatured in costume, accent, and vocabulary, portrayed as a rustic fool in an essentially comic role. If the *chula* character can be compared to the cockney on the nineteenth-century English stage, then the *gallego* is like the

43. Ibid., "Coro de chulas": El tabaco que el gobierno da / no es *na* [nada], 2; tableau 2, scene 1, no. 7. Tobacco workers engaged in frequent industrial struggles during this period, protesting against deteriorating working conditions caused by the government's provision of poor-quality tobacco (as mentioned in Granès's lyric), and the ever-present threat of mechanization. D. J. O'Connor, "Representations of Women Workers: Tobacco Strikers in the 1890s," in *Constructing Spanish Womanhood: Female Identity in Modern Spain*, ed. Victoria Lorée Enders and Pamela Beth Radcliff (Albany: State University of New York Press, 1999), 151–72.

44. From act 3 of Verdi's *Rigoletto*.

45. Granés and Reig, *Carmela*, tableau 1, scene 2, "Al relevo vienen ya."

Irishman, with a heavy brogue and slapstick stupidity. José's thick Galician accent, at times written into the script, provides a vivid contrast to the Madrid
argot that gives edge to Carmela's sharp wit. At their first encounter, Carmela
mockingly asks José if he is "*andaluz*," to which he responds in thickest accent—to her great amusement—that he is "*gallego*, though you wouldn't
know it."[46] This is a subtle reversal of Mérimée's novella, which also plays on
regional identity when Carmen claims to be from Navarre, like José.

Like Liern before him, Granés noted José's affectation of nobility, which
made him appear ridiculous to a Spanish audience, allowing Zuñiga to make
fun of José's claim that Gothic blood ran in his veins and insistence that he
be addressed as "don."[47] José's comic dialogue with Micaëla, in which they
discuss his grandmother in the village, reveals the grinding poverty of his
true origins, as illustrated by her pride in telling the neighbors that he had
stolen chickens for her as a boy.[48] Granés's stage direction indicates that
this scene should be played in a highly romantic, but *bufo* (in the style of a
comic opera), manner,[49] and Micaëla provides emotional bathos as well as an
added dimension to the regional comedy. José's role is largely relegated to
comedy, and he does not sing until near the end of the second tableau, when
he engages in a short recitative exchange with the bullfighter. He is even
denied the dignity of killing his faithless lover at the end of the show. After
an extended sung argument with Carmela in the third and final tableaux,
José draws a large knife and chases her around the stage, but it is Escamón,
emerging dazed from the bullring with his drawn sword still in his hand,
who accidentally runs Carmela through. The entire cast rises (including the
murdered Carmela) to close the work with a chorale-like Amen, after which
Carmela falls dead again.

Granés reserves serious treatment only for the *fiesta nacional*, without
exempting the bullfighter from ridicule. Although Escamón is mocked as
a self-aggrandizing but cowardly torero, his role is given greater dramatic
weight by an extended monologue, which dominates the second tableau.
The famous chorus greets his entry, accompanied by his *cuadrilla*, decked
out in full bullfighting regalia (tableau 2, scene 3). The music stays close to
Bizet's popular march, but ends with a reference to the Spanish Royal March,
matched with the more politically charged lyric "viva la Constitución" (long

46. Ibid., 13. "Jallego, / pero nun se me conoce."
47. Meilhac and Halévy have José respond to Zuñiga's question "Vous êtes Navarrais?"
with the fulsome reply "Et vieux chrétien. Don José Lizzarabengoa, c'est mon nom"
(act 1, scene 3).
48. Granés and Reig, *Carmela*, tableau 1, scene 5.
49. Ibid., "Toda esta escena romántica por todo lo alto, pero muy en bufo."

live the constitution).[50] Despite the claim that he is a brave torero ("Torero soy y bravo"), both Escamón and the chorus refer to his lack of prowess in the arena.[51] And Escamón replies, with swaggering movements, that when confronted by the bull, he is so afraid he never knows who will kill whom. The effective comic contrast between the uncertain lyric and the combined verve of music and action is reversed in the lengthy monologue in which Escamón describes an ideal bullfight. The directions indicate that the actor must simultaneously caricature every incident of the bullfight in mime, while the text itself is skillfully versified, combining technical description with colorful popular expressions, like the best call of a local sporting fixture. This moving speech presents a dramatic and gripping description of the *corrida* (bullfight), and imparts a sense of deep respect and affection. After describing the stirring chords of the military band and the shower of hats into the arena that mark the end of the fight, Escamón utters these closing lines:

> There is no show like it.
> We will remain free and brave
> while we conserve here
> this *fiesta nacional.*
> Anyone who is not convinced of this,
> does not deserve to see the sun,
> is neither honorable nor Spanish;
> indeed ... has no shame![52]

Despite the mime and slapstick surrounding the narration of the bullfight, this is an ardent defense of bullfighting in the context of contemporary debates surrounding the *fiesta nacional* and the nature of modern Spanish identity.[53]

50. The cry of "[l]ong live the constitution," while patriotic and liberal, could be construed as a contentious statement in late-nineteenth-century Barcelona. It could also be seen as a distant echo of "la liberté!" which concludes the second act of Bizet's opera.

51. Granés and Reig, *Carmela*, tableau 2, scene 3, "A ver si en la función, / le dan un revolcón, / que por lo regular / es lo que à Escamón / le suele pasar" (Let's see if Escamón gets tossed again at today's fight, because that's what usually happens).

52. Ibid., "No hay espectáculo igual. / Libres y bravos seremos / mientras aquí conservemos / esta fiesta nacional. / Quien de ello no se convenza / ni merece ver el sol, / ni es honrado, ni español; / vamos ... ¡ni tiene vergüenza!"

53. Despite the popularity of bullfighting in late-nineteenth-century Barcelona, there was also a lively debate in opposition to the practice, especially among early Catalanists. We are grateful to Francesc Cortès for pointing this out.

The third tableau is set at the bullring, and it follows Bizet's finale in being through-composed, with no spoken dialogue at all, effectively heightening the dramatic tension of the denouement. Extensive recitative-like passages alternate with more lyrical utterances, melodrama, and occasional quotations of Bizet's famous fate motive.

Despite Escamón's monologue about the bullfight, there are no heroes in Granés's *Carmela*. True to his name, Escamón was booed out of the bullring for his ineptitude and failure to kill the bull cleanly. Granés, like Liern before him, used the characterization of Carmela and José to declare cultural ownership of this adopted work, and to subvert issues of dominance in the relationship, which lie at the heart of the French original. *Carmela* distilled the Spanish core of *Carmen*, shifting power and cultural authority by using the weapon of humor. In this work that appeared at the height of the *género chico*'s popularity, Granés employed stereotypes that were to persist in the *zarzuela* for the next quarter of a century. As he reinscribed the North/South divide on a different axis, the play of insider and outsider—or civilized center making fun of exoticized peripheries—gained layers of complexity, as Catalan audiences laughed both with and at the Madrid characters and the Galician local color.

While taking its cue from the spate of *Carmen* performances in Barcelona, Granés and Reig's parody was intended for the broader *género chico* market, and within weeks of its successful premiere a Madrid production was in preparation. By the spring it was already attracting audiences in Seville, Granada, and other provincial centers, and it was staged at the start of the summer season at Madrid's Teatro Apolo (the acknowledged temple of the *género chico*), where audiences embraced the work and Granés and Reig took many curtain calls. In *La España artística* the reviewer claimed that Reig's wonderful score "glosses Bizet's principal themes with such mastery and ingenuity that the public could not stop applauding it." He also praised Granés's capacity to follow the most decisive moments of the opera's plot and highlight them with *gracia*, yet without becoming grotesque.[54] In the months that followed, *Carmela* attracted new audiences in cities throughout Spain, as well as in Havana, Buenos Aires, and Mexico City.

This first intense phase of Spanish engagement with *Carmen* exposes the fault lines between the French literary and theatrical vision of Spain, and Spaniards' representations of their own culture. The varying productions, translations, and adaptations that emerged in Madrid and Barcelona between

---

54. "Los teatros de Madrid: Apolo," *La España artística*, 8 June 1891, 2. *Carmela*'s progress through Spain and Latin America is chronicled in the pages of *La España artística*.

late 1887 and the early 1890s attempted to reconcile Bizet's *espagnolade* with elements of *costumbrista* theater, and render it more palatable to Spanish audiences. These were no ephemeral developments, but pointed the way forward for future stagings—and indeed impersonations of the protagonist—that were to evolve over the next quarter of a century.

PART III

Authenticating *Carmen* in the Age
of Verismo (1889–1908)

CHAPTER 5

☙

Gypsy Primitivism and the Rise of Emma Calvé

In February 1887 Paris thrilled to a new sensation in Spanish entertainment, so lively and authentic that a critic gushed, "the Parisians will give up going to Seville ... and the Sevillians will have to come to Paris."[1] More than just a stage show, "La Feria de Sevilla" at the Nouveau Cirque recreated the atmosphere of the celebrated Seville April Fair, which had become a significant tourist attraction since its foundation by the local council in 1847 (see Figure 5.1). In a program featuring *estudiantinas*, flamenco singers, clowns, and a real-life bullfight staged with *becerros* (bull calves) in the venue's drained swimming tank, the highlight was the voluptuous and provocative Spanish dance performed by a troupe starring the young Carmencita Dausset and her cross-dressed partner Trinidad Huertas "la Cuenca."

Dausset had started with this troupe as a child, first appearing in Paris as the "pearl of Seville" in 1884 at the age of sixteen. After a year in Paris she headlined a season in Barcelona during the 1888 Exposition, followed by another Paris season in 1889. That same year she made her transatlantic debut, finding success as a touring artist in the United States. Carmencita (as she became known) was the harbinger of the 1890s wave of Spanish entertainment that was to delight Paris and become a staple of variety programs in cosmopolitan centers of Europe, the Americas, and beyond. The 1890s was the great decade of the global music-hall industry and its celebrity stars, the courtesan performers. Once she had launched her New York career, Carmencita became perhaps the first of the Spanish dancers to dominate the stages of the Belle

---

1. Un monsieur de l'orchestre [Arnold Mortier], "La Soirée théâtrale: La Foire de Séville," *Le Figaro* (Paris), 8 March 1887, 3.

Figure 5.1 Adrien Marie, "La 'feria de Sevilla' au Nouveau Cirque, spectacle réglé par M. Agoust," reproduced in *Le Théatre illustré* [1887]. Performers from left to right: Mlle Carmencita, Mlle Cuenca, the clown Tony Grèce.
Credit: Private collection.

Époque, followed by Carolina "la Belle" Otero, Rosario "la Belle" Guerrero, and La Tortajada (Consuelo Tamayo Hernández). Their extraordinary popularity was part of a craze for Spanish dance and culture that was felt from the visual arts to the operatic stage.

But the context in which Carmencita appeared at the Nouveau Cirque tells us much about changing Parisian tastes in Spanish entertainment. The Catalan impresario who put the 1887 show together—and who later founded the Moulin Rouge and the Paris-Olympia music halls—discovered one of the keys to success in the competitive world of exotic spectacle: he won recognition for the authenticity of his production. By recruiting this new style of dancer directly from Spain, rather than from among the versatile *grisettes* of Montmartre or Batignolles, Josep Oller demonstrated his sound instinct for the Parisian market, simultaneously ensuring that his Spanish show included songs that were already popular in Parisian salons. Oller's production evoked the aural and visual markers of Spanishness, from castanets and guitars to oranges, cigarettes, and bullfighters, accompanied by drinks from the "cellars of the famous Lillas Pastia," a description that indicates how, by 1887, *Carmen* had become a standard point of reference for anything reminiscent of Seville.[2] From 1889, however, this idealized and somewhat simplified image of Spain—focused on Seville—expanded eastward to include Granada and the deeper shadow of its Arab legacy and gypsy culture.

With the Exposition Universelle of 1889 came a fresh and "primitive" style of performance, courtesy of the gypsies from Granada, the emergence of which was to shape the international representation of Spanish dance into the early twentieth century. And so the stage was set for a transformation in the look and sound of *Carmen* that was inflected by the 1890s styling of the Spanish entertainers in the music halls. The great operatic Carmen of this era, Emma Calvé, brought these elements together and added a crucial ingredient: the influence of the new Italian verismo school.

FLAMENCO AND NEW PROJECTIONS OF THE SPANISH GYPSY AT THE 1889 EXPOSITION UNIVERSELLE

The Exposition Universelle, which ran from May to October 1889, gave new impetus to Parisians' interest in all things Spanish. This great event, the fourth of five held in Paris in the later nineteenth century, celebrated both the centenary of the French Revolution and the progress of modernity, with exhibits in all fields of commercial and artistic endeavor (including the construction of the Eiffel Tower). It also featured a large colonial exhibit, which introduced mass audiences to world cultures, particularly those of France's colonies. Here, ethnography intersected with theater and entertainment, and visitors to the Exposition could undertake an imaginary journey to foreign lands, not least among them France's southern neighbor.[3]

> Do you love Spain? ... They have put it everywhere ... and I'm not complaining; it is such a beautiful country, so colorful and picturesque!
>
> The bullfights, the *fêtes espagnoles* (Spanish fiestas) at the Cirque d'hiver, the gypsies at the Exposition just carry us across the Pyrenees.[4]

Gaston Paulin thus summed up the superabundance of Spanish-themed activity not only within the Exposition but in numerous accompanying events as well. The French fascination with the picturesque brutality of bullfighting was indulged by the erection of two bullrings, one a commercial enterprise in the

2. Un monsieur de l'orchestre, "La Soirée théâtrale."

3. Annegret Fauser, *Musical Encounters at the 1889 Paris World's Fair*, Eastman Studies in Music (Rochester, NY: University of Rochester Press, 2005), esp. 139–278.

4. Gaston Paulin, "L'Espagne à Paris," *Le Guide musicale* 35, no. 33 (1889): 206.

Bois de Boulogne, and the other funded by the Spanish government next to the Exposition site on the Champs de Mars. Controversy over animal cruelty dogged the popularity of the French *corrida* even though the bulls were not killed, and by 1890 bullfighting was banned, having been declared a "socially dangerous" leisure activity on a par with café billiards and illegal gambling.[5]

The fascination with tauromachy in 1889 even found its way inside the theaters, which were capitalizing on the crowds visiting Paris for the Exposition. Oller remounted his 1887 success at the Nouveau Cirque, this time without Carmencita: *La Foire de Séville* instead featured La Cuenca playing all the (human) roles in a mimed bullfight, in a program bursting with local color reminiscent of the opening scenes of *Carmen*'s act 4. The Cirque d'hiver offered Spanish regional dance and popular song, with a cast of hundreds, while a more elevated audience could enjoy a light classical program at the ten Soirées Espagnoles held at the Théâtre du Vaudeville in late July. Under the auspices of a Spanish impresario and Catalan music director, these Spanish evenings boasted luminaries like Pablo Sarasate, Isaac Albéniz, and Elena Sanz (in national costume), singing items from contemporary French operas and well-known *zarzuelas*. Bizet's "Habanera" was performed alongside the most famous habanera of the *género chico* genre—Federico Chueca's "Tango de la Menegilda" from *La Gran Vía* (1886)—and the "Coro de las mujeres fumando" (Chorus of smoking women) from Manuel Fernández Caballero's *zarzuela Los sobrinos del Capitán Grant* (1877).[6] Tableaux presenting Spanish customs were also featured, in which popular Spanish songs and dances, including *jotas* and *seguidillas*, were performed by an orchestra and the inevitable *estudiantina*, which played an integral role in all these Spanish-themed spectacles—even the taverna at the Spanish national pavilion featured an *estudiantina sévillane* as its house band.[7] Meanwhile, Bizet's *Carmen* played at the Opéra-Comique on average once a week for the duration of the Exposition, achieving its 400th performance on 13 September.[8]

The craze for all things Spanish was only heightened by the appearance of a troupe of Andalusian gypsies, who joined the program at the Grand Théâtre de l'Exposition in mid-July.[9] Exotic dance became a central attraction of the great fairs with the 1889 Exposition Universelle, and such performances

5. Adrian Shubert, *Death and Money in the Afternoon: A History of the Spanish Bullfight* (New York: Oxford University Press, 1999), 12–13, 34.

6. Albert Soubies and Paul Milliet, "Vaudeville," *Almanach des Spectacles* 16 (1889): 39–40; Montserrat Bergadá, "Les Pianistes catalans à Paris entre 1875 et 1925" (PhD thesis, Université François Rabelais, 1997), 58–60.

7. Geraldine Power, "Projections of Spain in Popular Spectacle and Chanson, Paris: 1889–1926" (PhD thesis, University of Melbourne, 2013), 19; Fauser, *Musical Encounters*, 261.

8. Fauser, *Musical Encounters*, 59, 79, 261, 267.

9. Ibid., 263.

spilled over from theatrical programming, to be integrated with the ethnographic exhibits from countries as varied as Java, Vietnam, and Egypt. These dancers from Africa and Asia not only looked the part but also danced to the unfamiliar sounds of music from their own lands.[10] The authenticity of the indigenous performers posed a challenge to the exotic spectacle that had long drawn the wealthy to elite theaters to enjoy an Orientalism safely packaged with familiar Western music and choreography.[11]

Parisian audiences may have felt entitled to claim a certain familiarity with Spanish dance, either in its high-art manifestations on the operatic stage or as popular entertainment in the *café-concerts*. However, this wave of Andalusian gypsies presented something new, the effects of which were to ripple through both elite and popular entertainment. Seville had long been the source of colorful and sundrenched images of Spanish culture in the European imagination, with the gypsy elided seamlessly into this world. As the 1800s drew to a close, however, the "primitive" aspects of this constructed Spanishness were increasingly privileged, and the focus shifted from Seville to the fringes of Granada, where the cave-dwelling gypsies of the Sacromonte were acclaimed as more "authentic" practitioners of their supposedly ancient culture. Despite its irrelevance to Carmen's scenario, Granada gained increasing prominence as a source of "authentic" Spanish color in the strategies of numerous artists who sought to stage the opera or impersonate its protagonist over the coming years.

After the failure of the original "Spanish" act engaged for the Grand Théâtre de l'Exposition, its impresario actually traveled to the caves in the hills around Granada to sign up some "authentic" gypsies (see Figure 5.2). The result was — sensation![12] In the context of contemporary preoccupations with provenance and cultural authenticity, this troupe achieved a certain status by purporting to represent "the 'true' musical Spain," in contrast to that translated into European concert music or commodified into the popular styles of the French *café-concert*.[13] Performing on a stage set designed to look like a *posada* (inn), they convinced that noted connoisseur of the musical exotic, Julien Tiersot, that they were behaving "as they do at home."[14]

The Granadine gypsies performed seated in a semicircle, the typical formation of a flamenco *cuadro* (troupe). Rather than being accompanied by the *estudiantina* and castanets so familiar to French audiences, their music

10. Ibid., 224–26.

11. Fauser refers to the 1880 Paris production of Verdi's *Aida,* for which extensive Egyptological research was undertaken. Ibid., 224.

12. *Europa y América* (15 July 1889), cited in Bergadá, "Les Pianistes catalans," 58.

13. Fauser, *Musical Encounters*, 216–18, 63.

14. Julien Tiersot, *Promenades musicales à l'Exposition* (Paris: Fischbacher, 1889), 277, quoted in Fauser, *Musical Encounters*, 266.

Figure 5.2 Mlle Pepa and M. Picheri dancing at the Exposition Universelle, Paris (1889), in "Exposition Universelle.—Les gitanes de Grenade au Champs-de-Mars.—La danse du Tango. (D'après nature, par M. Parys)," *Le Monde illustré* 33, no. 1692 (31 August 1889): cover.

was provided by several (male) guitarists, with the women contributing the *cante* (song), *palmas* (rhythmic clapping), and *jaleo* (calls of encouragement and praise). The dancers—La Pepa, Soledad, and, most notably, La Macarrona (Juana Vargas de las Heras)—were colorfully dressed in long skirts and shawls, with flowers in their hair. They rose singly or in pairs to perform in the space in front of the chairs. Some critics described them as "naturally graceful," while others saw their "primitive" contortions as earthy, their heel stamping often contrasted with the ethereal artificiality of Spanish ballet on the contemporary operatic stage.[15] Rodolphe Darzens and Catulle Mendès described the dancers twisting, leaping, and bending with feverish enthusiasm, their finger snapping reminiscent of the sound of crackling gunfire. Compared with the Arab belly dancers who were also exciting considerable interest in 1889, the gypsies employed their arms, legs, and bottoms, but did not engage their stomachs.[16] Their "strange and brutal" charm emanated from their "animality," as "young wild beasts, who play, who leap."[17] Jean Lorrain found La Maccarona's twisting and circling frankly reptilian, and perhaps even fiery: she was "more than a grass snake, a salamander."[18] For such writers, the dancers' attraction was inseparable from their apparent savagery, and comparison with wild or sensual animals was typical of nineteenth-century commentary on exotic women and prostitutes. It is no surprise, therefore, that such vocabulary had been applied to Carmen herself, first by Mérimée, but memorably in the intemperate reviews of 1875, in which Galli-Marié's hip-swaying come-hither behavior as Carmen was likened to a filly from the Cordoba studs. The visiting Spanish author Emilia Pardo Bazán noted that the spectators who were crazy about La Maccarona considered her to be "a houri, a Carmen."[19]

Critics considered the troupe of Granadine gypsies to be both primitive and authentic, describing them variously as "'racially pure'" and "wedded to the earth of the South."[20] Such claims were unqualified by any awareness that the style they were bringing to Paris was the evolving flamenco genre that had developed in the urban cafes of Madrid and Seville, or the *zambras* (shows and festivities) of Granada staged for foreign travelers in search of the exotic. A Spanish observer, horrified that Spain should be represented by the

---

15. For a detailed account of the music and dance of the Granadine gypsies, and indeed the range of Spanish music on offer, see Tiersot's first column in his series "Promenades musicales à l'Exposition" in *Le Ménestrel* 55, no. 35 (1 September 1889): 276–77. Fauser, *Musical Encounters*, 260, Guy Ducrey, "L'Andalouse et l'Almée: Quelques Danseuses "sauvages" aux Expositions universelles," in *Sociopoétique de la danse*, ed. Alain Montandon (Paris: Anthropos, 1998), 470, cited in Anne Décoret-Ahiha, *Les Danses exotiques en France 1880–1940* (Pantin: Centre national de la danse, 2004), 33.

16. Fauser, *Musical Encounters*, 264.

17. Rodolphe Darzens and Catulle Mendès, "Gitanas," *Les Belles du monde* (Paris: Plon, 1889), 24–25, cited in Décoret-Ahiha, *Les Danses exotiques*, 33, 34.

18. Jean Lorrain, "La Macaronna: Coins de l'Exposition," *L'Événement* (11 August 1889), cited in Décoret-Ahiha, *Les Danses exotiques*, 33.

19. Luis Sazatornil Ruíz and Ana Belén Lasheras Peña, "París y la españolada: Casticismo y estereotipos nacionales en las exposiciones universales (1855–1900)," *Mélanges de la Casa de Velázquez* 35, no. 2 (2005): 279.

20. Fauser, *Musical Encounters*, 263–64, quoting from article in *Le Petit Journal*.

repugnant display of a flamenco *cuadro*, complete with its *capitán*, decried the troupe as a "prostitution of the expansive and special life of Andalusia."[21]

It was the dancers, above all La Maccarona, who achieved a certain celebrity, attracting a glittering society crowd to the troupe's nightly performances. Arthur Pougin noted that all the personnel of the Opéra had attended the *gitanas'* show, and *première danseuse* Rosita Mauri had been seen more than once applauding Soledad and Maccarona with all her might, perhaps reflecting on how this sensational new Spanish dance would affect audience tastes for her own style.[22] The success of the gypsy dancers at the 1889 Exposition gave new life to the phenomenon of the Spanish dancer in the music halls, which enjoyed a golden era during the 1890s and developed into a hybrid and internationalized style.

SPANISH DANCERS AND COSMOPOLITAN MUSIC HALLS OF THE 1890S

Local entrepreneurs were quick to exploit Spanish dance's return to favor and 1890s Parisian music halls and *cafés-concerts* offered a packaged version of Spanish dance, which brought together familiar styles with carefully mediated elements of the newer and more "primitive" flamenco forms. If Belle Époque audiences fetishized female beauty and risqué sensuality, they especially appreciated such women in exotic guise, and the new generation of Spanish dancers was poised to step into the spotlight. Carmencita (Dausset), La Tortajada, Otero, and Guerrero were recognized first in Spain and Paris, then across the world, and carried the fashion for Spanish dance through the 1890s and right up to World War I. Over these two decades, they exploited, popularized, and modernized the stereotypical foreign image of Spanish women as sensual, inconstant femmes fatales, in the process both drawing on and influencing the most pervasive embodiment of this stereotype: Carmen.

Spanish critics and connoisseurs at times dismissed them as mere courtesans, and they were notorious for their extravagant jewels and exalted liaisons, a status perpetuated by the willingness of Parisian audiences to accept as a stage entertainer any woman who attained scandalous celebrity.[23]

21. Quoting Josep Lluís Pellicer from his 1891 account of the 1889 Paris Exposition. Sazatornil Ruíz and Lasheras Peña, "París y la españolada," 279.

22. Arthur Pougin, *Le Théâtre à l'Exposition Universelle de 1889* (Paris: Librairie Fischbacher, [1890]), 109, cited in Fauser, *Musical Encounters*, 266.

23. Enrique Gómez Carrillo, *Bailarinas* (Madrid: B. Rodríguez Serra, 1902), 73–74. Gómez Carrillo explains dismissively that even a performer who may have no skill to start with, after two months has learned to dance and sing, and will be applauded and showered in gold.

But these women were not without talent, and the most influential were Spanish by birth and training. Using Paris as the first stage in their international careers, they shaped a new form of Spanish dance for transatlantic audiences. These performers broke with the tradition of the dance troupe, and were billed as solo acts, although they often appeared with a featured dance partner, associated artists, and backing musicians, or starred in a freestanding *spectacle* (theatrical entertainment). Whether singing, dancing, or both, they performed with a variety of accompaniments. Otero appeared with an *estudiantina* in Paris and often toured with her own plucked-string ensemble. Costumed in Spanish style, these instrumentalists also provided *jaleo*, their cries and handclapping creating atmosphere on stage.[24] When seeking a more intimate effect, Tortajada—an accomplished musician—was able to accompany herself on guitar or mandolin.

Dance was the defining element of staged Spanishness in this era, but these performers often included song and mime in their "turns." Carmencita sang only reluctantly, but the young Otero opened her performances with a few vocal items, which she drew from contemporary popular music. She sang French chansons, songs by composers like Francesco Paolo Tosti and Iradier (especially his ever-popular "La paloma"), and numbers drawn from *zarzuelas*, especially *género chico* works such as *La Gran Vía*. Otero's singing lacked power and even her abundant charm could not make up for it with some critics, but in later years she studied voice more seriously. La Tortajada considered herself predominantly a singer, despite her awareness that foreign audiences demanded some "moves" from her to prove that she really was Spanish, describing such gestures as "un poquito de meneo" (a bit of hip swaying). Tortajada's performances encompassed extended lyric works, composed by her husband and manager, Ramón Tortajada, in which she sometimes played all the roles.[25] Characterizing the vocal style of Otero and Tortajada without the benefit of recordings is tricky, but contemporary accounts suggest a voice production somewhere between the less refined flamenco voices of the *cafés cantantes* and the light operetta sound of the *género chico* singer, which prefigured the *cuplé*.

As dancers, the Belle Époque stars developed a hybrid art, mediating for an international public what they had studied in Spain or performed to Spanish audiences early in their careers, adding inflections from the range of contemporary international dance styles. As the oldest of the four, Carmencita offered

24. One London critic described Otero dancing, "interspersed with cries," accompanied by "music supplied by half a dozen compatriots, male and female, who were seated on the stage, and urged their principals to still wilder courses by discordant screamings." "The Alhambra," *Morning Post* (London), 16 May 1899, 5.

25. Carmen de Burgos, *Confesiones de artistas*, (Madrid: V. H. de Sanz Calleja, [1910–1920]), 2:28.

a graceful and expressive style that 1890s observers found somewhat lacking in the Spanish fire of more modern exponents. Arthur Symons described her dance as "a more civilized modification of what is undoubtedly, in its essence, barbaric, oriental, animal."[26] The basic elements included dances that had been the mainstay of early-to-mid-nineteenth-century Spanish exoticism, like the *fandangos* and *cachuchas* of the *escuela bolera*; the *sevillanas* and *jotas* of regional dance; while Carmencita's pirouettes were a nod to the Romantic ballet. Contemporary fashion was incorporated in the form of high kicks, reminiscent of the can-cans still popular in Parisian music halls, and any movement of hips or belly was interpreted by critics as *danse du ventre* (or belly dance), at a time when versions of the sensual Middle Eastern dances proliferated on Western stages. By the twentieth century, the acts might include new arrivals like the Brazilian *maxixe* and the American cakewalk, and by 1913 both Otero and Guerrero were performing the Argentine tango.

Apart from the notes of passion and sensuality always looked for in Spanish dance, it was the use of the whole body that distinguished these dancers from their more "Western" counterparts, in whose performances the focus was squarely on their footwork. The essential feature was the *meneo*, described dreamily by Paulin as "the graceful and serpentine undulations of the hips, the voluptuous postures," which gave the choreographic figures a sense of infinity (see Figure 5.3).[27] Their employment of hip movements and the famous back arch were typical, but the characteristic arm movements known as *brazear* were key indicators of authenticity and Carmencita was praised for her "snake-like, rhythmical arms." We will see that Calvé studied this art in order to make herself a distinctive and more Spanish Carmen. In describing the transition from the *escuela bolera* dances with their *jotas* and castanets—stylized versions of which still featured on the polite stages of the opera theaters—to the flamenco-inflected dances of the 1890s music hall, one Spanish critic declared that with their exaggerated affectations, dancers like Otero had converted Spanish dance into the Oriental belly dance.[28] It was noted that Otero used such scandalous moves in Paris, although not in London, yet she, Tortajada, and Guerrero all engaged in the heel stamping and sudden swirling turns that were considered so distinctively Spanish. Non-Spanish writers rarely used the term flamenco to describe their dances, even in relation to Guerrero, who seems to have employed flamenco dance styles as a primitivizing and dramatic element in her act.

---

26. Arthur Symons, "Dancing as Soul Expression," *Forum* 66 (1921): 314.
27. Paulin, "L'Espagne à Paris," 206.
28. Kasabal, "Las bailarinas," *Blanco y negro*, 17 June 1899, 6.

Figure 5.3 La Belle Otero, photograph by Reutlinger (1890s).
Credit: Bibliothèque Nationale de France.

Perhaps the clearest indication of the influence of flamenco on these performers was in their costume. Apart from the jewels and haute couture gowns, they were all willing to dress in character for certain numbers or dramatic scenas, affecting colorful folkloric garb like the short Spanish skirt (but not necessarily eschewing the jewels!). The embroidered fringed shawl known as the *mantón de manila*—worn by the Granadine gypsies of 1889—became a common item of Spanish costume at this time, especially tied around the waist, or even as a garment in itself (as worn in mildly risqué postcards by figures like Guerrero and even Calvé). This fashion led to a clear change in Carmen's dress, as singers abandoned the tight bodice and short bolero-style jacket of Galli-Marié's 1875 costume in favor of the new gypsy look (see Figure 5.4).

CALVÉ AND *CARMEN* AT THE OPÉRA-COMIQUE

This evolving landscape of Spanish entertainment posed a challenge to Carmens at the Opéra-Comique, where Léon Carvalho was still director, upholding the performance traditions of that theater and concerned not to offend his audiences. The new styles in Spanishness were, however, embraced by the young Emma Calvé, who debuted in the title role in December 1892. If

(a)

Figure 5.4 (a) La Habanera, *Paris illustré*, 63 (16 March 1889): 169; (b) Elena Sanz as Carmen, photograph by Pirou, in V. Emile-Michelet, "Une vie de diva: Elena Sanz," *Le Théâtre* 20 (August 1899): 24; (c) Georgette Leblanc as Carmen, photograph by Boyer, in Arsène Alexandre, "Mademoiselle Georgette Leblanc de l'Opéra-Comique," *Le Théâtre* 14 (February 1899): 16.
Credit: (a) Private collection; (b) and (c) State Library of Victoria.

Galli-Marié's Carmen had been viewed as naturalistic to the point of provocation, then Calvé introduced a different kind of realism. Her Carmen found such favor on the international circuit that she was forever identified with Bizet's gypsy and audiences accepted her interpretation as a benchmark well into the new century.

Chiefly associated with French and Italian opera during her early career, Calvé nevertheless claimed a Spanish heritage years before attempting Bizet's masterpiece. Calvé first declared herself to be Spanish (and six years younger than her actual age) when interviewed in the journal *Paris-Artiste* in

(b)

Figure 5.4 Continued.

January 1885, soon after her engagement by the Théâtre-Italien for its 1885 production of *Aben-Hamet* (1884). This new work by Théodore Dubois was based on Chateaubriand's novel of medieval Granada, *Les Aventures du dernier Abencérage* (1826). *Paris-Artiste* reported that Calvé had been born in Madrid to a Spanish father and French mother, that she had spent all her childhood in the "country of serenades and castanets," that her sister was a famous singer in Russia, and that Calvé was Paris's new star.[29] Although Calvé was indeed

29. Jean Contrucci, *Emma Calvé la diva du siècle* (Paris: Albin Michel, 1989), 92–93. Contrucci cites *Paris-Artiste* 47 (23 January 1885) as containing this article along with a glorious portrait of the beautiful singer.

Figure 5.4 Continued.

destined to become a star, none of her other claims can be substantiated. Indeed, in subsequent interviews Calvé claimed a Spanish mother and a French father.

Calvé was in fact born to French parents in the Cévennes in southern France, but her family spent four years living in a rural area of northern Spain during her early childhood. Although Calvé later identified publicly with her origins and settled in the Cévennes, she seems to have claimed Spanish ancestry as a young singer seeking to bolster her distinction and allure just as Spain was coming back into vogue. As a child she had learned Spanish, and her "southern" appearance further facilitated her assumption of this exotic background. In 1905 Enrique Gómez Carrillo, critic and connoisseur of Spanish dancers in Paris, described Calvé with "her large eyes full of languor, ... hair of dark silk, ... lips of geranium, and ... slender waist," most truly herself when clad, like Carmen, in a *mantilla*, with high comb and carnations in her hair.[30] Calvé could not have known in 1885 that Carmen was to become the signa-ture role of her career, and a more immediate explanation is suggested by the opera in which Calvé made her Paris debut, as Aben-Hamet's Christian sweet-heart, Bianca. In preparing for this role, Calvé immersed herself in the me-dieval world of Moorish life in the Alhambra and the reconquest of Spain, a fascination she again indulged when her preparation for *Carmen* took her to Granada early in the following decade.[31]

Calvé's career started slowly in the 1880s: after her operatic debut at the Théâtre de la Monnaie in Brussels and a few undistinguished roles in Parisian theaters, she sought new opportunities for study and perfor-mance in Italy in the latter half of the decade. There she discovered the great actress Eleanora Duse and began to follow her career, full of admi-ration for her spontaneity, her sincerity, and the intensity of her style. She was especially impressed by Duse's Santuzza in the original Giovanni Verga play of *Cavalleria rusticana*.[32] Continuing to take singing lessons, Calvé was simultaneously building her own reputation as an opera singer, achieving success in Rome in early 1889 in the role of Leïla in Bizet's *Les Pêcheurs de perles*.

In the meantime she extended her familiarity with Spaniards and Spanish culture. Calvé spent spring and early summer 1889 in Paris and may have seen some of the Spanish acts surrounding the Exposition. More impor-tantly, she enjoyed a close friendship with Elena Sanz. Both were contracted for the season of Théâtre-Italien at the Gaieté, during which Calvé impressed Parisian audiences with her greatly improved operatic performance, opening the season as Leïla in Bizet's *Les Pêcheurs*. Her hardwon Parisian success was applauded from a box by Sanz, and later that week they performed together at a private party.[33] This collaboration provides a possible context for one of

30. Enrique Gómez Carrillo, "Carmen," *Blanco y negro*, 11 March 1905, 17.

31. In her memoirs she describes reading and rereading the Chateaubriand novel, hardly sleeping, and dreaming of Granada, the Alhambra, and Boabdil. Calvé gives the date as 1883, but the work was not premiered until December 1884. Emma Calvé, *Sous tous les ciels j'ai chanté* (Paulhe, France: Lune de papier, [1940] 2004), 18.

32. Steven Huebner, "La Princesse Paysanne du Midi," in *Music, Theater, and Cultural Transfer: Paris, 1830–1914*, ed. Annegret Fauser and Mark Everist (Chicago and London: University of Chicago Press, 2009), 366–67. For a brief review of Calvé's early career, see also Karen Henson, *Opera Acts: Singers and Performance in the Late Nineteenth Century* (Cambridge: Cambridge University Press, 2015), 154.

33. Fourcaud, "Musique," *Le Gaulois* (Paris), 21 April 1889, 3; "Ce qui se passe: Échos de Paris," *Le Gaulois* (Paris), 26 April 1889, 1.

Calvé's (undated) anecdotes, in which she describes the two singers having a bit of fun while singing Spanish songs together:

> One day it occurred to us to try our luck in true Bohemian fashion. We disguised ourselves as wandering ballad singers and went out into the streets of Paris, to see whether we could not earn some pennies for the poor. We were both young and not ugly! Guitar in hand, scarf on head, off we went in search of adventure.

Failing to find an appreciative audience in the streets, Sanz suggested they accept an invitation to the Spanish Embassy, so they dressed up and sang for their social equals, telling their story to everyone's amusement. Sanz's access to Franco-Spanish high society can only have benefited her young friend, who may also have learned from Sanz's skill and charm in performing Spanish songs with simple accompaniment (Calvé's memoirs are notoriously vague and frequently inaccurate; sadly, she does not clarify which of them played the guitar, although it is more likely to have been Sanz).[34]

In 1890 Calvé began to reap the rewards of her persistence and hard work. Celebrated by Italian audiences for her dramatic interpretation of Santuzza in Mascagni's sensational first opera *Cavalleria rusticana*, this Italian success finally opened the doors of the Opéra-Comique, as Carvalho was keen to cash in on the novelty and likely popularity of Mascagni's new work. After delicate negotiations, Calvé was contracted to perform Santuzza, with another role to be selected by mutual agreement. In January 1892 Calvé's Santuzza introduced Paris audiences to her veristic realism, modeled on Duse's "naturalist," psychologized approach.[35] Although the critics disliked Mascagni's opera and resented its (foreign) presence on the Opéra-Comique's subsidized stage, Calvé herself received high praise. Seen as a carrier of the living tragic traditions of Italy, she portrayed Santuzza with a depth of truth, passion, and color not seen since Galli-Marié.[36] She was already being viewed as a possible successor to the original Carmen, who had retired only in 1887, and had last been heard at the Opéra-Comique at the Bizet celebration in 1890. Calvé's own accession to the role was announced in June 1892, and she was to project her newly minted version of Bizet's gypsy in contrast to Galli-Marié's much beloved interpretation.

Calvé's various narratives of her creation of Carmen dramatize her desire to overthrow tired convention in favor of a more "authentic" and modern representation both of Spanishness and the character herself. The details may

---

34. Emma Calvé, *My Life*, trans. Rosamond Gilder (New York and London: D. Appleton, 1922), 174–76.

35. Henson, *Opera Acts*, 155.

36. Contrucci, *Emma Calvé*, 136–42. Contrucci is citing the contemporary press.

vary slightly between contemporary press reports, the different volumes of her memoirs, and later biographical accounts, but more important than these historical discrepancies is that Calvé's construction of a sustained narrative around Carmen indicates a conscious campaign to claim authority in the role. Steven Huebner observes that "for Calvé ... an authentic performance was a conflation of research, life experience, and basic character,"[37] and despite her later disavowal of the character as antipathetic, it is clear that Calvé projected her identification with the gypsy in order to be recognized as the definitive Carmen of her age.[38]

Calvé constructed her new Carmen from several key elements: the physicality of the role, in gesture and movement; the look of the character, through novel costuming; and her vocal characterization. Around each of these she wove her narrative, an idiosyncratic mixture of claims that her Spanish blood and upbringing gave her an instinctive understanding of the role with an almost ethnographic commitment to painstaking research in her quest for authenticity. Calvé's thorough preparation began with her reading and rereading not only the libretto but also Mérimée's text. She wrote of the "intense concentrated effort" required to learn a new role, of her need to study "the character, the play, the period, in order to form an idea of the opera as a whole."[39] She also advocated what she termed the "absorption of one's personality in a rôle," to the extent that she quoted her family declaring, "'You are a stranger to us'" when they were confronted with the singer during this process.[40]

In summer 1892, Calvé embarked on a journey to Spain "for the purpose of acquiring the right local color," visiting Madrid, Avila, and Granada.[41] The French press reported that she had also visited Seville, that classic destination for people seeking out the true Carmen, but it was clear that Granada was her main goal.[42] Her choice of Andalusian destination was undoubtedly influenced by the celebrity of the Granadine gypsies at the 1889 Exposition,

---

37. Huebner, "La Princesse Paysanne du Midi," 372.

38. "I have often been asked whether Carmen is my favorite role. Indeed, it is not! I adore Bizet's music, but the character is, on the whole, antipathetic to me. Yet I have been a prisoner to that opera.... Carmen has only two redeeming qualities. She is truthful, and she is brave." Calvé, My Life, 83.

39. Ibid., 261–62.

40. Ibid., 256–57.

41. Hermann Klein, Great Women-Singers of My Time (London: George Routledge & Sons, 1931), 153; Georges Girard, Emma Calvé: La Cantatrice sous tous les ciels (Millau, France: Éditions Grans Causses, 1983), 252. Girard's Chronology suggests that Calvé was approached by the Opéra-Comique to sing Carmen in August 1891, and that she traveled to Spain during September, before singing Mascagni's L'amico Fritz in Rome in October, but La Presse did not announce her debut as Carmen at the Opéra-Comique until June 1892 and Contrucci confirms this timeline. "Courrier des Théatres," La Presse (Paris), 12 June 1892, 4.

42. "Théatres et Concerts," Le Journal des débats, 1 October 1892, 4.

performers who had reshaped the French image of "authentic" Spanish gypsy style as primitive and mystic. Calvé was not the first opera singer to seek authenticity south of the Pyrenees, but the breadth and focus of her study tour helped her create a unique and integrated characterization. Taking copious notes, Calvé attended bullfights, ventured into crowded alleyways, sought out the celebrated gypsy cavedwellings of Granada's Sacromonte district, and observed the women "at their work in the cigarette factories."[43] The press reported that in Granada Calvé learned from the gypsies "how to dance, how to do her hair; [and they] unveiled to her the mysteries of the tarot and of knife play," whetting Parisians' appetites for an "altogether remarkable" Carmen.[44]

Perhaps the keynote of Calvé's study tour in Granada was her engagement with the manner in which the gypsies comported themselves. Attending a gypsy dance spectacle in Granada, staged for tourists, Calvé registered not only the details of their dress but also their posture and gestures. As the young women danced in groups and solo, including fan dances, she noted their "natural pride," something she ascribed to an awareness of the ancientness of their race. She wrote in her notebook "don't forget that demeanor for Carmen."[45] In her notes she remarked on the distinction between Spanish gypsies and Montmartre bohemians, with their "exaggerated hip-swaying," who were so often used as a model by would-be operatic Carmens. Calvé described the beauty of the true gypsy gait as "lively, supple, nimble, light, free, harmonious."[46] Despite spending only a few short weeks in Spain, she claimed to have learned "flamenco" in Granada from a certain Lola, particularly the characteristic arm movements known as *brazear*, which she described as the arms and hand "twirling" around the head, the waist, and the length of the body.[47]

In her 1922 memoir, Calvé added a childhood anecdote to her narrative of study and ethnographic observation, a story that allowed her to claim an underlying "natural" flair for impersonating a gypsy. She relates that one day she followed a band of gypsies from her Basque village, staying with them until nightfall.[48] "Nothing about the gypsies enchanted me as much as their songs and dances. I positively thrilled with delight at the sound of the throbbing, rhythmic music."[49] When her family arrived to take her home, they found her "dancing and singing in the midst of the gypsy band, like a true *gitanella*."[50] Calvé continued,

43. Girard, *Emma Calvé*, 44, 252; Calvé, *My Life*, 81, 257; Contrucci, *Emma Calvé*, 165.
44. "Théatres et Concerts," *Le Journal des débats*, 1 October 1892, 4.
45. Contrucci, *Emma Calvé*, 166.
46. Girard, *Emma Calvé*, 51.
47. Contrucci, *Emma Calvé*, 166.
48. Calvé, *My Life*, 3, 10.
49. Ibid., 11–12.
50. Ibid., 13.

Was it because of this that, when I came to act Carmen, I never needed to be taught the dances and gestures of the Spanish gypsies? Was it because of these early years in Spain that I seemed to know by instinct how to carry the shawl, how to walk and move and dance, when I found myself impersonating the law-less *gitana* of Bizet's famous opera?[51]

This fascination with contemporary gypsy performance was increasingly important for an Opéra-Comique Carmen who could not avoid comparison with the Spanish dancing stars of the popular Parisian stage.

Despite consulting with Galli-Marié, especially about the right way to play the card scene, Calvé still sought to distinguish her new Carmen from the one consecrated by association with Bizet. She dramatized this quest in recollections of the stormy rehearsal process, marked by her insistence on being permitted to enact a novel conception of the role:

"How do you expect me to imitate Galli?" I protested. "She was small, dainty, an entirely different build. I am big. I have long arms. It is absurd for me to imitate any one but the gypsies themselves!"

Whereupon, I showed them the true dance of the *gitanas*, with its special use of arms and hands—a manner of dancing for which the Spaniards have invented the expression "el brazear."[52]

Always framing her arguments over production style as a battle for authenticity, Calvé never hesitated to use her Spanish experiences to promote her interpretation of Carmen. Her biographer, Georges Girard, quotes an unnamed American critic who questioned Calvé's studied failure to deny press stories about her association with gypsies, declaring that although it helped her create an illusion for her public, her performance was in fact quite distinct from the uncouth mediocrity of the standard Spanish gypsy dancer. He ascribed her uniquely dynamic take on the role to a devoted study of Mérimée, which had enabled her to create a complete personality from her own imagination and her own artistic composition.[53] But perhaps this author just succumbed to another of her compelling narratives.

Calvé explained how she leavened her innovations with a degree of historical and artistic perspective, stimulated by advice from Bizet's widow, with whom she had discussed the role before embarking for Spain. The singer already had the paintings of Velázquez in her sights, but Geneviève Straus-Bizet's recommendation of Goya's *majas* led her to spend hours in

51. Ibid., 13–14.
52. Ibid., 81.
53. Girard, *Emma Calvé*, 46.

contemplation of the most characteristic Spanish art, taking advantage of the recent resurgence in interest that led to an increase in the number of Goya's paintings on public display in Madrid galleries.[54] French collectors had been gathering Spanish art since the Napoleonic period, but the last decade of the century saw an increasing focus on Goya's portraits of women, distinguished by sensual detail (as in the portrayal of the fabrics they wore) and vibrant color seen to "breathe modernity as well as life into these pictures."[55] Goya's *majas* and *majos* just predated the period in which Mérimée set the original story of Carmen, so when singers like Calvé sought their authenticity in Mérimée, Goya could serve as an appropriate model for their visual style. Calvé was so taken with Goya's famous painting *La maja vestida* that she ordered an outfit in the same style: a dress of pale yellow satin and a mauve bolero covered in fine embroidery, finished with an ivory lace mantilla.[56] She intended this costume for act 4 of the opera. In the years that followed, singers increasingly presented themselves as Carmen in "authentic" costumes purchased in Spain and inspired by Spanish painting, culture, and fashion. Back in Paris, Calvé wore this Goyesque ensemble at a soirée hosted by Mme Straus-Bizet, during which she sang several scenes from the opera, winning over her audience with her freshness of approach and vocal command of the role.[57]

In the earlier part of the opera, Calvé renounced the bolero and short skirt used since Galli-Marié in favor of a costume that featured the *mantón de manila* that was fashionable among Spanish society ladies at the time (see Figure 5.5).[58] For the exotic set piece of the "Chanson bohème" she abandoned the traditional castanets (which were less typical of flamenco than of regional dances) for the startling innovation of a shawl dance, which she claimed to have learned in Spain, although this apparently left the Opéra-Comique's opening night audience indifferent.[59] She also adopted a coiffure typical among the gypsies she had visited, which focused on the use of comb and flowers rather than elaborate kiss-curls. Calvé thus distinguished herself visually from Galli-Marié's authoritative take on the role. When it came to fitting her novel conception of the role into the Opéra-Comique's production, sparks were bound to

54. Calvé, *Sous tous les ciels*, 73; Contrucci, *Emma Calvé*, 165; Girard, *Emma Calvé*, 43.

55. For an authoritative survey of responses to Goya's work, see Nigel Glendinning, *Goya and His Critics* (New Haven and London: Yale University Press, 1977), 16, 122. For a more general consideration of the French interest in Spanish art, see Gary Tinterow, Geneviève Lacambre, et al, *Manet/Velázquez: The French Taste for Spanish Painting* (New York: Metropolitan Museum of Art; New Haven & London: Yale University Press, 2003).

56. Girard, *Emma Calvé*, 43–44.

57. Contrucci, *Emma Calvé*, 169.

58. Calvé, *My Life*, 81.

59. Édouard Noël and Edmond Stoullig, "Théâtre Nationale de l'Opéra-Comique," *Les Annales du théâtre et de la musique [1892]* 18 (1893): 114.

MADAME EMMA CALVÉ AS "CARMEN."

FROM A COPYRIGHT PHOTOGRAPH BY JAMES L. BREESE.—[SEE PAGE 365.]

Figure 5.5 "Madame Emma Calvé as 'Carmen,'" from a photograph by James L. Breese, *Leslie's Weekly Illustrated*, 5 December 1895, cover.

fly, and Calvé described the rehearsals as stormy. As Director Carvalho believed in Opéra-Comique tradition, and perhaps still entertained the scruples that had caused the initially pale revival of 1883, before Galli-Marié's return, he was reluctant to allow Calvé to present an interpretation of excessive sensuality.

Hermann Klein recalled that "when [Calvé] essayed Carmen at the Opéra-Comique, her impersonation proved altogether too Spanish for the liking of the Parisians, who had been accustomed to the essentially French conception of the original—Mme Galli-Marié."[60] Others found her more Italian than Spanish, associating this with her love of picturesque and picaresque detail that resulted in a mannered style, in which she underlined each idea.[61] Her admiration for Eleanora Duse was recognized in gait and gesture, rendering her Carmen "a woman with a heap of pasts."[62] And yet there remained an element that was essentially French. Calvé managed to convey the character's humanity in a charming and picturesque manner, avoiding an excess of "brutal ardor."[63] This portrayal suggests that she did not confront the Opéra-Comique tradition too aggressively; indeed, Calvé claimed that Galli-Marié attended her debut and praised her warmly, for her "lovely voice" as well as for her boldness and originality.[64] This originality was seen by "Frimousse" as an expression of absolute modernity, which made Calvé's Carmen completely Parisian, so much so that Lillas Pastia's tavern reminded him of nothing so much as Aristide Bruant's cabaret.[65]

There was a general consensus that Calvé's most effective performance was in the "Card Aria" of act 3 (See Figure 5.6). The beauty and strength of her chest voice, and her ability to project the drama musically through her voice as well as her acting would have granted this scene considerable power. Without sacrificing the beauty of her tone to guttural effects she conveyed a wide variety of emotion and gesture in her singing, such that she was described as an "incomparable vocal actress."[66] Yet even from this early point in her career, she exercised considerable freedom with the score, leading Arthur Pougin to fulminate,

60. Klein, *Great Women-Singers of My Time*, 153.

61. F., "Musique: Opéra-Comique; Mlle Emma Calvé dans *Carmen*," *Le Gaulois* (Paris), 15 December 1892, 3.

62. Huebner, *"La Princesse Paysanne du Midi,"* 370. citing A. Gallus [Arthur Wisner], *Emma Calvé: Her Artistic Life* (New York: R. H. Russell, 1902), n.p.

63. E. D. H., "Courrier des Théatres," *La Presse* (Paris), 15 December 1892.

64. Mina Curtiss, *Bizet and His World* (New York: Vienna House, 1958), 434n3.

65. This was "une Carmen fin-de-siècle, dernier cri, dernier bateau, une Carmen bienparisienne, enfin." Frimousse, "La Soirée parisienne: Mlle Calvé dans 'Carmen,'" *Le Gaulois* (Paris), 15 December 1892, 3.

66. For a thoughtful reflection on Calvé's vocal style and its dramatic effect, see Huebner, "Music, Theater, and Cultural Transfer," 373–76.

Figure 5.6 Emma Calvé in act 3 of *Carmen* at the Opéra-Comique, photograph by Reutlinger, reproduced in Ludovic Halévy, "La Millième Représentation de Carmen," *Le Théâtre* 145 (January [I] 1905): 13.
Credit: State Library of Victoria.

What has happened, with Emma Calvé, to Bizet's adorable music? What has happened to the tempos, what has happened to the rhythms? Everything has changed, everything is upended, and the orchestra is confused, it is no longer able to follow, and not only are traditions broken, but so too is logic, even musical sense no longer exists.[67]

67. Arthur Pougin, "Opéra-Comique: Mlle Calvé dans *Carmen*," *Le Ménestrel* (1892): 403, trans. in Huebner, *"La Princesse Paysanne du Midi,"* 375.

Le tout-Paris crowded the Opéra-Comique for Calvé's debut on 14 December 1892 and greeted her with ovations, although the variety of critical responses to this new Carmen suggest that it was indeed a hybrid.[68] Calvé's Carmen certainly excited her Parisian audience, but despite her determined efforts, and in a faint echo of 1875, its Spanishness failed to be the main issue. Perhaps the contemporaneity of her appearance and her realist style were the most striking features of her performance. After a successful season as Carmen, she made a triumphant return in the role in late 1894, to a very warm response,[69] but Calvé did not routinely sing the role at the Opéra-Comique in the years following her debut. She sang in other operas, but was much occupied with a busy touring schedule in the United States and Europe, including her first Carmen at Covent Garden in May and at the Metropolitan Opera in December 1893. She was hugely influential, however, and every 1890s Carmen, whether operatic or not, owed something to Calvé. She welcomed the mantle of fame, with glamorous portraiture and a carefully cultivated public persona, building on her stories of Hispanic roots and a natural understanding of the role. Calvé was a true successor to Galli-Marié and Hauk, combining their commitment to the dramatic and emotional strength of the character with the new manifestations of operatic drama and ways of performing Spain to create a unique and long-lasting Carmen for the Belle Époque.

THE FRENCH IMAGE OF GRANADA AND *CARMEN* AT THE FIN DE SIÈCLE

Even though Calvé focused on other roles at the Opéra-Comique as the 1890s progressed, *Carmen* continued to enjoy its hard-won place at the heart of the theater's repertory. During the 1880s and 1890s *Carmen* was often the most performed work in the Opéra-Comique's annual lists, always among the top five when performances were totaled at the end of the year.[70] It even merited a new production when it opened the newly rebuilt theatre in 1898. The opera's dynamic relationship with the ongoing Parisian fashion for Spain in popular entertainment, which received a burst of new energy from the great Exposition Universelle of 1900, no doubt helped sustain its popularity, and its arrival at 1,000 performances in 1904 was marked by a grand celebration. This was the era in which *Carmen* became firmly established not only as an

---

68. Édouard Noël and Edmond Stoullig, "Théâtre Nationale de l'Opéra-Comique," *Les Annales du théâtre et de la musique [1892]* 18 (1893): 113.

69. Édouard Noël and Edmond Stoullig, "Théâtre Nationale de l'Opéra-Comique," *Les Annales du théâtre et de la musique [1894]* 20 (1895): 171.

70. Noël and Stoullig's *Les Annales du théâtre et de la musique* provide tables that summarize the number of performances of each work in their annual volumes.

institution at the Opéra-Comique but also as a recognized part of France's cultural patrimony.

Having taken over the directorship of the Opéra-Comique in January 1898, Albert Carré faced the challenge of staging a season across three different theaters and the honor of launching the (third) Salle Favart late in the year. After a glittering gala on 7 December, which featured no fewer than four overtures and four individual opera acts, including act 2 from *Carmen*, the real opening night took place on 8 December with a new production of *Carmen*. The choice of opera for this important event is a clear indicator of its established status at the Opéra-Comique, but it also demonstrates that Carré wanted to make his own mark on this central work.

Carré and his team had undertaken research in Spain to prepare the production, as was now *de rigeur*, and the new sets and costumes dazzled Parisian audiences with images of the "real" Spain in a complete "metamorphosis" from the familiar old stagings.[71] The costumes, including military uniforms, were based on the fashions of 1847, presumably to match the era of the novella's publication, rather than Mérimée's setting in 1830.[72] After the sharp contemporaneity of Calvé's 1892 debut, the Opéra-Comique had decided to try the "return to Mérimée" strategy for claiming authenticity.

As in 1875, critics reported that the sets were based on authentic sketches brought back from Spain, and each scene was intended to recreate the details of everyday life in all their color and variety.[73] Act 1 featured a pretty Sevillian square in the shadow of the Giralda, populated by street vendors, beggars, and curtain-twitching neighbors in addition to the expected soldiers and cigarette workers.[74] The familiar tavern scene in act 2 was replaced by an open-air patio, and the dancers—led by the noted flamenco dancer Trinidad la Gata—had been expressly imported from Granada, adding a more contemporary touch of choreographic authenticity.[75] Using the production as an excuse to write an extended travel piece about Granada, Gustave Larroumet recognized that Carré had shaped his stage exoticism around his desire to create "la couleur gitane" (gypsy color), resulting in a luminous depiction of sunny Spain on the

71. The sets were designed by Lucien Jusseaume, Marcel Jambon, and Alfred Lemeunier, while the costumes were created by Charles Bianchini. See Alfred Bruneau, "Les Théâtres: Opéra-Comique; Reprise de *Carmen*," *Le Figaro* (Paris), 9 December 1898, 4.

72. Edmond Stoullig, "Théâtre Nationale de l'Opéra-Comique," *Les Annales du théâtre et de la musique [1898]* 24 (1899): 134; Gustave Larroumet, "Carmen et les gitanes de Grenade," in *Nouvelles Études d'histoire et de critique dramatiques* (Paris: Librairie Hachette, 1899), 306.

73. Jean Lemarc, "Soirs Parisiens: La Vraie Carmen," *La Presse* (Paris), 9 December 1898, 2.

74. Stoullig, "Théâtre Nationale de l'Opéra-Comique," 134; Bruneau, "Les Théâtres," 4.

75. Stoullig, "Théâtre Nationale de l'Opéra-Comique," 134. Bruneau, "Les Théâtres," 4.

stage of the Opéra-Comique.[76] Despite its artistic charm, the obsessive attention to detail in the new version struck Alfred Bruneau as perhaps excessive.[77]

The soprano Georgette Leblanc worked hard in the title role. While needing
to differentiate herself from the notable Carmens who had preceded her, she
followed the established script when it came to preparation. She was reported
to have read and reread the Mérimée novella. She spent her vacation in Spain
so she could study the gypsies at close quarters during the *feria* of Seville and
may also have visited Granada and chatted with cigarette workers.[78] Naturally
fair, she donned a dark wig with heavy kiss-curls and darkened her skin,
declaring that she wanted her Carmen to be lifelike and real, even if it meant
"sacrificing an effect."[79] Despite her undoubted sincerity, Leblanc achieved a
mixed success, acclaimed by her audiences rather than the press. Viewed as
a slightly unconventional Carmen, perhaps she tried too hard, focusing on
her appearance and manner at the expense of the music (see Figure 5.4c).
Jean Favart described her as a true *bohémienne*, with lips of Granada and the
swaying walk of a Sevillian but a Parisian voice, while Bruneau criticized every
aspect of her musical execution.[80] Leblanc's artfully changed appearance made
her seem more gypsy than Spanish to Stoullig, performing with the "allures
of a primitive grace," but he queried whether the public did not see through
her so-realistic *gitane* to a "gigolette montmartroise."[81] The specter of the
Montmartre bohemian, so vehemently repudiated by Calvé, rose again to
haunt this new pretender to the "authentic" Carmen.

Carré's addition of a flamenco troupe from Granada to the established catalogue of Spanish stereotypes staged in *Carmen* confirms the contemporary
assumption that Granada was the most "authentic source" of this "primitive"
artifact, complementing Seville's long-standing role as the archetypal Spanish
town of heat, color, bullfighters, and dancers. The Spanish characteristics
represented by these two Andalusian towns were combined with the Moorish
or North African element of Spain's past, and this blend was represented at
Paris's great Exposition Universelle of 1900 in a lively demonstration of how
the 1890s had reconsolidated the fashion for Spanishness. Notwithstanding
the Spanish government's desire to project an image of a cultured, European,

76. Gustave Larroumet found the woman and child dancing as "inseparable from the
sun as the walls of the Alhambra," declaring that they had never before left the Albaicín
quarter of Granada. He continues with a long description of contemporary Granada.
Larroumet, "Carmen et les gitanes de Grenade," 308ff; J.-L. Croze, "Le Théâtre," *La
Presse* (Paris), 10 December 1898.
77. Bruneau, "Les Théâtres," 4.
78. Lemarc, "Soirs Parisiens," 2; Stoullig, "Théâtre Nationale de l'Opéra-Comique," 135.
79. Lemarc, "Soirs Parisiens," 2.
80. Ibid.; Jean Favart, "Le Théâtre: Il est ouvert!," *La Presse*, 7 December 1898, 2;
Bruneau, "Les Théâtres," 4.
81. Stoullig, "Théâtre Nationale de l'Opéra-Comique," 135.

and progressive nation, especially in the aftermath of its loss of empire in the disastrous Spanish-American War of 1898, the Exposition's organizers looked again to the Spanish topic for entertainment. One of the fair's most popular attractions was a 5,000-square-meter historical theme park in the Trocadero Gardens called *L'Andalousie au temps des maures* (Andalusia in the time of the Moors).[82] The title referred to the medieval heyday of Moorish Spain and the era of the great Romances during the reconquest by Christian monarchs, but the exhibit was also populated by contemporary North African desert tribes, fortune-telling gypsies, belly-dancing Arabians, and regional dancers of modern Spain, in an eclectic landscape that encompassed every possible Orientalist stereotype associated with the country south of the Pyrenees (see Figure 5.7).

Granada was evoked by a recreation of the gypsy cave dwellings of the Sacromonte and an impression of the Alhambra's iconic Patio of the Lions, albeit mixed with architectural elements of Seville's famous Alcazar. Seville was represented by a reconstruction of the Giralda Tower, which abutted a large arena where dramatic spectacles of Moors battling Christians and tribal attacks on North African caravans were staged beside gypsy weddings. A character dressed as Boabdil, the last Moorish king of Granada (to whom writers ascribed "The Moor's Last Sigh" upon his exile from the city), acted as master of ceremonies.[83] An additional 600-seat open-air theater was dedicated to nightly dance shows, ranging from the older-style regional dances to modern flamenco troupes. These performances attracted large crowds, particularly because they served food and drink into the night. When Calvé attended, her companion, Pierre Gailhard (director of the Opéra), introduced her to the *capitán* of the troupe of Albaicín gypsies as "la Calvé," and he replied, "By God, I should have known, it is she who is Carmen at the Opéra-Comique."[84] If Calvé's story is to be believed, it reinforces the crossover between Spanish-themed entertainments in Paris at this time.

The popularity of such live re-enactments perhaps encouraged what may have been the first performance of *Carmen* in the style of an arena spectacular at the Roman amphitheater of Nîmes in May 1901. It was not the first to use live animals—horses had appeared in the act 4 procession as early as the first Vienna production in October 1875—but the staging of a real bullfight as part of act 4 was unprecedented.[85] The audience was thus divided between

82. Sazatornil Ruíz and Lasheras Peña, "París y la españolada," 284.

83. In addition to Boabdil's centrality in *L'Andalousie au temps des maures*, the Spanish pavilion prominently featured a suit of armor that was purported to have belonged to him.

84. Don José, "Carmen," *Gil Blas* (Paris), 24 December 1904, 1.

85. Ludovic Halévy, "La Millième Représentation de *Carmen*," *Le Théâtre* 145 (January [I] 1905): 12.

(a)

(b)

Figure 5.7 (a) "L'Andalousie au temps des Maures: Les arènes"; (b) "L'Andalousie au temps des Maures: Les gitanes." (Andalusia in the time of the Moors: The arenas; The gypsies), *Le Panorama: Exposition universelle de 1900* (Paris: Librairie d'Art Ludovic Baschet, 1900, n.p.).

Figure 5.8 *Carmen*, 1901 production at the Arena of Nîmes, "Acte II: La posada," photograph by Bernheim, Nîmes, in Henri de Curzon, "Le Théâtre en province: Carmen aux Arènes de Nîmes," *Le Théâtre* 64 (August [II] 1901): 14–18.
Credit: State Library of Victoria.

opera lovers and bullfighting aficionados. Although bullfighting was banned by French authorities in 1890, prolonged legal action had led to its reinstatement in the southern *départements*, where it could be claimed as part of an "indigenous" tradition.[86] Performance style aside, here we see the incursion not just of realism but of "reality" into the fictional world of the opera, with Escamillo substituted by a genuine *torero* in an identical costume, who led a *cuadrilla* of *picadors* and *banderilleros* and finally killed a "little red bull."[87]

The Nîmes production seems to have been distinctive mainly for its elaborate sets and may have drawn inspiration from the architectural reconstructions of the 1900 Exposition, as well as Carré's 1898 production. The opera appeared against the backdrop of a panorama of Seville, which depicted its Roman ramparts (as mentioned in the first line of Carmen's act 1 "Séguedille"), the Gothic cathedral, and the Moorish Giralda tower (see Figure 5.8). For the four acts, typical settings were added in the foreground, and a curtain came down

86. Shubert, *Death and Money in the Afternoon*, 12, 34.

87. Henri de Curzon, "Le Théâtre en Province: *Carmen* aux Arènes de Nîmes," *Le Théâtre* 64 (August [II] 1901): 14, 16.

to allow for the changes of scene. This curtain depicted a scene apparently unrelated to *Carmen*'s plot: Boabdil's submission to the Christian conquerors. Boabdil had been a central figure in representations of Spain at the 1900 Exposition, and this conflation of Moorish and gypsy Granada with historic Spanish themes indicates a common desire to draw on a multiplicity of images of Spain's past to create spectacular entertainments in this era.[88]

In December 1904 the Opéra-Comique marked the 1,000th performance of Bizet's *Carmen* with a "solemn" and "magnificent" celebration.[89] The distinguished French author Jean Richepin penned a ceremonial poem that was recited at the end of the opera. A glittering audience of invited guests included performers from the premiere in 1875 and the sole surviving librettist, Ludovic Halévy. The illustrated journal *Le Théâtre* marked the occasion with a special issue: a full-length portrait of Calvé as Carmen graced the title page, and a long article by Halévy himself traced the troubled history of Bizet's *chef d'oeuvre* through its composition, premiere, international success, and eventual Parisian acceptance after the *seconde première* of 1883.[90]

It was to Emma Calvé that Carré turned for his Carmen on this occasion. Calvé had just retired from New York's Metropolitan Opera and remained unrivaled in the role, the "ideal Carmen" most applauded around the world. By now she had sung the role no fewer than 562 times, and she was to claim in 1920 to have sung it 1,389 times.[91] Lionized by the press, she did not miss the opportunity to reinforce her narrative of authenticity, describing an incident in the Albaicín district of Granada when the gypsies declared her countenance quite Andalusian and responded with incredulity to her avowals that she was French. Described as "la Duse lyrique" (the Duse of song), this performance set the seal on more than a decade when Calvé reigned supreme as the world's Carmen, with her "heart of gold, voice of diamonds, gesture of fire."[92]

88. De Curzon, "Le Théâtre en Province: *Carmen* aux Arènes de Nîmes," 16.

89. Un monsieur de l'orchestre [Arnold Mortier], "La Soirée: La Millième de *Carmen*," *Le Figaro* (Paris), 24 December 1904, 4.

90. Halévy, "La Millième Représentation de *Carmen*," 5–14.

91. Gabriel Fauré, "Les Théatres," *Le Figaro* (Paris), 24 December 1904, 4; Don José, "Carmen," 1; "Music: Emma Calve to Retire," *New York Times*, 8 August 1920, 73.

92. Don José, "Carmen," 1.

CHAPTER 6

cⱱɔ

Transatlantic Carmens in Dance
and Drama

Within a year of her 1892 debut as Carmen at the Opéra-Comique, Emma Calvé had been acclaimed in the role by audiences in London and New York. The novelty of her interpretation was undeniable in the 1890s, but its sustained success owed much to changing fashions in entertainment, particularly the fresh image of staged Spanishness that was ushered in by the 1889 Exposition Universelle and that continued to develop into the early years of the twentieth century. Paris was arguably the center of international entertainment at the *fin de siècle*, and the engine room of cosmopolitan Spanish-themed acts. London and New York, however, also formed a key part of the "transatlantic culture of spectacle" that provided such fertile ground for their propagation.[1] In this age of "metropolitan mass culture," the evolving image of Spanishness was disseminated by enterprises that catered to all tastes, ranging from "theaters, metropolitan newspapers, print and billboard advertising, World Fairs and exhibitions, amusement parks, plush restaurants, huge new department stores, traveling circuses and musical shows, and eventually ... dance halls, cabarets, nickelodeons and movie houses,"[2] many of which were to provide platforms for new adaptations of *Carmen*. Calvé's international celebrity as Carmen was the catalyst for two 1890s adaptations of the opera and novella: one in the legitimate theater, the other a ballet, both of which flourished in this transatlantic environment.

---

1. Susan A. Glenn, *Female Spectacle: The Theatrical Roots of Modern Feminism* (Cambridge, MA and London: Harvard University Press, 2000), 12.
2. Glenn, *Female Spectacle*, 12.

SPANISH ENTERTAINMENT IN LONDON
AND NEW YORK ... CALVÉ'S CARMEN

After the 1889 Exposition, and before Calvé donned the mantle of Bizet's gypsy, the taste for Spanishness was simmering quietly in the English capital. Londoners continued to enjoy *estudiantinas* and embraced the parodic shenanigans of *Carmen Up to Data*, but even this enjoyment did not lead to an immediate explosion of interest in Spanish dance. More highbrow audiences did, however, appreciate Spanish performances in the concert hall, offered by perennial favorites like Sarasate and relative newcomers like the pianist Isaac Albéniz, despite the debates they provoked about what constituted truly Spanish music.[3]

Cosmopolitan painter (and keen amateur musician) John Singer Sargent shared his passion for, and expertise in, all things Spanish by promoting Spain's culture and art among his friends on both sides of the Atlantic, contributing to a peculiarly US phenomenon described by Richard L. Kagan as a "Spanish Craze" that flourished between 1890 and 1930.[4] Wealthy art collectors like Isabella Stewart Gardner and Archer Huntington amassed Spanish paintings, furniture, and artifacts, and the very skyline of New York was shaped by the Spanish look. In 1890 a thirty-two-story reproduction of Seville's iconic Giralda tower crowned the newly rebuilt Madison Square Garden entertainment complex, towering over the city.[5] This fad for Hispanic culture provided a backdrop to the entertainment sensation of the year, which was the "battle" between two beautiful Spanish dancers for supremacy on New York's variety stage, Carmencita and Otero.

Dancing on the fringes of the 1889 Exposition, Carmencita Dausset was seen by Sargent and talent-spotted by the impresario Bolossy Kiralfy.[6]

---

3. Walter Aaron Clark, *Isaac Albéniz: Portrait of a Romantic* (Oxford: Oxford University Press, 1999), 77–84. For a consideration of Spanish music and musicians in late Victorian London, focused on Sarasate and Albéniz, see Kenneth James Murray, "Spanish Music and Its Representations in London (1878–1930): From the Exotic to the Modern" (PhD thesis, University of Melbourne, 2013), 77–115.

4. Richard Kagan, "The Spanish Craze: The Discovery of Spanish Art and Culture in the United States," in *When Spain Fascinated America* ([Madrid]: Fundación Zuloaga; Gobierno de España, Ministerio de Cultura, 2010), 25–46. This collection of essays addresses several aspects of the "Spanish Craze," with a particular focus on the painter Ignacio Zuloaga.

5. This second Madison Square Garden was built in 1890 to a Stanford White design and hosted everything from boxing to glamorous entertainments in its sports arena, restaurant, theater, concert hall, and roof garden, until its demolition in 1925.

6. Sargent described Carmencita performing in a tent on the Allée des étrangers, but this may have just been another pavilion of the many at the Exposition. The following discussion of Carmencita's early years in New York is based on M. Elizabeth Boone, Vistas de España: *American Views of Art and Life in Spain, 1860–1914* (New Haven and London: Yale University Press, 2007), 139–43; Camille Hardy, "Flashes of Flamenco: The American Debuts of Carmencita and Otero," *Arabesque: A Magazine of*

She accepted a booking to perform at the New York theater Niblo's Garden from August 1889, first dancing a *divertissement* in a production taken from London's Alhambra Theatre, then touring with the company for several months. New Yorkers found Carmencita to be the main attraction of this show, and by February 1890 she was starring as a featured artist in Koster and Bial's variety program. Her five-to-ten-minute turn showed off her use of castanets and *taconeo* (heel stamping), but she did not go in for high kicks. Well-informed viewers saw that she possessed both technique and grace, but most commentators were fixated by her flexible body and sinuous movements (especially her beautiful—and provocative—back bend). Carmencita's success made her a darling of the popular press, but society ladies, already deeply engaged by the fashion for Spain, could not risk their respectability by visiting a vaudeville venue like Koster and Bial's. So Carmencita was invited to perform at parties in private homes and offer dance lessons to society ladies. She attended a ball held in her honor at Madison Square Garden, and even had a waltz dedicated to her (see Figure 6.1). Sargent (who was painting Carmencita's portrait) used at least one of the private parties to recreate his famous 1882 painting *El Jaleo: Danse des gitanes*, complete with guitarists seated against the wall, makeshift footlights, and Carmencita dancing, as described by one guest:

> In the back I saw a row of men who were softly strumming on guitars.... [S]uddenly ... this thing leapt out of the darkness with a tiger skin wrapped around her and a red thing in her hair and began to dance—back and forth—back and forth—one minute she would be in the light and the next moment she was in the dark shade.... It was the most wild and primitive thing that I have ever seen in my life and the most artistic.[7]

It is clear that Carmencita was not dancing solely in the flamenco style of the Granadine gypsies; she drew her steps from Spanish classical and regional dance styles, and calm observers recognized the essential modesty of her art. Yet the American public and press primitivized her dance, describing her as "sensual," "uncivilized" and "untrained"—the latter two were far from

International Dance 9, no. 1 (1983): 17–19; José Gelardo Navarro and José Luis Navarro García, *Carmencita Dauset: Una bailaora almeriense* (Almería: La Hidra de Lerna/ Diputación de Almería, 2011), 29–57. A study of Carmencita's full stay in the United States can be found in Francisco Javier Mora Contreras and Kiko Mora, "Carmencita on the Road: Baile español y vaudeville en los Estados Unidos de América (1889–1895)," *Lumière* (2011), accessed 1 October 2016, http://www.elumiere.net/exclusivo_web/carmencita/carmencita_on_the_road.php.

7. From a 1927 interview with Dora Wheeler Keith, quoted in Boone, *Vistas de España*, 140, 243n93.

Figure 6.1 *Carmencita Waltz*, cover (Philadelphia: Wm. D. Dutton, 1891).
Credit: From the New York Public Library, https://digitalcollections.nypl.org/items/3e4cb0e0-ada5-01333e4a-00505686a51c.

the truth—and Carmencita understood the promotional benefit of playing to stereotypes born both of Orientalism and North American prudishness.

Carmencita's great success made Spanish dance such a drawcard that Koster and Bial's longtime rival (and neighboring establishment), the Eden-Musée, sent their talent scout to search France for an act that might compete with her and lure audiences back to their slightly higher-class venue. He found the as yet little-known Carolina Otero, who had danced in Spain and provincial France before her Paris debut in December 1889. After some intensive training to polish her act, the youthful Otero launched herself in Paris with a concert in which she sang and danced as she was accompanied by an *estudiantina* dressed in bullfighting costumes. This "Orchestra Espagnol" played a *Fantasie sur Carmen* among other popular numbers, many taken from *zarzuelas*, in a show that punctuated a ball at the Salons du Grand Véfours. Writing of this event in her memoirs, Otero described her success and quoted the journalist Hugues Le Roux, who found "all the East in her movements ... and in her eyes all the flames of passion, all the ardor of life, all the coquetry of woman."[8] These words accurately describe Otero's future persona, but her next step was an engagement at the Cirque d'été in May 1890. Although she was still working with an *estudiantina*, the focus seems to have moved to her dancing, and the press repeated claims of her genuine Spanishness (to distinguish her from the many "fake" Spaniards who sprang up in the wake of 1889). But the erotic sensuality of her performance remains the keynote of their response.[9]

When Otero arrived in New York in September 1890, the Eden-Musée's publicity machine had already whipped the local press into a frenzy about this "rival to Carmencita," and her introductions were bolstered by fantastical claims of noble birth, elevated education, and even abduction by the Spanish King Alfonso XII (her future liaison with his son Alfonso XIII was more credible). Billed as "The 'Queen' of Spanish dancers, the Nightingale of Seville— accompanied by her own company of guitarists and dancers,"[10] she was represented as a higher-class act than her predecessor. In a bizarre reversal of the actual situation, journalists created a dichotomy between the two Spanish dancers, in which Carmencita's voluptuous beauty was seen as the result of nature (a wildflower), while Otero's "chaste" performance and Madonna-like countenance could only be described as art (a conservatory bloom).[11] While it is likely that Otero had been instructed to adapt her act, reducing its Parisian excesses for a more moralistic New York audience, this interpretation of the dancers' relative merits shows the power not only of Orientalist stereotyping but also of public relations in shaping perceptions. The familiar tendency to portray Spanish dancers as Carmenesque characters was applicable to both Otero and Carmencita, the former with her penchant for taking lovers (usually wealthy and or socially elevated), the latter whose dance was described in animalistic terms similar to her fictional namesake. Their "struggle" for

8. Caroline Otero, *My Story* (London: A. M. Philpot, [1927]), 112–13.

9. Geraldine Power, "Projections of Spain in Popular Spectacle and Chanson, Paris: 1889–1926" (PhD thesis, University of Melbourne, 2013), 28–31.

10. "Eden-Musee," *Sun* (New York), 28 September 1890, 9.

11. "Otero Comes and Conquers," *Sun* (New York), 2 October 1890, 3.

supremacy in New York was reported across the world and set the stage for the next scene in Carmen's operatic journey.

While this panorama of Spanish dance shaped productions of the opera and audience expectations of the protagonist, the darker dramatic elements of Bizet's opera were waiting to be unlocked by new interpretative modes in acting that swept the stage during the 1890s. Many sought to emulate the great European actresses of the age, Eleanora Duse and Sarah Bernhardt, who embodied contrasting styles of performance, the one spontaneous and "natural," the other a "paragon of beautiful intonation and sculptural elegance."[12] The operatic Carmen of the 1890s was transformed by Calvé, a disciple of Duse, who also channeled the lyricism and charm of the Opéra-Comique tradition.

Calvé took London by storm in summer 1893, where she was immediately judged "the ideal Carmen."[13] Yet George Bernard Shaw, who considered Calvé a truly great artist, declared that her Carmen "shocked me beyond measure." He criticized her for denying the gypsy any redeeming feature, neither "honesty, courage [nor] honor," in a performance that was at times frankly lewd. Calvé's depiction of Carmen's death focused the attention of London critics and was described in the *Times* as "horrible in its intensity."[14] Shaw found it all too real: "to see Calvé's Carmen changing from a live creature, with properly coordinated movements, into a reeling, staggering, flopping, disorganized thing, and finally tumble down a mere heap of carrion, is to get much the same sensation as might be given by the reality of a brutal murder."[15]

The passage of time (and possibly modifications in Calvé's performance) allowed Shaw a more balanced appreciation of her Carmen in 1896. Shaw had identified Calvé's role in the transformation of the "Mérimée Carmen" into the "Zola Carmen," as part of the "naturalistic movement which was presently to turn Carmen into a disorderly, lascivious, good-for-nothing factory girl."[16] He concluded that Calvé's performance cheapened the character, with its echoes of the contemporary popular stage:

---

12. Steven Huebner, *"La Princesse Paysanne du Midi,"* in *Music, Theater, and Cultural Transfer: Paris, 1830–1914*, ed. Annegret Fauser and Mark Everist (Chicago and London: University of Chicago Press, 2009), 366–67.

13. Hermann Klein, *Great Women-Singers of My Time* (London: George Routledge & Sons, 1931), 153–54.

14. "The Opera," *Times* (London), 31 May 1893, 10.

15. George Bernard Shaw, *Music in London 1890–94 by Bernard Shaw* (London: Constable, 1932a), 3: 227–28. From review originally published in *World*, 30 May 1894.

16. George Bernard Shaw, "Miss Nethersole and Mrs Kendal [June 1896]," in *Our Theatres in the Nineties* (London: Constable, 1932b), 2: 154. Review originally published in *Saturday Review*, 13 June 1896.

Calvé, an artist of genius, divested Carmen of the last rag of romance and respectability: it is not possible to describe in decent language what a rapscallion
she made of her.... Here you had no mere monkey mimicry of this or that antic
of a street girl, but great acting in all its qualities, interpretation, invention, selection, creation, and fine execution, with the true tragi-comic force behind it.
And yet it was hard to forgive Calvé for the performance, since the achievement,
though striking enough, was, for an artist of her gifts, too cheap to counter-
balance the degradation of her beauty and the throwing away of her skill on a
study from vulgar life which was, after all, quite foreign to the work on which
she imposed it.[17]

While Shaw did not reference the Spanishness of Calvé's performance, he was
undoubtedly aware of the contemporary tendency to imbue operatic Carmens
with the primitivism ascribed to gypsy performers and the traits of music-hall
Spanish dancing girls.[18] He exhibits a rare sensitivity, however, in discerning
that this "vulgar" Carmen was discordant with the essentially 1870s conception of Bizet's score and drama, a disharmony emphasized when combined
with the passionate drama of Calvé's verismo-inspired interpretation.

Calvé went on to even greater success in New York, first as Santuzza,
then as Carmen. She presented the Metropolitan Opera with its first French
Carmen, although she had to fight management for the privilege of breaking
their tradition of singing it in Italian (or even in German). On being told that
no tenor was available to sing the role in French, she flatly refused to perform
the opera in Italian and enlisted a friend, the great actor Coquelin, to approach
Jean de Reszke, even though Don José was not yet in his repertory.[19] Calvé
got her way. She even claimed to have resorted to subterfuge over costume,
appearing in a threadbare shawl in the first act, similar to the chorus, in direct
contravention of the director's order that Carmen as cigarette girl should appear à la Galli-Marié, in black bolero and fringed cap.[20]

Calvé made her New York debut only two short years after Otero and
Carmencita had polarized local opinion with their distinctive versions of
Spanish entertainment. She introduced her Carmen to the Met's audiences
on 20 December 1893, and was warmly received, apart from some
objections to the heightened sensuality of her interpretation. Although
the opera singer also caused some consternation among the critics for her

17. Shaw, "Miss Nethersole and Mrs Kendal," 154–55.
18. See Shaw's review of Otero in her first London season: Shaw, *Music in London*,
2: 169. From review originally published in *World*, 19 October 1892.
19. Emma Calvé, *Sous tous les ciels j'ai chanté* (Paulhe, Fance: Lune de papier, [1940]
2004), 101.
20. Georges Girard, *Emma Calvé: La cantatrice sous tous les ciels* (Millau, France: Éditions
Grans Causses, 1983), 144–45.

apparently lascivious dancing, she was not compared with her predecessors from the music halls. She seems to have used a gestural language based on movement and the creation of distinctive poses with her arms and hips, and this language prompted comparisons with generic exotic dance, probably of the "hoochy-coochy" or belly-dance varieties, recently seen among the titillating acts on the Midway Plaisance at the 1893 Chicago World's Fair. On opening night, her performance in act 2 was said to approach "the boundaries of the hazardous."[21] But she quickly toned down the sexualized aspect of her performance that had characterized her early appearances as Carmen, and Henry Krehbiel credited Calvé with an awareness of her audience's sensibility that led her to rely more on "the charm with which she infallibly at that time imbued every character that she essayed."[22] The hybrid nature of her Carmen interpretation led American writer and critic Willa Cather to observe that she possessed "all France in her smile and all Spain in her eyes."[23]

Reappearing as Carmen season after season, Calvé achieved such popularity that the Met's management came to rely on her to fill the auditorium (and their coffers) until her retirement from that theater in 1904.[24] No other singer could gain traction in the role while Calvé reigned as Carmen in New York. According to Carl Van Vechten, it was with Calvé's interpretation that "*Carmen* became a fetish"; audiences were completely "fascinated" by her.[25] Like her idol Duse, Calvé offered constant variations in her impersonation of the character, creating a sense of spontaneity.[26] Whether appearing as Santuzza or as Carmen, Calvé stood out from her operatic peers through her flair for acting, and her equal commitment to the dramatic and the musical elements of her performance. According to Krehbiel,

21. The official title of the exhibition was "World's Fair: Columbian Exposition." "'Carmen' at the Opera," *New York Times*, 21 December 1893, 2.

22. Martin Mayer, *The Met: One Hundred Years of Grand Opera* (London: Thames and Hudson, 1983), 68; Henry Edward Krehbiel, "Notable Carmens of Last Four Decades," *New York Tribune*, 13 December 1914, 7.

23. Cather wrote this opinion after hearing Calvé in concert in 1897. Willa Cather, *The World and the Parish: Willa Cather's Articles and Reviews, 1893–1902*, ed. William M. Curtin (Lincoln: University of Nebraska Press, 1970), 1: 409.

24. Calvé performed Carmen twenty-nine times (out of thirty) in her first Met season alone, and although she did not return to the Met for eighteen months, she then claimed ownership of the role, appearing in it nearly every year until 1904 (the exceptions were 1898 and 1903). "Met Careers: Calvé, Emma [Soprano]," MetOpera Database, accessed 13 July 2011, http://69.18.170.204/archives/frame.htm.

25. Carl Van Vechten, *The Music of Spain* (London: Kegan Paul, Trench, Trubner, 1920), 153.

26. Duse "cultivated a more spontaneous impression, changing details according to the emotional temperature and her state of mind." Huebner, "*La Princesse Paysanne du Midi*," 366–67.

[s]he lifted the physical element in the character into prominence.... But what was more admirable than her appeal to the senses in her acting was the manner in which she captivated the imagination by her singing. That was as completely unconventional as were her poses, her gestures and her play of features.... She could not have sung as she did if she had not been able to act as she did. The two modes of expression were not merely complementary of each other in her case—they were one in origin and one in aim. She did not subordinate nature to art, but presented art vitalized by nature.[27]

Van Vechten noted that "Calvé had the power, as few singers have possessed it, to color her voice to express different emotions, and her vocal treatment of the part in the beginning was a delight."[28] Calvé's innovative approach introduced a modern dramatic sensibility to the role of Carmen, opening up the stage for other performers to break with the limitations of operatic convention and expose the work to new trends in theatrical realism.

The Met's *Carmen* was not the only version circulating in the United States at the time. Kristen Turner has traced an alternate reading that was practiced by several touring companies, which featured the addition of a pantomime scene at the very end of act 3, in which Carmen attempts to stab José in the back during the orchestral postlude. This violent outburst is more graphic than other examples of Carmen's temper, for her attack on the cigarette worker in act 1 occurs offstage. When combined with cuts to the opening scenes of act 4, it served to underline José's justification for murdering Carmen and reduce sympathy for the errant gypsy.[29]

OLGA NETHERSOLE AND THE "CARMEN KISS"

In December 1895, another novel approach was presented to New York audiences in the guise of a new melodrama entitled *Carmen: A Dramatic Version of Prosper Mérimée's Novel*, commissioned from the prolific English playwright Henry Hamilton by actor and theatrical manager Olga Nethersole.[30] *Carmen* functioned as a star vehicle for Nethersole on her second American tour, and it achieved both controversy and success as she performed it around

27. Krehbiel, "Notable Carmens," 7.

28. Van Vechten, *Music of Spain*, 153.

29. Kristen M. Turner, "Opera in English: Class and Culture in America, 1878–1910" (PhD thesis, University of North Carolina at Chapel Hill, 2015), 344–48.

30. Henry Hamilton (1853?–1918) was initially an actor and then a playwright. Many of his works were adapted into silent films. Nethersole performed in several of Hamilton's plays earlier in her career, including *Harvest*, which constituted her very first professional engagement, touring provincial theaters in the United Kingdom in 1887.

the northeastern United States into spring 1896. After six years of acting, the young Englishwoman had launched her career as a manager in 1893, establishing her international reputation on the back of eleven American tours undertaken between 1894 and 1914. Actor-managers required appropriate leading roles to expose their talents, and while men were well catered to, Nethersole found few plays that allowed her to transcend contemporary expectations of a woman on the stage, described by Elizabeth Robins as the "knack of pleasing."[31] Nethersole set about creating a repertory for herself by commissioning adaptations, translations, and original material. She promoted herself as the English Bernhardt, playing on her friendship with the divine Sarah, and performed English versions of many plays famously associated with Bernhardt.[32] A specialist in playing "fallen women," Nethersole satisfied her predilection for emotional and dramatic roles by adapting operatic subjects to the legitimate stage.[33]

Nethersole, who claimed that her mother was Spanish, played a variety of Latin types during her career, including a character possibly based on Lola Montez in *The Silver Falls* (1888), a fifteenth-century Spanish princess in *The Termagant* (1898), and Nedda in a theatrical adaptation of *I Pagliacci* (1907).[34] She claimed in a 1907 interview that "there is a strain of Spanish blood in my veins. It surges and flows with great intensity and controls me, particularly when I am acting."[35] The addition of a work like *Carmen* to her repertory thus enhanced her established profile and granted further opportunity

31. Elizabeth Robins, *Both Sides of the Curtain* (London: William Heinemann, 1940), 242. The way in which expectations of women on stage mirrored societal expectations during the 1890s is discussed in a close study of Robins's autobiography in Mary Jean Corbett, "Performing Identities: Actresses and Autobiography," in *The Cambridge Companion to Victorian and Edwardian Theatre*, ed. Kerry Powell (Cambridge: Cambridge University Press, 2004), 110–11.

32. Nethersole's short run in *Carmen* at London's Gaiety Theatre in 1896 was supplemented with a special matinee on Thursday 18 June, given for "Madame Sarah Bernhardt," who had "expressed some curiosity as to the 'Carmen kiss.'" "Music and the Drama," *Glasgow Herald*, 15 June 1896; Joy Harriman Reilly, "From Wicked Woman of the Stage to New Woman: The Career of Olga Nethersole (1870–1951); Actress-Manager, Suffragist, Health Pioneer" (PhD thesis, Ohio State University, 1984), 121, 124.

33. Nethersole commissioned numerous adaptations and translations from French novels, plays, and operas during her career, presenting English versions of celebrated works like Victorien Sardou's *Tosca, Camille* by Alexandre Dumas fils, Meilhac and Halévy's *Frou-Frou*, Alphonse Daudet's *Sapho*, and several works by Paul Hervieu. Reilly, "From Wicked Woman," 26, 50–52, 148, 61, 306–9.

34. *The Silver Falls* was a melodrama written in 1888 for London's Adelphi Theatre by George R Sims and Henry Pettitt, who also wrote *Carmen Up to Data*.

35. Nethersole's mother was said to be Spanish, although Reilly has not been able to trace her name. "Olga Nethersole: Actress and Philanthropist," *Theatre Magazine* 7 (1907): 194, quoted in Reilly, "From Wicked Woman," 128; 31, 67.

to exploit her alleged Mediterranean blood, while appealing to English tastes for Spanish entertainment.

Nethersole promoted her unconventional approach, which was characterized by the play's most scandalous effect, the "Carmen kiss." New York critics agreed that her performance "out-Calved Calve," offering a "danse du ventre in four acts" that made the audience positively uncomfortable with its similarity to a "long study of the couchee-couchee" from the Midway Plaisance.[36] Despite the controversial elements, the opening-night audience at New York's Empire Theatre passed from "critical observation to close interest, to absorbed attention, to even-handed applause," ending up in a state of "complacent surrender to the star."[37]

Nethersole enjoyed sufficient success during her 1896 US tour to take *Carmen* and her company to London for a brief summer season (lasting barely two weeks) at the Gaiety Theatre. London's musical elite were curious and Nethersole drew an audience that included soprano Emma Albani, composer Arthur Sullivan, the celebrated Carmen Zélie de Lussan, and impresario Augustus Harris.[38] Despite claims that she played to sold-out houses during the two-week London run, the *Glasgow Herald* commented laconically that *Carmen* had "not created so great a sensation in London at mid-summer as it did in New York in the winter."[39] The short run was intentional, allowing Nethersole to take a holiday before embarking on her third American tour, but she judged it sufficiently successful to take the work into her repertory, playing it for another ten years.[40]

While Mérimée is referenced in the work's subtitle, Hamilton's lengthy play (running to four hours) was closely based on the operatic scenario and attempted to cash in on the elements of the opera that provided opportunities for realism and melodrama, presenting what was effectively an "operatic" work without the singing. The verbose script was belittled as "a monologue entertainment" and a "star-actress version," a response confirmed by Shaw, who found the whole play "tedious, inept, absurd, and at its most characteristic moments positively asinine."[41]

The production made use of music from Bizet's score as overture, interludes, and melodramatic accompaniment, and to create spectacle with a few "spirited" dance numbers.[42] Cather noted that Carmen's first entry is

36. "The Nethersole Kiss," *Indianapolis Journal*, 27 December 1895, 3.

37. "Nethersole's 'Passion-Dyed' Carmen," *Indianapolis Journal*, 25 December 1895, 3.

38. "Music and the Drama (from our special correspondent)," *Glasgow Herald*, 8 June 1896, 9.

39. "Music and the Drama," *Glasgow Herald*, 15 June 1896.

40. Reilly, "From Wicked Woman," 54–55.

41. "Miss Nethersole as Carmen," *Pall Mall Gazette*, 8 June 1896; Shaw, "Miss Nethersole and Mrs Kendal," 153.

42. The dances were arranged by Señor Espinosa. "The London Theatres: The Gaiety," *Era* (London), 13 June 1896.

"attended by the Carmen motif played vigorously by the orchestra."[43] Other musical items were interleaved with Bizet's music, such as Frank A. Howson's undistinguished song "Make Love All Round" (lyrics by Hamilton), sung by Nethersole and released as sheet music that same year. The banal lyrics and melody were given an exotic feel by the relentless accompanimental figure outlining a stereotypical bolero-type dance rhythm.[44] As for dancing, despite being convinced of Nethersole's picturesque and appropriate appearance, the *Era* critic considered "a fandango in the real Spanish style ... as yet, beyond her powers."[45] Cather, who saw Nethersole in Pittsburgh and may have been less familiar with Spanish dance than the London critics, describes how her dance for Don José rendered her "fascinating," an effect that dissolved when she was in repose.[46]

Nethersole espoused an emotional and physically demonstrative acting style that enjoyed some vogue during the 1890s. Influenced by naturalism and an idiosyncratic interpretation of "realism," as well as popular melodrama, she was criticized for an exaggerated manner by some American and English critics, who viewed her as part of a more continental tradition. Despite longstanding comparisons between her and Bernhardt, Nethersole's style was also characterized by mobility and constant variation, linking her with Calvé and Duse. As one observer described it,

> Miss Nethersole belongs to the sensational, realistic school which aims to give an actual transcript of life. Nothing is softened, nothing toned down, ... In one of the scenes. . . she makes a rush for the toreador, and seizing him as a tiger seizes his prey, she kisses him again and again, almost in an ecstasy of madness.[47]

She proudly colored her performance with a number of other "innovative realistic touches," including turning her back to the audience, whispering, biting, and scratching, the infamous kiss, and crawling off stage to behind the rocks near the end of act 3, an effect at least one critic found "irresistibly funny."[48]

It was perhaps in her death scene that Nethersole took her commitment to realism to its extreme.[49] In Shaw's words,

43. Cather, *World and the Parish*, 1: 433.

44. Frank A. Howson and Henry Hamilton, *Make Love All Round* (Boston: Oliver Ditson Company, 1896).

45. "London Theatres: The Gaiety," *Era*, 13 June 1896.

46. Cather, *World and the Parish*, 1: 433.

47. "Broadbrim's New Year Letter," *Kapunda Herald* (South Australia), 6 March 1896, 4.

48. Reilly, "From Wicked Woman," 54; "London Theatres: The Gaiety," *Era*, 13 June 1896.

49. W. Moy Thomas criticized Nethersole for applying "some false theory of artistic realism." "The Theatres: Carmen," *Graphic* (London), 13 June 1896.

[a]nd Carmen, after being stabbed, and dying a screaming, gurgling, rattling, "realistic" death, compounded of all the stage colics and convulsions ever imagined, suddenly comes to life and dies over again in the older operatic manner ... , warbling "I love you, I love you." What is a critic expected to say to such folly?[50]

Nethersole dressed realistically in tattered lace with holes in her stockings, and underlined the physicality of the character by consuming copious quantities of candy, oranges, and cakes throughout the performance; Cather observed "she is always eating when she isn't drinking or kissing."[51] But her attempt to impersonate streetwise Spanishness could not convince London critics all too familiar with Spanish entertainment. Shaw ridiculed her display of "the old-fashioned modish airs and graces, the mantilla, comb, fan, castanets, and dancing-shoes of the stage Spanish gipsies whom our grandmothers admired."[52] He lambasted her inept combination of hackneyed stage Spanishness in her costume and mannerisms with "the realistic sordidness and vulgarity of a dissolute ragpicker."[53] The critic of *The Era* concurred, arguing that instinctive sensuality should have been the keynote of the character, rather than the calculated vice that Nethersole overplayed in her "leering streetwalker, with a ready mercenary smile, winking at all the men, tickling them, patting their faces, and allowing and taking every sort of liberty."[54] Such responses echo within an 1890s urban context the critical misgivings first associated with Galli-Marié's 1875 Carmen in relation to the sordid elements of Parisian street life.

Whereas *Carmen Up to Data* had clothed its common characters in humor and charm, Hamilton and Nethersole's melodramatic lower-class *Carmen* exhibited "in a lurid light every repulsive trait in Carmen's repulsive character," tearing "away the veil of pretty music that has up to now hidden the infamy of Carmen from the public gaze."[55] Without the ameliorating effect of the musical lyricism within an operatic setting, Nethersole's Carmen set itself apart from those of her operatic contemporaries. She denied the character any redeeming feature, sparing nothing "that could accentuate the demoniacal side of Carmen's nature."[56] If this reading prevented the audience from establishing any sympathy or rapport with her, it must also have undermined the effect of the final tragedy.[57]

50. Shaw, "Miss Nethersole and Mrs Kendal," 153.
51. Cather, *World and the Parish*, 1: 433 34.
52. Shaw, "Miss Nethersole and Mrs Kendal," 155.
53. Ibid.
54. "London Theatres: The Gaiety," *Era*, 13 June 1896.
55. "Miss Nethersole as Carmen," *Pall Mall Gazette*, 8 June 1896.
56. "Last Night's Theatricals: 'Carmen' at the Gaiety," *Lloyd's Weekly Newspaper* (London), 7 June 1896.
57. Thomas, "Theatres: Carmen," *Graphic*, 13 June 1896.

But Nethersole as Carmen is clearly connected with Calvé, who also exploited her reputed Spanish ancestry and was arguably the first Carmen to adopt a naturalistic approach to the role. Cather observed that "their intellectual conception of the part is the same, but Miss Nethersole is thin and English; she has to do something dangerously violent to accomplish what Calvé does by a look."[58] Cather admitted to being impressed by Nethersole's expressive eyes, her mobile lips (which Cather compared to Bernhardt's), and her ability to fascinate in the absence of beauty or a commanding physique. Nethersole exploited only the histrionic potential of the role, lacking both Calvé's appreciation of contemporary gypsy culture and her comic charm (see Figure 6.2). Cather identified Nethersole's nervous intensity, rather than sensuality, as the keynote of her performance style, but found her desire to reveal the spiritual element of the character to be in constant tension with her misguided conflation of naturalism with exoticist coloration, "forever being driven back and drowned by the click of the castanets that is always recurring."[59] Nor did she demonstrate a sense of fun in the role: Shaw declared that "she has not a spark of humor," whereas it was just this quality that rendered Calvé's "comedy of . . . audacities . . . irresistible" to him.[60]

The "most titillating effect" of Nethersole's *Carmen* was her famous kiss, which created considerable scandal in the United States. Nethersole described it as "languorous, passionate and of the sunny South," and explained that she simply kissed "as I know Carmen must have done."[61] Far exceeding the outrage caused by her other naturalistic touches (bare feet, cigarette smoking, nose blowing, and general wildness), her kisses were distinguished both by number and duration,[62] and provoked considerable comment:

> Miss Nethersole's kisses have made a good deal of talk in town, and you may or not, according to the sort of person you are, regard their fervor, duration and audible unctuousness necessary to the artistic depiction of Carmen's character.[63]

58. Cather, *World and the Parish*, 1: 410.

59. Ibid., 432–35.

60. Shaw, "Miss Nethersole and Mrs Kendal," 155, 154.

61. "Music and the Drama (from our special correspondent)," *Glasgow Herald*, 8 June 1896, 9.

62. Reilly, "From Wicked Woman," 135–36; Vanessa Toulmin and Simon Popple, eds., *Visual Delights Two: Exhibition and Reception* (Eastleigh: John Libbey, 2005), 99.

63. *New York Herald* (29 December 1895), 4D, cited in Nancy Mowll Mathews and Charles Musser, *Moving Pictures: American Art and Early Film, 1880–1910* (Manchester, VT: Hudson Hills Press in association with Williams College Museum of Art, 2005), 6.

Figure 6.2 Olga Nethersole as Carmen, Ogden's Cigarette Card (mid-1890s).
Credit: Private collection.

and

> It is no exaggeration to assert that if Miss Nethersole were to reduce the dura-
> tion of her kisses one-half, the performance would be over considerably more
> than a half-hour before midnight.[64]

A New York critic was moved to describe the performance in almost
pornographic terms:

> Olga twisted and writhed and wriggled with passion, her sinuous body and
> limbs trembling, her eyes burning, her lips quivering. Her lips—ah! Those lips of
> hers, large lips, red lips, pulpy lips, juicy lips, clinging lips—lips forbidden by the
> church, but of great pith and moment to the flesh and the devil—lips that leered
> and smiled and tempted—we shall say no more about those lips lest trouble
> come. Olga kissed everybody on the stage in general and her lovers in particular.
> Such kisses! ... Before the evening was over Don Jose was a physical wreck and
> the spectators were in a cold perspiration.... The leading actor cannot live the
> season out. He will dwindle and pine away, and some night Olga will swallow
> him by slow suction, as a snake does a rabbit.[65]

Cather was surprised to find the celebrated kiss not a "prolonged bit of
[cheap] stage business," but instead intoxicating and as terrible as a lightning
bolt or earthquake. This impression forced her admiration, even though she
remained unsure whether she approved, concluding that it was "great, elemental, volcanic, and true, true, true!"[66] Audiences flocked, both in North
America and in London, to see for themselves whether the act was realism or
pornography. Nethersole's "Carmen" kiss created such a furor that its fame
lasted well beyond 1896, and her biographer Joy Hariman Reilly quotes a
1908 article in which the writer states "we have been brought up on stories of
the Nethersole kiss."[67]

Such was its celebrity that the well-known actress May Irwin burlesqued
the kiss on Broadway that same year, inserting it into the musical comedy
The Widow Jones by John McNally. This spoof on the "Nethersole kiss" was
then filmed by the Edison Manufacturing Company in early 1896, screened
as *The Kiss* by Vitascope in May of that year, featuring at Koster and Bial's as
well as many other vaudeville venues. American critics distinguished between

64. Quoting from the New York *Dramatic Mirror*: "Before the Curtain," *Sunday Times*
(Sydney, NSW), 16 February 1896, 7.
65. "The Nethersole Kiss," *Indianapolis Journal*, 27 December 1895, 3.
66. Cather, *World and the Parish*, 1: 434.
67. Reilly, "From Wicked Woman," 139.

the risqué European sensuality projected by Nethersole and the wholesome American coyness of Irwin's take on it.[68]

Nethersole seems to have inspired other dramatic versions of *Carmen*, such as the 1896 production starring Rosabel Morrison, which compensated for the more demure comportment of its heroine by projecting a ten-minute motion picture of a bullfight behind the relevant scenes, as played by the Eidoloscope (see Figure 6.3).[69] This hybrid approach shows *Carmen* productions at the forefront of technical innovation, in service of the constant need to compete with other attractions.

Nethersole maintained *Carmen* in her repertory until near the end of her career and in 1907 even performed it in Paris, when she took a lease on Bernhardt's theater for a season. Albert Carré of the Opéra-Comique promptly took out an injunction to prevent her staging *Carmen*, but the ensuing court case vindicated both parties: Nethersole was able to perform her *Carmen*, but only when it was billed as *The Spanish Gypsy* and without the use of Bizet's music.[70] Reilly claims that Nethersole was given a favorable reception in France, where her famed intensity was more appreciated than by Anglo-Saxon audiences.[71] Freedom from restrictions allowed more scope for *Carmen* adaptations to emerge outside of France, and this latitude was certainly the case with the most important ballet version of the Belle Epoque, starring Rosario Guerrero.

CROSSING THE ATLANTIC: SPANISH DANCE AND *CARMEN* AS BALLET

London's love affair with Spanish dance, which had waxed and waned through the nineteenth century, still promised a warm reception to any turn offering Spanish fire, passion, and, where possible, a knife fight, a predilection that had facilitated the welcome given to Bizet's *Carmen* when it finally arrived on

---

68. Mathews and Musser, *Moving Pictures: American Art and Early Film, 1880–1910*, 6, 32–33; *Visual Delights Two*, 99–101. The "May Irwin Kiss," with John Rice, as filmed for Edison Vitascope in 1896, can be viewed on the Library of Congress website, and was promoted at the time as "[a]n osculatory performance by May Irwin and John Rice. The most popular subject ever shown." Accessed 20 December 2016, https://www.loc.gov/item/00694131.

69. Charles Musser, "A Cornucopia of Images: Comparison and Judgment across Theater, Film and the Visual Arts during the Late Nineteenth Century," in *Moving Pictures: American Art and Early Film, 1880–1910*, 31.

70. "Miss Nethersole as Carmen: English Actress Settles Her Difficulty with Albert Carre in Paris," *New York Times*, 11 June 1907; Reilly, "From Wicked Woman," 80, 83, 84.

71. Reilly, "From Wicked Woman," 298–99.

Figure 6.3 Rosabel Morrison in *Carmen*, theatrical poster (*c.* 1896).
Credit: Library of Congress, http://www.loc.gov/pictures/item/2014636161.

the English stage. But opera was more popular than ballet in London during the 1870s and 1880s. Although audiences tolerated the divertissement type of ballet, which did not present a storyline and might be inserted into an opera, they had lost interest in the narrative genre of the *ballet d'action*, particularly its use of pantomime to convey the plot. The *ballet d'action* was revived in the mid-1880s when the two grand music halls on Leicester Square, the Alhambra and the Empire, began to build their variety programs around the key attraction of original narrative ballets.[72] Often led by Italian choreographers and *premières danseuses*, the mainly English corps de ballet was schooled in the Italian tradition, which distinguished between mime and dance roles. As in burlesque, male leads were traditionally played as mime roles *en travesty*; the "principal boy" was a drawcard in Leicester Square just as it was at the Gaiety, while the corps de ballet exercised a perennial appeal.[73]

Apart from these two great halls, which maintained ballet as a central attraction, dance on the English stage was reduced to a specialty turn in variety programs. When Otero made her London debut at the Empire in 1892, it was noted that Spanish acts enjoyed a surprisingly low profile when they were compared with the proliferation of character dancing, step dancing, skirt dancing, and serpentine dancing.[74] Otero's usually winning combination of an almost hypnotic hauteur with considerable charm and flirty sensuality did not immediately win over the largely male audience of the Empire, whose expectations of her performance had been elevated by press reports of her sensational New York debut. She opened her show with three "foreign" songs (sung in French and Spanish), followed by a "poignant, most meaning dance ... intensely felt,"[75] displaying elements of flamenco in her heel stamping and her quick turns. But there was a fundamental modesty to her first appearances, which failed to satisfy the audience's desire for something more immediately titillating, perhaps with high kicks, associated with their preconceptions of

72. The newly built Empire opened in April 1884, and rebadged itself as Empire Theatre of Varieties in 1887; ballet was part of its variety programs from the start. The Alhambra went through a variety of managers and programming styles from its initial incarnation as the Royal Panopticon of Science and Art in 1854, but its late-nineteenth-century glory era really began in October 1884, when it "became the Alhambra Theatre of Varieties, with Ballet now as its chief and permanent attraction." By 1899, they advertised themselves as the "original home of ballet" and the "home of ballet" respectively. See Mark E. Perugini, *A Pageant of the Dance and Ballet* (London: Jarrolds, 1946), 213–14, 23; "[Classified]," *Times* (London), 7 July 1899, 8.

73. The corps often danced in travesty costumes characterized by figure-accentuating tights and short tunics. Alexandra Carter, *Dance and Dancers in the Victorian and Edwardian Music Hall Ballet* (Aldershot, UK: Ashgate, 2005), 35, 64–65.

74. Silhouette, "Otero," *Star* (London), 24 September 1892. In *Caroline de Otero: Receuil*, Rés. Fol. S.W. 191, Arts du spectacle, Bibliothèque Nationale, f64.

75. George Bernard Shaw, "Visiting the Halls (*World*, 19 October 1892)," in *Music in London 1890–94 by Bernard Shaw* (London: Constable, 1932a), 2: 169.

Spanish "passion." When Carmencita, after five years of North American success, made her London debut at the Palace in 1895, she also faced the "solid
phalanx of British indifference," her charm and grace seen as "the reverse
of 'showy,'" characterized instead by "simplicity and directness."[76] She was,
however, considered both voluptuous and very Spanish and it was noted
that she appeared in a "Carmenesque scene."[77] Both Carmencita and Otero
were invited into London society, performing in private salons or for charity.
Carmencita had the precedent of her association with John Singer Sargent
and intimacy with New York's social elite,[78] but Otero, who fulfilled London
engagements in 1898, 1899, and 1902, must have been known as one of the
Prince of Wales's favorite companions in Paris and Monte Carlo. Although her
London appearances became less modest in terms of dress and decorum as the
decade wore on, she danced in late 1898 for high society at a bazaar held in aid
of victims of the Spanish-American War.[79]

While Carmencita and Otero embodied Carmen and Spanish dance for transatlantic audiences, the opera itself gave rise to balletic reinterpretations, which
condensed the action into a form that could be communicated exclusively in
movement and music. These dramatic works were quite distinct from the dance
interludes and divertissements that formed part of the opera's action, or were
inserted to add color and spectacle, traditionally to acts 2 and 4. Many writers
attribute the very first ballet treatment of Mérimée's story to Marius Petipa,
who claimed to have devised *Carmen et son torero* (1845/46) during his sojourn
in Madrid in the mid-1840s. In his memoirs, Petipa described his creation of
this one-act ballet for a gala celebration in honor of Queen Isabel II's marriage
(which took place in late 1846), but he did not explicitly connect it with the
Mérimée, nor have scholars uncovered evidence of its Spanish performance.[80]

76. "Carmencita," *Saturday Review* 79, no. 2058 (1895): 441; "The Theatres," *Graphic*
(1895): 246.

77. "In London Town," *Penny Illustrated Paper and Illustrated Times*, 2 March 1895, 136.

78. Carmencita sang in ordinary dress to her husband's piano accompaniment at a
private party, where she "fairly charmed us by her singularly expressive *chansons*, illustrated by a variety of *chic* and piquant *pas* which gave such intense dramatic force
to her unique performances." "In London Town," *Penny Illustrated Paper and Illustrated
Times*, 23 March 1895, 184.

79. "Bazaar at Downshire House," *Standard* (London), 2 December 1898, 2. This bazaar
was the culmination of a concerted campaign by Ana de Osma y Zabala, the Condesa de
Casa Valencia, wife of the former Spanish Ambassador to London (1895–1897). For
more information on her works in aid of victims of the war, and on Spanish bazaars
more generally, see Kirsty Hooper, "'Moorish Splendour' in the British Provinces, 1886–
1906: The Spanish Bazaar, from Dundee to Southampton," in *Contact and Connection
Symposium* (Coventry, UK: University of Warwick Institute of Advanced Study, 2013),
accessed 1 June 2015, http://www.kirstyhooper.net/2013-06_PAPER_Bazaars.pdf.

80. It seems likely that, writing his memoirs in old age, Petipa chose to make a claim
to *Carmen*. Other ballets from his Madrid period include *The Pearl of Seville*, *The Flower
of Granada*, and *The Departure for the Bullfight*. Marius Petipa, *Russian Ballet Master: The*

The Spanish Royal Ballet's 1879 performance of *The Torrera or Spanish Bull Fight* at the Alhambra (see Chapter 2) was programmed on a double bill with the first British ballet adaptation of *Carmen*, a half-hour show in four scenes announced by the Alhambra in late October as a "Grand Original Romantic Ballet d'Action."[81] *Carmen* provided an unusually dramatic plot for a ballet, and this production was clearly designed to capitalize on the success of Bizet's opera at its London debut the previous year. The Alhambra management found that copyright restrictions on Bizet's score meant their indefatigable house composer, Georges Jacobi, had to create an original score, but he satisfied audience expectations by including a sweet and charming habanera and the inevitable melodic reminiscence of the "Toreador Song" from the opera.[82] Both José and Escamillo were presented as trouser roles, adding the titillation of an all-female principal cast.[83]

It was a Spanish star who inspired and headlined perhaps the most celebrated ballet production of *Carmen* of the prewar era at the Alhambra in 1903. Although little is known of her background, Rosario Guerrero had already appeared at iconic Paris music halls, including the Olympia and the Folies Bergère, when she debuted in London in the Alhambra's summer 1899 variety program.[84] She seems to have played for about two-and-a-half weeks, and Arthur Symons considered her a charming addition, declaring in late June that he had "gone wild over a new Spanish dancer ... quite a splendid creature."[85] The management of the Alhambra must have seen even more potential in her, because she returned for a four-week season between Continental engagements in September 1902 with her own dramatic sketch *The Rose and*

Memoirs of Marius Petipa, trans. Helen Whittaker, ed. Lillian Moore (London: Dance Books, 1958), 16.

81. [Classifieds], *Times* 18 October 1879, 8; *Standard* 3 December 1879, 4

82. Georges Jacobi was conductor and musical director of the Alhambra in 1872–98, after conducting the Bouffes-Parisiens for several years before the Franco-Prussian War. Deborah Bull, "Ballet Goes to the Music Hall [music feature]," (BBC Radio 3, 2011).

83. Ivor Guest, *Ballet in Leicester Square: The Alhambra and the Empire 1860 1915* (London: Dance Books, 1992), 16, 30, 33.

84. Rosario Guerrero took her place in the program alongside two *ballets d'action* that had been playing since January and April respectively, and the usual mixed bag of artists, including the "Bedouin Arabs" and the famed music-hall artiste Letty Lind. "[Classified]," *Times*, 7 July 1899, 8. Guerrero has been largely ignored by scholarly research, and one of the best sources of material on her life and career, although largely focused on her American tours, is the website Rosario Guerrero Spanish Dancer maintained by Sarah Stovin across various sites, which have included a rich and varying collection of press quotations and illustrations, especially postcards from the era. Sarah Stovin, Rosario Guerrero Spanish Dancer, accessed 14 November 2016, http://rosarioguerrerospanishdancer.weebly.com/history.html.

85. Arthur Symons, *Arthur Symons: Selected Letters, 1880–1935* (Basingstoke, UK: Macmillan, 1989), 132.

the Dagger, set to music by Paul Lacombe. Guerrero's difference from the usual run of English and Italian dancers at the Alhambra was an important element of her appeal. She was famous for her "pantomimic sketches," as well as her typically Spanish beauty, and her dancing was considered particularly fascinating and uniquely Spanish in its combination of "dash and distinction, coupled with *allure*."[86]

The Rose and the Dagger capitalized on all her strengths: beauty, mime, and Spanish dance. Guerrero's character arrives at an inn on a stormy night to face an innkeeper who tries to steal her diamond ring at knifepoint. Dropping her hooded cloak to reveal her literally stunning beauty, she then bewitches him with her dancing and persuades him to swap his dagger for the rose in her hair. Overcome with passion, he "throws himself" upon her and she stabs him in self-defense, his death surely reminding audiences of Bizet's finale, despite the role reversal. Her mime partner, Alexander Volbert, took the part of the innkeeper, and together their mime enacted a high level of emotion and drama.[87] When it came to Guerrero's dance, Volbert stood aside for a specialist and they performed that classic of Spanish dance, the *sevillana*.[88]

In 1903 the Alhambra team created a new *ballet d'action* based on *Carmen*, specifically as a vehicle for Guerrero's talents in dance and pantomime, announcing it as a new "Grand dramatic ballet." Magnificent costumes and picturesque scenery framed the forty-five-minute action, which condensed the dramatic elements of Bizet's opera into five scenes: a square in Seville, outside the cigarette factory; the military prison; the inn of Lillas Pastias; the rocky mountain pass; outside the bullring. The additional scene depicted José in prison, seeing visions of his mother, a clever substitution for the letter scene, which depended on the character of Micaëla, who does not appear in this version.

George Byng, the Alhambra's house composer, made a careful adaptation of Bizet's score, keeping all the famous melodies and inspiring the *Times* critic to comment that Bizet's music had been "very respectfully treated."[89] A full Alhambra ballet had to feature the famous corps de ballet, so Byng added a few extra dance numbers, namely a cigarette dance for the opening scene, a Hungarian dance for the inn scene (which also featured Guerrero's dance and a tambourine dance), a bolero, and a *grande valse*. A students' dance and

---

86. Italics in original. "La Belle Guerrero," *Sketch*, 3 September 1902.

87. At least one critic explicitly preferred Guerrero's dance to her mime. Astral, "At the Music-Halls," *Topical Times* (London), 20 September 1902, 2.

88. Troy Kinney and Margaret West Kinney, *The Dance: Its Place in Art and Life* (New York: Frederick A. Stokes, 1914), 137, 39.

89. "The Alhambra," *Times* (London), 8 May 1903, 7. Byng was also praised for exercising "a wise discretion." "'Carmen.' The Alhambra's New Ballet," *Music Hall and Theatre Review* 29 (1903): 293.

a colorful march of bullfighters graced the finale. Although the beautifully costumed chorus lines and comic travesty effects were very pleasing, they created a certain incongruity with the harsh tragedy of the plot, especially when contrasted with the dramatic mime "brilliantly" presented by Guerrero as Carmen and Volbert as Don José. The expected trouser role was provided by Edith Slack as Escamillo, who received acclaim for her mime of "the glories of a bullfight" set to Bizet's "Toreador Song,"[90] but whose presence in such a virile role was considered inappropriate by some, who thought it should embody "exuberant masculinity."[91]

Guerrero debuted in this work on 7 May 1903 and drew international attention (see Figure 6.4). Her portrayal became a yardstick for operatic Carmens for years to come, mainly because of her magnetism as an actress. One of Calvé's appearances as Carmen in London coincided with Guerrero's run at the Alhambra. This overlap facilitated a comparison: "One represented the cigarette-girl as a deliberate flirt not altogether without heart; the other imbuing the character with a certain devilish unscrupulousness and deliberation which is, to me, somewhat revolting." This critic clearly favored Calvé, but for him the essential appeal lay in the story, for "no matter how presented, this love tragedy is so true to life ... that it never fails to appeal to the heart. Carmen's frailties are forgiven in the anguish of her death." It was noted that both played to packed houses, despite the contrast between their interpretations.[92]

As late as 1906 a London critic claimed that her Carmen "caused Guerrero to be ranked among the operatic stars who enjoy the advantage over her of speech in their impersonation of the character."[93] She was described as possessing animal qualities like savagery and daring, but the versatility that enabled her to project anything from "dazzling, unconscionable charm" to the premonition of "a tragic, overhanging doom" (in the card scene) led Mark Perugini to declare her work "not acting but reality, the real Carmen of Mérimée."[94] Despite appearing on an admittedly elite music-hall stage, she was thus praised for achieving a dramatic truth that brought her closer to that fabled Carmen "of Mérimée" than most of her operatic colleagues. Even Calvé was reported in the American press as having declared Guerrero "the embodiment of Bizet's cigarette girl."[95]

90. "Alhambra," *Times*, 8 May 1903, 7; "'Carmen.' The Alhambra's New Ballet," 293.
91. *Era*, 9 May 1903, quoted in Guest, *Ballet in Leicester Square*, 67–68.
92. X., "Meditations in Music Halls," *Sunday Times*, 28 June 1903, 6.
93. *Bystander*, 4 July 1906.
94. Mark E. Perugini, *The Art of Ballet* (London: Martin Secker, 1915), 268.
95. This much-quoted endorsement could have been an invention of Guerrero's public relations machine or might indicate that Calvé saw *Carmen* at the Alhambra in London as this newspaper article predates Guerrero's New York debut as Carmen. Whatever its

Figure 6.4 Rosario Guerrero and M. Volbert in *Carmen* at London's Alhambra Theatre, featured on the cover of popular Parisian journal. *Paris qui chante* 1, no. 28 (2 August 1903).
Credit: Special Collections, University of Melbourne.

London critics quickly recognized the passion, fire, and sensuality that distinguished Guerrero from the usual run of Alhambra dancers. Responses to her pairing with Volbert clarify the exotic qualities of their dramatic and emotional performance:

source, its importance lies in its contribution to the development of Guerrero's reputation as the "true" Carmen. "Roof Garden and Music Hall: This Week's Amusements for New Yorkers," *Sun* (New York), 3 July 1904, 5.

La Belle Guerrero makes a magnificent Carmen, alluring, impudent, and se-ductive in turn. She speaks volumes with her lang[u]orous eyes and arching brows. Monsieur Volbert, as Don Jose, is cold and restrained at first, but after succumbing to Carmen's charms, fierce and passionate.[96]

[Volbert] was not afraid to let himself go; and thus imparted to the char-acter a reality of passion that would have been probably lacking in an English performer.[97]

Volbert's passionate impersonation of José parallels the growing impact of verismo on the operatic character by the turn of the century (see Figure 6.5).

Although *Carmen* fitted in with the Alhambra's tradition of *ballets d'actions* in many respects, Guerrero's peculiarly Spanish dancing owed more to the tra-dition of exotic entertainment, and her dual command of mime and dance harked back to earlier traditions, like that of Elssler. In a 1903 interview, Guerrero explained that she had studied mime in Paris, with an eye to more serious roles than were usual in the music hall, and even wished to train with an opera coach in dramatic works like *Aida*, not because she could sing, but for the sake of conveying great tragedy in pantomime form. She considered the Alhambra *Carmen* a "grand production" and her best work.[98]

The work was thus something of a hybrid, but this aspect did not inhibit its success. Guerrero's allure was amplified by the unusual appeal of a ballet featuring a convincing and coherent dramatic plot, which together prefigured the successful combination of exoticism with dramatic musical coherence that was to be such a feature of the Ballets Russes productions when the company arrived in London in 1909. Unlike the overtly English style of *Carmen Up to Data*, or the French affectations of Nethersole's reading, Guerrero's interpreta-tion advanced the process of Hispanicizing Carmen for English audiences. She played Carmen for several months, eventually replaced by another Spaniard, Maria la Bella, and the Alhambra's *Carmen* enjoyed an exceptionally long run, just short of eleven months (see Figure 6.6).[99] In October 1903 Guerrero took ship for New York, under contract to Florenz Ziegfeld, to appear in his production of the comic opera *The Red Feather*. She also launched herself on the American vaudeville circuit, and spent the next six months performing her sketches, including *The Rose and the Dagger*, in variety theaters around New York and touring to other cities.[100]

96. "'Carmen.' The Alhambra's New Ballet," 293.

97. *Pall Mall Gazette* (London), 8 May 1903, 8.

98. "How the Beautiful Spanish Dancer, Guerrero, Outrivaled Otero," *Sunday Telegraph* (New York), 22 November 1903, 2.

99. Guest, *Ballet in Leicester Square*, 67.

100. Guerrero arrived in New York on 20 October to star in Ziegfeld's show *The Red Feather*, but after a dispute over star billing, she opened up in vaudeville to perform her own sketches, before appearing for Ziegfeld as contracted. "News of Plays and Players," *New York Time*, 21 October 1903, 8.

Figure 6.5 "Guerrero and Mons. Volbert in the Grand Ballet 'Carmen,'" Raphael Tuck post-card, *Carmen Alhambra set*. Theatrical Souvenirs series (*c.* 1903).
Credit: CC BY-SA 3.0 (TuckDB Postcards), https://tuckdb.org/postcards/60663.

Guerrero arrived at a time when early-twentieth-century New Yorkers must have felt that Spain greeted them at every turn. Far from being exhausted by the touring stars of the 1890s, North Americans and their fascination with everything Hispanic embraced architecture, art, and theater alongside music and dance. The increasingly confident nation had acquired many formerly Spanish colonial territories during the nineteenth century, and victory in the Spanish-American War of 1898 brought Puerto Rico, Guam, the Philippines, and Cuba under US jurisdiction.[101] The tensions created by this conflict ranged

101. The United States acquired Florida in 1819, annexed Texas in 1845, and won California in 1848. María Dolores Jiménez-Blanco, "Spanish Art and American

Figure 6.6 "'Carmen' at the Alhambra. Mons. Volbert and Signora Maria la Bella. Carmen Tempts Don Jose," photograph by W. and D. Downey, *Black and White* (19 December 1903): 362.
Credit: Private collection

from anti-Spanish propaganda dredging up images from the Black Legend to discomfort at the "increasingly imperialistic actions" of the United States.[102] Growing recognition of Spain's contribution to the "civilization" of the New World found expression in the emergence of the long-lasting architectural style known as "Spanish Revival," which drew on both Spanish and Spanish colonial

Collections," in *When Spain Fascinated America* ([Madrid]: Fundación Zuloaga; Gobierno de España, Ministerio de Cultura, 2010), 62–63.

102. This sensation of "dis-ease" could be "soothed" by "evocations of romantic Spain." Boone, *Vistas de España*, 188.

architecture. It shaped building designs from the Chicago World's Fair (1893), which commemorated four hundred years since Columbus's discovery of the New World, to Buffalo's Pan-American Exposition (1901), for which organizers adopted a Spanish architectural theme "in the belief that this particular style best embodied the idea of 'America.'"[103] The incorporation of the new territories ushered in a new phase in the relationship between American cultural elites and all things Hispanic. Appreciation of Spain's Golden Age, along with the art and architecture of the Spanish Baroque, was now bolstered by a sense of kinship with Spain's imperial achievements and the opportunity, even responsibility, to "appropriate the patrimony" of a weakened nation no longer in a position to preserve its "many artistic and architectural treasures."[104]

In 1904 cultural philanthropist and longtime collector Archer Huntington founded the Hispanic Society of America. He envisioned an institution almost like the British Library, dedicated to "advancement of the study of the Spanish and Portuguese languages, literature, and history," and housing a collection of books, manuscripts, arts and crafts.[105] When its magnificent Upper Manhattan building opened to the public in 1908, it housed a library, a publishing house, and a museum. Here Huntington displayed works by the great artists of Spain's past, such as Velázquez, Murillo, Zurbarán, El Greco, and Goya, while also promoting contemporary artists.[106] In 1909 the Hispanic Society staged exhibitions that introduced the American public to two of Spain's greatest contemporary painters and their starkly contrasting visions of their homeland. Joaquín Sorolla's depictions of sunny Spain met with immediate acclaim, while Ignacio Zuloaga's darker representations of Spanish scenes and characters achieved less instant success, but resulted in subsequent solo shows in 1916 and 1925.

New York had long been home to a Spanish-speaking community with its own cultural outlets, including newspapers and theatrical activity.[107] The

103. Richard L. Kagan, "The Spanish *Craze* in the United States: Cultural Entitlement and the Appropriation of Spain's Cultural Patrimony, ca. 1890–ca. 1930," *Revista Complutense de Historia de América* 36 (2010): 40–41, 51–52; Richard L. Kagan, "The Spanish Craze: The Discovery of Spanish Art and Culture in the United States," in *When Spain Fascinated America* ([Madrid]: Fundación Zuloaga; Gobierno de España, Ministerio de Cultura, 2010), 37–39.

104. Kagan, "Spanish Craze," 54.

105. Mitchell Codding, "Archer Milton Huntington, Champion of Spain in the United States," in *Spain in America: The Origins of Hispanism in the United States*, ed. Richard L. Kagan (Urbana and Chicago: University of Illinois Press, 2002), 154, 158.

106. Kagan, "Spanish Craze," 34; Jiménez-Blanco, "Spanish Art and American Collections," 64–65. For more information on the Hispanic Society Museum and Library, see its website, accessed 15 December 2016, at http://hispanicsociety.org.

107. Spanish-speaking immigrants had lived in New York since as early as 1654, but Hispanic cultural life began to flourish in the public sphere with the foundation of

community's numbers swelled in the 1890s with an influx of expatriates from Spain's last remaining Latin-American colonies, who gathered in New York to foment their respective independence struggles, and again in the 1910s with refugees from the Mexican Revolution.[108] A shared taste for *zarzuela* and Spanish-language theater was catered to by amateur theatricals but especially by touring companies who worked the Hispanic "empire" circuit, from the Iberian peninsula to Cuba and various countries in Latin America. With this local Hispanic community ready to welcome visiting Spanish artists, alongside mainstream New York audiences in both elite and more popular entertainment venues, a beautiful Spanish performer headlining the ultimate Spanish tale was bound to succeed.

Guerrero finally launched her *Carmen* at the New York Roof Garden in early July 1904. Summer in New York was the season of the big international stars, when many of the ordinary theaters were closed, so this timing gave *Carmen*'s debut an even greater cachet. Volbert arrived from Europe to reprise his role as José, and the production was made even more spectacular with "a company of seventy-five people costumed with grand opera picturesqueness."[109] Advance publicity advised it would include "a realistic Spanish bullfight with live bulls and horses."[110] Guerrero's success in New York saw *Carmen* playing there until mid-August. She then began to appear at different vaudeville houses, always as a headline act, before returning to Europe at the end of the year.

Guerrero's career continued on both sides of the Atlantic, with Paris, Madrid, and the United States all favored with repeated presentations of her distinctive Spanish-themed sketches featuring dance and mime, many of which mined the themes of the Carmen story. In addition to *The Rose and the Dagger*, which she performed as *Le Couteau et la rose* at Paris's Théâtre Marigny as late as 1911, she staged *The Daughter of the Mountain* and the one-act pantomime *La gitana*. This last was a story of two women fighting for the love of a bullfighter, quite literally with daggers in the final scene, resulting in tragedy, surely recalling act 1 (and even act 4) of Bizet's opera.[111]

As Guerrero's celebrity increased, she began to identify publicly with the dramatic role that represented the artistic peak of her career. Her claims to have been born in Seville, and to have grown up dancing, are consistent with

Spanish-language newspapers in the late 1820s. For an outline of theatrical activities in these communities, see Nicolás Kanellos, *A History of Hispanic Theater in the United States: Origins to 1940* (Austin: University of Texas Press, 1990).

108. Kanellos, *History of Hispanic Theater*, 105.
109. "Plays and Players," *Theatre Magazine* 4, no.42 (August 1904): 188–89
110. "Plays and Players," *Theatre Magazine* 4, no. 37 (March 1904): 60.
111. "Plays and Players," *Sunday Times* (London), 23 April 1905, 2.

a Carmenesque image.[112] She was not afraid to avow Carmen's Spanishness, even granting Bizet honorary status, as she declared her enjoyment of the role:

> Ah, yes. I felt that I was in my element there; Bizet's music lends itself to my coloring. It is Spain, and the rattle of the castanets can be felt in the orchestration. Bizet was a Parisian by birth, but a Spaniard in feeling, or he could not have written the "Toreador Song."[113]

The dramatic instinct that allowed her to inhabit so completely the role of Carmen was fully matched by her ability to project herself as the ideal Spanish "product" in her dealings with the press, not missing the opportunity to play on her exotic charm. Obviously aware that her passionate performances were one of her chief drawcards, she spoke about playing the character: "I revelled in it. I felt that I was Carmen, and, do you know, I verily believe that my Don Jose was now and again really afraid of me. He once declared that he could see murder in my eye."[114]

Guerrero's career went even a step beyond Bizet's *Carmen* when various American papers reported in May 1906 that she had been confined to an insane asylum, violently mad: "She dances all the time, rising from her bed in the middle of the night to dance till she falls exhausted on the floor."[115] Although these reports conflict with her known performance engagements at London's Palace Theatre from late May of that year, the connection between the acute intensity of Guerrero's performances and such a breakdown must have seemed plausible to her public.[116]

LATE AND CAPRICIOUS CALVÉ

The extreme passion of Guerrero's Carmen was a logical extension of the dramatic development of the role spearheaded by Minnie Hauk, who made the opera

112. "Oh yes. I was born dancing—I think most Spanish girls are; it is in our blood. We love the old national dances, and I think they are more beautiful than the set figures of the dance of society. Don't you? They mean something, too; every step interprets a seguidilla or a malagueña." "How the Beautiful Spanish Dancer, Guerrero, Outrivaled Otero," 2.

113. Edgar Lee, "A Chat with La Guerrero," *Illustrated Sporting and Dramatic News* (London), 22 April 1905, 272.

114. Lee, "Chat with La Guerrero," 272.

115. "Excessive Dancing Makes Famous Guerrero Mad," *Evening Telegram* (New York), 18 May 1906, 3. The story does not appear to have been all that widespread, but was reported in the *Washington Times, Philadelphia Inquirer*, and the *Post-Standard* (Syracuse, NY).

116. "Plays and Players," *Times*, 30 May 1906, 14. This article announced that Guerrero was "now appearing every evening (9.45) in a pantomime at the Palace Theatre."

so popular in New York when she introduced it in 1878. Local interpretations of the opera had emphasized the gypsy protagonist's sensual and unruly nature, playing up her violent temper, and Calvé must have been aware of this emphasis, given her annual appearances and extensive touring. With New York audiences under the spell of her unique impersonation of the gypsy, Calvé's *Carmen* dominated the Met's repertory from the mid-1890s until 1908, although the turn of the century saw its sway threatened by Wagner's operas and Gounod's *Faust*, and the introduction of the new Italian operas from 1903.[117]

Calvé was aged in her mid-thirties when she first presented her energetic and unpredictable impersonation of Carmen to New York audiences. Still offering this interpretation more than a decade later, she was accused of a capricious and exaggerated style. We can judge Calvé's vocal interpretation only from the recordings she made in several sessions late in her career and after her retirement.[118] On some records her *Carmen* arias were accompanied by piano, on others by full orchestra, and one can hear her lovely vocal tone and clear diction. Calvé did not use altered vocal timbre or attack for emphasis or to convey heightened emotion, although her full, rich chest notes convey the sensuality of her Carmen, in contrast to her effortless and lyrical upper register. Expression resides more in her unpredictable rubato and extended durations, a habit so ingrained that critics decried her cavalier approach to Bizet's score. Her practice of rushing one part of a phrase, while lingering over another part, resulted in an erratic pulse that would have made her habanera very difficult to dance to. She particularly favored broad ritardandos in the last line of a stanza, and even broader ones in the last few lines of an aria, with extended durations on high or penultimate notes, which surely garnered her great applause. Apart from a coquettish and operatic giggle in her 1902 recording of the "Séguedille" (an embellishment affected by many singers in recordings of the era), her recordings are relatively straight, perhaps because of the constraints of the new medium. This lack of affectation might suggest that accusations of caprice and eccentricity were largely based on her stage business, with histrionics that emerged before a large audience.

This very personal approach had always been central to Calvé's reading of the role, although the balance between charm and mannerism clearly shifted as she aged:

Before her artistic ideals degenerated to the point whence she could not see anything in the opera but an opportunity to exploit her personality Mme Calvé used

117. Henry Edward Krehbiel, *Chapters of Opera*, 2nd ed. (New York: Henry Holt, 1909), 276, 318–19, 61.

118. Calvé made recordings in 1902 for Gramophone (as the Gramophone and Typewriter Company) in London and for Lionel Mapleson at the Met; for Victor in 1907, 1908, and 1916, and for Pathé in 1920.

to present Carmen as a woman thoroughly wanton but equipped with witcheries which, despite their viciousness, offered some explanation, possibly even some palliation, for the errant conduct of Don José.[119]

A journalist's anecdote suggests that Jean de Reszke himself had found her mannerisms intolerable when he appeared as Calvé's very first New York Don José in 1893. Despite having learnt the role expressly for this production, "after two performances, in which the tenor never knew where to turn to find his gypsy sweetheart, de Reszke decided, unlike the public, that her interpretation was too capricious for him, and he refused to reappear."[120] Another story relates to Calvé's appearance in the *millième* performance at Paris's Opéra-Comique in 1904, when, instead of listening calmly from a chair as Edmond Clément sang his "Flower Aria," she "threw herself in a paroxysm of pretended passion on [his] breast," forcing him to gasp for breath (and upstaging his key lyrical moment).[121]

By the new century, Calvé's commitment to a realist and dramatic Carmen had fallen victim to her success. "The star has risen above the work," noted the New York critic James Huneker in 1904, "Mme Calvé's Carmen is a thing of the past" (see Figure 6.7).[122] Calvé famously championed a ragged Carmen early in her career but increasingly became known for her grand gowns. She was not beyond justifying her choice of a "gorgeous red silk petticoat" for the first act with her usual narrative of authenticity:

"When I decided to sing Carmen," she replied, "I went to Seville, the very place where the scene of the opera is laid, to make studies on the spot. I often stood outside the cigarette factories and watched the girls coming to and going from their work. On one occasion I followed one of them to a second-hand costumer's, and saw her buy a brilliant red skirt. The next day she wore it, and occasionally lifted her dress a little so as to give a glimpse of the skirt and flirt with it. I went directly to the same costumer and bought the exact duplicate of the skirt. I have it on now, and as soon as you see me go on the stage you will see that I flirt with it just as I saw the cigarette girl in Seville do."[123]

119. Krehbiel, "Notable Carmens," 7.

120. "Some Tenors in 'Carmen,'" *New York Times*, 21 January 1917, X8.

121. "Musical America's Open Forum [Letter from George E. Shea]," *Musical America* 23, no. 20 (1916): 26.

122. Quaintance Eaton, *The Miracle of the Met* (New York: Meredith, 1968), 124–25.

123. Gustav Kobbé, *Opera Singers: A Pictorial Souvenir*, 6th ed. (Boston: Oliver Ditson, [1901] 1913), n.p.

Figure 6.7 "Mr John Cort presents Calvé," poster (*c.* 1907).
Credit: Library of Congress, http://www.loc.gov/pictures/item/2014635507.

But this was far from her worst excess, and she was described in 1906 as the "spangled, Worth-clad Carmen."[124] Retreating youth, and the slow loss of all the "vocal and physical allure" that goes with it, increased perceptions of the eccentricity of Calvé's reading, while her dominance in the role cost New York

124. *Sun* (New York), 30 December 1906, 5.

the chance for any other singer to build a following as Bizet's gypsy.[125] Van Vechten cites W. J. Henderson saying that

> Mme. Calvé's bold, picturesque and capricious impersonation of the gipsy became the idol of the American imagination, and thereby much harm was wrought, for whereas the gifted performer began the season with a consistent and well-executed characterization, she speedily permitted success to turn her head and lead her to abandon genuine dramatic art for catch-penny devices aimed at the unthinking. The result has been that opera-goers have found correct impersonations of Carmen uninteresting.[126]

By the early twentieth century, Calvé's Carmen, initially hailed for its realism, had been rendered passé by a new wave of verismo performance and evolving representations of Spanishness that was to culminate in the first internationally renowned Spanish Carmen: Maria Gay.

---

125. "No 'Carmen' to Succeed Calvé," *Sun* (New York), 27 February 1910, 7.
126. Van Vechten, *The Music of Spain*, 155, note.

CHAPTER 7

✧

Finding a Spanish Voice for Carmen

Elena Fons and Maria Gay

Spanish theaters gradually incorporated Bizet's *Carmen* as part of their repertory in the last decade of the nineteenth century, after working through initial qualms about its exoticism and inaccuracies. In a process mediated by Italian opera and the rise of verismo, *Carmen* became a model to which many Spanish composers looked for inspiration in creating their own nationalist school. In tandem with this evolution, a renewed engagement with Bizet's opera can be identified, led by the first Spaniards to gain international renown as Carmen: Elena Fons and Maria Gay.

ELENA FONS: A CARMEN FROM SEVILLE

Reflecting on the 1910 season in Madrid, the eminent Spanish critic Cecilio de Roda declared that

> *Carmen* triumphed yet again. But how did it triumph? Soaked in syrup, paired off with Rosina, of the same yoke as *Linda* and *Dinorah*; converting herself to the utmost as a diabolical woman, a naughty girl or a scatterbrain. This is how Carmen has been portrayed by nearly all the singers I have seen—apart from Calvé, who interpreted the role from a French point of view, Elena Fons and Maria Gay.[1]

1. Cecilio de Roda, "El año musical," *La España moderna* 22, no. 256 (1910): 37.

In the course of 1910 both Elena Fons and Maria Gay, Spanish singers at the height of their careers, presented their mature interpretations of Carmen in Madrid. Over the previous decade these two divas had become the most renowned Spanish protagonists of the opera, building in their own distinct ways upon the legacy of Emma Calvé.

The proliferation of *Carmen* productions in Spain in the 1890s had seen a number of singers from the Iberian peninsula impersonating the role in cities from Barcelona to Seville, but one in particular came to be seen as the fin-de-siècle embodiment of Carmen in Spain and Latin America. This was the soprano Elena Fons, born in Seville in 1873, who was to shape the role of Carmen around the evolving musical and theatrical projections of Andalusian identity, while asserting a sense of authenticity that emanated from her birth in the city in which the opera is set. Fons enjoyed an international career in Italian opera, *zarzuela*, and popular Spanish song, and created a charming Carmen much beloved by Spanish audiences.

In the 1870s Seville had a thriving musical life, which ranged from a variety of popular styles through to a strong operatic presence, particularly in the decade following the 1874 restoration of Alfonso XII.[2] In fact, *Carmen* had made its way to Seville within a year of its Madrid premiere, performed in Spanish by a *zarzuela* company in the summer gardens of the Eslava Theater on 27 July 1889. This was followed in April 1890 by a touring Italian company's production of the opera with Giuseppina Pasqua—the diva who first portrayed Carmen at Madrid's Teatro Real—in the title role, and several other stagings of the work throughout the 1890s.[3]

In terms of popular styles of music-making, Seville had a burgeoning flamenco scene, which is corroborated by the city's key role in the establishment of *cafés cantantes* as locales for its evolution and dissemination. Seville had been at the vanguard of the development of flamenco and its modes of presentation since the 1860s, and leading flamenco historian José Blas Vega categorized the 1880s and 1890s as the golden age of the *cafés cantantes*.[4] The singing styles associated with the *cafés cantantes* are suggestively described by John Singer Sargent—who was a flamenco *aficionado*—in a letter from Seville dating from 1880:

> You wished some Spanish songs. I could not find any good ones. The best are what one hears in Andalucia, the half African Malagueñas & Soleás, dismal, restless chants that it is impossible to note. They are something between a

2. Andrés Moreno Mengíbar, *La ópera en Sevilla en el siglo XIX* (Seville: Universidad de Sevilla, Secretariado de Publicaciones, 1998), 322.

3. See Moreno Mengíbar, *La ópera en Sevilla en el siglo XIX*, 205–98.

4. José Blas Vega, *Los cafés cantantes de Sevilla* (Madrid: Cinterco, 1987).

Hungarian Czardas and the chant of the Italian peasant in the fields, and are generally composed of five strophes and end stormily *on the dominant*, the theme quite lost in strange fiorituras and guttural roulades. The gitano [gypsy] voices are marvellously supple.[5]

These two important facets of Seville's music-making—opera and flamenco—were influential in shaping the career of Elena Fons, and formed part of her earliest training under Enriqueta Ventura de Doménech, with whom she studied piano and voice from the age of ten. Doménech was one of the first pianists to publish arrangements of flamenco *palos*, in her collection *Trozos flamencos* (1880), which included *Seguidillas gitanas*, *Panaderos*, and a *Malagueña granadina*, pieces in which she retained some of the structures and harmonic idiosyncrasies of the flamenco forms (see Figure 7.1).[6] Doménech is likely to have imparted this love of flamenco to her pupil, who was to become one of the few classical divas to be an *aficionado* of many *palos* and to record as a flamenco artist.

After training in Seville with Doménech and Francisco Reynés, Fons received a scholarship from the Council of Seville to further her studies in Madrid. In late 1894 she made her debut at the Teatro Real, initially as Venus in *Tannhäuser*, but by December of that year she was singing Micaëla in the Real's production of *Carmen*, receiving very positive reviews for her passion and dramatic presence, not virtues normally associated with this role: "Elena Fons ... had a complete triumph. Her Micaëla was adorable, with a beautiful and well-modulated voice, which gained her much applause. She sang the romance with passion, and attained great heights as an actress."[7] These performances of *Carmen* spread through January into February 1895, during which time Emma Calvé also performed at the Teatro Real, in Ambroise Thomas's *Hamlet*, and as Santuzza in *Cavalleria rusticana*, another of the roles that became a cornerstone of Fons's repertory.

Calvé's Madrid performances in early 1895 had created much expectation among the Spanish public and were preceded by articles that spread claims about her own Spanish origins.[8] Her visit coincided with public uproar at the Teatro Real related to dissatisfaction with the management, and although she managed to charm the audience into allowing her to sing *Hamlet* and several

5. John Singer Sargent, letter to Vernon Lee, 9 July 1880, in M. Elizabeth Boone, Vistas de España: *American Views of Art and Life in Spain, 1860–1914* (New Haven and London: Yale University Press, 2007), 124, 240n30; Richard Ormond, "John Singer Sargent and Vernon Lee," *Colby Quarterly* 9, no. 3 (1970): 163.

6. See Guillermo Castro Buendía, "Las 'seguidillas gitanas' y 'del cambio' de Enriqueta Ventura de Doménech," *Sinfonía Virtual* 24 (2013): 1–26.

7. *La crónica del sport* (Madrid), 31 December 1894, 383.

8. *El nuevo mundo*, 3 January 1895.

Figure 7.1 T[omás] Povedano, cover image for Enriqueta Ventura de Doménech, *Trozos flamencos* (Seville: Enrique Bergali, 1880).

other works, she declared herself frightened by the aggressive manners of Madrid audiences and did not stay to complete her contract.[9] Despite a stipulation in her contract, she did not essay Carmen before a Spanish public,

9. Emma Calvé, *My Life*, trans. Rosamond Gilder (New York and London: D. Appleton, 1922), 125–29; Jean Contrucci, *Emma Calvé la diva du siècle* (Paris: Albin Michel, 1989), 212–13.

even though preparations for the production were well under way, and she was taking dance lessons with the famous *bailaora* (flamenco dancer) La Macarrona, who had amazed the crowds at the 1889 Exposition Universelle and was currently performing in Madrid. From newspaper reports it appears as though Calvé had wished to perfect the art of the *sevillanas* dance, which was to be incorporated into act 1 of the opera.[10] In the end, the excuse given by Calvé was that the sudden illness of her mother necessitated her immediate return to France. But one is left wondering whether issues concerning the Teatro Real's management, or perhaps even some misgivings about being able to sell her impersonation of Carmen to the demanding audience of the Real, may have underpinned her inordinate haste to quit the Spanish capital. At any rate, this incident gave Fons the opportunity to study Calvé at close quarters, whether observing her in *Hamlet* or *Cavalleria rusticana*, or in preparation for *Carmen*. Fons was to make her debut in the title role of *Carmen* only a couple of months later, in April 1895, to a highly appreciative home audience at Seville's Teatro de San Fernando.

By the early 1900s Fons had made a name for herself as Carmen throughout Spain, Portugal, and Italy, with the occasional appearance in European centers as far afield as Saint Petersburg. She was also identified with the role in Latin America, particularly via repeated tours to Cuba, Mexico, and Argentina. Apart from *Carmen*, she was also known for singing in verismo operas, in particular *Cavalleria rusticana* and *I Pagliacci*, and works like Verdi's *Otello* and Meyerbeer's *L'Africaine*. Despite these successes, in 1909 the Parisian daily *Le Figaro* noted that "Elena Fons, an authentic Sevillian who passes in Spain as the best interpreter of Carmen," had not reproduced her success beyond the Pyrenees.[11]

Fons played up her status as a true Andalusian, exploiting her familiarity with popular song and dance styles of the region. Her career was not confined to the operatic stage, and she was a celebrated performer of *zarzuela*, regional song, and *cuplé*, even recording as a flamenco artist in the early twentieth century.[12] In Spain and South America Fons was seen as an opera singer who was capable of projecting the character of a genuine Andalusian woman. She played Carmen with animation and seductive charm, emphasizing the Andalusian—and peculiarly Sevillian—quality of *gracia*, which inflected not only her singing, movement, and dancing, but every aspect of her performance

10. Reported in *El guadalete*, 1 February 1895. The rehearsal with La Macarrona is said to have taken place the previous day.
11. Serge Basset, "Courrier des théatres," *Le Figaro* (Paris), 28 November 1909, 6.
12. A 1922 advertisement for the recordings produced by the Spanish branch of His Master's Voice (Discos "La voz de su amo") lists her singing flamenco song beside such stellar flamenco names as Niña de los Peines. "[Advertisement]," *ABC* (Madrid), 21 January 1922, 29.

Figure 7.2 Elena Fons in *Carmen*, photograph by Antoni Esplugas.
Credit: Centre de Documentació i Museu de les Arts Escèniques de l'Institut del Teatre (MAE), Top. 11128 Col. Paris. Catàleg documents Sedó.

as well. Fons combined this easy grace and wit with a transfer of the characteristic stereotypes of regional Spain from the *zarzuela* tradition into Bizet's opera, embodying a Sevillian Carmen instantly recognized by her Spanish audiences. In the process, she was embraced by Hispanic audiences as a true "Carmen andaluza," who "brought honor to her native land" (see Figure 7.2).[13]

13. "Triunfos personales: Elena Fons," *El arte del teatro* 2, no. 30 (1907): 11; "Nuestros Grabados: Elena Fons," *Eco artístico* 2, no. 9 (1910): [2].

The flamenco recordings that Fons made in 1908, at a time when she was still being hailed for the purity of her operatic Desdemona, indicate her ability to modulate her voice and style to the more animated, rhythmically dynamic, and guttural sounds of flamenco, while maintaining aspects of her lyric suppleness. This versatility is noted in many reviews, such as the following description of an 1898 concert in Salamanca, where she sang arias and duos from *Gioconda* and *Cavalleria rusticana* to great acclaim:

> The echo of the applause had not been extinguished when the *soprano* transformed herself as if by magic into a delightful Andalusian *cantaora*, with more wit and charm than that contained in all of Andalusia.
>
> The crowd became delirious, with thunderous applause, and from everyone's lips came forth the praise that we can condense into a single expressive phrase: "*Gitana!*"[14]

In her performances of *Carmen*, Fons was capable of bringing aspects of this popular delivery to performative numbers such as the "Habanera" and the "Séguedille," while projecting a heightened dramatic lyricism when required. Her movement and dance in these numbers and the "Chanson bohème" were likewise deemed to be authentic in their reflection of theatrical dance styles associated with Seville. Following her marriage in 1899 to Angelo Angioletti, the stage name for the Catalan tenor Jaume Bachs, Fons often paired with him in the role of José (until his death in 1909) and performed more often in Barcelona. This partnership and her evolving artistry gave her scope to develop in the role over time, as was commented on in *El arte del teatro* in 1907:

> We already knew the Carmen of Elena Fons, which is known and applauded in the major theaters of Europe and of South America. Here, in Barcelona, we had applauded her, but we are always struck by an Andalusian Carmen who is seductive, full blooded, daring, with a fine voice, and above all who feels the character.... Fons had never before reached the heights of the performance she gave yesterday, above all in the card aria of the third act.... [She] fully embodied the character of the Sevillian cigarette worker conceived by Mérimée, and has known how to give the action the animated yet somewhat restrained movement which is true to those Andalusian workers.[15]

Fons's ability to embody the Sevillian Carmen convincingly for Hispanic audiences contrasts with the strategy of Calvé and a number of the Parisian

14. *El adelanto* (Salamanca), 11 September 1898, 3.
15. "Triunfos personales: Elena Fons," 12. This review relates to performances of *Carmen* given in Barcelona earlier that year.

interpreters, who opted for the primitive associations of the *gitanas* from the Granada caves when selling their portrayals in northern Europe. The increasing association of Bizet's opera with verismo in Spain (and elsewhere) from the 1890s further underscored the importance of the local color being credible for audiences, from sets and costumes to the performance style of the singers (see Figure 7.3).[16] In this context Fons was able to bring to life Bizet's protagonist for the opera-going public south of the Pyrenees.

SPANISH OPERA AND *CARMEN*

Even before the appearance of Fons as Carmen, Spanish audiences and composers of the 1890s had begun to reassess the opera's human drama and Bizet's projection of Spanishness in the light of their increasing familiarity with Italian verismo operas.[17] As early as 1887, the critic of *El imparcial* had signaled the importance of local color to the Spanish reception of the opera's music:

> Bizet has realized an exceptional task in welding Spanish songs, in which there is a preponderance of what we could call absolute melody, with the most difficult art of the Wagnerian school. The public could appreciate the color and inspiration of the former, but until it hears the opera on numerous occasions it will not be able to fully appreciate . . . the triumphs achieved by the maestro in harmony and the perfection that he has imprinted on the orchestration.[18]

The combination of Spanish musical sources and tropes with advanced compositional techniques that critics identified in Bizet's score not only challenged local audiences, but also opened new horizons for Spanish composers searching for a nationalist voice.

Carmen's considerable influence on the development of new operas by Spanish composers was heightened because its establishment in Spain coincided with the arrival of verismo operas, beginning with Mascagni's *Cavalleria rusticana* in Madrid in 1890. Seeing *Carmen* again in 1892, Peña

---

16. The 1908 production of *Carmen* at Madrid's Teatro Real seems to have drawn on the set designs created by Luigi Manini for the 1884 premiere of *Carmen* at the Teatro de São Carlos in Lisbon. We are grateful to David Cranmer for making us aware of the Manini designs. Marina Arnal Ferrándiz, "Luigi Manini (1848–1936) en el Teatro de São Carlos de Lisboa, o un futuro incierto para la herencia de los Bibiena" (PhD thesis, Universidad Complutense de Madrid, 2015), 130, 229, 234, 238.

17. Luis G. Iberni, "Verismo y realismo en la ópera española," in *La ópera en España e Hispanoamérica*, ed. Emilio Casares Rodicio and Álvaro Torrente (Madrid: ICCMU, 2002), 2:215.

18. "Teatro de la Zarzuela: *Carmen*," *El imparcial* (Madrid), 3 November 1887.

TEATRO REAL: ÓPERA «CARMEN», DE BIZET,
ADMIRABLEMENTE CANTADA POR NUESTRA COMPATRIOTA ELENA FONS

Figure 7.3 Images from production of *Carmen* at the Teatro Real (Madrid), starring Elena Fons, reproduced in "Teatro Real: Opera 'Carmen,' de Bizet; Admirablemente cantada por nuestra compatriot Elena Fons," *El album ibero americano* 26, no. 9 (7 March 1908): 103.
Credit: Biblioteca Nacional de España.

y Goñi revealed in his comments the perceived magnification of the human drama in Bizet's masterpiece:

> What seemed small before on the vast stage of the Teatro Real, now starts to seem large. The beauties of the work impress in their own right; the ear now perceives perfectly what previously sounded strange to it; and from this moment on it is the human note that is highlighted in this admirable creation of Bizet, the verismo which the opera breathes and is imposed on the spectator through the slow but irresistible impulse of genius.[19]

While Italian verismo would eventually influence both Spanish opera and *zarzuela* composition, its most immediate impact was the creation of verismo-inspired plays with Spanish settings, such as *La Dolores* by Josep Feliu y Codina. The 1892 Barcelona premiere of Feliu y Codina's play prompted immediate comparisons with *Carmen*: "From the outset, when we are transported to an Aragonese tavern, to its tragic conclusion, which takes place amid amorous rivalry, defamatory remarks and a well-aimed knifing, we miss the possible contribution of the unfortunate Bizet."[20] In fact *La Dolores* was soon to be set to music by one of the leading fin-de-siècle Spanish opera and *zarzuela* composers, Tomás Bretón. Madrid's Teatro Real had a well-established practice of excluding operas by Spanish composers, and the chances for a Spanish verismo opera composed during the 1890s were diminished by the continuing success of *Cavalleria rusticana* and *Carmen*. Bretón's bitter experience seeking performances for his early opera *Los amantes de Teruel* prevented him from even offering *La Dolores* to the Real, and it made a very successful debut at the Teatro de la Zarzuela in 1895, before enjoying significant international exposure in an Italian translation. Several Madrid critics felt that they had to defend the work in relation to *Carmen*, among them the prominent music activist Guillermo Morphy:

> Bretón's *La Dolores* is, for me, the most complete of his works … I believe that posterity will view it as the template of a realized ideal. Bizet's *Carmen* has circled the world, and apart from the talent of its author, this has been in part because of its supposed Spanish color, as false in its literary aspect as in the musical, which is without doubt inspired and beautiful, but improper for a popular Spanish plot.[21]

---

19. Antonio Peña y Goñi, "Carmen," *La época* (Madrid), 20 January 1892, quoted in Luis G. Iberni, "Cien años de Antonio Peña y Goñi," *Cuadernos de música iberoamericana* 4 (1997): 9.
20. J. Roca y Roca, "La semana en Barcelona," *La vanguardia*, 13 November 1892: 4.
21. G. Morphy, "*La Dolores* de Bretón," *La correspondencia de España*, 18 March 1895.

The similarities between the two works include Bretón's use of a descending theme reminiscent of the *Carmen* fate motive and the violent ending with a rapid denouement, which it shares with both *Cavalleria rusticana* and *Carmen*.[22]

Soon after *La Dolores* took off, Enrique Granados adapted another play by Feliu y Codina into the Spanish opera *María del Carmen*, with some features of verismo. Premiered in Madrid in 1898, it was again compared favorably with *Carmen*, the principal foreign yardstick of local color and orchestration. While the plot avoids the habitual tragic ending, there are musical similarities to *Carmen* in the use of leitmotiv technique, and a keen sense of orchestration that highlights the brilliant local color of the score, enlivening the play's setting in Murcia (a region of southern Spain adjacent to Andalusia).[23]

The influence of *Carmen* and verismo extended to the one-act *zarzuelas* of the *género chico*. This genre was the only medium that provided a livelihood for Spanish composers writing for the lyric stage, although some of its more successful exponents (including Bretón) also composed for the concert hall and were committed to writing Spanish operas in a nationalist mold. Such was the case with Ruperto Chapí (1851–1909), whose *zarzuela grande, La bruja*, had followed *Carmen* at the Teatro de la Zarzuela in 1887. In his hugely successful *género chico zarzuela, La revoltosa* (1897/8), the duo of Mari-Pepa and Felipe is reminiscent of *Carmen*, while there are more marked similarities in his later *zarzuelas*. In *Entre rocas* (1907/8), the influence of *Cavalleria rusticana* and *Carmen* are evident in the treatment of the theme of *contrabandistas* (smugglers), while *Carmen* is the model for choral interventions and the definition of some of the characters.[24]

Carmen also served as an important model for Manuel de Falla's *La vida breve* (1905), a landmark Spanish opera of the period that eventually gained widespread international exposure—the only Spanish nationalist opera to achieve this status.[25] Falla's detailed study of *Carmen* was possibly undertaken at the instigation of his teacher, Felipe Pedrell, although he knew the opera before coming into contact with the Catalan maestro. The impact of Bizet's opera is most prominent in the local color of the dances and the fiesta scene. The descending melodic motive associated with fate in Falla's opera employs

22. For further details see Víctor Sánchez, *Tomás Bretón* (Madrid: ICCMU, 2002).

23. Teresa Cascudo García-Villaraco, "¿Un ejemplo de modernismo silenciado? *María del Carmen* (1898), la primera ópera de Enrique Granados, y su recepción madrileña," *Acta Musicologica* 84, no. 2 (2012): 225–52. Cascudo points out that *María del Carmen* cannot be defined as a verismo opera.

24. For further details see Luis G. Iberni, *Ruperto Chapí* (Madrid: ICCMU, 1995).

25. Unlike Spanish nationalist operas, a number of *zarzuelas*, especially of the *género chico* variety, enjoyed an international trajectory. These included Federico Chueca and Joaquín Valverde's *La Gran Vía* (1886), and Tomás Bretón's *La Verbena de la paloma* (1894).

four pitches. *La vida breve*'s location in Granada was also in line with fin-de-siècle stagings of gypsy primitivism and the evolving characterizations of Carmen. In its quest for ethnographic "authenticity," *La vida breve*, like Chapí's *La chavala* (1898) before it, presented the Andalusian protagonist Salud in a more chaste light than Carmen. This aspect was stressed by the Spanish composer and musicologist Pedro Morales in his preface to Carl van Vechten's *The Music of Spain* (1920):

> Every "gitana" ... no matter how low she may have fallen, bears the seed of fidelity, ready to blossom, deeply rooted in her heart. The operatic character, Spanish par excellence, is not Carmen, but Salud, the heroine of Manuel de Falla's opera, *La vida breve*.[26]

More recent commentators have concurred with this depiction of Salud in terms of a verismo-inspired character whose demise is caused by personal betrayal and social pressures, rather than the gay or scheming exotic gypsy stereotype who controls her own fate.[27]

The strength of *Carmen* as an international stereotype of Spanishness led Falla to consider writing a one-act sequel to the opera after his arrival in Paris in 1907. Entitled *La muerte de Carmen* (The death of Carmen), it was to be based on Mérimée's novel and dedicated to Bizet. He discussed the idea with the soprano and popular Carmen impersonator Lucienne Bréval, who discouraged him because the subject was "near-sacred" for her, but the critic Pierre Lalo advised him that as a Spaniard he would be an ideal composer for such a project, and sent him to call on Bizet's widow. She, however, was opposed to the plan, and he abandoned it.[28] At any rate, a revised version of *La vida breve*, with added passages that heightened the opera's local color and an accelerated denouement, became the first work by a Spanish composer to be performed at the Opéra-Comique in late 1913.

This production of *La vida breve* was probably facilitated by the growing closeness of Franco-Spanish relations at the time, which also gave greater agency to Spanish composers and performers in the framing of Spanish musical identity in Paris. The rapprochement is particularly evident in the early years of the twentieth century, following the signing of the Entente Cordiale between France and Britain in 1904 (an agreement that recognized Spain's

26. Pedro Morales, "Preface," in *The Music of Spain,* by Carl Van Vechten (London: Kegan Paul, Trench, Trubner, 1920), xvi–xvii.

27. Antoine Le Duc, "De la zarzuela à *La vida breve*: Continuité/rupture," in *Manuel de Falla: Latinité et universalité*, ed. Louis Jambou (Paris: Presses de l'Université de Paris-Sorbonne, 1999), 53.

28. Jaime Pahissa, *Manuel de Falla: His Life and Works,* trans. Jean Wagstaff (London: Museum Press, 1954), 109.

Figure 7.4 T. Bianco, *Fêtes Franco-Espagnoles*, Intimate dance at the Elysée Palace, postcard (1913). Caricature of Alfonso XIII of Spain dancing with France's President Poincaré, both dressed as bullfighters.
Credit: Private collection.

interests in Morocco), and came to a head with Alfonso XIII's state visit to Paris in May 1913. Numerous cultural events ensued, including an October performance by the Orquesta Sinfónica de Madrid conducted by Enrique Fernández Arbós, with a program highlighting music by Spanish composers. During this period Alfonso XIII was repeatedly caricatured through the employment of Carmenesque stereotypes, such as his depiction as a bullfighter (see Figure 7.4), and at times with reference to his liaisons with Spanish entertainers (most notably La Belle Otero).[29]

The Parisian critical reception of Falla's *La vida breve* was also underscored by comparisons with *Carmen*. Little wonder that this was the case, given that *Carmen* had been the chief repertory work at the Opéra Comique since the 1890s. The house production of 1898 was still in use, and its decor and costumes had been drawn upon for a series of Franco-Hispanic works at the Opéra Comique, including Ravel's *L'Heure espagnole* (1911). However, for *La vida breve* Carré commissioned a new production, one aimed at providing even greater verisimilitude in its projection of local color for a work by an "authentic" Spaniard. On the whole, French critics viewed *La vida breve* as an authentically Spanish verismo opera, unlike Italian and French forays into

29. Geraldine Power, "Projections of Spain in Popular Spectacle and Chanson, Paris: 1889–1926" (PhD thesis, University of Melbourne, 2013), 235.

Hispanic verismo. It was likewise contrasted with *Carmen*, which seemed picturesque by comparison, not because of the ways in which the composer had infused it with local color, but because of the two operas' differentiated narratives in the portrayal of customs and violence.[30]

In a sense *Carmen*, viewed as a proto-verismo opera, had established a template for Hispanic verismo that made it difficult for Spanish operas to succeed at home and abroad. The clichés of Spanishness established by the opera, and perpetuated through its impact on literature and spectacle, meant that Spanish operas had to measure up to or explicitly counter these expectations, often by arguing for the greater authenticity of the constituent elements of their works, as was the case with Enrique Granados and his opera *Goyescas* in 1915. This argument was even promulgated by French authors of Hispanic operas and their partisan critics. The most notable of these composers was Raoul Laparra, who premiered his opera *La habanera* at the Opéra-Comique in 1908, and followed this up with *La jota* in 1911.[31] However, it was to be another Spanish singer, rather than a composer, who most successfully navigated the issues of authenticity and verismo in her international projection of Carmen in the early twentieth century.

MARIA GAY: THE REVOLUTIONARY CARMEN

Maria Gay was not the first Spanish singer to be identified with the role of Carmen, but she could be described as the first cosmopolitan Spanish Carmen, acclaimed from Saint Petersburg to London and Boston to Buenos Aires. In contrast to some of the more coquettish French Carmens of the Belle Époque, Gay's Carmen encompassed the complete spectrum of emotions, radiating *gracia*, vitality, and earthiness.

Born Maria Pichot i Gironès into a bourgeois Catalan family in 1879,[32] Gay was raised in an artistic milieu among siblings including the well-known artist (and friend of Pablo Picasso) Ramón Pichot, and professional musicians Luis Pichot (a violinist), and Ricardo Pichot (a cellist). Growing up during the 1890s, Gay would have witnessed the *Carmen* phenomenon that swept Barcelona early in this decade, with all its interpretative variety; she is likely to have heard Elena Fons in the role and may even have seen the parody *Carmela*,

---

30. For an extended discussion of the Parisian critical reception of *La vida breve* and the discourse of Spanishness, see Samuel Llano, *Whose Spain? Negotiating Spanish Music in Paris, 1908–1929* (New York: Oxford University Press, 2013), 136–60; Elena Torres Clemente, *Las óperas de Manuel de Falla: De* La vida breve *a* El retablo de maese Pedro (Madrid: Sociedad Española de Musicología, 2007), 203–28.

31. Llano, *Whose Spain?*, 185–86.

32. Some sources give her birth date as 1876, others as 1879.

the success of which extended into the 1900s. She moved in circles devoted to the cause of Catalan art and culture, a movement that expressed itself not only in *modernisme*, but also in varying degrees of Catalan activism, at times considered revolutionary by the Spanish state. The story that a youthful Gay was arrested and imprisoned for singing patriotic Catalan songs is part of her mythology, but it is consistent with this milieu and the heightened political tensions of fin-de-siècle Barcelona.[33] Although training to be a sculptor, Gay was already singing with Barcelona's important choral societies when she decided to focus her energies on becoming a professional singer.[34]

She married the conductor and composer Joan Gay i Planella while still in her teens, and in 1900 they moved to Paris together to "finish" her training and advance their work in promoting Catalan music. While in Paris, Gay studied with the American soprano Ada Adini (1855–1924), and continued her concert career, making her French debut in December 1900 when she performed works by Wagner and Franck with the Lamoureux orchestra.[35] She rapidly consolidated her reputation as a concert artist who specialized in lieder, touring with pianists like Raoul Pugno and Alfred Cortot. Miguel Salvador declared that Gay was the only Spanish lieder singer to have achieved success outside Spain, praising her expressivity, her ability to create a powerful characterization within aesthetic limits, and her deep intimacy with the poetic and lyric elements of the genre.[36] These techniques were to prove a crucial element of her operatic career.

For opera was Gay's destiny, and she later told the press that Calvé herself had advised her to study for the "lyric stage," as she was "born to play Carmen."[37] This claimed encouragement proved prescient, for Gay made her operatic debut by singing Carmen at the Théâtre de la Monnaie in Brussels on 25 September 1904, giving many performances throughout the two subsequent seasons.[38] According to a family story, Gay's extreme nerves when

33. Gay herself cited her eight-day incarceration as a "political offender" for "singing a Catalan song in public," and declared her allegiance with the liberal, republican, anticlerical cause when speaking to an English journalist just a few months after the bloody events of Tragic Week (July 1909) in Barcelona. "The New 'Carmen' Talks to 'Mail' Readers," *Daily Mail* (Hull), 27 October 1909, 3.

34. Gay sang as a soloist with the Orfeo Catalá, with the choir Catalunya Nova, and at the Institució Catalana de Música and the Ateneu Barcelonès. L'Associació Musical de Mestres Directors, "Joan Gay i Planella," accessed 1 July 2013, http://www.assmmd.org/biografies/jgayplanella.htm.

35. "Programmes des concerts," *Le Ménestrel* 66, no. 49 (1900): 389.

36. M[iguel]. Salvador, "Notas del Real: Carmen III," *El globo* (Madrid), 23 November 1909, 2.

37. Ramón Reig Coromines, "La soprano Maria Gay," *Revista de Girona* 16 (1961): 64–65.

38. Sources give a wide variety of dates for Gay's operatic debut, ranging from 1902 to 1907, but most refer to her appearance as Carmen at the Théâtre de la Monnaie in Brussels. This debut date is taken from the digital opera archives of La Monnaie, http://carmen.demunt.be.

she started rehearsal in Brussels led her to confess in a panic that she had never appeared on the operatic stage before. She worked hard to learn the necessary stage business and enter into the character's psychology. After a shaky first night, when nerves detracted from her singing, Gay won over her audience with five performances to full houses, and thus established herself as an original and innovative Carmen.[39] Having launched her international operatic career with what became her signature role, Gay performed in the French provinces and embarked on a touring schedule that included Belgium, Germany, Switzerland, Russia, and North Africa in the 1905–6 season alone.[40] In 1906 she broke into the top rank, with successive debuts at the Opéra-Comique in April, Covent Garden in November, and La Scala in December.

After nearly two decades of Carmenesque Spanish stars at the most glamorous heights of music hall and pantomime in Paris, most productions of Bizet's opera relied on tired convention, and Gay's bold new Carmen shocked and delighted a world ready for a genuinely Spanish opera singer to reinvent the role. She publicly declared her desire to "wring out of Carmen all the wildness, the witchery ... the 'nature,'" and mounted a challenge to accepted theatrical interpretations.[41] Writing of her Opéra-Comique debut, the critic Noziére (Fernand Weil) observed, "Maria Gay doesn't linger on elegant and foolish conventions, but in her simplicity and even her vulgarity, she presents us with a cigarette maker of Seville. We don't have before us a Bohemian of the Opéra-Comique or of a melodrama. This is reality itself" (see Figure 7.5).[42]

Gay told the press that she loved the opera and its leading role, describing it as the "most subtle and attractive part in all opera I know," but she was also clear that Bizet's music "is absolutely French."[43] Her Carmen may have been perceived as "Spanish" and "real," but it was not built on a foundation of market-saturating exotic stereotypes. Gay approached opera with an attitude shaped by her training in non-dramatic genres such as Spanish and Catalan song, lieder, and concert performance of Wagner, which had fostered her extraordinary vocal expressivity and a close attention to bringing the literary text to life in all its intensity.

39. Gay's debut was attended by family members and distinguished friends such as the composer Isaac Albéniz and the writer Eduardo Marquina. Reig Corominas, "La soprano Maria Gay," 65; "New 'Carmen' Talks to 'Mail' Readers, 3.
40. Besides *Carmen*, Gay's operatic repertoire ranged from Gluck's *Orfeo* to Saint-Saëns's *Samson et Dalila*, and included works by Wagner, Verdi, and Puccini.
41. "New 'Carmen' Talks to 'Mail' Readers," 3.
42. We are grateful to Jessica Trevitt for her assistance in translating this article. Nozière [Fernand Weil], "Le Théâtre," *Gil Blas* (Paris), 1 May 1906, 3.
43. "New 'Carmen' Talks to 'Mail' Readers," 3.

Figure 7.5 Maria Gay as Carmen in act 1.
Credit: Centre de Documentació i Museu de les Arts Escèniques de l'Institut del Teatre (MAE), Top. F311-29

London society's interest in Spanish dance and culture had only increased with the alliances of the early twentieth century, fostered by the long-term friendship of the young Spanish king with Edward VII, which had developed during his long service as "Bertie," Prince of Wales. The strategic marriage of Victoria Eugenie of Battenberg (Queen Victoria's granddaughter) to Alfonso XIII, which took place in May 1906, intensified interest in Spain, including *Carmen* as a manifestation of "Spanish" culture. Maria Gay's Covent Garden debut as Carmen took place on 21 November 1906, and her triumph attracted capacity audiences who appreciated her genuine Spanishness in dance and gesture. Many critics declared her the "best Carmen" they had ever seen, but she was also recognized as the most "truthful" Carmen since Minnie Hauk. When her return a year later again filled the Royal Opera House, the *Times* observed that she "took a place second only, if not equal, to Mme. Calvé."[44] Although her singing was not considered faultless, Gay was praised for creating the "atmosphere of old Spain" with complete truth. "She moved with a perfect grace; the piquancy of her gestures, her little stage devices, were Spanish; and when she danced one lost all consciousness of surroundings and was back again in the cafés of [Seville]."[45]

It was during her 1906 Covent Garden season that Gay's debut at La Scala was announced. According to *Le Guide musical* the Milan theater had not staged *Carmen* for a while, for want of a satisfactory protagonist. In Gay, however, they had found their dream Carmen, fresh from "revolutionizing" the role in Berlin and London.[46] This new contract brought Gay into a company shaped by the leadership of Giulio Gatti-Casazza under the musical direction of Arturo Toscanini and introduced her to her future life partner, the great verismo tenor Giovanni Zenatello, who had created the role of Pinkerton in the 1904 premiere of Giacomo Puccini's *Madama Butterfly*. In Gay's first Italian season they appeared together in Verdi's *Aida* and *Carmen* and they began to develop a fresh dramatic interpretation of the relationship between Carmen and José, which reached its fullest expression in the opera's finale. Both the contemporary press and later recordings testify to the visceral quality of their performance, which they overlaid with the clichés that had accrued to styles of verismo performance: Gay shouted and Zenatello sobbed as they played out the desperate and raw emotion of José and Carmen's final encounter. Although Zenatello debuted at the Metropolitan at the same time as Gay, he did not appear with her in *Carmen* (an honor that was reserved for Caruso and other New York favorites). But they toured South America in the roles, and after Gay had left her husband and children for Zenatello, they settled together in the United States. where they continued their work together in many memorable seasons in Boston and with a teaching practice based in New York (see Figure 7.6).

Gay was fully formed as an opera singer when she joined the ensemble at La Scala, but the fact that its singers exemplified the new directions emerging from the "Italian school" of the turn of the twentieth century must have encouraged the development of more emotional and even violent aspects in her interpretations. Commentators such as Edward Dent have dismissed the veristi as "typical products of the modern Italian opera stage, the wobbling

44. "Royal Italian Opera," *Musical Times* 47, no. 766 (1 December 1906): 832; "The Great Discovery at the Opera: The New Carmen," *Illustrated London News* (1 December 1906): 803; "Royal Opera," *Times* (London), 8 October 1907, 6.

45. "Music," *Illustrated London News* (1 December 1906): 820.

46. "Nouvelles," *Le Guide musical*, 52, no. 50 (16 December 1906): 809.

Figure 7.6 Maria Gay and [Giovanni] Zenatello (*c.* 1910–15), Bain News Service.
Credit: George Grantham Bain Collection, Library of Congress, http://www.loc.gov/pictures/item/ggb2005016085.

soprano who is never on her true note, and the gulping tenor always on the verge of collapsing into tears,"[47] but as the new century progressed, the Italian commitment to emotionally charged performance continued to shape interpretations of *Carmen*. This ever-heightened pitch of exaggerated drama did not suit all audiences, and Gay's Carmen aroused controversy.[48] For all

47. Edward J. Dent, *Opera*, rev. ed. (Harmondsworth, UK: Penguin, 1949), 115.
48. This controversy applied equally to men singing in the new style: Gatti-Casazza pointed out in his memoirs that a tenor who achieves "tremendous success in Spain or South America may be severely criticized for his style in New York," and Francesc Cortès notes that Caruso's first performances in Barcelona were not well received. Giulio Gatti-Casazza, *Memories of the Opera* (New York: Vienna House, [1941] 1973), 227; Francesc Cortès, private communication, May 2016.

the reviewers who would happily have echoed J. Coudurier's declaration that Gay represented "Carmen as she should be and as one has never before seen her,"[49] there were always a few who remained unmoved, who interpreted her nuanced vocal inflections as bad intonation or were disgusted by her energetic and sexualized stage business. Some identified parallels between these performative "excesses" and the expressive techniques employed by contemporary artists, in which context Gay's association with leading avant-garde Spanish artists, including Picasso and Ignacio Zuloaga is noteworthy.

> It makes one think of a painter with too much paint on his palette, who is daubing a bit randomly. But often, it has the desired effect, the product of reflection, intelligence, a powerful artistic sense, evoking a vigorous and gripping reality. And the ensemble comes alive, colored, with a strong and irresistible seduction.[50]

The perception of reality was strengthened by Gay's addition of a different brand of "Spanishness" to her conception of the role. By drawing on her own upbringing in an educated and artistic Catalan milieu, she based her Carmen on her observation of the characters of the multifaceted Barcelona scene, which boasted a resident Andalusian community and every kind of entertainment. All these features set Gay's Carmen apart from the customary, even for Spanish audiences. When Gay debuted as Carmen at Madrid's Teatro Real in late 1909, after four years of international success, critics feared yet another Carmen constructed to please foreign tastes. Leading Spanish critic Cecilio de Roda was fed up with singers whose attempts to be charming displaced any thought of dramatic realism, degrading the feisty gypsy into a mischievous and impudent little girl.[51]

The Teatro Real was well versed in Italianate *Carmen* productions, and its audiences had cherished Giuseppina Pasqua as their first Carmen. But Gay was competing with a popular local Carmen who was a great favorite at the Teatro Real, her contemporary Elena Fons. Despite comparison with Fons, and all her distinguished predecessors, Gay's Carmen met with considerable support among Madrid's critics. Salvador declared that she "appeared to have been born to play Carmen." For this discerning critic all preceding Carmens, however talented, were missing a vital element, but Gay's Carmen was complete, from her appearance and her nervous and passionate movements to

49. J. Coudurier, "Le Théâtre," *Figaro*, 24 November 1906, 2.

50. "Une Carmen," *Le Monde artiste* 46, no. 13 (1906): 201.

51. The management of the Teatro Real had been trying to book Gay for several years, but her busy touring schedule had prevented an earlier appearance. "Las noches del Real," *ABC* (Madrid), 18 November 1909, 10; Roda, "El año musical," 37.

her careful characterization, informed by study of the gypsy's psychology.[52] Madrid's critics were surprised by the strength of Gay's rich voice in the lower register, and she—like Fons—was honored with the acknowledgment of that uniquely Spanish virtue, *gracia*.

While Gay's energetic, even wild, reading of the title character in acts 1 and 2 provoked much debate among the Madrid critics, she was considered especially good in the more dramatic scenes of acts 3 and 4, interrupted by "bravos" and applause after various numbers and called repeatedly at the end of each act.[53] Her performance inspired new responses to the standard queries about the validity of the work's depiction of "Spanish" life, prompting Roda to deny the plot's absurdity, for it could well have appeared in a court report.[54] In the pages of the daily *ABC*, the critic mused, if a Spanish audience was willing to accept Carmen as scripted—featuring a Sevillian *cigarrera* who cheats on her lovers and is a smuggler and a heroine of tavern orgies—this "woman would have to speak and act like Maria Gay's Carmen. And if this kind of woman doesn't exist? Well, we have to blame Mérimée, who invented her; but if we admit her into the theater, then it is the Carmen of Mérimée that Maria Gay creates."[55]

So how did Gay come up with a Carmen who convinced the skeptical Madrid press of her reality, "a creation so much her own, that it is like no-one else"?[56] She danced along the conceptual tightrope between her own sense of national and personal identity—which was at odds with the opera's depiction of the gypsy—and her desire to create an "authentic" version of the character, based on her nuanced understanding of the work's cultural stereotypes. She allowed her character to hint at images of political engagement, but did not hesitate to incorporate bold sensuality into Carmen's spectrum of moods. At no stage did Gay claim, "I am Carmen," a stance that had been adopted either implicitly or explicitly by many of her predecessors in an attempt to give their impersonations an aura of prestige or authenticity. Instead, she made two very different claims: one based on her Catalan identity, the other on Spanish nationalist rejection of foreign stereotypes.

Arriving in New York for her Met debut, Gay told the press: "I am a native of Barcelona, the city in which Carmen lived. She is there still and I have seen her on the streets often."[57] Gay thus acknowledged the existence of Carmen as a Spanish type in the international cultural imagination, beyond the confines

52. M[iguel]. Salvador, "Notas del Real: Carmen [II]," *El globo* (Madrid), 22 November 1909, 1.

53. "Las noches del Real," 11.

54. Roda, "El año musical," 37.

55. "Las noches del Real," 10.

56. Ibid.

57. "Singers for Both Houses," *Sun* (New York), 1 November 1908, 9.

of opera theater, but, as a Catalan, she declared her difference. She later explained to an interviewer,

> One reason why "Carmen" is not in any case a picture of Spain, ... is because it draws with exaggeration the manners of Andalusia, the people of which are almost a separate race from the pure Spaniard, possessing many Moorish characteristics, and such a love of the picturesque in dress that foreign painters always reproduce them in their pictures.[58]

Gay's delineation of the picturesque Andalusian as "almost a separate race" identifies the people of this region directly with their visual, literary, and theatrical representations in *costumbrista* art. A rare critic understood this perception, and alluded to parallels with the ways in which Spain was evoked in the other contemporary arts. He described her performance as "putting Spain on the stage" in a "remarkable victory of artistic impressionism ... a realistic race-study."[59] Gay's separation of herself from this type further distinguishes her from Sevillian soprano Elena Fons. By virtue of her class and Catalan regional identity, Gay assumed the role of an independent and informed observer, from which vantage point she could construct her Carmen. It should be noted, however, that Gay's public biography eventually encompassed many of the situations and emotions experienced by her character—from imprisonment, through a marriage breakdown, to chasing a new man—and these parallels gave her embodiment of the errant *bohémienne* unique authority.

Despite this kind of publicity, Gay sought to distinguish herself from the fiction of the opera by contrasting the opera's imaginary Andalusia with modern Spain. She was indignant "that the opera gives foreigners the false idea that Spain is peopled with smugglers and *filles de joie*! ... The real Spanish woman is serious, grave, and domestic in her tastes, preferring to tend the flowers in her little window garden rather than wear them in her hair."[60] This extract reveals Gay's agreement with contemporary opinion among Spanish intellectuals about the true nature of Spanish womanhood and its debasement by exotic stereotypes. Such attitudes, commonplace among progressive Spaniards, were reinforced for English-speaking audiences only a few years later by Pedro Morales, when he insisted that Carmen was "not a prototype, but a very extraordinary type of Spanish woman."[61]

---

58. This article, authored by Maria Gay in an unidentified New York paper, is reported at some length in "Music and Drama," *Sydney Morning Herald*, 1 November 1913, 4.

59. "Before the Footlights: The Spanish Jade; 'Carmen'—as Realized by Madame Gay," *Daily Mail* (Hull), 2 November 1909, 3.

60. "Music and Drama," 4.

61. Morales, "Preface," xvi–xvii.

Humor was a more unexpected facet of Gay's interpretation, concordant with her ability to look dispassionately at the opera and its protagonist. She shared vivacity with Calvé, but Gay's Carmen was "impishly, at times devilishly, mischievous,"[62] and was on occasion inclined to make "sport of the role," as she seems to have done in Boston in 1914, before a familiar and affectionate audience. She thus combined "earnest interpretation" with "holding a scene at arm's length once in a while and laughing at it," demonstrating that she could "seriously enact a part and burlesque it at the same time."[63]

Educated and politically aware, Gay deployed a fresh set of associations to redefine the character. She referred to the contemporary plight of real cigarette-makers, recalling the issues that were linked with the opera in the season of its Madrid premieres (1887–88), and which had been further exacerbated by increasing mechanization of the industry as it entered the twentieth century.

> It is true that the cigarette-makers have a reputation for song and scandal. Still, these smoke-clouds rising from the factory girls cover a social struggle rather than a tempest of the heart. Such girls are much occupied with labor politics, bull fights, dancing saloons, and the thousand and one national distractions from their hard-working life. Other Spanish women do not smoke, the city men rarely drink and the rustics are never intoxicated.[64]

Presumably aware of Gay's liberal sympathies, Parisian critics explicitly linked Gay's portrayal of Carmen with historic social struggles. At her Opéra-Comique debut, she is described as shouting "la liberté!" in the tavern scene of act 2 "with the revolutionary fervor of that figure on the barricade ... painted by Eugène Delacroix."[65]

Gay considered every detail and effect that would help her realize the character's psychology.[66] Building on her experience singing Italian opera (including Mascagni's *Cavalleria rusticana*), she did not shy away from the less acceptable qualities of her character, describing Carmen as a savage, a "girl of the people" not afraid to alienate the audience's sympathy with her death.[67]

---

62. "Before the Footlights: The Spanish Jade," 3.
63. "'Carmen' Sung," *Christian Science Monitor* (Boston), 14 March 1914, 21.
64. "Music and Drama," 4.
65. This reference is probably to Delacroix's celebrated painting *Le 28 Juillet: La Liberté guidant le peuple (28 juillet 1830)* (28 July: Liberty leading the people [28 July 1830]) (1830, Musée du Louvre). "Une Carmen," 201.
66. Eduardo Muñoz, "Carmen," *El imparcial* (Madrid), 28 November 1910, 4.
67. This comment emerges from a comparison with Zélie de Lussan's more "winsome, attractive, and refined" Carmen, who did not seem to deserve the tragic death, as reported from the *Glasgow News*. Amphion, "Musical and Dramatic Notes," *West Australian* (Perth), 20 November 1909, 3.

Gay, who was aware that her portrayal was criticized as vulgar, particularly in comparison with Calvé's more refined approach, declared, "I think so was Carmen.... Also, she had what you call 'sex.' It is true to life; ... I play as I see."[68] If even Spanish critics recognized in Gay a "figura gitana,"[69] foreign critics saw her as the classic Spanish woman; her full figure suited fin-de-siècle tastes and enhanced the character's sensual appeal, like Carmencita, Otero, and Guerrero before her.

> Mlle. Maria Gay ... is a remarkable woman, young and beautiful, with great masses of wavy black hair, divided at the side, and dark, lustrous eyes that glisten with expression. She is a woman of fine physique—broad shoulders and good height.[70]

Launching herself in Paris, Gay declared herself a thoroughly modern Spanish Carmen by presenting herself in costume and makeup designed by Zuloaga, who had created innovative portraits of gypsies and Andalusian women and is also renowned for his reconfiguration of the landscapes and imagery of Castile and southern Spain.[71] Gay's costume was at least partly inspired by Goya, whose influence was reshaping Zuloaga's representations of Spain. In a Paris gripped by renewed interest in Goya, this link did not go unnoticed.[72] Gay seems to have worn the same vividly green shawl for act 1 of her Met debut, in which one critic noted its striking contrast with her "plain frock of dull red of a cheap quality that befitted her station."[73] In an age when divas often wore their haute-couture gowns for every role, Gay's commitment to realism was lauded, along with her "exquisite" taste in costume.

Salvador was so impressed with Gay's appearance in the 1909 Madrid production that he described her outfit for every act, explaining that she had dismissed Mérimée's imagery for a fresh interpretation. He classified her act 1 ensemble as "zuloaguesco": a dark frock with large red print, fresh flowers, white stockings, and small green scarf. In act 2 she wore a shawl of beautiful green, perhaps the same as in Paris and New York, but not in the style of a vulgar gypsy, more a "modern interpretation of the international Spanish genre." She affected the blanket garment of the Andalusian region of Jerez with appropriate accessories for the mountains of act 3, but her act 4 gown

68. Amphion, "Musical and Dramatic Notes," *West Australian* (Perth), 29 January 1916, 10.

69. "Las noches del Real," 11.

70. "Picked Out for a Winner," *Los Angeles Herald*, 13 January 1907.

71. Reig Corominas, "La soprano Maria Gay," 65. Zuloaga's 1908 portrait of Lucienne Bréval as Carmen displays elements of both these tendencies.

72. "Une Carmen," 201.

73. Sylvester Rawling, "Maria Gay Shows the Quality of Her Carmen at the Metropolitan," *Evening World* (New York), 4 December 1908, 10.

Figure 7.7 Maria Gay as Carmen in act 4, photograph by A. Dupont.
Credit: Library of Congress, http://www.loc.gov/pictures/item/2002715558.

was luminous: pale pink bordered with silver, the skirt underlined with black lace, wearing her mantilla in a Goyesque manner over the high comb in her hair.[74] The combination of modernity and historical sensibility in Gay's visual presentation is demonstrated by the recognition of both Zuloaga and Goya in her look (see Figure 7.7)[75]

Equally "Spanish" when she moved, Gay was a proficient castanet player and an accomplished dancer with an acute rhythmic sensibility, which she

74. Salvador, "Notas del Real: Carmen [II]," 1.
75. "Las noches del Real," 11.

proved in some productions by dancing on a table in act 2. But her stage business went far beyond these basic clichés of theatrical Spanishness.[76] Gay had perfected an alluring, dance-like gait, used to spectacular effect in the act 1 "Habanera" as she worked her way gracefully through the crowd of admirers to José.[77] Salvador observed that "all her movements show the poise and lightness of a *bolera* (dancer of classicized regional dance),"[78] while her rendition of a *seguidilla* and a *romalis* showed even a foreign critic

> how the hands could interpret the meaning of a dance as well as the feet and the body. To see Madame Gay dance is an experience in itself. The short, sharp stamps of the feet, the swaying of the body, the invitation of the glances, and, above all, that incessant play of flexible gestures by those wonderful hands.[79]

Clearly, Gay went beyond the *brazear* so trumpeted by Calvé and could convey a range of features of the theatrical Spanish dance styles so beloved of audiences at this time. The description of stamping and expressive but precise hand movements suggests that at least part of her choreography was based on current flamenco practice.

Gay's peculiar histrionic touches were in keeping with her thoughtful approach to the role, and she injected realism by running in pursuit of José, spitting, and blowing her nose (admittedly into a handkerchief), behaviors that an actress like Nethersole may have embraced but that were considered shocking on the operatic stage.[80] She must have exacted a nightly toll on the props when she threw a tambourine halfway across the stage, smashed her fan to pieces, and tore the "roses from her waist."[81] The Spanish diva was not the first to spice up the role with dramatic, even violent, touches: Minnie Hauk had famously smashed plates to create castanets (a feat still remembered in 1908[82]),

76. The Geneva correspondent for *Le Monde artiste* said her dancing of a "Romalio" (perhaps the *romalis*?) on a table captivated the local audience, and that she was Spanish from head to foot, in costume, gesture, dance, and skill in handling the castanets. After a London performance she is described as using the castanets "with a virtuosity no other prima donna ever equalled." "Etranger: Genève," *Le Monde artiste* 46, no. 7 (1906): 106; "Opera Notes from Europe," *Sun* (New York), 30 December 1906, 5.

77. Nozière, "Le Théâtre," quoted in Koehler, "Etranger: Cologne," *Le Monde artiste* 46, no. 41 (1906): 537.

78. Salvador, "Notas del Real: Carmen [II]," 1.

79. "Before the Footlights," 3.

80. "Maria Gay is not above nose-blowing and expectoration in her interpretation of Carmen, physical acts in the public performance of which no Spanish cigarette girl would probably be caught ashamed." Carl Van Vechten, *Music and Bad Manners* (New York: Alfred A. Knopf, 1916), 18.

81. "Carmen Not Well Given," *Sun* (New York), 4 December 1908, 5; Rawling, "Maria Gay Shows," 10.

82. "Music: A New Carmen at the Metropolitan," *New York Tribune*, 4 December 1908, 7.

while Calvé was renowned for throwing chairs around the stage, a risky undertaking calculated for maximum sensation. In contrast, Gay's gestures seemed to explode from Carmen's internal frustration, her physicality neither capricious nor played simply for effect. Quickly changing from one mood to the next, her facial expressions, vocal style, and physical gestures combined to create a Carmen who could be both simple and vulgar without sacrifice of complexity (see Figure 7.8).

Numerous critics describe Gay's mesmerizing effect—once on stage, she was the focus of all attention, and her naturalistic, dynamic acting made her a

Figure 7.8 "A New Carmen: Miss Maria Gay Achieved a Great Success in London," photograph by [Ernest Walter] Histed (*c.* 1906), clipping from unidentified German periodical, no. 50 [1906]: 2209.
Credit: Private collection.

uniquely compelling Carmen—but she was noted for being able to make "her dramatic points by her singing rather than her acting."[83] As the first contralto who truly owned the role, she was comfortable in all the registers of her remarkable range, from her effortless top notes to the astonishing power and breadth of her chest voice, in which she could match sound with her tenors. Critics frequently described the "warmth" and the rich quality of her sound, her extraordinary technique and control of the instrument. The ability to employ a "burnt" sound in the low register suggests that she may have been evoking—albeit in a stylized operatic manner—the more gravelly vocal production of some flamenco singers of the time, without recourse to the popular style of folk or *aflamencado* singing affected by Fons (and possibly Sanz) in their renditions of Carmen's main arias.[84] Indeed, if verismo had permitted the exaggeration of emotion through the operatic inflection of styles adopted from "folk" practices, then flamenco was surely one of the Spanish equivalents of rustic southern Italian folk styles at this time. In addition to this dark quality, sometimes criticized as a technical fault, Gay's repertoire of vocal characterization included an extraordinary variety of timbre and color, including non-sung sounds, ranging from sighs, gasps, and sobs to half-sung speech and unabashed shouting.

Even if we match the most vivid critical accounts with her recordings of the "Habanera," "Séguedille," the "Card Aria," and the finale, we can only glimpse shadows of Gay's performance.[85] Recordings reveal her distinctive approach to musical gesture and phrasing, driven by a sense of pulse and her at times explosive projection of the text. Gay's dramatic range as a singer is best gauged from her 1910 recording of the "Card Aria" and her later performance with Zenatello of the final scene of act 4, recorded in New Jersey in 1930. But some critics convey an impression of the dramatic effect of her musical interpretation.

Gay's first appearance in act 1, as she sang her way through the throng of would-be admirers to fix her attention on José, was subtly provocative. Without resorting to coquettish excess, she used the "Habanera" to circle him like a bird of prey, slowly intensifying her sensual attack through timbral gradation. Always full-voiced, her tone slowly became richer, earthier, and more emotional through the second and third stanzas. Gay established a steady

83. *New York Herald*, [December 1908], cited in the Metropolitan Opera Archives, accessed 1 November 2016, http://archives.metoperafamily.org/archives/frame.htm [Met Performance] CID: 42230, *Carmen* {199} Metropolitan Opera House: 12/3/1908.

84. It should be noted that the flamenco styles of vocal production in the late nineteenth and early twentieth century can differ significantly from the flamenco voice types of the early twenty-first century.

85. Maria Gay, *Carmen (Bizet): Habanera; Air des Cartes*, recorded 1 December 1910, Columbia, A-5279; Giovanni Zenatello, *Carmen: Sei tu? Final Duet Part 1; No, mai Carmen non cedera! Final Duet Part 2*, recorded 3 December 1930, Victor 7314.

rhythm in the famous descending lines that open the number, suggesting the sensual dance, and she maintained the music's forward momentum until carefully judged rubato and an increased warmth of sound emphasize the low notes at the end of the phrases. Her easy swaying motion underlies an attentive delivery of the text, with a clear and projected diction that shapes the lyrical line as much as the melody. Gay's interpretation is distinctive in her time for the attention she paid to the rhythmic and phrasal integrity of the score, in contrast with the freely scattered rubato of many of her contemporaries, and she has no recourse to momentary coquettish effects to create moments of charm.

If Gay performed act 1's "Séguedille" with "a whirlwind of sensual passion," her play of Spanish performativity reached its climax in the "Chanson bohème." In a uniquely rhythmic performance, she projected "unaccustomed liveliness," shocking Nozière, who had never "seen an artist who gave it such rhythm." He declared Gay's rendition of the "Card Aria" the "best of the best." Its static quality calls for maximum vocal expressivity and its low tessitura gave her scope to explore the breadth and nuance available to her in this register. For Nozière this represented the pinnacle of her impersonation:

> In the card trio she showed an unforgettable simplicity and depth of emotion. We were thus able to appreciate the richness and range of her voice, the grandeur of her style. It was at that moment that she was a sublime artist.[86]

Gay was not afraid to "dirty" her sound in the visceral cry, "la mort," nor to sob and gasp in her breath as she faced Carmen's fate. It was as if she had channeled the timbres and exclamations of the more somber flamenco *palos* (like the *soleá* and *siguiriya*, often referred to as *cante jondo*) through the operatic prism of verismo. Her approach to the "Card Aria" prefigured the exclamatory style of her declamation in the finale, replete with shrieks and gasps. This depth of emotion conveyed by a flexible vocal interpretation, coupled with her exuberant physicality in the role, meant that Gay's Carmen was more veristic than French. When she performed with an Italian company, or to an audience accustomed to Italian style (as in Madrid), she appeared in a context congenial to this characterization. But in theaters accustomed to a more French tradition of Bizet performance, Gay's gypsy could be shocking, if not distasteful. The modernity of Gay's Carmen resulted from an intelligent distillation of operatic convention and innovation with the clichés of staged Spanishness, and it was thrown into sharp relief by the proliferation of manifestations of these stereotypes across various sites of entertainment in Europe and North America.

86. Nozière, "Le Théatre," 3.

PART IV

Carmen as Popular Entertainment
(1900–15)

CHAPTER 8

༠⅄ఎ

Carmen's Music-Hall Embrace

Spanish-styled theatrical entertainment retained its appeal as Paris entered the twentieth century, gracing the popular stage in the form of mime, short sketches, dance turns, and, of course, that essential genre of the Parisian scene, the *chanson*. In these years leading up to the outbreak of the war that brought the heady era of the Belle Époque to a close, we can trace parallel evolutionary processes in theatrical Spanish dance and in its elite cousin, the ballet. In Paris, flamenco began to enter mainstream entertainment in the wake of its success at the 1900 Exposition Universelle, and was increasingly included in hybrid *spectacles* alongside more familiar forms of Spanish dance. The advent of the Ballets Russes in 1909 modeled innovation in every aspect of danced drama, from plot and music to design and choreography, transforming the landscape of theatrical dance. Against a background of rapid aesthetic change, *Carmen* continued to be subject to reconfiguration, its themes and characters re-emerging in song, dance, and mime as theatrical representations of Spanishness became increasingly associated with dramatic dance. And so *Carmen* enabled the ultimate transformation, as La Belle Otero—the great music hall star of the Belle Époque—sang (and danced) the title role of the opera, on the very stage of the Opéra-Comique itself.

THE CARMENESQUE *CHANSON* IN THE PARISIAN MUSIC HALL

The *chanson*, an emblematic genre of the Belle Époque, embraced the Spanish fashions of the era, and even gave rise to a subgenre often identified as the *chanson espagnole*. This genre drew freely upon the well-worn musical, literary, and scenic tropes of the nineteenth-century *espagnolade* and on features associated with *Carmen*, reworking them within comic or dramatic narratives that resonated with the music-hall audiences of the new century. Although these *chansons* were frequently composed and sung by French artists, the Spanish performers who continued to flock to Paris in the new century also made a significant contribution to the ongoing development of this form of Spanish-themed song in the French capital.[1] Stars like the *cupletista* Fornarina (Consuelo Vello) and La Tortajada mostly performed material written expressly for them, often singing in Spanish, and they were confident enough to play with the very stereotypes of Spanishness that were their main selling point. The ubiquity and popularity of the style is demonstrated by Tortajada's self-titled 1903 "chanson espagnole," in which she claimed her authenticity as the real Tortajada from Granada, letting fly with a chorus of "Olé" and nonsense syllables to evoke the clatter of Spanish dancing in a self-aware, tongue-in-cheek play with the markers of the popular *espagnolade*.[2] Tortajada's implication is that she is the genuine artifact, unlike the many imitators and "fake" Spaniards of the era. The importance of Spanish stars like Otero, Guerrero, and Tortajada in the Parisian scene is evident from topical references to them in song lyrics or parody songs explicitly imitating their style.[3]

The rise of the *chanson* (and the *chanson espagnole*) coincided with a boom in sheet-music publication and the emergence of recordings, which worked alongside live performance to foster the genre's dissemination and popularity. Sheet music had the added advantage of a visual element, and in the early 1900s this was not confined to photographs promoting the singer who had popularized the particular song, as song sheets were adorned with attractive artwork that could illustrate the Spanish theme. All these songs traded on the long-established set of Spanish stereotypes, often with specifically Andalusian inflections, harking back to the *género andaluz* so popular during the Second Empire—although at times updated to reflect contemporary stage fashions—demonstrating that Andalusia was still considered emblematic of Spain as a

---

1. Much of the discussion in this section is indebted to the groundbreaking work on Hispanic popular music in Paris by Geraldine Power in "Projections of Spain in Popular Spectacle and Chanson, Paris: 1889–1926" (PhD thesis, University of Melbourne, 2013).

2. Power, "Projections of Spain," 89–91. Tortajada, "La Tortajada (chanson espagnole)," *Paris qui chante* 1 (4 October 1903): 8–9.

3. In 1903 the cross-dressing performer Bertin featured several numbers in "imitation" of Otero and Tortajada, the sheet music of which depicts him dressed and posing like the women in question, while Celia Galley launched *Nina l'espagnole*, a song parodying Otero's persona, in 1907. Bertin's parody songs, *Madame Rasta (chanson espagnole)* and *Une fête à Madrid*, as well as the instrumental number *Flor d'amor (baile español)*, which was dedicated to "Madame Guerrero," were all published in the 2 August 1903 issue of *Paris qui chante*. This weekly journal was devoted to the entertainment scene and included a sheet-music supplement. Power, "Projections of Spain," 83–87, 118–19.

whole. Whether depicted in the lyrics or as illustrations on published sheet music, many of the places and situations featured in *Carmen* are referred to in the songs, with characters including bullfighters, dancers, gypsies, and Spanish women who were by turns beautiful, defiant, and unfaithful, loved desperately by men whose jealousy might drive them to violence.[4] Musically, the markers of Spanishness in the *chansons* varied from adopting dance styles like the habanera or *jota*, with their distinctive syncopations and rhythmic patterns, to the inclusion of triplet turns, or allusions to the Andalusian scale and cadence, always within a simple harmonic framework. The recycling and recombination of these apparently infinitely reproducible Spanish topics seems to have been more than just a frank attempt to profit from a popular exotic commodity.

If ubiquity and cliché invited parody, the industry also offered a self-conscious acknowledgment of the way in which this hybrid genre had grown out of a uniquely Parisian Franco-Spanish cultural exchange: this was the case with the emergence of a song type designated by terms like "chanson hispano-montmartroise" or "chanson montmartro-espagnole."[5] The compound subtitles indicate that these songs functioned on multiple levels, both as easily digestible exotic commodities for a music-hall audience seeking entertainment (and perhaps a little titillation), and as sly commentary on the depth of this Parisian *espagnolade* tradition. Referential humor was based on older *espagnolades* (like *Carmen* or Iradier's habaneras) and the famous Spanish performers and composers of the tradition. In the case of this new genre designation, however, lyrics often explicitly acknowledged the local performers based in the notorious entertainment districts of Paris, notably Montmartre, where Spanish and French stage and artistic types mingled, competed, and collaborated.

Into this vibrant Franco-Spanish landscape entered the young Spanish composer Quinito Valverde (Joaquín Valverde Sanjuán), son of the great *zarzuela* composer Joaquín Valverde Durán, who had cowritten *La Gran Vía*. The younger Valverde had made a name for himself in Madrid by composing topical, urban *revistas* (reviews), *género chico* works, songs, and operettas. Equally proficient in Spanish and contemporary European styles, he displayed a particular flair for dance numbers. But he had his eye on the lucrative French market, and having worked with La Fornarina in Spain before she launched herself in Paris in 1907, he composed many of the French-language *chansons* with which she established her international career, including several that

---

4. Power, "Projections of Spain," 74–75, 138.

5. Examples of this hybrid genre include *La Likette (chanson danse hispano-montmartroise)* of 1909; *La Chiquilla espagnola (chanson montmartro-espagnole)* of 1913, both published in *Paris qui chante*. See Power, "Projections of Spain," 127–29, 229–30, 376–77.

Figure 8.1 J. [Quinito] Valverde (music), Gabriel Montoya (lyrics), *Chanson pour Pepa, Havanaise* (Madrid: Casa Dotesio, 1907).
Credit: ICCMU (Instituto Complutense de Ciencias Musicales).

played with elements of the plot and musical style of *Carmen*. These include the *Chanson pour Pepa (havanaise)* of 1907, which quotes the immortal line, "Prends garde à toi," from the "Habanera" and features a lover who threatens to kill his girl if she won't love him truly (see Figure 8.1).[6]

6. Power, "Projections of Spain," 131–35.

These songs by Valverde prefigure a number of Parisian Spanish-themed *chansons* dating from about 1910 to 1915, which gravitated increasingly toward intertextual subject matter that could be related to *Carmen*.[7] Geraldine Power describes a group of songs that mimic many aspects of the opera's storyline and cast of characters, and are frequently set to habanera rhythms. Some echo musical motives from the opera's famous numbers, like the opening figure from the refrain of the "Chanson bohème," or the incipit of the opera's overture, while others repeat famous lines in their lyrics, especially "Prends garde à toi."[8] Just as Otero began to publicize her ambition to sing the title role on the operatic stage (of which more follows), the growing fixation with Bizet's *Carmen* is demonstrated by the 1910 release of a new version of Iradier's celebrated habanera *La paloma*, now titled *La Vraie Paloma!* (The True Paloma/Dove!). The original lyrics, in which the singer's affection is communicated to his distant beloved by a gentle dove, are substituted by a new French text in which a jealous Andalusian beauty stabs her faithless lover with a dagger.[9] Despite the role reversal, the parallels with *Carmen* are unmistakable: the most famous of Iradier's habaneras is subsumed into the Carmen narrative, almost mirroring the way his "El arreglito"—as adapted by Bizet—had come to define the opera and its protagonist. The combination of habanera and Carmenesque themes is also evident in *Bravade andalouse* of 1909 and *Carmen l'andalouse* of 1910.[10]

The early 1900s had seen the proliferation of the habanera in Paris, where it infiltrated a variety of musical styles. In terms of popular music, it retained its appeal in part because of the fashion for syncopated song and dance styles, including ragtime and the *maxixe* (which in fact owed their derivation in part to the habanera's rhythmic template). The vogue for the habanera was also perpetuated by Carmen's aria, which had breached its operatic confines and frequently appeared as a self-contained item on the popular stage. Two further numbers from Spanish *género chico zarzuelas* were well known to Parisian audiences: the "Tango de Menegilda" from Chueca and Valverde's *La Gran Vía* (1886) and "Donde vas con mantón de Manila" from Bretón's *La Verbena de la paloma* (1894).[11] The "Tango de Menegilda" depicts a Madrid maid being able

7. Ibid., 215–33.

8. These references to the opera can be found in *La Morena* (1911), and *La Gitane jalouse* (1912). Power, "Projections of Spain," 222, 226–28. Another example, *Le Chauffeur amoureux* (1906), refers to love as a "gypsy child," quoting the second stanza of Carmen's famous "Habanera."

9. Power, "Projections of Spain," 215.

10. Ibid., 135–36, 216–18.

11. *La Gran Vía* was adapted into French and had a successful run at the Olympia in Paris in 1896, although the "Tango de Menegilda" had been performed in Paris by La Belle Otero as early as 1889.

to get ahead only by employing guile and her sexual charms, while "Donde vas con mantón de Manila" depicts an argument between a strong-willed woman and her lover.

The habanera's reach also extended to some of the most innovative instrumental and orchestral music being produced in fin-de-siècle Paris. By the late nineteenth and early twentieth centuries it had attained a certain independence from its original poetic allusions and had become a key marker of musical Spanishness. From Bizet, through Chabrier, Albéniz, and Ravel, and to Debussy, the habanera had been transformed from a sensuous song to a nostalgic utterance, often evoking the night music of Granada (especially in works such as Debussy's "La Soirée dans Grenade ..." and "Parfums de la nuit" from his orchestral suite *Ibéria*), a site increasingly associated with *Carmen* at the turn of the century.[12]

The established popularity of the habanera was also to facilitate the Argentine tango's acceptance in Paris from around 1908, another dance that owed its origins in part to the same rhythmic template. This nexus between the habanera and the tango is even more direct in the case of the *tango-chanson*, a form of song cultivated by French, Spanish, and Argentine composers in the French capital in the years prior to World War I, and that at times drew on the narratives associated with *Carmen* to underscore its identity as a sexualized social dance.[13] Power draws attention to the hybridity of the *tango-chanson*, highlighting the case of *Mimi Bohême* of 1909, a collaboration between the French lyricist Léo Lelièvre and Spanish musician Manuel Sarrablo, in which they adapted the popular Argentine melody *La Morocha* by Enrique Saborido. This tango was marked as a "Tempo di Habanera," a more familiar tempo and genre indication for Parisian audiences of the time, and is colored by Carmenesque allusions to "gypsy hearts" and "treachery."[14] In Paris, Spanish performers were also integral to the dissemination of the Argentine tango, at times investing it with Andalusian inflections of dance and dress, as had been the case with the earlier arrival of Latin-American song and dance styles such as the *maxixe*.[15]

12. See Michael Christoforidis, "Isaac Albéniz, Claude Debussy and Views of the Alhambra from Paris," in *Manuel de Falla and Visions of Spanish Music* (London and New York: Routledge, 2018), 47–67.

13. Power, "Projections of Spain," 237–54.

14. Ibid., 240–44.

15. K. Meira Goldberg notes the incorporation of ragtime elements into Spanish dance and flamenco in the early twentieth century. See K. Meira Goldberg, "*Jaleo de Jerez* and *tumulte noir*: Primitivist Modernism and Cakewalk in Flamenco, 1902–1917," in *Flamenco on the Global Stage: Historical, Critical and Theoretical Perspectives*, ed. K. Meira Goldberg, Ninotchka Devorah Bennahum, and Michelle Heffner Hayes (Jefferson, NC: McFarland, 2015), 124–42.

SPANISH DANCE IN THE AGE OF THE BALLETS RUSSES

As the *spectacle* struggled to retain its popularity in the fast-changing scene of the early 1900s, impresarios staged a number of theatrical entertainments incorporating Hispanic dance styles—including recent manifestations of flamenco and the latest trend of the Argentine tango—in an attempt to capitalize on the interest in dance created by Diaghilev's Ballets Russes. This new dance company arrived in Paris in 1909, taking both the fashionable and artistic worlds by storm as it reinvigorated the theatrical dance spectacle. The Ballets Russes's formula for success included compelling storylines, expressive and dramatic pantomime, fine music (often by great composers), lavish and innovative sets and costumes, and superb dancing in a style that transcended the Romantic ballet tradition, incorporating elements of the folk, primitive, and exotic. With works like the Polovtsian Dances from Alexander Borodin's *Prince Igor* (1909) or *Schéhérazade* (1910) to music by Nikolai Rimsky-Korsakov, the Russians reworked the conception of exotic dance, simultaneously demonstrating fresh possibilities for dance as a vehicle for narrative. Performing across the Continent and in London, the company had an incalculable impact on modern ballet, and its success resulted in a recalibration of the Spanish dance spectacle on both sides of the English Channel.[16]

Power observes that whereas flamenco had mainly appeared in "mediated spots in review-type *spectacles*," from around 1908 there was also a "surge in music-hall *spectacles* incorporating Andalusian and flamenco dance." With the arrival of outstanding flamenco performers like La Macarrona (still remembered by some for her watershed appearance with the Granadine gypsy troupe at the 1889 Exposition Universelle) and Antonio de Bilbao, the gypsy dance style once considered of only ethnographic interest won over mainstream Parisian audiences, who were becoming more interested in primitivist art. This new generation of flamenco dancers and impresarios replicated the Spanish *tablao* (flamenco venue), most notably in the Parisian locale known as La Feria, which opened in 1912. Here patrons could enjoy dinner and sherry, while watching the dancers perform with their troupe of guitarists and singers lined up behind them. It was a site frequented by the Spanish community in Paris and at times hosted a blend of Spanish styles, with guest appearances by artists like Valverde and La Fornarina.[17]

Valverde became a key player in the staging of Spanish dance in Paris from 1909. He decided to build on his success as a composer of *género chico* and *revista*

16. Members of the Ballets Russes were to get their first taste of Spanish dance and flamenco in the venues of Paris, witnessing the hybrid dance spectacles of Valverde, or the *tablaos* set up in local cafes, before the company embarked on extended tours through Spain during World War I.

17. Power, "Projections of Spain," 153–64, 210.

in Madrid by embracing the hybrid Spanish entertainments that appealed to audiences in the French capital. Teaming up with various French librettists, between 1909 and 1913 Valverde produced a series of four *spectacles* with Spanish storylines and plenty of song and dance. Performed by mixed casts, the *spectacles* had French principals in the dramatic leads, but Spanish dancers and subsidiary characters were an important feature. Valverde's *La Maison de danses* premiered at the Théâtre du Vaudeville in November 1909, telling the tale of a Carmen-like character, a dancer in a dance school who attracted too many lovers, culminating in a violent confrontation. Despite the dark undertones of the dramatic plot, the setting provided ample opportunities for choreographed numbers, accompanied by *estudiantina* ensembles of guitarists and mandolinists, all of whom were rehearsed by Valverde himself.[18] His other *spectacles* conformed to a more frivolous mood, with farcical plots and picaresque characters.

L'Amour en Espagne, which debuted at the Parisiana in August 1909 but was revived a year later at the Moulin Rouge, was described as an "opérette-bouffe franco-espagnole." Despite this hybrid nomenclature, the whole production was a showcase for Hispanic dance styles, including habanera and Andalusian tango. Its 1910 iteration featured the Paris debut of La Argentina (Antonia Mercé), who became a legendary figure in Spanish dance and negotiated the fault lines between classical and popular styles. Notable elements of *L'Amour en Espagne* were its flamenco numbers, danced by a troupe of Granadine gypsies, its finale, and "La corrida" choreographed by Antonio de Bilbao.[19] This winning formula then formed the basis for *La Rose de Grenade* (staged at the Olympia in early 1912) and *La Belle Cigarière* (Moulin Rouge, 1913), both light-hearted French-authored shows playing on Spanish stereotypes (see Figure 8.2). In spite of the presence of cigarette manufacturing and smuggling in the plot of *La Belle Cigarière*, these works moved away from the more dramatic Carmenesque themes. French actors filled the leading roles, but they starred La Argentina and Maria la Bella respectively, and offered both old and new in their music and dance, as represented by *estudiantinas* and flamenco troupes. Flamenco rose in status and recognition in Paris after being showcased in Valverde's operettas.[20]

The upsurge in the staging of Spanish dance was also reflected in productions at the Opéra and the Opéra-Comique in the 1910s. These productions included the dance sequences of Raoul Laparra's opera *La jota*, produced at the Opéra-Comique in 1911, and the addition of an extra dance and importation

18. Ibid., 173–74, 85.
19. The show also seems to have included a comic bullfight involving a real bull. Ibid., 186–200.
20. Ibid., 192–207.

Figure 8.2 Images from Quinito Valverde's *La Rose de Grenade*, *Le Music-Hall*, 15 February 1912, 5.
Credit: Bibliothèque Nationale de France.

from Spain of *bailaoras* (flamenco dancers) for the Opéra-Comique production of Falla's *La Vie brève* in late 1913. The Opéra also competed in this space, in a more pointed rivalry with the Ballets Russes, when Jane Catulle-Mendés provided a narrative thread to Chabrier's score for the staging of the ballet *España* in May 1911. The production's emphasis on design was complemented by the choreography created by Léo Staats with the Opéra's former *première danseuse* Rosita Mauri. By the 1910s it also became much more common for French productions of *Carmen* to incorporate flamenco *bailaoras*—first employed in the 1890s—for some of the dance sequences of the opera (most notably the "Chanson bohème"). Even the legendary gypsy dancer and entertainer Pastora Imperio served in this capacity in the 1918 French production of *Carmen* at Madrid's Teatro Real. The Ballets Russes was to fully encounter Spain when the troupe toured that country during World War I. Elements of Spanish dance and flamenco were incorporated into the Ballets Russes production of Manuel de Falla's *The Three-Cornered Hat* (1919), and Diaghilev even staged a flamenco show, the *Cuadro flamenco*, under the aegis of his company (1921).

Just as it had done in Paris, the Ballets Russes electrified the London dance world with its debut season at Covent Garden in late autumn 1911. After years in which English ballet had stagnated, the Russian productions were hailed by the local press for their "inventive genius" and for presenting "a whole range of ideas such as we have never met before."[21] Their imaginative innovations

21. "Music: The Russian Ballet," *Times* (London), 24 June 1911, 13.

inspired local producers, while critics speculated that the quality of the music that accompanied the dance was more important than might have hitherto been recognized in an artform that focused on the visual element.[22] In this context, the Alhambra's Anglo-Australian manager, Alfred Moul, announced in January 1912 that he was restaging the theater's *Carmen* ballet, perhaps hoping to emulate the success achieved when Rosario Guerrero had created the role in dance and mime back in 1903.

But Moul was careful to explain that he was not simply reviving the 1903 production. While this new *Carmen* was still based on Byng's "reverent" adaptation of the Bizet score—which was considered "first-rate ballet music"[23]— scenario and design were created anew by Dion Clayton Calthrop, and costumes prepared with considerable care, including some "lovely shawls from Seville" to add a further touch of authenticity.[24] Moul had initially announced that Carmen would be played by Anna Gaschewska, a dancer from the corps de ballet of the Ballets Russes, in a clear indication that he was seeking to cash in on the latest fashion in theatrical dance. But contractual difficulties forced him to replace Gaschewska with the Spanish dancer Maria la Bella, who had starred as the Alhambra's Carmen in 1903, after Guerrero left for the United States, and was enjoying success on the Parisian stage. Moul again returned to the 1903 cast when he hired the distinguished French mime artist Volbert to reprise his impersonation of José, but he abandoned the Alhambra's (by now outdated) travesty tradition by casting another French mime, Emile Agoust, as Escamillo. The strength of this cast of principals was in dramatic pantomime, and Maria la Bella proved especially adept at combining dance with mime to "very poignant dramatic effect," appearing "at once alluring and dramatic, as Carmens should be" (see Figure 8.3).[25] She thus lived up to the expectations created by long familiarity with the opera, and in particular the interpretations of singers like Calvé and Gay. Despite a suitably tragic finale, Calthrop emphasized the "lighter and brighter side of the plot," in which Maria la Bella shone as the "fascinating cigarette girl [rather] than as the faithless sweetheart."[26]

In perhaps his most significant change, however, Moul updated the work significantly in terms of its Spanishness, in contrast to 1903 when Guerrero had been the unique exponent of Spanish dance, surrounded by the Alhambra's chorus line. Moul proudly reported to the press that he had imported "a great

22. "Music: The Russian Ballet: A Retrospect," *Times* (London), 5 August 1912, 9.

23. "New Ballet at the Alhambra," *Times* (London), 25 January 1912, 8.

24. "Mr Alfred Moul on the Coming 'Carmen,'" *Referee*, 21 January 1912, 4.

25. "The Spanish Dancers," *Manchester Guardian*, 25 January 1912, 6; "New Ballet at the Alhambra," 8.

26. Tristram, "The Variety Stage: 'Carmen' at the Alhambra," *Referee*, 28 January 1912, 4.

MARIA LA BELLA

Figure 8.3 Maria la Bella as Carmen at the Alhambra Theatre (London), *Le Music Hall* 2, no. 10 (15 May 1912): 30.

deal of real Spanish local color," giving "some of the Spanish national dances [to] artists who have never, up to the present, performed out of Spain." He was even more excited to present a dancer of the "Andalusian Flamenco or Gipsy type."[27] This was La Malagueñita, partnered by Antonio de Bilbao, who headed a troupe of Spanish dancers. She performed several flamenco numbers on a tabletop, dressed in a white *torero* outfit and playing castanets, giving new life to this enduring image of Spanish abandon (see Figure 8.4). Antonio wowed the audience with his *zapateado*, but so much heel stamping and gypsy flamenco proved slightly too much for some elements of the Alhambra audience. London had not been exposed to as much flamenco as Paris, and the allegiance of the *Referee*'s critic was clearly still with the Alhambra's charming chorus girls:

> The troupe of Spanish Dancers, headed by La Malagueñita, execute sundry measures in accepted Spanish style, but I don't think that they add much to the

27. "Mr Alfred Moul on the Coming 'Carmen,'" 4.

Figure 8.4 La Malagueñita in the *posada* scene of *Carmen*, depicted by Dudley Hardy, "From Sunny Spain to Gloomy London: A Scene in 'Carmen,' the New Ballet at the Alhambra," *Graphic*, 3 February 1912, 139.

attractiveness of the ballet. There is such a deal of foot-stamping in this style of dancing. An extra dance or two for the stock corps de ballet might have proved a happier idea.[28]

28. It should be noted that Czech ballet master Augustin Berger provided the choreography for the Alhambra's dancers in 1912. Tristram, "The Variety Stage," 4.

Moul's valiant attempt to compete with the Ballets Russes at Covent Garden, by proving that English theater still had something to offer, was recognized by the critic of the *Manchester Guardian*: "The new production of Bizet's 'Carmen' at the Alhambra to-night was rather heartening. Evidently the Russians do not utterly carry it away."[29] This was truly a modernized *Carmen*, designed for audiences that had already encountered the energy of the Ballets Russes and the new flamenco styles that spread from 1900.[30]

LA BELLE OTERO AS CARMEN

Amidst this burgeoning scene of Spanish-themed entertainment, the aging Carolina Otero continued to draw audiences and to dream of new conquests: in the twilight of her career, she aspired to sing Bizet's Carmen at the Opéra-Comique. In 1912, at the very end of the Belle Époque, that august theater allowed her to make the almost unprecedented transition from music-hall performer and elite courtesan to opera star, if only for a single benefit performance. The idea of a dancer performing Carmen in the opera itself was more easily contemplated because of the way the operatic role itself had changed over the previous decade. By the early years of the twentieth century, *Carmen*—in the company of Richard Strauss's *Salome* (with its infamous Dance of the Seven Veils)—began to attract stars who could dance as well as sing and act the title role. This tendency developed with the Ballets Russes as the company found new ways to entwine narrative with dance, and by 1914 was presenting operas like Rimsky-Korsakov's *Le Coq d'or* as mimed and danced spectacles, with the singers forming part of the offstage music ensemble.[31]

Otero had built her career around a Carmenesque persona, combining her classic Spanish beauty with a magnetic stage presence, sensual dancing, and adroit self-promotion. Although she seems to have been born into a poor Galician family from the north of Spain, Otero publicized various versions of her biography, including frequent claims of noble ancestry, or, alternatively, Andalusian origins.[32] The tale she told in her memoirs, published in the 1920s,

29. "The Spanish Dancers," 6.

30. Ivor Guest, *Ballet in Leicester Square: The Alhambra and the Empire 1860–1915* (London: Dance Books, 1992), 81–82; "Mr Alfred Moul on the Coming 'Carmen,'" 4.

31. See Davinia Caddy, *The Ballets Russes and Beyond: Music and Dance in Belle-Époque Paris* (Cambridge and New York: Cambridge University Press, 2012).

32. Where possible we have checked the popular biographical sources on Otero against accounts in the contemporary press. Javier Figuero and Marie-Hélène Carbonel, *Arruíname, pero no me abandones: La Belle Otero y la Belle Époque* (Madrid: Espasa-Calpe, 2003); Arthur H. Lewis, *La Belle Otero* (New York: Trident, 1967); Carolina Otero, *Les*

demonstrates that she finally decided a narrative related to *Carmen* was the most fruitful:

> My mother, Carmen, ... was an unusually beautiful gypsy whose early life was passed on the open roads of Andalusia.... Carmen earned her living as a Spanish gypsy earns it. She danced: she sang: she told fortunes.[33]

In this tale of Otero's origin, her father was a handsome Greek officer whose mad passion led him to pursue her independent gypsy mother across Andalusia, finally winning her heart and hand after abducting her near Seville and settling with his young family in Galicia, before his wife's unfaithfulness led the family to tragedy.[34] Otero lived up to this confected ancestry, both in her beauty and her liking for the company of wealthy men. During her years of stardom the press was particularly devoted to reporting on her "private" life. She was notorious for her many affairs, especially with members of noble and even royal families, including the Prince of Wales and Alfonso XIII of Spain. Through these liaisons Otero amassed a dazzling collection of jewelry and was reported to have caused much heartbreak, even suicides, among her spurned lovers, as she upheld her freedom to choose whom she would "love." Otero (and her managers) sustained intense public interest by manipulating the media, not really a difficult task, given the contemporary journalistic predisposition to perpetuate stereotypes of the exotic performer.

During the 1890s Otero was one of the brightest stars of the international variety stage, confirming her celebrity status by wearing her extravagant jewels on stage at every opportunity. Branded as a genuine Spaniard (in a market flooded by imitators), Otero was infamous for her sexualized Spanish dance that distilled the passion associated with the South from an eclectic mixture of regional dance, flamenco, and contemporary music-hall styles. Although her sensuality must be seen within the context of 1890s mores, she made good use of her notoriously flexible spine (her backbends were justly famous, as can be discerned in surviving 1898 film footage depicting her dancing), and some of her costumes were flagrantly revealing. Between her international tours, performing in cities from London to New York and Berlin to Saint Petersburg—Otero appeared on the bills of the best Parisian *café-chantants* and music halls, frequently heading the program at the Folies-Bergère. Such was Otero's continued fame and iconic

---

Souvenirs et la vie intime de la belle Otero (Paris: Le Calame, 1926); Caroline Otero, *My Story* (London: A. M. Philpot, [1927]).

33. Otero, *My Story*, 11.
34. Ibid., 12–20.

style that as late as 1908 Geraldine Farrar (already an internationally celebrated opera singer) was reported to have modeled her "coiffure" as Nedda in Ruggero Leoncavallo's *I Pagliacci* on Otero's hairstyle.[35] By the start of the twentieth century Otero gradually shifted the format of her act from a combination of songs and dances, culminating with dance, toward more dramatic pantomime turns, following the prevailing fashion. In her choice of stage characters, Otero managed to perpetuate her persona as a Spanish beauty and femme fatale, with plots that focused on passion, jealousy, tragedy, and fate, all motives closely aligned with Carmen and the stereotype of the Spanish woman perpetuated in European and North American culture.

When she was a young performer, Otero's vocal production had been weaker than her dancing, despite her boasting in her early publicity that she had sung opera in Spain. She seems to have worked on her singing, maintaining it as part of her act throughout the 1890s, but she did not publicize her study of vocal technique until the 1900s, when she announced that she had decided to launch herself onto the operatic stage, initially targeting the role of Carmen. Perhaps she was encouraged in this ambition by the success of her young competitor, the beautiful Italian Lina Cavalieri, whose variety career took her from Italy in 1894 to rivalry with Otero on the stage of the Folies-Bergère in 1896. They were pitted even more directly against each other when they appeared on the same bill at the Saint Petersburg Aquarium in summer 1898.[36] The following year Cavalieri announced her retirement from variety to pursue a career in opera and proceeded to sing principal roles with Italian companies from Lisbon to Saint Petersburg before debuting at the Met in 1906 and Covent Garden in 1908. Despite repeated announcements that she was studying Carmen and was keen to play the role, Cavalieri seems to have been wary of Bizet's gypsy.[37] When she finally sang Carmen opposite Zenatello's José for Oscar Hammerstein's Manhattan Opera in the 1909–10 season, her beauty and charm were not enough to carry a role that had come to require a truly dramatic delivery. Despite praise for her dancing, Cavalieri's Carmen was judged "too much of the lady and too little of the animal," featuring laughing naughtiness rather than allure and devilry, while musically it sat too low for her limited vocal capabilities.[38] After five performances for Hammerstein,

35. "[Debussy Thanks Campanini]," *Musical America* 7, no. 20 (1908): 7.

36. Paul Fryer and Olga Usova, *Lina Cavalieri: The Life of Opera's Greatest Beauty, 1874–1944* (Jefferson, NC: McFarland, 2004), 18, 22–23.

37. Ibid., 86. The Met even announced that she would make her debut as Carmen in their 1908–09 season.

38. "Cavalieri Gay in Role of 'Carmen,'" *Musical America* 11, no. 4 (1909): 8; "Cavalieri Gay in Role of Carmen," *New York Times*, 26 November 1909.

Cavalieri sang Carmen only a few more times in Russia, having found it an uncongenial role.

The first decade of the twentieth century had witnessed a procession of Carmens at the Opéra-Comique, some of whom—like the Anglo-Belgian mezzo-soprano Marguerite Sylva—had come to that institution with a mixed theatrical pedigree. Although she had essayed Bizet's gypsy in England and the United States, Sylva came to the Salle Favart from a successful New York career in operetta, musical comedy, and vaudeville at the turn of the century, bringing to the role elements of staged Spanishness from the dance turns thriving in contemporary popular theatres (see Figure 8.5). Commenting on the rousing ovation she received from her Parisian audience at the end of the 1906–7 season, Sylva noted to an interviewer:

> You saw how demonstrative it was. Well, almost every one of that immense crowd knows the score of "Carmen" as well as I do. They have seen every Carmen that the world has ever known right here in this theatre, where the opera was first produced nearly thirty-two years ago and has been played on an average perhaps twice a week ever since.[39]

Carmen's status at the Opéra-Comique meant that the work's lead functioned as a presentation role for many aspiring sopranos and mezzo-sopranos. While Parisian audiences and press could be critical, they could also be open to innovation, given that no one singer embodied the role at the Opéra-Comique in the way that Calvé had dominated at the Met. These circumstances, along with Otero's notoriety and social connections, allowed her to aspire to performing the role at the Salle Favart.

Otero had been developing her dramatic abilities since 1900 as she focused increasingly on pantomime, learning skills that prepared her to express the tragic destiny of Bizet's gypsy protagonist, and enhanced her already undisputed status as the embodiment of Spanishness on the Parisian stage. She showed the first evidence of this versatility in her pantomime debut, when she danced, sang, and mimed in a one-act show entitled *Une fête à Séville*, which was staged at the Théâtre Marigny during the 1900 Exposition Universelle. It was declared "necessary" that Otero, as one of Paris's "celebrities or curiosities," be "displayed during the Exhibition to the innumerable visitors coming to Paris."[40] Produced as a star vehicle for Otero, *Une fête à Séville* had many Carmenesque features: this tale of a

39. "Sylva Ends Season at Opera Comique: Former Light Opera Star Tells of Her Career in French Capital," *Musical America* 6, no. 8 (6 July 1907): 16.

40. Adolphe Aderer, "Théatre Marigny: Une Fête à Séville," *Le Théâtre* 43 (October [I]) 1900): 22.

Figure 8.5 "Mme Marguerita Sylva as Carmen, of the Opéra-Comique," photograph by Boissonas (*c.* 1906–15).
Credit: George Grantham Bain Collection, Library of Congress, http://www.loc.gov/pictures/item/ggb2004003862.

bullfighter (played by Paul Franck) was set in a square outside Seville's bull-ring. After his death is foretold in the cards by a fortune teller, he is stabbed accidentally by his jealous mistress, who had been aiming for his new lover, Mercedes, played by Otero. She made her entrance with a Spanish song

Figure 8.6 Otero as Mercedes in scene 3 of *Une fête à Séville*. "Le tango de la table," reproduced in Adolphe Aderer, "Théatre Marigny: Une fête à Séville," *Le Théâtre* 43 (October [I] 1900): 20.
Credit: State Library of Victoria.

before performing the rest of the work in mute pantomime and dance, winning praise for her dramatic portrayal of a wide variety of moods (see Figure 8.6).[41]

Otero continued to perform as a mime artist throughout the first decade of the century, honing her skills under the tutelage of her costar, the eminent mime artist Georges Wague. She played a variety of roles, but was usually called on to display her ability as a sensual dancer specializing in Hispanic characters, much like the dramatic sketches performed by her renowned compatriot (and Carmen impersonator) Rosario Guerrero. Carmenesque themes reappear in the storylines of her pantomimes, many of which featured gypsies, dance, passion, and betrayal, and culminated in murder. Otero played either victim or perpetrator in works like the dark tale of *Nuit de Noël* (Christmas Eve, 1908) or the tragic but picturesque *Giska la bohémienne* (Giska the Gypsy, 1908), in which she played a Breton gypsy who is killed for taking a new lover.

Despite her ongoing pantomime career, Otero was clearly considering her options as she approached her mid-forties. In 1910 she announced her

41. For a more detailed discussion of the reception of *Une fête à Séville*, see Power, "Projections of Spain," 51–53.

intention to found a school for the training of Spanish dancers, with branches in Seville and Paris, financed by the sale of her jewels. Speaking to an American journalist of these plans, Otero deplored the hard life of the Spanish dancer, especially the flamenco artist, whose exertions aged her prematurely, explaining that she had been able to adapt her own "flamenco" style to foreign audiences and spare herself this fate. Her "academy of Spanish national dances" was intended to elevate genres like the "seductive seguidilla, the ferocious fandango, the blustering bolero and the flamenco" out of the low-life world of smoky bars into "honorable ... surroundings before fashionable publics," and address the lamentable ignorance of foreigners about the Spanish dance they flocked to see. There is no evidence that Otero ever realized this plan, and she famously lost most of her fortune at the gambling tables of the French Riviera.[42] She did, however, embrace new dance fashions, such as the Argentine tango, featuring as a demonstration dancer in a season of "tango teas" at the London Opera House alongside her music-hall engagements in autumn 1913.[43]

But January 1909 saw the announcement of Otero's ambition to perform Carmen on the operatic stage, amid reports that she was studying with renowned singing teacher (Marquis Ange-Pierre de) Trabadelo, who had taught many other opera singers, including Mary Garden and Geraldine Farrar. Otero "believes she has a powerful dramatic voice" suited to the role, wrote *Musical America*'s satirical columnist Mephisto, closing his notice with this cynical statement: "I wish her luck, but scarcely think she will erase the memory of some of the Carmens we have heard and seen."[44] Otero did not achieve the next stage in her quest until summer 1912, but the lapse of several years suggests her intense determination to fulfill this aspiration. By then she had been studying with Lucien Fugère, famous baritone and teacher at the Paris Conservatoire. After several months of rehearsal, Otero performed act 1 of *Carmen* at a matinee benefit for "Trente Ans de Théâtre" (Thirty Years of Theater) at the Théâtre de Variétés in June 1912 (see Figure 8.7). Partnered with opera singer Thomas Salignac as José, she appeared with the chorus and orchestra of the Opéra-Comique. Rumors immediately arose that Otero would soon appear in a regular production at the Salle Favart.[45]

André Nède of *Le Figaro* reported that Otero playing Carmen would have fulfilled a dream for Henri Meilhac, librettist for *Carmen*. According to Nède, Meilhac had declared Otero to be his ideal to play the Spanish gypsy (in the wake of Galli-Marié), not just because she embodied the character physically, but also because he was confident that—given her intelligence and theatrical

42. "The Dancing Girls of Spain: Otero Has Found a Use for Her Wealth of Jewels," *Sun* (New York), 19 June 1910, 7.

43. "The Theatrical Season. The Variety Theatres," *Times*, 27 October 1913, 12.

44. Mephisto, "Mephisto's Musings," *Musical America* 9, no. 12 (1909): 7.

45. "Paris et départements," *Le Ménestrel* 78, no. 24 (15 June 1912): 191.

Le chœur des Enfants : *Voici la garde montante...*

Figure 8.7 Caricature of Otero rehearsing to sing the role of Carmen. "Une débutante," *Le Music hall* 2, no. 10 (15 May 1912): 18.

talent—she could rise to the challenge of an operatic role.[46] Despite her heavy Spanish accent, which had been considered an obstacle to her appearance in French-language theater, Robert Brussel thought that Otero performed the "Habanera" and "Séguidille" to great effect. He described her Carmen as "spirited, passionate, ironic, above all superficial and very beautiful, and perhaps that is not the worst way of conceiving the character."[47] Brussel's ascription of "irony" suggests that Otero's ability to create a convincing persona as Carmen owed as much to her audience's recognition that she had lived many aspects of the role, and her knowing acknowledgment of this awareness, as it did to her stagecraft and allure. That her Spanish accent did not count against her, however, is an indicator of the extent to which the projection of a Hispanic persona had become integral to portrayals of Carmen and the quest for scenic realism in the role. Otero's achievement in this single act, and the aspirations it allowed her to articulate, are summed up by the correspondent for *Musical America*:

> Her acting was found by many to be superior to her singing. But this is natural in one so long a queen of pantomime. She appeared to be the ideal Carmen. As she had announced beforehand, she played the part with "fury," but her Spanish

46. André Nède, "Un gala aux variétés," *Le Figaro* (Paris), 14 June 1912, 1. Meilhac died in 1897, so he must have seen a younger Otero in the full flush of her success as star of music hall and *café-concert*.
47. Robert Brussel, "Mme Caroline Otero dans *Carmen*," *Le Figaro* (Paris), 20 June 1912, 5.

Figure 8.8 Otero in costume for act 4 of *Carmen* (1912).
Credit: Bibliothèque Nationale de France.

realism was so strong that her interpretation seemed more truthful than the
traditional presentation of the part.[48]

The ascription of "fury" to Otero's characterization recalls Guerrero's interpretation of the role, but this was not to be the end of Otero's operatic quest (see
Figure 8.8). In January 1913 she appeared in a full performance of *Carmen*
for the Opéra-Comique, not as part of their regular season but in the course

48. "'The Ring' Successful in Paris: Otero as 'Carmen,'" *Musical America* 16, no. 10
(1912): 26.

of a "matinée extraordinaire" for the benefit of dramatic artists, again singing opposite Salignac. Despite some doubts among the Parisian press, she was praised for her graceful movements (especially her dance in the second act), for the quality of her voice in the upper register, and even for the charming effect on the dialogue of her strong Spanish accent.[49] Otero was, however, well aware of the opposition to her presence on the stage of the Salle Favart.

> My worst crime ... was to come straight from the music halls to carry off the great role that professional singers quarrel over with increasing vigor. I remember many of them sitting with their scores in their hands while I was singing, watching like lynxes to pounce on any mistakes.[50]

While she may have been unnerved by the singers in the audience, Otero maintained a façade of self-assuredness, insolence, and bravado, qualities that had facilitated her association with the figure of Carmen over the previous two decades. Otero's biographer reported that, when asked if she had been nervous, she declared,

> Not a goddamned bit! All those smug women sitting out there, waiting for me to make a fool of myself; I'd laid half their husbands and the other half would have enjoyed the experience if they could have afforded me.[51]

Otero confidently announced her plans to continue her operatic career: she would sing Carmen at the Opéra-Comique and in the French provinces and then branch out into other dramatic roles suited to her Mediterranean temperament, in works such as Puccini's *Tosca*, Mascagni's *Cavalleria rusticana* and Massenet's *La Navarraise*.[52] There were even rumors that she had been invited to perform at the Metropolitan in New York.[53] Otero reported in her memoir that she achieved a *succès fou* as Carmen in Rouen, but "there ended, unhappily, my playing the part of Carmen, because of certain jealousies and pecuniary difficulties," including a lawsuit preventing her planned appearance at Deauville.[54] Blaming her troubles on the rivalry of "female singers," Otero abandoned opera, and with the outbreak of World War I she largely retired from performing.

49. "Mlle Otéro dans Carmen," *Comoedia* (Paris), 22 January 1913, 2; A. M., "Opéra-Comique: Mme C. Otero dans *Carmen*," *Le Monde musicale* 2 (1913): 23.
   50. Otero, *My Story*, 257.
   51. Lewis, *La Belle Otero*, 221.
   52. "'The Ring' Successful in Paris: Otero as 'Carmen,'" 26.
   53. Lewis, *La Belle Otero*, 222.
   54. Otero, *My Story*, 255–57.

By the time she appeared as Carmen at the Opéra-Comique in January 1913, Otero had performed Spanishness on the international stage for more than twenty years and had made a significant contribution to the Belle Époque personification of Carmen, imitated by many of the gypsy's operatic impersonators. Her knowing play with notions of exoticism and authenticity, and her audacity in aspiring to the operatic stage, at times enabled her to break the fourth wall, sharing the fun with her audience. But Otero's genuine dramatic gifts and onstage charisma meant that she also convincingly embodied the tragedy and dark emotions that had become essential to the portrayal of Bizet's Carmen by the second decade of the twentieth century.

CHAPTER 9

༄

Reproducing *Carmen*
in the United States

Geraldine Farrar, the Met, and Beyond

W hen Geraldine Farrar made her debut as Carmen at the Metropolitan Opera in November 1914, no one could have predicted the notoriety she was soon to achieve as the Spanish gypsy, first in moving pictures, and again upon her subsequent return to the operatic stage. As Carmen, the American Farrar repackaged traditions of staged Spanishness and modes of performing Bizet's gypsy that had been enacted on New York stages since the 1880s. This chapter explores the modern ubiquity of Bizet's opera as it found itself at the intersection of newly emerging technologies, which offered mass dissemination and transformed opera singers into multimedia superstars. In an age when opera enjoyed widespread popularity in North America,[1] entrepreneurs and innovators recognized in *Carmen* a work that bridged elite and popular entertainment, and the early years of the twentieth century saw both the music and story of this beloved opera disseminated widely not only from the live stage but also on new platforms such as phonograph recordings and film. This Carmenesque panorama was untouched by the debut of Enrique Granados's new opera *Goyescas* at the Met in early 1916, with its rival claims to Hispanic authenticity. Forty years after its first performances at the Opéra-Comique *Carmen* remained a touchstone for the representation of Spanish music and dance, a genre of exotic entertainment that still enjoyed immense

---

1. David Suisman, *Selling Sounds: The Commercial Revolution in American Music* (Cambridge, MA: Harvard University Press, 2009), 107.

popularity after more than a decade of currency in music halls on either side of the Atlantic.

CARMEN AT THE METROPOLITAN IN THE POST-CALVÉ ERA

Despite its undisputed place at the heart of the international operatic repertory, by 1914 Bizet's opera had been absent from the stage of New York's Metropolitan Opera for more than five years, something the *Evening Post* critic considered an "absolutely inexcusable neglect" for such an audience favorite.[2] Its last airing had been in 1908, starring Maria Gay in her one and only season at the Met. Gay was invited by the Met's newly appointed Italian manager, Giulio Gatti-Casazza, who replaced Heinrich Conried in mid-1908 as General Manager of the company. Fresh from running La Scala in Milan, Gatti-Casazza brought conductor Arturo Toscanini with him, and popular opinion assumed they would favor Italian operas above all else. Their first Metropolitan season was launched in November 1908 with a mixture of Wagner and Italian operas, and ventured into French works only after about three weeks, when they staged their first *Carmen* on 3 December 1908.[3] This served as Maria Gay's North American debut, singing in French with a stellar cast.[4] Playing José, Enrico Caruso was the established star, ably supported by the well-loved local singer Geraldine Farrar in the role of Micaëla and the mature Belgian baritone Jean Noté, a regular performer at the Paris Opéra, appearing in his first season with the New York company.

The Met had all but abandoned *Carmen* after Calvé's retirement in April 1904, although it was performed elsewhere in New York during this hiatus. In November 1904, the management tried to replace Calvé with the great Wagnerian prima donna Olive Fremstad, whose independent and fresh interpretation, replete with sensuality and power, was free of the mannerisms and capricious exaggeration that had come to characterize Calvé's impersonation. In 1906 Fremstad sang Carmen opposite Caruso, in his first serious venture outside Italian opera since his 1903 Met debut.

---

2. Unsigned review in the *Evening Post*, cited in the Metropolitan Opera Archives, accessed 1 November 2016, http://archives.metoperafamily.org/archives/frame.htm [Met Performance] CID: 58030, Carmen {207} Metropolitan Opera House: 11/19/1914.

3. The company performed Gounod's *Faust* at the Brooklyn Academy on 14 November 1908, but the official season opening was at the Metropolitan Opera House itself on 16 November, when Toscanini made his debut by conducting Verdi's *Aida*.

4. Gay sang in seven *Carmens* at the Met itself, plus one performance each at the Academy of Music in Brooklyn and the Academy of Music in Philadelphia.

Arriving in New York, Gay must have hoped that her bright reputation as one of Europe's most fêted Carmens would fend off the long shadow cast by Calvé. Although gushing reports of her operatic successes in London had been relayed in the New York papers, this publicity proved to be a mixed blessing, as expectations were perhaps raised too high. And her artistic reputation could not drown out gossipy reportage of her extramarital "pursuit" of the Italian tenor Giovanni Zenatello (who had headlined Hammerstein's opera season at the Manhattan Opera House the previous year) in the tabloid press. Gay's reputation for political engagement also formed part of her public image, so that even before she set foot in New York she was represented as an independent, and possibly uncontrollable, character; perhaps even a "new woman."[5] After Calvé's capricious charm, and Fremstad's sensual but gracious Carmen, Gay's original and unsentimental portrayal of Bizet's gypsy did not immediately find favor in the United States. Her Spanish-inflected stage business and gestures struck some as irredeemably vulgar, although others praised the "marvellous consistency and effectiveness" of her acting.[6]

Gay, Caruso, Noté, and Farrar were performing together for the first time, and most had never played *Carmen* at the Met. The first night seems to have had some shortcomings, with criticism of Caruso's French accent, Farrar not in full voice, and Gay's vocal production disparaged as lacking color and dramatic expression. Although critics reported growing confidence as the run of eight performances proceeded, and the singers became accustomed to the Met's cavernous spaces, Gay did not win over this toughest of audiences, leading the critic of the *New York Sun* to look back in 1910, reflecting that "in spite of this uncommon cast New York once more sniffed at the best 'Carmen' that the Metropolitan had to offer."[7]

With the graciousness born of hindsight (and her own stellar career as Carmen), Farrar wrote at length about the Met's 1908 production in her memoirs:

And now a native Spanish artist was to come forward in the roly-poly Maria Gay, of sparkling eye and flashing smile. For her, Mr. Gatti entertained justifiable hopes for enduring success in this particular role.

---

5. The term "new woman" had been associated with opera stars, in particular Olive Fremstad and her portrayal of *Salome* in the Met's 1904 production of Richard Strauss's opera. See Joseph Horowitz, *Artists in Exile: How Refugees from the Twentieth Century War and Revolution Transformed the American Performing Arts* (New York: Harper, 2009), 337.

6. Rawling, "Maria Gay Shows . . . ," *Evening World*, 4 December 1908, 10.

7. "No 'Carmen' to Succeed Calvé," *Sun* (New York), 27 February 1910, 7.

I fear as Micaela, I made a less passive character than was the usual pattern, for in the tussle of the third act, I recall I, too, had a hand in the rough-and-tumble between Carmen and her infuriated Don José.

Farrar reflected on Gay's performance as a way of contextualizing criticism of her own alleged "assault" on Caruso when she herself had graduated to the title role in the Met's 1914 revival of *Carmen*:

> The tempestuous daughter of Iberia ... kicked and spat, till even the blasé New York dowagers were moved to raise their fans to shocked faces, to screen some of her more frank and realistic attempts at seduction. A shower of orange juice precipitated with accuracy toward the unfortunate hero surprised not only him, but the audience in general, to general protest. Other studied bits of realism made an unfortunate impression on the aristocratic Metropolitan stage, quite as objectionable, in their frank vulgarity, apparently, to the powers-that-be, as was the *Salome* episode of previous heated discussion, and ban.
>
> Maria Gay, however, is nonetheless a singer of experience and interest, ... [and] has enjoyed an excellent professional reputation in other lands less critical of elementary physical display.[8]

Farrar hints that Gay's vulgar excess as Carmen, and the Met audience's response to it, should be viewed in light of the scandalous *Salome* production of the previous year, which had set a new limit for what was unacceptable on the operatic stage. If *Salome* pushed the boundaries of moral behavior and physicality (including sensual dance) that limited female protagonists, it perhaps also allowed Carmens new scope to challenge previously established norms.[9] Before Gay shocked New Yorkers with her own interpretation of Carmen, her establishment in the role across Europe had coincided with the explosion of Strauss's *Salome* onto the international stage.

Henry Krehbiel, who had seen every New York Carmen from Hauk's creation of the role onward, described Gay as "an all too fleshly Carmen":

> There was an unquestionable personal note in her impersonation.... She placed herself unmistakably in the gallery of Carmens of which operatic cognoscenti will think for a considerable period, not by any charm of manner of song, but because she was the only one who instead of giving pleasure awakened disgust.[10]

---

8. Geraldine Farrar, *The Autobiography of Geraldine Farrar: Such Sweet Compulsion* (New York: Greystone, 1938), 126–27.

9. Kristen M. Turner, "Opera in English: Class and Culture in America, 1878–1910" (PhD thesis, University of North Carolina at Chapel Hill, 2015), 390–91.

10. Henry Edward Krehbiel, "Notable Carmens of Last Four Decades," *New York Tribune* (New York), 13 December 1914, 7.

Unable to replace Calvé in the audience's confidence, the Met seem to have decided that they could not win with *Carmen* during this period. Indeed, *Carmen* was not presented at New York's Metropolitan after Gay's last performance on 17 February 1909, until Farrar debuted as the gypsy on 19 November 1914, in a new production featuring box-office and recording stars Farrar and Caruso, under the baton of Toscanini, to the approval of an enthusiastic public (see Figure 9.1).

Figure 9.1 Geraldine Farrar and Enrico Caruso in *Carmen* at New York's Metropolitan Opera, photograph by Herman Mishkin (1915).
Credit: ©The Metropolitan Opera Archives.

Farrar was convincing in her new role, both in her singing and her acting, but her Carmen was inevitably judged against the high standard set by her predecessors Gay, Calvé, and even (for those with longer memories) Hauk. Critics noted her tendency toward a "pert" and animated reading, and although she was praised for avoiding "coarseness or depravity," they missed a seductive sensuality. This attribute had characterized the more mature renditions of Gay and Calvé, and was considered an essential feature of Spanish or gypsy women.[11] Familiarity with Farrar rendered the critics charitable, however, and they were disposed to allow her time in which to develop what was at this early stage a reading that "did not offer much in the way of striking innovation."[12] Farrar admitted in later years that she "had always wanted to go to Spain for local color and a study of the gypsy type there," before she presented her idea of Carmen. But in 1914 she was yet to realize this dream, relying instead on her imagination, and what she later described as her "definite and natural feeling for this role, so grateful in its dramatic impulse, so physically animated in song and movement."[13] Perhaps as a consequence Farrar's early Carmen was found to lack "the smoldering Mediterranean fire ... that is an essential quality of the character. There is a certain lack of rude elemental force in this sophisticated maiden, sometimes too prettily coquettish, too little of the soil."[14] Farrar had not yet incorporated the lessons of Maria Gay's independent, passionate Carmen into her own stage persona, but many felt that in time she would do so. As the critic for the *Evening Post* observed,

[t]hose who have followed Miss Farrar's career know that, however hard and long she may have studied a new operatic rôle, her début in it is only the beginning for her. It took her two years in each case to make [the Goosegirl and Tosca, Zerlina and Madama Butterfly]—and several others—exactly as she wanted them, and even now she introduces changes in them. It is very safe to predict that those who were charmed by her Carmen last night will be still more fascinated as her conception of the part deepens and she tries out the variants she is sure to have in her mind.[15]

Farrar lived up to these expectations. Within only a few months, *Musical America* declared her Carmen "wholly original," having "grown from

11. "Geraldine Farrar a Distinctly Individual Carmen," *Musical America* 21, no. 4 (1914): 2; "Carmen in Philadelphia," *Musical America* 21, no. 26 (1915): 1.

12. "Carmen in Philadelphia," 1.

13. Farrar, *Autobiography of Geraldine Farrar*, 137.

14. "New Production of Bizet's *Carmen*," *New York Times*, 20 November 1914, 9.

15. *Evening Post*, cited in [Met Performance] CID: 58030 Carmen [207] Metropolitan Opera House: 11/19/1914.

performance to performance," well on the way to being one of the greatest successes of an already "triumphant career."[16]

CARMEN IN THE AGE OF MECHANICAL REPRODUCTION

Carmen's popularity was never limited to the audiences that could afford a ticket to an operatic performance, nor indeed to those who lived in a town large enough to host such productions. In addition to the emblematic numbers that might be performed by amateur singers, potpourris and medleys were disseminated via sheet music and in public performance by pianists and bands. With the new century, means of mechanical reproduction began to be more affordable, and the pianola, the phonograph, and even live accompaniment to silent films brought a wide variety of musics to new audiences. Bizet's opera was both a beneficiary and vehicle of these developments as the new technologies extended *Carmen's* reach. A work that was simultaneously popular and high art was of inestimable value as a means to elevate public taste and could serve the marketing goals that associated the phonograph with cultural distinction.

Ever since its 1875 premiere, excerpts from Bizet's score had been heard in parodies and music-hall programs, played by barrel organs in the streets, and read from sheet music in countless homes. By the turn of the twentieth century even manufacturers of player pianos used *Carmen* as a promotional hook. At the deluxe end of the market, advertising for the Aeolian Orchestrelle (a roll-operated reed organ) depicted a swirling gypsy dancer above an image of this imposing "orchestra in a single instrument" (played by a respectably suited gentleman). These images were captioned by the bold statement "[a] perfect orchestrelle rendering of 'Carmen' in your own home" (see Figure 9.2)[17]

The individual arias were undeniably popular, and abbreviated reconfigurations of *Carmen* exercised a consistent appeal. Each such reassembly created its own narrative, and instrumental medleys served as aural equivalents to the opera's adaptations as ballet or pantomime. In Sarasate's perennial showpiece, the violin impersonated Carmen herself, primarily through a selection of her lively and sensual vocal numbers from acts 1 and 2, which emphasized the charm of Spanish local color. John Philip Sousa's band focused on the numbers best suited to its celebrated military style in a medley that encompassed an opening bugle call, the overture to act 1, the entr'acte to act 4, and the "Toreador Song."[18] Other bands showcased their soloists by including

16. "Mephisto's Musings," *Musical America* 21, no.10 (1915): 7.
17. Advertisement for Aeolian Orchestrelle, *Illustrated London News*, 8 November 1914, 771.
18. See, for example, the recordings made for Victor by Sousa's Band of an arrangement by Fred Godfrey entitled "Carmen Selection." Victor 35000: Matrix Number

Figure 9.2 Advertisement for Aeolian Orchestrelle, *Illustrated London News*, 8 November 1914, 771.
Credit: State Library of Victoria.

renditions of the "Habanera" (a solo trumpet could imitate the singer's voice to great effect) or featuring their brilliant ensemble work in the dramatic *accelerando* of the "Chanson bohème."[19] In Anton Seidl's regular summer orchestral concerts at Coney Island's Brighton Beach Resort, his avowed focus on Wagner and the German symphonic tradition notwithstanding, a medley from *Carmen* was the "single most-performed selection" of the 1896 season.[20]

As the commercial recording industry established itself in the early 1900s, some of the big companies, such as the Gramophone Company (in the United Kingdom) and Victor (in the United States) increasingly focused their marketing on opera and opera stars. Enrico Caruso made his first appearance in London in 1900, but his international stardom really dated from the release of his first recordings there in 1901. By 1903, Caruso's first Victor recordings hit the US market as he prepared to debut at New York's Metropolitan opera, and quickly established him as a popular favorite with New York audiences. Caruso was described as the first star of the "modern music industry"; his celebrity was driven by this convergence, and his prestige was a key factor in the success of Victor's "Red Seal" catalogue, which was dominated by opera and offered "great" voices singing "great" music. From its English beginnings at the Gramophone Company, the Red Seal series recorded all the leading voices of the era. This series made high art available to the aspirational masses, with the added cachet of deluxe presentation and higher price.[21]

Record companies were very aware of contemporary developments in the operatic world. Victor took advantage of the Met's late 1914 revival of *Carmen*, including selections from the opera recorded by the company's high-profile cast in their February 1915 catalogue: four records featured Farrar, while Frances Alda sang Micaëla's aria, supplementing the back catalogue of discs by Caruso and Pasquale Amato (who played Escamillo). The *Boston Globe* admired Victor's "enterprise ... [giving] everyone the opportunity to hear this all-star cast in this great success."[22]

C-2058/2, 16 December 1904; Matrix Number C-2058/3, 13 December 1911. Listed in Library of Congress National Jukebox, accessed 1 November 2015, http://www.loc.gov/jukebox/recordings/detail/id/5939.

19. William Reitz, for example, recorded a "Carmen selection" for xylophone solo with orchestral accompaniment (Victor 16892, Matrix Number B-10219/2, 28 April 1911). See early-twentieth-century recordings listed in Library of Congress "National Jukebox," accessed 1 November 2015, http://www.loc.gov/jukebox/recordings/detail/id/2222.

20. Joseph Horowitz, *Moral Fire: Musical Portraits from America's Fin-de-Siècle* (Berkeley: University of California Press, 2012), 158. By the early 1900s, references to the characters and music of *Carmen*—principally to the "Habanera" and the "Toreador Song"—can be found in some popular novelty songs. See Larry Hamberlin, *Tin Pan Opera: Operatic Novelty Songs in the Ragtime Era* (Oxford: Oxford University Press, 2011), 105, 196, 278.

21. Suisman, *Selling Sounds*, 109, 28.

22. "Revival of Carmen," *Boston Globe*, 28 January 1915, 5.

Figure 9.3 Geraldine Farrar as Carmen (with Victrola), wearing the same outfit as she wears in the tavern sequence of Cecil B. DeMille's film (*c.* 1915).
Credit: Library of Congress, http://www.loc.gov/pictures/item/2003665637.

The notion that the popular category of "song" could be identified with the elite genre of opera was argued as late as 1935, when George Gershwin defended his use of songs in his own opera *Porgy and Bess* by pointing out that "many of the most successful operas of the past have had songs. . . . 'Carmen' is almost a collection of song hits."[23] Arias from *Carmen* appeared frequently in recordings from all the major companies, the opera's emblematic numbers gaining in familiarity and enduring appeal, and allowing the record labels to exploit the fame of opera's most beloved stars.[24]

Celebrity endorsement assisted in the promotion of such records, and the machines that played them, while advertising materials often depicted the opera stars listening to their own voices on the phonograph (see Figure 9.3).

23. George Gershwin, "Rhapsody in Catfish Row," *New York Times*, 20 October 1935, X1. Edward J. Dent even claimed that Puccini's later operas were carefully constructed so that they were "all divisible into sections that would each make a gramophone record." Edward J. Dent, *Opera*, rev. ed. (Harmondsworth, UK: Penguin, 1949), 116.

24. See, for example, the selection of early record catalogues scanned and freely available on the British Library website, accessed 1 November 2015, http://sounds.bl.uk/Sound-recording-history/Early-record-catalogues.

Their blurbs promised listeners at home the same experience as those fortunate enough to hear the singers live in the theater. One advertisement presented Farrar in full costume as Carmen, next to her Victor disk, accompanied by the following claim:

> Both are Farrar.
>
> The Victor Record of Farrar's voice is just as truly Farrar as Farrar herself.
>
> The same singularly beautiful voice, with all the personal charm and individuality of the artist.
>
> To hear the new Carmen records by Farrar is to be stirred with enthusiasm, just as were the vast audiences—the largest ever assembled in the Metropolitan Opera House—which greeted her performance of Carmen, and acclaimed it the supreme triumph of this great artist's career.[25]

While this copy from May 1915 played upon the prestige Farrar had attained as Carmen, she was already a seasoned recording artist, having made her first records in Berlin, years before establishing herself as a homegrown star at the Metropolitan.[26]

The growth of the recording industry also helped Emma Calvé to prolong her career. If we look at her recordings of *Carmen* alone, after early sessions in 1902 (at the Met and for Gramophone), she recorded for Victor in 1907, 1908, and 1916, while her 1920 Pathé sessions included the "Habanera," the "Chanson bohème," and the "Card Aria." Despite her much-heralded retirement from the operatic stage, Calvé continued to undertake concert tours, and in 1912 she treated her US fans to concerts that featured a "two-scene tabloid version of Carmen" as the second half of her program. Calvé toured the work with her new husband, the Italian tenor Galileo Gasparri, and a pianist. This "condensed" *Carmen* was advertised as covering the whole story of Bizet's opera, performed only by the characters Carmen and José, costumed and acted. Their revised narrative began with the "Habanera" (sung in the tavern), progressing through José's "Dragon d'Alcala" and the long sequence from act 2 that includes their duets and the "Flower Song." The second scene encompassed Carmen's "Card Aria" and their dramatic final duet. The aging (and increasingly stout) Calvé did not attempt the dance numbers, choosing the lyrical and dramatic over the spectacular, and building on her reputation for singing as well as acting the role, and doing "both in superlatively excellent manner."[27]

---

25. Advertisement for Victor talking-machine record, *Ladies Home Journal* (May 1915).

26. Farrar, *Autobiography of Geraldine Farrar*, 109.

27. Walter Anthony, "Tetrazzini to Give Farewell Concert at Dreamland Rink," *San Francisco Call*, 17 March 1912, 53; "Madame Calve to Come in Concert on Friday Next," *Washington Times*, 20 October 1912. Calvé offered an alternate program of selections from *Cavalleria rusticana* during this tour.

Calvé's "tabloid" *Carmen*, like the many medleys drawn from Bizet's score, demonstrated the possibility of extracting numbers to represent specific moods or imagery. Thanks to the opera's widespread popularity, its score became a fertile source for the musical accompaniment to early film. *Carmen* had been regularly mined for theatrical overtures in the late nineteenth century, and Rick Altman notes that operas provided the majority of scores used to accompany early films in the 1890s and first years of the new century. The practice of showing "illustrated songs," in which live singers performed popular numbers against a background of projected images, started in vaudeville theaters back in the days of magic-lantern slides (often with the audience joining in). Soon it was adopted by moving pictures, and became a popular feature of nickelodeons.[28] These hybrid attractions were widely used to cross-promote newly published sheet music, but also featured opera selections, and early listings of short films on the Carmen theme suggest that the "Toreador Song" was a favorite.[29]

Collections of musical cues for use by musicians accompanying films initially featured original compositions, but by 1911 these publications grouped arrangements of popular and familiar pieces under useful headings. Extracts from *Carmen* appear in nearly all of them, with the "Toreador Song" frequently listed to represent Spain under the category of "National Tunes."[30] This practice developed considerably with the establishment of film music libraries, for which musical extracts were classified according to their emotional valence in order to match the atmosphere of each scene. *Carmen* again offered useful selections and by the early 1920s the use of its most famous arias was codified by writers like George W. Beynon, whose guide to cinema musicians recommended the "Habanera," "Toreador Song," and "Flower Song" among other familiar "Grand Opera Arias" for matching prevailing emotions, or even establishing a "likeness between the screen actor and the opera principal."[31] After achieving success as a film actress, Farrar herself compiled a list of "appropriate musical selections," drawing mainly on the operatic repertoire with which she was most familiar. She included two recommendations for numbers from *Carmen*: the entr'acte to act 4 for "vivacity" and the "Toreador Song" for "pride."[32]

28. Rick Altman, *Silent Film Sound* (New York: Columbia University Press, 2004), 107, 82.

29. See the Filmography listings in Phil Powrie et al., *Carmen on Film: A Cultural History* (Bloomington and Indianapolis: Indiana University Press, 2007), 243–48.

30. Altman, *Silent Film Sound*, 32, 251, 58.

31. George W. Beynon, *Musical Presentation of Motion Pictures* (New York: G. Schirmer, 1921), 68.

32. Altman, *Silent Film Sound*, 368–69. Other emotions included contentment, joy, melancholy, love, courage, desire, hope, despair, regret, jealousy, anger, pain, and gratitude.

The 1914 opening of New York's first large picture palaces ushered in an era of longer, prestige films, which were to be accompanied by purpose-written scores played by full orchestra. Samuel L. "Roxy" Rothapfel's model picture palace, the Strand, which seated 3,500, quickly became known for its "high-class" orchestral accompaniment of films, and selections from *Carmen* were included in the score for Jesse L. Lasky's *Rose of the Rancho* (1914), highlighting the Hispanic theme of David Belasco's play set in California.[33]

Filmed versions of the Carmen narrative appeared regularly around the world, and it is claimed as "probably the most adapted story on screen after Bram Stoker's ... *Dracula*."[34] Phil Powrie's filmography traces such works back to 1906, listing no fewer than seventeen films entitled *Carmen* by 1913.[35] The story offered spectacular elements ideally suited to silent film, like Spanish dancing and the bullfight. Such scenes had already been explored in the experimental films of the 1890s, Edison's 1894 film of Carmencita, for example, or a bullfight filmed in Mexico in 1896, which was then used as back-projection to act 4 in a theatrical production of *Carmen*. In 1915 the burgeoning US film industry embraced *Carmen*, with two high-profile features competing for attention. As soon as word got out that Lasky and Cecil B. DeMille were planning a *Carmen* film, their rival Raoul Walsh persuaded William Fox to create a *Carmen* of his own, starring Theda Bara, who had just catapulted to fame as the movies' first "vamp."[36] These two films opened within a day of each other (31 October and 1 November), and were followed a few weeks later (18 December) by Charlie Chaplin's *A Burlesque on Carmen*.

ADAPTING *CARMEN* AS CINEMATIC SPECTACLE

Lasky's decision to recruit Met star Geraldine Farrar to headline his new project developed the nexus between the operatic stage and the moving picture industry, despite the strange irony of a performer known for the sound of her voice becoming a silent film actress.[37] This link had already been pioneered by Marguerite Sylva (another operatic Carmen known in New York), who starred in an Italo-Spanish film based on Bizet's opera in 1913.[38] Farrar's casting was

33. Ibid., 290.

34. For an outline of *Carmen* films in the silent period and an extensive filmography of the subject, see Powrie et al., *Carmen on Film*: ix–x, 8–12, 243–48.

35. Ibid., 243–45.

36. Ibid., 41–42.

37. See also Melina Esse, "The Silent Diva: Farrar's Carmen," in *Technology and the Diva*, ed. Karen Henson (Cambridge: Cambridge University Press, 2016), 94–95.

38. Ann Davies and Phil Powrie, Carmen *on Screen: An Annotated Filmography and Bibliography* (Woodbridge, UK and Rochester, NY: Tamesis, 2006), 7.

explained in the preface to the published "photoplay" of Lasky and DeMille's 1915 film, a publication that hints at the cinematic coup the studio hoped to achieve with her films:

> To-day, *Carmen* is one of the most popular operas of the lyric stage. The greatest singers of the world have sung the parts of Carmen, Don José, and Escamillo. Last winter, Miss Geraldine Farrar sang the part for the first time at the Metropolitan Opera House in New York, and her success in the role was instantaneous and triumphant.
>
> So closely did Miss Farrar become identified with the part of the Spanish gypsy, that arrangements were made for her to appear in a motion picture produced by the Jesse Lasky Company, under the personal direction of Mr. Cecil B. DeMille. It was the first time that a grand-opera artist had acted before the camera, and no detail was neglected in making of it a great artistic success.[39]

For this new *Carmen*, DeMille drew together varying elements from the *Carmen* phenomenon that had pervaded fin-de-siècle American culture, and created an early example of the spectacular feature film.

The increase in multireel feature films around this time began to consolidate the attraction of moving pictures to middle-class audiences, many of whom had hitherto dismissed the new medium as addressing the working class through fairground and nickelodeon. Already drawing writers, plots, and actors from the legitimate theater, filmmakers like DeMille and Lasky developed the strategy of "exploit[ing] the congruence of cultural forms in the genteel tradition by focusing on the intertextuality of feature film and grand opera."[40] Farrar and *Carmen* provided the ideal package for this enterprise, all the more because Farrar had already declined to appear on the vaudeville stage, guarding her prestige.[41]

DeMille shot *Carmen* in just three weeks (June–July 1915), with a budget of $23,429, and the film grossed six times that amount.[42] The premiere took place on 1 November 1915 at Boston's Symphony Hall, a venue chosen by Farrar as the temple of high art in her hometown, and attracted an "all-night ticket line, capacity crowds, and intense press coverage."[43] DeMille seems to have taken note of D. W. Griffith's success with *Birth of a Nation*, which had premiered in February 1915. Large orchestras accompanied its prestige

39. Geraldine Farrar, *Carmen [Photo Drama Edition]* (New York: A. L. Burt, 1915), xii–xiii.

40. Sumiko Higashi, *Cecil B. DeMille and American Culture: The Silent Era* (Berkeley: University of California Press, 1994), 20. See also Esse, "Silent Diva," 94.

41. Higashi, *Cecil B. DeMille*, 21.

42. Simon Louvish, *Cecil B. DeMille and the Golden Calf* (London: Faber & Faber, 2007), 101, 106.

43. Altman, *Silent Film Sound*, 295.

screenings, playing an eclectic assembly of folk and popular song, extracts from the classics, and original music. For *Carmen*, however, DeMille set a new standard, commissioning Hugo Riesenfeld to arrange a score from Bizet's music, which resulted in a coherent and carefully constructed musical accompaniment to the film, presented by a large orchestra and (on occasion) singers performing selected numbers from the opera.[44] Publicity highlighted the filmmakers' aspiration to achieve perfect synchronization between music and screen action, with claims that "trained composers" were present on set, making "careful musical notations," and that Farrar herself "gave the staff the benefit of her wide knowledge," playing a significant role in the development of the musical score.[45]

In adapting the story to the relatively new format of a feature film, William deMille (Cecil B. DeMille's older brother) had to abandon his first draft of the screenplay because the copyright holders of the opera libretto demanded a prohibitive fee. Therefore, he rewrote the story "as if it were formally based on the original novel by Prosper Mérimée," while retaining key scenes from the opera.[46] With a running time of just under an hour, DeMille's film was similar in length to Guerrero's ballet, but unlike the Alhambra version, which had condensed the opera's action, the film offers a fresh reconfiguration of the story. The writers treated both the novella and the libretto as mere starting points. They revised or discarded scenes and characters (Micaëla does not appear in the film), added new elements, and restructured the action into a cohesive plot, relieved of the discursive and even reflective passages that extend the operatic fabric. The production drew on the appeal of picturesque Spain in the choice of locations, sets, and costumes, and exploited the widespread popularity of musical medleys from the opera. The film's realistic depiction of passion and violence was reinforced by the wild, sensual qualities of the title character, traits increasingly associated with her Spanishness. If Meilhac and Halévy's libretto presented Carmen as an exoticized cipher, successive interpreters from Galli-Marié to Hauk and Gay had gradually invested the character with agency and wit. The film inscribes this transformation structurally: this is Carmen's story, not José's, as much a departure from the opera as from Mérimée's conception of his title character.

The dramatic thread of this silent film is communicated primarily as pantomime supported by musical accompaniment, while the narrative is articulated by intertitles. The film is structured around several spectacular set pieces, including Carmen dancing at Pastia's tavern, Carmen fighting with her fellow worker at the cigarette factory, and the grand spectacle

44. Ibid.
45. "Music Score of 'Carmen' Pictures," *Boston Daily Globe*, 19 September 1915, 47.
46. Louvish, *Cecil B. DeMille*, 103.

surrounding the denouement, which features sensational footage of an especially staged live bullfight before the lengthy final altercation between José and Carmen outside the bullring.[47] Filmed bullfights had been associated with *Carmen* since the 1890s, and had been filmed specifically for Carmen films (as had been the case in 1913 for Sylva's film, for which the bullfight had been staged at the arena of Nîmes). The press gave extensive coverage to the arrangements for and filming of this piece of cinematic realism.[48]

Violence is a keynote of DeMille's film, portrayed in scenes shocking enough to draw the attention of the censors.[49] The film boasts no fewer than four fight scenes: the scene in the tobacco factory where scantily clad women tear at one another's clothing with abandon; José's fight with his fellow soldier in Pastia's tavern; Carmen and José's violent argument in the mountains; and their final, fatal struggle at the bullring. After the abandon of the factory brawl, one reviewer could only conclude that

> [a] Spanish cigarette maker is, to judge from what the audience witnessed yesterday, a combination of tigress and lightweight slugger, with a tendency to go about all the time in a state of undress. . . .
>
> There must hereafter be a recognized line between the Carmens who have feathers and scratch and those that have whiskers and bite. At all events Maria Gay's Carmen seems all prunes and prisms compared with the Spanish Gypsy that Miss Farrar is revealing at the Strand Theater.[50]

Carmen herself is characterized by this violent tendency, even beyond the principal narrative thread of the film, such as when she casually knocks down and kicks a man who obstructs her entry into Pastia's tavern. Both the violent and the sensual scenes achieve a sense of realism, and Farrar reveled in the relative freedom she was given to act out the character's physicality, as when she wrestled with her costar, Wallace Reid, near the smugglers' camp (see Figure 9.4).

The difference between the media of opera and silent film is most strikingly drawn in the final scene. The opera allows an extensive vocal exchange between the two as José pleads with Carmen and she denies him, insisting that she must remain free even in the face of death, which comes quickly. In the film, words and music cannot be combined in the same way. A few brief

47. Louvish, *Cecil B. DeMille*, 103.

48. Esse, "Silent Diva," 91. Impresario Morris Gest declared that this was the first bullfight ever held in Los Angeles.

49. Ibid., 89.

50. "Farrar a Tigress as Screen 'Carmen,'" *New York Sun*, 1 November 1915, 7.

Figure 9.4 Carmen and José wrestling (Geraldine Farrar and Wallace Reid). "'You are the devil,' José said. 'Yes,' she answered." Geraldine Farrar, *Carmen [Photo Drama Edition]* (New York: A. L. Burt, 1915), facing 110.

intertitles are followed by an extended sequence in which Carmen tries to escape José by climbing a gate into the bullring. He pulls her back down, agonizingly, by her hair, forces her to her knees, and nearly slits her throat, but the camera stays on her face as he finally stabs her in the chest. After she collapses, and Escamillo appears through the gate, José kisses her and stabs himself. This shocking sequence lasts a full three minutes and brings the film to a climactic conclusion.

The desire for realism and authenticity is conveyed with equal conviction in the film's design, which recreates the visual clichés of Spain in all their picturesque detail, yet manages to avoid a feeling of staginess. This realistic sense

Figure 9.5 Scene outside the bullring. "Many officers passed José, some with their sweethearts, and all joyous and care-free." Geraldine Farrar, *Carmen [Photo Drama Edition]* (New York: A. L. Burt, 1915), between 160 and 161.

of location means that the viewer is transported to foreign landscapes, as the camera follows the smugglers from the coast through the mountains with their pack mules to their camp.[51] Pastia's tavern evokes the imagery of a rustic Spanish *posada*, complete with its courtyard, guitarists, and couples dancing *sevillanas*, while the bullring is a fine edifice, offering intimate spaces and dramatic lighting, which contrast with the sunlit crowds outside the gate and the spectacle in the arena itself (see Figure 9.5). DeMille creates evocative and dramatic effects with his use of light and shadow, and the application of color tinting, like amber for the tavern, where Carmen dances, or red for the firelit smugglers' camp, where Carmen reads her doom in the cards.

Equal care was lavished on the costumes, with the possible exception of Carmen's more formal dresses, which suggest the influence of contemporary fashion. Smugglers, bullfighters, and working women are presented in costumes appropriate to their occupation and the occasion. The fine distinction between the bullfighter's everyday outfits and the *traje de luces* (suit of lights) he dons only for the fight itself was rarely upheld in such productions,

51. Ibid.

but is beautifully realized here. Carmen herself achieves a strong visual identity as the Spanish gypsy through consistent and characteristic use of shawls, hair combs, and fans, utterly convincing one critic, who declared, "This picture play is thoroughly Spanish in revelation of every physical characteristic of 'Carmen.'"[52]

Gillian Anderson recreated the orchestral score from the incomplete materials found on copyright deposit in the Library of Congress, as they had been prepared by Hugo Riesenfeld, and from reports in the contemporary press. This realization, which accompanies a modern release of the film, offers twenty-first-century viewers a tantalizing insight into the experience *Carmen* offered cinemagoers in 1915.[53] The score as presented by Anderson does not function as an orchestral medley of selections from the opera. Instead, Riesenfeld seems to have approached the opera as a source of evocative extracts that he could then employ as thematic loops underlying specific scenes, drawing not only on the famous vocal numbers, but also on instrumental passages and the commonly interpolated ballet music from Bizet's earlier opera *La Jolie Fille de Perth*. In line with contemporary practice for musical accompaniment to silent films, each musical fragment was associated with a character, an emotional state, a situation, or an activity.

The themes are instantly recognizable, but as they are remapped against the altered narrative of deMille's screenplay they are not necessarily paired with the same action as they are in the opera. For example, the music that opens act 4 to accompany the crowds outside the bullring is applied in the film to the jostling and scantily clad workers in the tobacco factory. The central tavern scene exemplifies both the transformation of the narrative and the sophisticated remapping of the music. While act 2 of the opera opens with the "Chanson bohème," and proceeds via some dialogue to the Toreador's celebrated "Couplets," the film's seven-minute sequence in Lillas Pastia's tavern presents multiple points of view. With the narrative articulated by seven intertitles, it tracks the development of Carmen's relationships with both Escamillo and José, and her duty to the smugglers. Rather than representing a

---

52. Ibid.

53. The discussion of the score is based both on reports in the contemporary press and on Gillian Anderson's reconstruction and performance of the film score with its accompaniment. The piano-conductor score she found lacked clear cue indications, rendering synchronization with the film partly guesswork. For details of the surviving performance materials and their reconstruction, see Gillian B. Anderson, "Geraldine Farrar and Cecil B. DeMille: The Effect of Opera on Film and Film on Opera in 1915," in Carmen: *From Silent Film to MTV*, ed. Chris Perriam and Ann Davies (Amsterdam, NY: Rodopi, 2005), 29–33.

Carmen [DVD], George Eastman House; A Diamond Time restoration for the Classic Movie Project; Produced by Bruce Higham & Douglas Schwalbe; Produced and directed by Cecil B. DeMille (Pleasantville, NY: Video Artists International, [2006]).

single emotion, which could have been scored to one number like the "Chanson bohème," this sequence is accompanied by a network of musical cues that distill key musical elements from throughout the opera, creating their own sense of dramatic momentum.[54] It opens with the "Séguedille" as soldiers drink and the assembled crowd dances; Escamillo is then introduced by his "Toreador Song," which alternates with "Si tu m'aimes, Carmen" (act 4), during his flirtation with Carmen, a melody that recurs for each of their four tender encounters as the film progresses (see Figure 9.6). Once Carmen sets herself to her task of José's seduction the "Habanera" is heard, but her dance atop the table is set to the wordless song that in the opera follows her recitative "Je vais danser en votre honneur" (act 2). With José on one side of the table, and Escamillo on the other, this scene of Carmen's dance graphically depicts the fatal conflict that drives the remainder of the film, but eschews the opera's emblematic numbers like the "Habanera" or "Chanson bohème." As Carmen falls into José's arms at the end of her dance, we see and hear the trumpets calling him back to barracks, and the remainder of this scene is accompanied by her dance theme overlaid and alternating with the fanfare.

The fragmentation and repetition of musical passages from the opera accommodates the cinematic editing. However, this process often leads to abrupt juxtapositions when a scene changes and the music must keep up. Unlike the truncation of the score in its use for ballet or "tabloid" versions—most of which retained some semblance of the opera's numbers and its smaller-scale lyric structures—the adaptation to film accompaniment deprives the music of its more autonomous musical structures. Structural integrity and development now largely reside in the fabric of the film, where the narrative is mediated and inflected by the visual effects and editing techniques. The technique of repeating musical fragments until a scene or topic is complete is best exemplified by DeMille's use of the smugglers as a unifying thread throughout the film. Whether depicted trekking their contraband around Spain, in their mountain camp, or in Pastia's tavern, they are invariably accompanied by repetitions of the "walking" theme that opens act 3 of the opera.

In the creation of a new set of cues the connections between music and action in the operatic original were often severed. The reconstructed score does not feature José's "Flower Song," whereas his offstage song "Dragon d'Alcala" ("Halte là, qui va là," act 2) serves to introduce José's first appearance. Carmen's entries are frequently indicated by the contracted "fate" motive, and she retains much of her musical characterization from the opera. The film's score features selections from all her main utterances, both the performative—like the "Habanera," the "Chanson bohème," and the "Séguedille"—and more private

---

54. The omission of the "Chanson bohème" at this point is striking, but it had been used earlier in the film when Carmen first visited Pastia's tavern, during daylight hours, and conferred with the smugglers.

Figure 9.6 [Carmen and Escamillo (Geraldine Farrar and Pedro de Cordoba) at the bull-ring.] "The saints be praised! But she was a vision of beauty, he thought." Geraldine Farrar, *Carmen [Photo Drama Edition]* (New York: A. L. Burt, 1915), facing 170.

utterances—like "Là-bas, là-bas dans la montagne" (after the "Flower Song," act 2), which accompanies her passionate encounter with José at the breach in the wall, as her kisses distract him from the passing smugglers. There is even a reference to the "Card Aria" in the red-tinted firelight scene in the mountain camp. When the film was screened in major theaters, the musical accompaniment varied, and it is possible that different theaters interpolated the favorite arias at will, disregarding the musical cues indicated by the studio.[55] At New York's

55. Esse, "Silent Diva," 96–98. Esse compares live performances at various screenings in 1915.

Strand Theater in November 1915 the audience enjoyed a selection of sung arias, including the "Habanera" (during the tavern scene), the "Flower Song" (for José's courtship) and the "Toreador Song," and even one piece by another composer.[56]

Critic Olin Downes confessed that he preferred Farrar and the opera on the operatic stage, but admitted that "the spectacle was wholly satisfactory" for audiences with a taste for "moving pictures of the more melodramatic variety."[57] Despite her earlier creation of Bizet's gypsy at the Met, in DeMille's film Farrar found new scope to develop a distinctively individual reading of the character. She revealed aspects of her vision of Carmen to the press in numerous interviews and articles, including an extended piece entitled "The Psychology of Carmen," in which she hinted at her awareness of her place in an extended lineage of Carmens:

> The reason that so many modern stage singers have attempted the rôle of Carmen is simply that there is so much in the character to be expressed—or, rather, so many different things. Each one of us probably sees something that the others have not seen—or thinks she does—and that "something" is *her individual Carmen.... Carmen* has, seemingly, as many variants as there are stage folk ready to express their varying ideas of her.[58]

In this interview, Farrar posited Carmen's descent from ancient Egyptian priestesses of the god Thoth, an interpretation apparently based on the purported origins of gypsies, fortune telling, and tarot cards, which validated her sensual and primitivized reading of the character.[59] Farrar thus recalled and elaborated on Calvé's description of gypsies as carrying in their spirits and bodies the pride and dignity of an ancient race. This attitude contributed to a burgeoning image of Carmen as an empowered, almost modern woman, comparable to Farrar's own reputation as a New Woman. Already an icon of "glamorous female independence," [60] Farrar imbued her Carmen with a sense of agency, and enacted certain characteristics of the New Woman for her newly acquired mass audience.

Farrar characterized Carmen as intelligent, rather than a creature of instinct, and was keenly aware that the ability to exert "more than a merely

56. "Farrar a Tigress," 7.

57. Olin Downes, "Boston Sees Miss Farrar as 'Carmen' in Moving Pictures," *Musical America* (9 October 1915): 4, quoted in Anderson, "Farrar and DeMille," 26.

58. Geraldine Farrar as recorded by Frederic Dean, "The Psychology of Carmen," *Bookman* 42 (1915): 414, 15. Emphasis in original.

59. Farrar and Dean, "The Psychology of Carmen," 412–17. Susan Rutherford interprets this article in terms of domination and subjection, describing Farrar as a "diva of desire." See Susan Rutherford, "'Pretending to Be Wicked': Divas, Technology, and the Consumption of Bizet's Carmen," in *Technology and the Diva*, ed. Karen Henson (Cambridge: Cambridge University Press, 2016), 84.

60. Powrie et al., *Carmen on Film*, 52.

sensual appeal" was essential if Carmen was to garner any audience sympathy, a problem that had been encountered by many earlier Carmens.[61] Farrar's Carmen combines a bold and at times wild sensuality with the calculating cleverness of someone used to operating outside the law, and she does not lose control of herself or her situation until the very end.

After the tight discipline and vocal strain of operatic production and performance, Farrar delighted in the relative freedom of the moviemaking process, describing her pleasure at being able to sing and declaim the role "in French or Italian as I chose," without any "curtain to rise" or "orchestra to overwhelm." DeMille gave her the freedom to "emote" to her heart's content, without any risk to her voice.[62]

> Mr. DeMille's long and varied experiences in the legitimate theater gave him an uncanny reading into his actors' psychology.... We were not cautioned to beware of undue emotion, disarranged locks, torn clothing, etc. We were allowed free action as we felt it; so we acted our parts as if we were engaged in a theater performance ...
>
> It was then that I asked Mr. DeMille if we might have music during our scenes, as I was so accustomed to orchestral accompaniment for certain tempi and phrasings, I felt I could better pantomime the rhythm of the effects.[63]

A pianist was duly provided, and Farrar described how having "a musician at my elbow ... inspired all my scenes," providing a "soulful throb" that "did more to start my tears than all the glycerine drops or onions more frequently employed by other less responsive orbs."[64] Farrar's dancing must have benefited from music being played on set, and she even took some lessons with the ex– Ballets Russes dancer Theodore Kosloff, who had found employment at the New York Roof Garden and later starred with Farrar and Reid in *The Woman God Forgot* (1917). Kosloff would have been aware of the Spanish dance traditions prevalent in Paris, stylized in later Ballets Russes productions, and given that Anna Pavlova was dancing the ballet sequences in *Carmen* for US audiences in the prewar years, this Russian-inflected interpretation of Spanish dance would have been deemed both acceptable and effective. Farrar's dancing was undisciplined but energetic and, despite her lack of grace, provided a further platform for her to develop that flirtatious side of her characterization of Carmen.

61. Anderson, "Farrar and DeMille," 25–26.
62. Geraldine Farrar, *The Story of an American Singer by Herself* (Boston and New York: Houghton Mifflin, 1916), 112–13.
63. Farrar, *Autobiography of Geraldine Farrar*, 168–69.
64. Ibid., 169.

Farrar made some fifteen films between 1915 and 1920, and became known for playing independent women (like her celebrated 1916 portrayal of Joan of Arc in *Joan the Woman*). Her clear marketability as a Spanish type led her to play a Mexican (Aztec), Irish-Mexican, or Spanish character in no fewer than six films, this casting made credible by her dark good looks and ability to perform passion and sensuality with absolute conviction. She noted, "Strangely enough, my most ardent movie fans were from South America; they repeatedly called for more and more roles featuring me in a Spanish type." Asking her friend, the Spanish soprano Lucrezia Bori (who sang Micaëla to her Carmen at the Met), why this might be, Farrar was told that "in Spain there was a gypsy type with dark hair and grey eyes like my own, which, added to my usual vivacity of the screen picturisations easily conveyed the impression that I, too, might be indigenous to her home country."[65]

GOYESCAS AND THE COMPETING SPAIN OF CARMEN

Just before Farrar made her triumphant return as to the Met as Carmen, a new Spanish opera made its debut, sparking debates about the authenticity of staged Spanishness. Enrique Granados arrived in New York in mid-December 1915 to launch his new opera *Goyescas*, the Metropolitan Opera premiere doubly welcome after his disappointment in trying to secure the work's debut both in Barcelona and Paris. Fêted by the press, and new to the United States, Granados seized the opportunity to "spread the gospel of Spanish music," and offer himself and his work as representing what he considered to be true Spanish culture.[66] In composing *Goyescas* Granados had tried to embody and abstract what he described as "the very soul of Spain," and in depicting the goyesque epoch he rejected the colorful Spain celebrated by and marketed to foreigners.[67] This foreign stereotyping of Spain not only reduced the affective range that audiences looked for in Spanish music, but also polarized the representation of both Spaniards and Spanish art into either the sunny joyous type or austere sadness, always shadowed by their inescapable reputation for passionate sensuality.

> Granados declared to the journalists that they, like many others, know nothing of the real musical contributions of Spain. The musical interpretation of Spain is not to be found in tawdry boleros and habaneras, in Moszkowksi,

---

65. Ibid., 214.
66. H. F. P. [Herbert F. Peyser], "Granados Here for Production of 'Goyescas,'" *Musical America* 23, no. 8 (1915): 4.
67. Ibid., 3.

in "Carmen," in anything that has sharp dance rhythms accompanied by tambourines or castanets. The music of my nation is far more complex, more poetic and subtle.[68]

With this comprehensive list, Granados dismissed New Yorkers' well-established tastes in Spanish and Spanish-styled music. Writing for *Musical America*, Herbert Peyser upbraided the composer for this comment: he accused Granados of composing music that was "conventionally Spanish" and suggested that his comments should "be construed as his own ignorance of American knowledge and musical experience."[69]

Granados was clearly unaware that his visit to the city coincided with a high point in its exposure to Spanish performers, and a fashion for all things Spanish. Carl Van Vechten, writing about Spain and its music in 1916, had observed "New York's real occupation by the Spaniards" in that fateful second decade of the new century, and declared that "the winter of 1915–16 beheld the Spanish blaze."[70] The war in Europe had brought many European artists to the United States, among them Spaniards like the cellist Pablo Casals and guitarist Miguel Llobet. Local and touring pianists were performing recent scores by Albéniz and Granados, while fashionable women were adopting the *mantón*, the mantilla, and hair and dress styles from different periods of Spanish costume. The exhibitions of Joaquín Sorolla (in 1909) and Ignacio Zuloaga (in 1909 and 1916) reignited a long-standing interest in Spanish art, fostered from the early years of the Gilded Age by collectors like Archer Huntington and Isabella Stewart Gardner, who amassed Spanish paintings, furniture, and artifacts.

However, the orchestral and operatic works that represented Spain at the turn of the twentieth century—and remained at the heart of popular programming in New York—were mostly composed by non-Spaniards. Orchestral showpieces like Chabrier's *España* and Rimsky-Korsakov's *Capriccio espagnol* held their own in the repertory, and both Debussy's *Ibéria* and Ravel's *Rhapsodie espagnole* were performed in New York before the war.[71] The "Malagueña" from Moritz Moszkowski's 1892 opera *Boabdil* was—according to Van Vechten— "still a favourite *morceau* with restaurant orchestras" in 1916.[72]

68. Ibid., 4.

69. Herbert F. Peyser, "'Goyescas' in World Première: A Fair Success," *Musical America* 23, no. 14 (1916): 4.

70. Carl Van Vechten, *The Music of Spain* (London: Kegan Paul, Trench, Trubner, 1920), 9–11.

71. The New York Philharmonic Leon Levy Digital Archives offer comprehensive program listings for the orchestras associated with this organization.

72. Van Vechten, *Music of Spain*: 9. *Boabdil* was staged in New York in 1893 at Oscar Hammerstein's Manhattan Opera House, and the ballet suite from the opera enjoyed some life in orchestral concerts.

Granados's unguarded remarks about Bizet's *Carmen,* the ultimate example of this phenomenon, suggest that he was unaware of its hold on local audiences, whose taste for Spanish local color embraced artists who played up the passionate, even violent, aspects of the Spanish stereotype. Granados and his librettist Fernando Periquet did play into preexisting stereotypes to a limited extent, as they sought to explain their new opera and its depiction of Goya's Madrid. Perhaps they thought an American audience would appreciate the democratic quality in crossing class boundaries that characterized the period, but Periquet also described the opera as "full of the joy of Spanish life, of the sadness of our untamable passions."[73]

Goyescas was favored with extensive press coverage before its premiere, as the Met fostered excitement about its first ever staging of a Spanish opera, or an opera sung in Spanish. The dress rehearsal was unusually well attended,[74] and the premiere on 28 January 1916 had a gala feel. Granados and his opera were greeted enthusiastically by a large (and vocal) contingent from New York's Hispanic community alongside the cream of New York high society and musical luminaries. The sets and costumes were magnificent and based on considerable research,[75] an "authenticity" welcomed by critics who were only too aware that the "Spanish music" they knew had largely been created by composers of other nationalities. Peyser responded warmly to the "glowing and animated stage pictures, replete with Spanish atmosphere, ... heightened by ... alluring and characteristic music."[76] The critic of the *New York Times* was convinced that *Goyescas* was "intensely Spanish in its whole texture and feeling.... coming from the brain and heart of a real Spaniard."[77] He appreciated Granados's rejection of the stereotype, praising his refusal to "fall into the easy commonplaces to which Spanish tunes and rhythms are so often a tempting invitation. There is here something deeper, more profoundly felt. The Spain that is pictured in 'Goyescas' is something very different from the 'hot night disturbed by a guitar' that has been ironically said to be the sum and substance of Spain in music."[78]

Despite this recognition of the composer's admitted aim, and the success of the premiere, interest in the work waned, and it closed after only five performances.[79] Many criticized the opera's dramatic weaknesses, while its

73. "Joys and Passions of Spanish Life Set Forth in 'Goyescas,'" *Musical America* 23, no. 13 (1916): 31.

74. Walter Aaron Clark, *Enrique Granados: Poet of the Piano* (New York: Oxford University Press, 2006), 155.

75. Ibid., 157.

76. Peyser, "'Goyescas' in World Première," 3.

77. "World's Premiere of Opera 'Goyescas,'" *New York Times,* 29 January 1916, 7.

78. Ibid.

79. Walter Clark posits a number of reasons for its failure in New York, including problems with the musical interpretation of conductor Gaetano Bavagnoli and a lukewarm response from Gatti-Casazza. Clark, *Enrique Granados,* 158.

orchestration—described by Van Vechten as "muddy and blatant"[80]—did not measure up to the standard set by Spanish orchestral showpieces, or even Bizet. Further criticism was reserved for Granados's vocal writing and text setting. But *Goyescas* was also fated to be judged against familiar standards for staged representations of Spain; inevitably, aspects of the work were compared with *Carmen*. Pepa's entrance in the first tableau, costumed "à la Carmen,"[81] and courted by the chorus of *majos*, reminded Peyser of Carmen's act 1 entry. He also heard passing echoes of Chabrier's *España* and Waldteufel's *Estudiantina Waltz*. Several critics found aspects of tableau 2 reminiscent of *Carmen*'s second act: the set was strikingly similar to Lillas Pastia's inn, and featured Spanish dances accompanied by castanets and *palmas*.[82]

The notoriously sharp-tongued critic Lawrence Gilman had noted Granados's passing disparagement of *Carmen*, and despite freely admitting that the Bizet was not beyond reproach, he lamented that "when [Granados] has to deal with drama and emotion at their highest … he can produce nothing better than … a superior order of salon-music, gracefully sentimental in melody, and prettily harmonized in the fashion of the day before yesterday: a kind of tonal rose-water sprayed over the dramatic situation."[83] Gilman's harsh critique may not have been shared by the majority of operagoers, but the Met seemed to have little appetite for Granados's Goyesque Spain. The desire for operas with more compelling storylines was soon to be satisfied by Farrar's triumphant return to the Met as Bizet's gypsy only three weeks after *Goyescas*' debut.

FARRAR RECASTS *CARMEN*

After all the excitement surrounding the Lasky film, Farrar revived her operatic Carmen at the Metropolitan Opera on 17 February 1916, introducing to the stage sensational innovations inspired by the dramatic interpretation she had developed for her screen role.[84] On opening night, Farrar's earthy and violent stage business created shock waves among audience, critics, and performers alike. In her memoirs Farrar provided a sanitized reminiscence of her transition from the world of the film back to the operatic stage:

80. Van Vechten, *Music of Spain*, 110.

81. Mephisto, "Mephisto's Musings," *Musical America* 23, no. 14 (1916): 7.

82. Peyser, "'Goyescas' in World Première," 3; "World's Premiere of Opera 'Goyescas,'" 7.

83. Lawrence Gilman, "Drama and Music," *North American Review* 203, no. 724 (1916): 453.

84. The following account is based on a selection of reviews, many of which are quoted in the piece from *Musical America*: "Mephisto's Musings," *Musical America* 23, no. 17 (1916): 7–8; see also "Geraldine Farrar a Lively Carmen," *New York Times*, 18 February 1916, 9; "Resents Farrar Slap," *Boston Globe*, 20 February 1916, 14.

I [had] garnered material for the first act of the Metropolitan's scene, that is usually indicated by a phlegmatic chorus line-up, waiting for a Carmen who seldom looks as if she had done anything more vigorous than drink a glass of orange juice in the wings. As in the movies, therefore, and with her willing connivance, in the opera version I fell upon a chorus girl in the provocative first act, seized and kicked her, and bowled her over in an exciting tussle that entertained even her blasé colleagues, looking on.[85]

Like Calvé, Farrar wanted to enliven Carmen's entrance with her novel realism, but contemporary observers suggest that her fury exceeded the above description. Farrar's costume was as shocking to the opera audience as her behavior: her dress torn to reveal petticoat and undergarments, she wrestled the poor chorus girl to the ground, scratching and throttling as well as kicking, before swaggering around the stage.

> In the first act especially, Mme. Farrar seemed like an energumen seized and shaken either by the evil spirits or by several quarts of her ancestral beverage which rendered her entirely incapable to check and control herself. I am not mentioning her impossible make-up, her torn and tattered dress, her arm and right breast entirely naked, her boorish poses, her sudden sallies towards her fellow cigar-makers, and the rest with all its concomitants of altered or interrupted melodic lines which reduced the scene to the proportions of a Los Angeles film.[86]

Farrar's musical interpretation seems to have suffered as she acted her heart out, with lapses in vocal quality and problems staying rhythmic and in time, especially in her castanet playing. Throughout her career she claimed that for her the drama was paramount, explaining to Carl Van Vechten that "In my humble way I am an actress who happens to be appearing in opera. I sacrifice tonal beauty to dramatic fitness every time I think it is necessary for an effect, and I shall continue to do it."[87]

In the tavern scene, she provided an unexpected thrill by throwing herself flat on a table, and when she threw her ring back in Jose's face (in act 4), she served him a resounding slap (echoing the slap she had already delivered in act 1). Apparently Caruso knocked Farrar down in act 3, although this was said to have been an accident and Farrar played gamely on, but given the reports that her energetic and incessant stage business not only upstaged him but

85. Farrar, *Autobiography of Geraldine Farrar*, 170.

86. E.V., "The Fourteenth Week at the Metropolitan, a Farrar Movie Thriller," *International Music and Drama* (1916); Anderson, "Farrar and DeMille," 28.

87. Carl Van Vechten, *Interpreters*, rev. ed. (New York: Alfred A. Knopf, 1920), 54–55.

also interfered with his singing, one must wonder. In the final sequence of act 4 she struggled so fiercely against him that he found it hard to hold on to her.

The press had a field day with these antics. Even six weeks later it was reported that a vaudeville act on Broadway was "regaling [its] public twice daily with: 'Say, if you fellows think we're rough, you ought to go to a real show at the Metropolitan Opera House and see Gerry Farrar kick a chorus girl in the snoot.'"[88] Despite verbatim reports of heated exchanges between Farrar and Caruso, all was smoothed over. Farrar toned down her stage business in later performances, and—some moralistic protests notwithstanding—undeniably good box office resulted from the production's notoriety. In light of this success, Farrar was happy to recall the warnings that she would threaten her operatic reputation by flirting with the moving pictures, and that her fans would not pay six dollars to hear her perform live when they could see her "in pictures" for fifty cents. In 1919 she described the consequences as highly satisfactory: "many a movie admirer has become an opera convert, still, however, remaining faithful to the silver sheet, and many an opera devotee has become, in addition, a movie fan" (see Figure 9.7).[89]

Farrar continued to appear in opera throughout her period as a film star, but she retired from the operatic stage in 1922, aged only forty, farewelled by her legions of fans. She did not stop singing, however, continuing to tour as a concert artist. In 1924 she launched her own opera company for an ambitious four-month tour in which she staged her own truncated version of *Carmen*, giving 123 performances in 125 days. It was described as "a tabloid opera for people and places unfamiliar with grand opera in the grand manner,"[90] and Farrar condensed the opera's four acts into three, discarding all of act 3 but the "Card Aria," which she moved to act 1 and—along with the "Chanson bohème"—assigned to the singer playing Mercedes, perhaps in acknowledgement of the limitations of her aging voice. She had clearly learned from her experience in the movies, and critics noted that the "distinctly novel feature of the modernized 'Carmen' is the elimination of all material that tends to interfere with the continuity of the dramatic action." To this end, and presumably in her efforts to streamline the work for a small touring company, Farrar also dispensed with the chorus, their parts performed in pantomime by dancers.[91] The design—inspired by the paintings of Zuloaga—was modern and minimal, using lighting effects and colored curtains that showed off the elaborate costumes to their best advantage.[92] Farrar's acting was again the highlight

88. "Point and Counterpoint," *Musical America* 23, no. 22 (1916): 29.

89. Geraldine Farrar, "The Story of My Life," *Photoplay* 15, no. 4 (1919): 52–53.

90. P. R., "Farrar in 'Carmen' at Symphony Hall," *Boston Daily Globe*, 12 April 1925, A6.

91. "Farrar Presents Modern 'Carmen,'" *Boston Daily Globe*, 27 September 1924, 4.

92. R., "Farrar in 'Carmen' at Symphony Hall," *Boston Daily Globe*, 12 April 1925, A6; "Farrar Is Fascinating," *Seattle Daily Times*, 24 November 1924, 11; Everhardt

Figure 9.7 "Geraldine Farrar as 'Carmen.'" Geraldine Farrar, *Carmen [Photo Drama Edition]* (New York: A. L. Burt, 1915), frontispiece.

of her performance, with all the intensity and nuance she had learned working in Hollywood, but more controlled and mature than her return to the stage of the Metropolitan in the immediate wake of the film's release.

Farrar's influential creation of a Carmen for the new century, both on the operatic stage and on film, ushered in a new phase of the *Carmen* story. She is the first historical Carmen who can be seen and heard from our twenty-first century vantage point (although in different media). Her presence on film and record enabled a new set of intertextual discourses to be embodied in future productions, adaptations, and even parodies of *Carmen*. But Farrar also represents a summation of the opera's Belle Époque trajectory from its *opéra comique* roots to its modern status as an international phenomenon, routinely adapted into a variety of genres and media. Farrar's Carmen indicates a conscious embrace of recent trends in dramatic realism overlaid with popular

Armstrong, "Farrar Gives Revised *Carmen*," *Seattle Post-Intelligencer*, 24 November 1924, 6; "Geraldine Farrar Goes Back to Opera," *New York Times*, 9 April 1924, 24.

traditions of Spanish entertainment. Clearly aware of her immediate debt to
Gay and Calvé and the lineages they inherited, Farrar offered an impersonation that also points forward. The modernity of Farrar's Carmen resides in
her stylization of the character's Spanishness—her sensuality, her passion,
and even her look—in potent combination with a mass celebrity that was almost independent of her earlier fame as an opera diva. Farrar thus provided
a touchstone for many of the reinventions of *Carmen* during the interwar period, when the opera—and its adaptations—continued to act as the principal
cosmopolitan vehicle for the staging of Spain.

SELECT BIBLIOGRAPHY

Albaicín, Curro. *Zambras de Granada y flamencos del Sacromonte: Una historia flamenca en Granada*. Granada, Spain: Almuzara, 2011.

Alonso, Celsa. *La canción lírica española en el siglo XIX*. Madrid: ICCMU, 1998.

Alonso, Celsa. "En el espejo de 'los otros': Andalucismo, exotismo e hispanismo." In *Creación musical, cultura popular y construcción nacional en la España contemporánea*, edited by Celsa Alonso. 83–103. Madrid: ICCMU, 2010.

Altman, Rick. *Silent Film Sound*. New York: Columbia University Press, 2004.

Álvarez Cañibano, Antonio. "El viaje de Glinka por España." In *Relaciones musicales entre España y Rusia*, edited by Antonio Álvarez Cañibano, Pilar V. Gutiérrez Dorado, and Cristina Marcos Patiño. 81–100. Madrid: Centro de documentación de música y danza, 1999.

Alvarez Junco, José. "The Nation-Building Process in Nineteenth-Century Spain." In *Nationalism and the Nation in the Iberian Peninsula*, edited by Clare Mar-Molinero and Angel Smith. 89–106. Oxford and Washington, DC: Berg, 1996.

Anderson, Gillian B. "Geraldine Farrar and Cecil B. DeMille: The Effect of Opera on Film and Film on Opera in 1915." In Carmen: *From Silent Film to MTV*, edited by Chris Perriam and Ann Davies. 23–35. Amsterdam, NY: Rodopi, 2005.

Baker, Evan. "The Scene Designs for the First Performances of Bizet's 'Carmen.'" *19th Century Music* 13, no. 3 (Spring 1990): 230–42.

Barrios, Antonio. "Los toros en la zarzuela." *Gaceta taurina* 2, no. 9 (April 1997): 11–13.

Bell, Archie. *Olga Nethersole*. Paris: Herbert Clarke, 1907.

Bentivegna, Patricia. *Parody in the Género Chico*. New Orleans, LA: University Press of the South, 2000.

Bergadá, Montserrat. "Les Pianistes catalans à Paris entre 1875 et 1925." PhD thesis, Université François Rabelais, 1997.

Bergadá, Montserrat. "Musiciens espagnols à Paris entre 1820 et 1868: État de la question et perspectives d'études." In *La Musique entre France et Espagne: Interactions stylistiques 1870–1939*, edited by Louis Jambou. 17–38. Paris: Presses de l'Université de Paris-Sorbonne, 2003.

Bizet, Georges. *Carmen*. Edited by Gary Kahn. Richmond, UK: Overture, 2013a.

Bizet, Georges. *Carmen: Opéra-Comique in Four Acts*. Edited by Richard Langham Smith. London: Peters Edition, 2013b.

Blas Vega, José. *Los cafés cantantes de Sevilla*. Madrid: Cinterco, 1987.

Boone, M. Elizabeth. Vistas de España: *American Views of Art and Life in Spain, 1860–1914*. New Haven and London: Yale University Press, 2007.

Booth, Michael R. *Theatre in the Victorian Age*. Cambridge: Cambridge University Press, 1991.

Bray, D. P. Eduardo de. *Carmen: Zarzuela en 4 actos y en verso, basada en la ópera del mismo nombre; Letra de D. P. Eduardo de Bray; Música del maestro Georges Bizet.* Barcelona: José Cunill, 1890.

Bretón, Tomás. *Diario (1881–1888).* Edited by Jacinto Torres. Madrid: Acento, 1995.

Calvé, Emma. *My Life.* Translated by Rosamond Gilder. New York and London: D. Appleton, 1922.

Calvé, Emma. *Sous tous les ciels j'ai chanté.* Paulhe, France: Lune de papier, (1940) 2004.

Carter, Alexandra. *Dance and Dancers in the Victorian and Edwardian Music Hall Ballet.* Aldershot, UK: Ashgate, 2005.

Cascudo García-Villaraco, Teresa. "¿Un ejemplo de modernismo silenciado? *María del Carmen* (1898), la primera ópera de Enrique Granados, y su recepción madrileña." *Acta Musicologica* 84, no. 2 (2012): 225–52.

Cather, Willa. *The World and the Parish: Willa Cather's Articles and Reviews, 1893–1902.* Edited by William M. Curtin. Lincoln: University of Nebraska Press, 1970.

Celik, Zeynep, and Leila Kinney. "Ethnography and Exhibitionism at the Expositions Universelles." *Assemblage* 13 (1990): 34–59.

Chabrier, Emmanuel. *Correspondance.* Edited by Roger Delage and Frans Durif. Paris: Klincksieck, 1994.

Charnon-Deutsch, Lou. *The Spanish Gypsy: The History of a European Obsession.* University Park: Pennsylvania State University Press, 2004.

Christoforidis, Michael. "Issues in the English Critical Reception of *The Three-Cornered Hat.*" *Context: Journal of Music Research* 19 (Spring 2000): 87–93.

Christoforidis, Michael. "Isaac Albéniz's Alhambrism and Fin-de-Siècle Paris." In *Antes de Iberia, de Masarnau a Albéniz: Actas del Symposium FIMTE 2008*, edited by Luisa Morales and Walter Clark. 171–82. Garrucha, Spain: Asociación Cultural LEAL, 2009.

Christoforidis, Michael. "Georges Bizet's *Carmen* and Fin-de-Siècle Spanish National Opera." *Studia Musicologica* 52, nos. 1–4 (2012): 419–28.

Christoforidis, Michael. "Reimagining the *Reconquista*: Massenet's *Le Cid* and the 1900 Exposition Universelle." In *The Eighteenth-Century Italian Opera Seria: Metamorphoses of the Opera in the Imperial Age*, edited by Petr Macek and Jana Perutková. 264–71. Prague: KLP, Koniasch Latin Press, 2013.

Christoforidis, Michael. "Serenading Spanish Students on the Streets of Paris: The International Projection of Estudiantinas in the 1870s." *Nineteenth-Century Music Review* 15, no. 1 (2017): 23–36.

Christoforidis, Michael. *Manuel de Falla and Visions of Spanish Music.* London and New York: Routledge, 2018.

Cincotta, Vincent J. *Zarzuela: The Spanish Lyric Theatre; A Complete Reference.* Rev. ed. Wollongong, Australia: University of Wollongong Press, 2003.

Clark, Robert L. A. "South of North: *Carmen* and French Nationalisms." In *East of West: Cross-Cultural Performance and the Staging of Difference*, edited by Claire Sponsler and Xiaomei Chen. 187–216. New York: Palgrave, 2000.

Clark, Walter Aaron. *Isaac Albéniz: Portrait of a Romantic.* Oxford: Oxford University Press, 1999.

Clark, Walter Aaron. *Enrique Granados: Poet of the Piano.* New York: Oxford University Press, 2006.

Clinton-Baddeley, V. C. *The Burlesque Tradition in the English Theatre after 1660.* London: Methuen, 1952.

Colomé, Delfín. "El ballet en España y Rusia: Influencias mutuas." In *Relaciones musicales entre España y Rusia*, edited by Antonio Álvarez Cañibano, Pilar V. Gutiérrez

Dorado, and Cristina Marcos Patiño. 121–35. Madrid: Centro de documentación de música y danza, 1999.

Contrucci, Jean. *Emma Calvé la diva du siècle*. Paris: Albin Michel, 1989.

Cortès, Francesc. "La ópera en Cataluña desde 1900 a 1936." In *La ópera en España e Hispanoamérica*, edited by Emilio Casares Rodicio and Álvaro Torrente. 2:325–62. Madrid: ICCMU, 2002.

Cortizo, María Encina, and Ramón Sobrino. "Los salones musicales madrileños: Nuevos espacios sociales para el cultivo de la música de concierto en la segunda mitad del XIX." *Ad Parnassum: A Journal of Eighteenth- and Nineteenth-Century Instrumental Music* 13, no. 25 (2015): 209–43.

Curtiss, Mina. *Bizet and His World*. New York: Vienna House, 1958.

Davies, Ann, and Phil Powrie. *Carmen on Screen: An Annotated Filmography and Bibliography*. Woodbridge, UK and Rochester, NY: Tamesis, 2006.

Dean, Winton. *Bizet*. London: Dent, 1948.

Dizikes, John. *Opera in America: A Cultural History*. New Haven and London: Yale University Press, 1993.

Eaton, Quaintance. *The Miracle of the Met*. New York: Meredith, 1968.

Esse, Melina. "The Silent Diva: Farrar's Carmen." In *Technology and the Diva*, edited by Karen Henson. 89–103. Cambridge: Cambridge University Press, 2016.

Farrar, Geraldine. *Carmen [Photo Drama Edition]*. New York: A. L. Burt, 1915.

Farrar, Geraldine. *The Story of an American Singer by Herself*. Boston and New York: Houghton Mifflin, 1916.

Farrar, Geraldine. "The Story of My Life." *Photoplay* 15, no. 4 (1919): 52–54, 106.

Farrar, Geraldine. *The Autobiography of Geraldine Farrar: Such Sweet Compulsion*. New York: Greystone, 1938.

Farrar, Geraldine, as recorded by Frederic Dean. "The Psychology of Carmen." *Bookman* 42 (December 1915). 412–17.

Fauser, Annegret. *Musical Encounters at the 1889 Paris World's Fair*. Eastman Studies in Music. Rochester, NY: University of Rochester Press, 2005.

Figuero, Javier, and Marie-Hélène Carbonel. *Arruíname, pero no me abandones: La Belle Otero y la Belle Époque*. Madrid: Espasa-Calpe, 2003.

Flint, Ralph. "Zuloaga and His Hour." *International Studio* (April 1925): 3–14.

Flitch, J. E. Crawford. *Modern Dancing and Dancers*. London: Grant Richards, 1912.

Fryer, Paul, and Olga Usova. *Lina Cavalieri: The Life of Opera's Greatest Beauty, 1874–1944*. Jefferson, NC: McFarland, 2004.

Furman, Nelly. "The Languages of Love in *Carmen*." In *Reading Opera*, edited by Arthur Groos and Roger Parker. 168–83. Princeton, NJ: Princeton University Press, 1988.

Gallus, A. [Arthur Wisner]. *Emma Calvé: Her Artistic Life*. New York: R. H. Russell, 1902.

Gänzl, Kurt. "Carmen Up-to-Data." In *The Encyclopedia of the Musical Theatre*, 226. Oxford: Blackwell, 1994.

García Carretero, Emilio. *Historia del Teatro de la Zarzuela de Madrid*. Madrid: Fundación de la Zarzuela Española, 2006.

Gatti-Casazza, Giulio. *Memories of the Opera*. New York: Vienna House, (1941) 1973.

Gelardo Navarro, José, and José Luis Navarro García. *Carmencita Dauset: Una bailaora almeriense*. Almería, Spain: La Hidra de Lerna/Diputación de Almería, 2011.

Girard, Georges. *Emma Calvé: La Cantatrice sous tous les ciels*. Millau, France: Éditions Grans Causses, 1983.

Glenn, Susan A. *Female Spectacle: The Theatrical Roots of Modern Feminism*. Cambridge, MA and London: Harvard University Press, 2000.

Goldberg, K. Meira, Ninotchka Devorah Bennahum, and Michelle Heffner Hayes, eds. *Flamenco on the Global Stage: Historical, Critical and Theoretical Perspectives*. Jefferson, NC: McFarland, 2015.

Gómez Carrillo, Enrique. *Bailarinas*. Madrid: B. Rodríguez Serra, 1902.

González de Molina, Manuel, and Miguel Gómez Oliver. *Historia contemporánea de Andalucía (nuevos contenidos para su estudio)*. 2nd ed. Granada, Spain: Proyecto Sur de Ediciones, 2000.

González López, Carlos, and Montserrat Martí Ayxelá. *Pintores españoles en París: 1850–1900*. Barcelona: Tusquets, 1989.

Granés, Salvador María, and Tomás Reig. *Carmela: Parodia-lírica de la ópera "Carmen" en un acto y tres cuadros*. Madrid: Velasco, 1891.

Guest, Ivor. *Fanny Elssler*. London: Adam & Charles Black, 1970.

Guest, Ivor. *The Romantic Ballet in England: Its Development, Fulfilment, and Decline*. Middletown, CT: Wesleyan University Press, [1972].

Guest, Ivor. *Ballet in Leicester Square: The Alhambra and the Empire 1860–1915*. London: Dance Books, 1992.

Halévy, Ludovic. "La Millième Représentation de *Carmen*." *Le Théâtre* 145 (January [I] 1905): 5–14.

Hamberlin, Larry. *Tin Pan Opera: Operatic Novelty Songs in the Ragtime Era*. Oxford: Oxford University Press, 2011.

Hardy, Camille. "Flashes of Flamenco: The American Debuts of Carmencita and Otero." *Arabesque: A Magazine of International Dance* 9, no. 1 (1983): 16–23.

Hauk, Minnie. *Memories of a Singer*. Repr. ed. New York: Arno (1925) 1977.

Henson, Karen. *Opera Acts: Singers and Performance in the Late Nineteenth Century*. Cambridge: Cambridge University Press, 2015.

Henson, Karen, ed. *Technology and the Diva: Sopranos, Opera, and Media from Romanticism to the Digital Age*. Cambridge: Cambridge University Press, 2016.

Higashi, Sumiko. *Cecil B. DeMille and American Culture: The Silent Era*. Berkeley: University of California Press, 1994.

Hoffmann, Léon-François. *Romantique Espagne: L'Image de l'Espagne en France entre 1800 et 1850*. Paris: Presses Universitaires de France, 1961.

Hollingshead, John. *Gaiety Chronicles*. London: Constable, 1898.

Hollingshead, John. *Good Old Gaiety: An Historiette and Remembrance*. London: Gaiety Theatre Company, 1903.

Hooper, Kirsty. "'Moorish Splendour' in the British Provinces, 1886–1906: The Spanish Bazaar, from Dundee to Southampton." In *Contact and Connection Symposium*, 1–10. Coventry, UK: University of Warwick Institute of Advanced Study, 2013.

Horowitz, Joseph. *Moral Fire: Musical Portraits from America's Fin-de-Siècle*. Berkeley: University of California Press, 2012.

Howarth, David, and Christopher Baker. *The Discovery of Spain: British Artists and Collectors, Goya to Picasso*. Edinburgh: National Galleries of Scotland, 2009.

Huebner, Steven. *French Opera at the Fin de Siècle: Wagnerism, Nationalism, and Style*. Oxford and New York: Oxford University Press, 1999.

Huebner, Steven. "*La Princesse Paysanne du Midi*." In *Music, Theater, and Cultural Transfer: Paris, 1830–1914*, edited by Annegret Fauser and Mark Everist. 361–78. Chicago and London: University of Chicago Press, 2009.

Hughes, Robert. *Barcelona*. New York: Alfred A. Knopf, 1992.

Iberni, Luis G. *Pablo Sarasate*. Madrid: Instituto Complutense de Ciencias Musicales, D.L., 1994.

Iberni, Luis G. *Ruperto Chapí*. Madrid: ICCMU, 1995.

Iberni, Luis G. "Controversias entre ópera y zarzuela en la España de la Restauración." *Cuadernos de música iberoamericana* 2–3 (1996–97): 157–64.

Iberni, Luis G. "Cien años de Antonio Peña y Goñi." *Cuadernos de música iberoamericana* 4 (1997): 3–13.

Iberni, Luis G. "Verismo y realismo en la ópera española." In *La ópera en España e Hispanoamérica*, edited by Emilio Casares Rodicio and Álvaro Torrente. 2:215–26. Madrid: ICCMU, 2002.

Kagan, Richard L., ed. *Spain in America: The Origins of Hispanism in the United States*. Urbana and Chicago: University of Illinois Press, 2002.

Kanellos, Nicolás. *A History of Hispanic Theatre in the United States: Origins to 1940*. Austin: University of Texas Press, 1990.

Kertesz, Elizabeth. "*Carmen* Meets *Carmela*: Hispanicising a 'Spanish' Opera." In *The Eighteenth-Century Italian Opera Seria: Metamorphoses of the Opera in the Imperial Age*, edited by Petr Macek and Jana Perutková. 272–77. Prague: KLP, Koniasch Latin Press, 2013.

Kertesz, Elizabeth, and Michael Christoforidis. "Confronting *Carmen* beyond the Pyrenees: Bizet's Opera in Madrid, 1887–1888." *Cambridge Opera Journal* 20, no. 1 (2008): 79–110.

Kinney, Troy, and Margaret West Kinney. *The Dance: Its Place in Art and Life*. New York: Frederick A. Stokes, 1914.

Klein, Hermann. *Thirty Years of Musical Life in London 1870–1900*. London: William Heinemann, 1903.

Klein, Hermann. *The Reign of Patti*. New York: Century, 1920.

Klein, Hermann. *Great Women-Singers of My Time*. London: George Routledge & Sons, 1931.

Klein, Hermann. *The Golden Age of Opera*. London: George Routledge & Sons, 1933.

Klein, John W. "Bizet: Opportunist or Innovator?" *Music & Letters* 5, no. 3 (July 1924): 230–38.

Klein, John W. "Bizet's Early Operas." *Music & Letters* 18, no. 2 (April 1937): 169–75.

Klein, John W. "Bizet's Admirers and Detractors." *Music & Letters* 19, no. 4 (October 1938): 405–16.

Klein, John W. "Bizet and Wagner." *Music & Letters* 28, no. 1 (January 1947): 50–62.

Krehbiel, Henry Edward. *Chapters of Opera*. 2nd ed. New York: Henry Holt, 1909.

Lacombe, Hervé. "La Réception de l'oeuvre dramatique de Bizet en Italie." *Mélanges de l'école française de Rome* 108, no. 1 (1996): 171–201.

Lacombe, Hervé. "The Writing of Exoticism in the Libretti of the Opera-Comique, 1825–1862." *Cambridge Opera Journal* 11, no. 2 (July 1999): 135–58.

Lacombe, Hervé. "L'Espagne à l'Opéra-Comique avant *Carmen*: Du *Guitarrero* de Halévy (1841) à *Don César de Bazan* de Massenet (1872)." In *Échanges musicaux franco-espagnols XVIIᵉ–XIXᵉ siècles*, edited by François Lesure. 161–93. Paris: Klincksieck, 2000a.

Lacombe, Hervé. *Georges Bizet: Naissance d'une identité créatrice*. Paris: Fayard, 2000b.

Lacombe, Hervé. *The Keys to French Opera in the Nineteenth Century*. Translated by Edward Schneider. Berkeley: University of California Press, 2001.

Lacombe, Hervé. "L'Espagne à Paris au milieu du XIXᵉ siècle (1847–1857): L'Influence d'artistes espagnols sur l'imaginaire parisien et la construction d'une 'hispanicité.'" *Revue de musicologie* 88, no. 2 (2002): 389–431.

Lacombe, Hervé, and Christine Rodriguez. *La Habanera de Carmen: Naissance d'un tube*. Paris: Fayard, 2014.

Langham Smith, Richard. "*Carmen*: From Mérimée to Bizet." In Carmen: *Georges Bizet*, edited by Gary Kahn. 9–34. Richmond, UK: Overture, 2013.

Laparra, Raoul. *Bizet et l'Espagne*. Paris: Librairie Delegrave, 1935.

Leicester, H. Marshall. "Discourse and the Film Text: Four Readings of *Carmen*." *Cambridge Opera Journal* 6, no. 3 (1994): 245–82.

Lewis, Arthur H. *La Belle Otero*. New York: Trident, 1967.

Liern, Rafael María. "Carmen: Zarzuela en cuatro actos." Autograph libretto. Madrid: Sociedad General de Autores y Editores, [1887].

Linares, Maria Teresa, and Faustino Nuñez. *La música entre Cuba y España*. Madrid: Fundación Autor, 1998.

Llano, Samuel. *Whose Spain? Negotiating Spanish Music in Paris, 1908–1929*. New York: Oxford University Press, 2013.

Locke, Ralph P. "Nineteenth-Century Music: Quantity, Quality, Qualities." *Nineteenth-Century Music Review* 1, no. 1 (2004): 3–41.

Locke, Ralph P. "Exotic Operas and Two Spanish 'Gypsies.'" In *Musical Exoticism: Images and Reflections*. 150–74. New York: Cambridge University Press, 2009a.

Locke, Ralph P. *Musical Exoticism: Images and Reflections*. New York: Cambridge University Press, 2009b.

Locke, Ralph P. "Spanish Local Colour in Bizet's *Carmen*: Unexplored Borrowings and Transformations." In *Music, Theater, and Cultural Transfer: Paris, 1830–1914*, edited by Annegret Fauser and Mark Everist. 316–60. Chicago and London: University of Chicago Press, 2009c.

López, Mar Soria. "Modern *Castiza* Landscapes: Working Women in *Zarzuela*." *Bulletin of Spanish Studies* 88, no. 6 (2011): 821–38.

Louvish, Simon. *Cecil B. DeMille and the Golden Calf*. London: Faber & Faber, 2007.

Lutz, Meyer. *Carmen up to Data, Burlesque Opera [vocal score]*. Edited by P. F. Campiglio. London: E. Ascherberg; New York: Novello, Ewer, 1890.

Macdonald, Hugh. *Bizet*. The Master Musicians. Oxford and New York: Oxford University Press, 2014.

Malherbe, Henri. *Carmen*. Paris: Albin Michel, 1951.

Mapleson, James Henry. *The Mapleson Memoirs: The Career of an Operatic Impresario, 1858–1888*. Edited by Harold Rosenthal. London: Putnam, (1888) 1966.

Martín Sárraga, Félix O. *Mitos y evidencia histórica sobre las tunas y estudiantinas*. Lima: Cauces, 2016.

Marvin, Roberta Montemorra. "Verdian Opera Burlesqued: A Glimpse into Mid-Victorian Theatrical Culture." *Cambridge Opera Journal* 15, no. 1 (March 2003): 33–66.

Mathews, Nancy Mowll, and Charles Musser. *Moving Pictures: American Art and Early Film, 1880–1910*. Manchester, VT: Hudson Hills Press in association with the Williams College Museum of Art, 2005.

Mayer, Martin. *The Met: One Hundred Years of Grand Opera*. London: Thames and Hudson, 1983.

McClary, Susan. *Georges Bizet*, Carmen. Cambridge: Cambridge University Press, 1992.

McQueen, Alison. *Empress Eugénie and the Arts: Politics and Visual Culture in the Nineteenth Century*. Farnham, UK; Burlington, VT: Ashgate, 2011.

Mora Contreras, Francisco Javier, and Kiko Mora. "*Carmencita on the Road*: Baile español y vaudeville en los Estados Unidos de América (1889–1895)." In *Lumière* (2011). Published electronically 28 October 2011. Accessed 1 October 2016. http://www.elumiere.net/exclusivo_web/carmencita/carmencita_on_the_road.php.

Moral Ruiz, Carmen del. *El género chico: Ocio y teatro en Madrid (1880–1910)*. Madrid: Alianza, 2004.

Morales, Pedro. "Preface." In *The Music of Spain*, by Carl Van Vechten. ix–xx. London: Kegan Paul, Trench, Trubner, 1920.

Mordey, Delphine. "Carmen, Communarde Bizet, 'Habanera' (Carmen), Carmen, Act I." *Cambridge Opera Journal* 28, no. 2 (2016): 215–19.

Moreno Mengíbar, Andrés. *La ópera en Sevilla en el siglo XIX*. Seville: Universidad de Sevilla, Secretariado de Publicaciones, 1998.

Murphy, Kerry. "Carmen: *Couleur locale* or the Real Thing?" In *Music, Theater, and Cultural Transfer: Paris, 1830–1914*, edited by Annegret Fauser and Mark Everist. 293–315. Chicago and London: University of Chicago Press, 2009.

Murray, Kenneth James. "Spanish Music and Its Representations in London (1878–1930): From the Exotic to the Modern." PhD thesis, University of Melbourne, 2013.

Musser, Charles. "A Cornucopia of Images: Comparison and Judgment across Theater, Film and the Visual Arts during the Late Nineteenth Century." In *Moving Pictures: American Art and Early Film, 1880–1910*, edited by Nancy Mowll Mathews, Charles Musser, and Marta Braun. 5–38. Manchester, VT: Hudson Hills Press in association with the Williams College Museum of Art, 2005.

Nagore Ferrer, María. *Sarasate: El violín de Europa*. Madrid: ICCMU, 2013.

Nuñez, Faustino. "La música española y lo español en *Carmen*." *Carmen* (program of the Teatro Real). Madrid: Teatro Real, 1999. 140–51.

O'Connor, D. J. "Representations of Women Workers: Tobacco Strikers in the 1890s." In *Constructing Spanish Womanhood: Female Identity in Modern Spain*, edited by Victoria Lorée Enders and Pamela Beth Radcliff. 151–72. Albany: State University of New York Press, 1999.

Otero, Carolina. *Les Souvenirs et la vie intime de la belle Otero*. Paris: Le Calame, 1926.

Otero, Caroline. *My Story*. London: A. M. Philpot, [1927].

Parakilas, James. "The Soldier and the Exotic: Operatic Variations on a Theme of Racial Encounter; Part I." *Opera Quarterly* 10 (1993): 33–56.

Parakilas, James. "How Spain Got a Soul." In *The Exotic in Western Music*, edited by Jonathan Bellman. 137–93. Boston: Northeastern University Press, 1998.

Perriam, Chris, and Ann Davies, eds. *Carmen: From Silent Film to MTV*. Amsterdam, NY: Rodopi, 2005.

Perugini, Mark E. *A Pageant of the Dance and Ballet*. London: Jarrolds, 1946.

Petipa, Marius. *Russian Ballet Master: The Memoirs of Marius Petipa*. Translated by Helen Whittaker. Edited by Lillian Moore. London: Dance Books, 1958.

Petipa, Marius. *The Diaries of Marius Petipa*. Translated by Lynn Garafola. Edited by Lynn Garafola. Pennington, NJ: Society of Dance History Scholars, 1992.

Power, Geraldine. "Projections of Spain in Popular Spectacle and Chanson, Paris: 1889–1926." PhD thesis, University of Melbourne, 2013.

Powrie, Phil, Bruce Babington, Ann Davies, and Chris Perriam. *Carmen on Film: A Cultural History*. Bloomington and Indianapolis: Indiana University Press, 2007.

Ramirez, James. *Carmencita, the Pearl of Seville*. New York: Press of the Law and Trade Printing Co., 1890.

Reilly, Joy Harriman. "From Wicked Woman of the Stage to New Woman: The Career of Olga Nethersole (1870–1951); Actress-Manager, Suffragist, Health Pioneer." PhD thesis, Ohio State University, 1984.

Robinson, Peter. "Mérimée's *Carmen*." In *Georges Bizet*, Carmen, edited by Susan McClary. 1–14. Cambridge: Cambridge University Press, 1992.

Rutherford, Susan. "'Pretending to Be Wicked': Divas, Technology, and the Consumption of Bizet's *Carmen*." In *Technology and the Diva*, edited by Karen Henson. 74–88. Cambridge: Cambridge University Press, 2016.

Sala, Emilio. *The Sounds of Paris in Verdi's* La traviata. Translated by Delia Casadei. Cambridge: Cambridge University Press, 2013.

Santana Burgos, Laura. "Diálogos entre Francia y España: La traducción de los libretos de *Carmen* y *El retablo de Maese Pedro*." PhD diss., Universidad de Granada, 2013.

Sazatornil Ruíz, Luis, and Ana Belén Lasheras Peña. "París y la españolada: Casticismo y estereotipos nacionales en las exposiciones universales (1855–1900)." *Mélanges de la Casa de Velázquez* 35, no. 2 (2005): 265–90.

Schoch, Richard W., ed. *Victorian Theatrical Burlesques*. Aldershot, UK: Ashgate, 2003.

Sentaurens, Jean. "*Carmen*: De la novela de 1845 a la zarzuela de 1887; Cómo nació 'la España de Mérimée.'" *Bulletin Hispanique* [104], no. 2 (December 2002): 851–72.

Sentaurens, Jean. "La España de Mérimée les sienta demasiado bien a los españoles. El fabuloso destino del 'cuentecillo gracioso' de la Señora de Montijo." In *La cultura del otro: Español en Francia, francés en España/La Culture de l'autre; Espagnol en France, français en Espagne*. 2–14. Seville: Universidad de Sevilla, 2006.

Seymour, Bruce. *Lola Montez: A Life*. New Haven, CT: Yale University Press, 1996.

Shaw, George Bernard. *Music in London 1890–94 by Bernard Shaw*. Vol. 3. London: Constable, 1932a.

Shaw, George Bernard. *Our Theatres in the Nineties*. Vol. 2. London: Constable, 1932b.

Shubert, Adrian. *Death and Money in the Afternoon: A History of the Spanish Bullfight*. New York: Oxford University Press, 1999.

Simonson, Mary. "'The Call of Salome': American Adaptations and Re-creations of the Female Body in the Early Twentieth Century." *Women and Music: A Journal of Gender and Culture* 11 (2007): 1–16.

Sims, George R., Henry Pettitt, and Meyer Lutz. "Carmen Up to Date [typescript]." In New York Public Library Performing Arts Research Collections—Theatre. New York, [1890].

Sims, George R., Henry Pettitt, and Meyer Lutz. *Carmen von Heute: Burlesque in vier Akten*. Vienna: Verlag des k.k. priv. Carl-Theaters, 1892.

Sobrino, Ramón. "Alhambrismo musical español de los albores románticos a Manuel de Falla." In *Manuel de Falla y la Alhambra*, edited by Francisco Baena and Yvan Nommick. 39–69. Granada, Spain: Patronato de la Alhambra y Generalife; Fundación Archivo Manuel de Falla, 2005.

Spies, André Michael. *Opera, State and Society in the Third Republic, 1875–1914*. Studies in Modern European History. Edited by Frank J. Coppa. New York: Peter Lang, 1998.

Steingress, Gerhard. *. . . Y Carmen se fue a París*. Cordoba, Spain: Almuzara, 2006.

Sturman, Janet L. *Zarzuela: Spanish Operetta, American Stage*. Urbana and Chicago: University of Illinois Press, 2000.

Suárez-Pajares, Javier, and Xoán M. Carreira, eds. *The Origins of the Bolero School*. Studies in Dance History 4, no. 1. Madison: University of Wisconsin Press for Society of Dance History Scholars, 1993.

Suisman, David. *Selling Sounds: The Commercial Revolution in American Music*. Cambridge, MA: Harvard University Press, 2009.

Symons, Arthur. "A Spanish Music-Hall." In *Cities and Sea-Coasts and Islands*. 145–57. New York: Brentano's, (1892) 1919.

Symons, Arthur. "Dancing as Soul Expression." *Forum* 66 (July–December 1921): 308–17.

Traubner, Richard. *Operetta: A Theatrical History*. New York: Routledge, 2004.

Turner, Kristen M. "Opera in English: Class and Culture in America, 1878–1910." PhD thesis, University of North Carolina at Chapel Hill, 2015.

Van Vechten, Carl. *The Music of Spain*. London: Kegan Paul, Trench, Trubner, 1920.

Van Vechten, Carl. *When Spain Fascinated America*. [Madrid]: Fundación Zuloaga; Gobierno de España, Ministerio de Cultura, 2010.

Wright, Lesley. "A New Source for *Carmen*." *19th-Century Music* 2, no. 1 (July 1978): 61–71.

Wright, Lesley. "*Carmen* and the Critics." In *Tan-yin-lun-yue: Conference Proceedings of "Musical Research and Music Practice," 1999*. 47–67. Taipei: Gao-Tan, 2000.

Wright, Lesley, ed. *Georges Bizet, Carmen: Dossier de presse parisienne (1875)*. Weinsberg. Germany: Lucie Galland, 2001.

Wright, Lesley. "Une critique revisitée: Réflexions sur l'accueil de *Carmen* à Paris en 1883." In *Musique, esthétique et société au XIXe siècle: Liber amicorum Joël-Marie Fauquet*, edited by Damien Colas, Florence Gétreau, and Malou Haine. 187–97. Wavre, Belgium: Éditions Mardaga, 2007.

Wright, Lesley. "Rewriting a Reception: Thoughts on *Carmen* in Paris, 1883." *Journal of Musicological Research* 28, no. 4 (2009): 282–92.

Wright, Lesley. "*Carmen* and the Opéra-Comique." In *Carmen: Georges Bizet*, edited by Gary Kahn. 35–55. Richmond, UK: Overture, 2013.

INDEX